The
Challenge
of
Democracy

The Challenge of Democracy

Government in America

Brief Edition

Third Edition

Kenneth Janda   NORTHWESTERN UNIVERSITY

Jeffrey M. Berry   TUFTS UNIVERSITY

Jerry Goldman   NORTHWESTERN UNIVERSITY

Abridged by Earl Huff

CALIFORNIA POLYTECHNIC STATE UNIVERSITY,
SAN LUIS OBISPO

Houghton Mifflin Company   Boston   New York

Sponsoring editor: Melissa Mashburn
Associate editor: Lily Eng
Senior project editor: Rosemary Winfield
Senior production/design coordinator: Carol Merrigan
Senior manufacturing coordinator: Marie Barnes
Marketing manager: Sandra McGuire

Cover design: Judy Arisman; Cover image: Gabrielle Keller

Printed in the U.S.A.

Library of Congress Catalog Card Number: 97-72492

ISBN: 0-395-77449-7

123456789-QF-0100 99 98 97

Contents

3

The Dynamics of Federalism 63

The Developing Concept of Federalism 68

From New Federalism to New Age Federalism 71

Other Governments in the Federal System 74

Contemporary Federalism and the Dilemmas of Democracy 76

Federalism and Pluralism 76

Summary 78

4

PUBLIC OPINION, POLITICAL SOCIALIZATION, AND THE MEDIA 80

Public Opinion and the Models of Democracy 82

Political Socialization 84

Social Groups and Political Values 84

From Values to Ideology 90

5

12

13

Appendices   A-1

References   R-1

Index   I-1

Preface

The third edition of *The Challenge of Democracy,* Brief Edition, is an abridged and updated version of the very popular fifth edition of *The Challenge of Democracy.* Again, our goal was to streamline the larger text without diminishing any of the qualities that have made it so successful. Additionally, we sought to make the text as current as possible by incorporating examples from events occurring later in 1997 after the publication of the larger text. Among these examples are several significant Supreme Court decisions.

Through the process of writing five editions of the larger text, however, what we are most struck by is how enduring our original framework is. *The Challenge of Democracy* is built around two themes that remain as relevant today as they were when we first conceived of this project. The first is the *clash among the values of freedom, order, and equality,* while the second focuses on the *tensions between pluralist and majoritarian visions of democracy.* Knowledge of these conflicts enables citizens to recognize and analyze the difficult choices they face in politics.

Because we wanted to write a book that students would actually read, we sought to discuss politics—a complex subject—in a captivating and understandable way. American politics isn't dull, and its textbooks needn't be either. But equally important, we wanted to produce a book that students would credit for stimulating their thinking about politics. While offering all the essential information about American government and politics, we believed that what was most important was to give students a framework for analyzing politics that they could use long after their studies ended. Based on the reactions to our earlier editions, we believe we succeeded in developing a lively book built on a framework that fulfills our goals.

Thematic Framework

As noted above, two themes run through our book. One deals with the *conflict among values,* and the other with *alternative models of democracy.* In Chapter 1, we suggest that American politics often reflects conflicts between the values of freedom and order and between the values of freedom and equality. These value conflicts are prominent in contemporary American society, and they help to explain political controversy and consensus in earlier eras.

For instance, in Chapter 2 we argue that the Constitution was designed to promote order, and it virtually ignored issues of political and social equality. Equality was later served, however, by several amendments to the Constitution.

In Chapter 12, "Civil Liberties and Civil Rights," we demonstrate that many of this nation's most controversial issues represent conflicts among individuals or groups who hold differing views on the values of freedom, order, and equality. Views on issues such as abortion are not just isolated opinions; they also reflect choices about the philosophy citizens want government to follow. Yet choosing among these values is difficult, sometimes excruciatingly so.

The second theme, also introduced in Chapter 1, asks students to consider two competing models of democratic government. One way that government can make decisions is by means of *majoritarian* principles—that is, by taking the actions desired by a majority of citizens. For instance, in Chapter 8, "Congress," we discuss the Republicans' Contract with America as an effort to move the national government to a more majoritarian system. A contrasting model of government, *pluralism,* is built around the interaction of decision makers in government with groups concerned about issues that affect them. Pluralism is a focus of Chapter 13, "Public Policy," which discusses issue networks in the nation's capital.

These models are not mere abstractions; we use them to illustrate the dynamics of the American political system. In Chapter 9, "The Presidency," we discuss the problem of divided government. More often than not over the past forty years, the party that controlled the White House didn't control both houses of Congress. When these two branches of government are divided between the two parties, majoritarian government is difficult. As Bill Clinton found out during 1993 and 1994, even when the same party controls both branches, the majoritarian model is not always realized.

Throughout the book we stress that students must make their own choices among the competing values and models of government. Although the three of us hold diverse and strong opinions about which choices are best, we do not believe it is our role to tell students our own answers to the broad questions we pose. Instead, we want our readers to learn firsthand that a democracy requires thoughtful choices. That is why we titled our book *The Challenge of Democracy.*

Features of the Third Brief Edition

The third edition maintains the basic structure of the previous edition while updating the political events of the past few years. We have also drawn on the latest research in political science to make sure that *The Challenge of Democracy* continues to represent the state of the art in our discipline.

To accommodate the major changes and new issues in politics that have occurred since the last edition, every chapter in the text has been thoroughly revised. One of the most significant changes we've made is in Chapter 1. Previous users of the book will notice that in our framework encompassing four different ideologies, we have replaced the term *populist* with *communitarian.* In contemporary usage, *populist* is used in many different ways, and we worried that students might find it confusing that politicians of both the left and the right claim to be populists, while journalists, pundits, and social scientists all have their own definitions of what it means to be a populist. As explained in Chapter 1, *communitarian* more clearly evokes the political thinking underlying a preference for order and equality.

Chapter 4, "Public Opinion, Political Socialization, and the Media," examines the landmark telecommunications deregulation law as well as the recent megamergers in the telecommunications industry that increasingly raise the issue of concentration of private ownership of media companies. In Chapter 6, "Political Parties, Campaigns, and Elections," and Chapter 8, "Congress," the Contract with America is discussed in detail. We follow the Contract from the fall campaign of 1994 through the first one hundred days and then close our discussion by documenting the final outcome on all the Contract legislation (Table 8.1 and accompanying text). More broadly, throughout the book we focus on the Contract with America in the context of the majoritarian model of democracy. Full coverage of the 1996 presidential and congressional elections is offered in Chapters 6, 8, and 9 ("The Presidency"). In addition, Chapter 9 fully incorporates an analysis of the Clinton presidency. Chapter 13, "Public Policy," takes up the controversial welfare reform law. Will it really "end welfare as we know it"?

In this edition, we provide a new, close connection between the words in our text and external computer resources. The rich resources of the Internet are featured in several ways. Each chapter concludes with "World Wide Web Resources," a list of World Wide Web sites that includes the URL and a brief description of each site. Another important resource for faculty and student users of our text is *The Challenge of Democracy Web Site* <http://www.hmco.com/college/COD/home.html> (see below for more details). These advances keep *The Challenge of Democracy* at the leading edge of technology in studying American government.

As in previous editions, each chapter begins with a vignette. The purpose of each vignette is to draw students into the substance of that chapter, while suggesting one of the themes of the book. Chapters with new vignettes include Chapter 3, "Federalism," where we look at Louisiana's minimum drinking age law; Chapter 5, "Participation and Voting," which begins with a vignette on the Viper Militia, asking students whether membership in a militia is a form of political participation; Chapter 6, "Political Parties, Campaigns, and Elections," which opens with an account of the recent efforts of Ross Perot's Reform Party and considers the problems of a third party in a two-party system; Chapter 10, "The Bureaucracy," which uses the tragic story of the ValuJet crash as a means of introducing the subject of regulation, a primary focus of the chapter; and Chapter 12, "Civil Liberties and Civil Rights," which opens with the story of a University of Michigan student who put fictional accounts of his fantasies on the Internet and was expelled, arrested, and jailed. Was his freedom of speech abridged?

In the last edition we introduced a new series of features, "Politics in a Changing America," designed to illustrate changes over time in the political opportunity, participation, and status of groups such as women, African Americans, youth, Hispanics, and religious fundamentalists. These features allow us to highlight many controversial and complex issues in American society, and we have continued them in this edition. Some of the original features have been kept, and others updated.

Through every edition of our book, we have believed that students can better evaluate how our political system works when they compare it with politics in other countries. Once again, several chapters have a boxed feature called "Compared with What?" that treats its topic in a comparative perspective. Do American television reporters color the news with their commentary more than reporters do in other countries? Are women better represented in other nations' national legislatures than in our own? To what extent do other countries have disagreements over affirmative action programs?

Each chapter concludes with a brief summary, a list of key terms, a short list of recommended readings, and the World Wide Web Resources feature described above. At the end of the book, we have included a copy of the Declaration of Independence and the Constitution.

The Teaching Learning Package

When we began writing *The Challenge of Democracy,* we viewed the book as part of a tightly integrated set of instructional materials. We have worked closely with some very talented political scientists and with educational specialists at Houghton Mifflin to produce what we think is a superior set of ancillary materials to help both instructors and students.

For the Instructor: Innovative Teaching Tools

The *Instructor's Resource Manual with Test Items,* written by the authors and Lori Brainard and carefully updated by Earl Huff of California Polytechnic State University, San Luis Obispo, provides teachers with material that relates directly to the thematic framework and organization of the book. The *Instructor's Resource Manual* includes learning objectives, chapter synopses, parallel lectures covering the material in each chapter, and suggestions for class projects and activities. The *Test Items* section provides hundreds of identification, multiple-choice, and essay questions.

Software ancillaries available to instructors include a *Computerized Test Bank* test generation program in Macintosh and IBM-compatible formats, containing all the items in the printed *Test Items.*

A transparency package, containing thirty full-color overhead transparencies from the main text, is available to adopters of the book.

The Challenge of Democracy Web Site <http://www.hmco.com/college/COD/home.html>, allows students and faculty users of the third edition access to a host of materials including links to web sites, downloadable versions of IDEAlog, and additional resources. The World Wide Web is transforming how we gather information and communicate ideas. We are committed to using new information technologies to assist users of our text in their search for current knowledge and information about American government and politics.

The *Houghton Mifflin American Government Web Site* located at <http://www.hmco.com/college> contains a complete array of resources to accompany our American government titles, including an extensive *Documents Collection* with accompanying discussion questions and web exercises, various instructor's resources, web-based research activities, an annotated collection of links to innovative and useful web sites, as well as a downloadable, updated version of the award-winning *Crosstabs,* a computerized software program allowing students to cross-tabulate survey data on the 1996 presidential election and the 1994 to 1995 voting records of members of Congress in order to analyze voter attitudes and behavior.

For the Student: Effective Learning Aids

The *Study Guide,* written by Melissa Butler of Wabash College and updated by Earl Huff, is designed to help students master the content of *The Challenge of Democracy,* Brief Edition. The *Study Guide* provides chapter summaries, research topics and resources (both in print and on the World Wide Web), exercises in reading tables and graphs, sample multiple-choice exam questions, and advice on improving study skills, finding internships, and participating in American politics.

IDEAlog 3.0, winner of the 1992 Instructional Software Award from the American Political Science Association, is closely tied to the text's "value conflicts" theme. A Java version of *IDEAlog 3.0* can now be found (along with the DOS/Windows and Macintosh versions) on our web site <http://www.hmco.com/college/COD/home.html>. Students answer twenty questions dealing with the conflicts of freedom vs. order and freedom versus equality. Their responses are then classified according to libertarian, conservative, liberal, or communitarian ideological tendencies.

We invite your questions, suggestions, and criticisms of the teaching/learning package and *The Challenge of Democracy.* You may contact us at our respective institutions, or, if you have access to an electronic mail service, you may contact us through our collective e-mail address <cod@nwu.edu>.

Acknowledgments

In the fifth edition of *The Challenge of Democracy* we acknowledged the contributions of many individuals whose advice and assistance have been of great value. We remain in their debt. They are Robert H. Angell, University of Texas, Brownsville; Margaret Ellis, James Madison University; JeDon A. Emenhiser, Humboldt State University; Daniel W. Fleitas, University of North Carolina, Charlotte; Scott C. Hefner, De Anza College; Thomas J. Mortillaro, Nicholls State University; and Edward E. Platt, Indiana University of Pennsylvania.

K. J.
J. M. B.
J. G.
E. H.

The
Challenge
of
Democracy

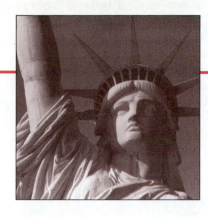

1

Dilemmas of Democracy

Suppose you are terminally ill and suffer excruciating pain. Do you have a "right" to die in this country? Does the state (that is, the government) have the right—even the duty—to prevent you from committing suicide? How about preventing a doctor from helping a doomed and tormented patient commit suicide?

From 1990 to 1996, Dr. Jack Kevorkian, a retired Michigan pathologist, assisted in at least twenty-seven suicides involving gravely ill people.[1] He had eluded conviction after the 1992 arrest for murder because he was careful to let his patients trigger the lethal action. But in 1992, Michigan outlawed assisted suicide. Facing prosecution, Kevorkian said, "I have never cared about anything but the welfare of the patient in front of me. I don't care about the law."[2] Put on trial three times, he was acquitted by juries each time and continued his macabre mission.

In contrast to the government's position in Michigan, Oregon voters in 1994 passed a law that allowed doctor-assisted suicide. Test your own feelings about this controversial issue. On what basis would you decide whether the government's interest in protecting life outweighs the freedom of individuals to end their own lives?

Which is better: to live under a government that allows individuals complete freedom to do whatever they please or to live under one that enforces strict law and order? Which is better: to allow businesses and private clubs to choose their customers and members or to pass laws that require them to admit and serve everyone, regardless of race or sex?

For many people, none of these alternatives is satisfactory. All pose difficult dilemmas. The dilemmas are tied to opposing philosophies that place different values on freedom, order, and equality.

This book explains American government and politics in light of these dilemmas. It does more than explain the workings of our government; it encourages you to think about what government should—and should not—do. And it judges the American government against democratic ideals, encouraging you to think about how government should make its decisions. As its title implies, *The Challenge of Democracy* argues that good government often involves difficult choices.

Compared with What? 1.1 (continued)

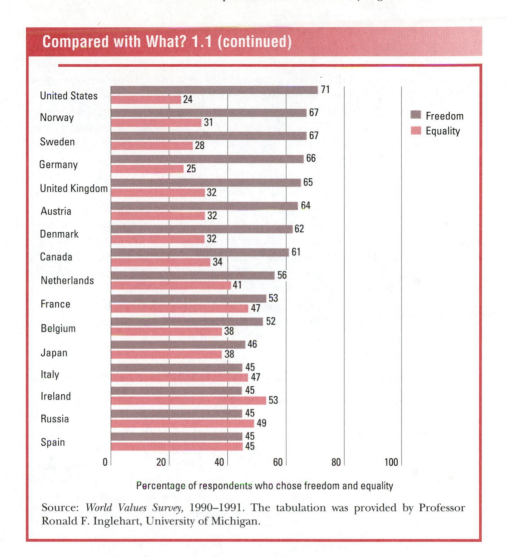

Percentage of respondents who chose freedom and equality

Source: *World Values Survey*, 1990–1991. The tabulation was provided by Professor Ronald F. Inglehart, University of Michigan.

range of political thought. On one side are people commonly called *liberals*; on the other are *conservatives*. In popular usage, liberals favor more government, conservatives less. This distinction is very clear when the issue is government spending to provide public goods. **Liberals** see a positive role for government in helping the disadvantaged. They favor generous government support for education, wildlife protection, public transportation, and a whole range of social programs. **Conservatives** want smaller government budgets and fewer government programs. They support free enterprise, arguing against government job programs, regulation of business, and legislation of working conditions and wage rates.

In other areas, liberal and conservative ideologies are less consistent. Their differences no longer hinge on the narrow question of the government's role in providing public goods. Liberals still favor more government and conservatives less, but this is no longer the critical difference between them. Today, that difference stems from their attitudes toward the purpose of government. Conservatives support the original purpose of government—maintaining social order. They are willing to use the coercive power of the state to force citizens to be orderly. Conservatives would not stop with defining, preventing, and punishing crime, however. They tend to want to preserve traditional patterns of social relations—the domestic role of women and the importance of religion in school and family life, for example.

Liberals are less likely than conservatives to want to use government power to maintain order. Liberals do not shy away from using government coercion, but they use it for a different purpose—to promote equality. They support laws ensuring that homosexuals receive equal treatment in employment, housing, and education; laws that require the busing of schoolchildren to achieve racial equality; laws that force private businesses to hire and promote women and members of minority groups; laws that require public transportation to provide equal access to the disabled.

Conservatives do not oppose equality, but they do not value it to the extent of using the government's power to enforce equality. For liberals, the use of that power to promote equality is both valid and necessary.

A Two-Dimensional Classification of Ideologies

To classify liberal and conservative ideologies more accurately, we have to incorporate the values of freedom, order, and equality into the classification. We can do this using the model in Figure 1.2. It depicts the conflicting values along two separate dimensions, each anchored in maximum freedom at the lower left. One dimension extends horizontally from maximum freedom on the left to maximum order on the right. The other extends vertically from maximum freedom at the bottom to maximum equality at the top. Each box represents a different ideological type: libertarians, liberals, conservatives, and communitarians.*

Libertarians value freedom more than order or equality. (We will use this term for people who have libertarian tendencies but may not accept the whole philosophy.) In practical terms, libertarians want minimal government intervention in both the economic and the social spheres. For example, they oppose affirmative action laws and laws that restrict transmission of sexually explicit material. Liberals value freedom more than order, but not more than equality. Liberals oppose laws that ban sexually explicit publications but support affirmative action. Conservatives value freedom more than equality but would restrict freedom to preserve social order. Conservatives oppose affirmative action but favor laws that restrict pornography.

---

*The ideological groupings we describe here conform to the classification in William S. Maddox and Stuart A. Lilie, *Beyond Liberal and Conservative: Reassessing the Political Spectrum* (Washington, D.C.: Cato Institute, 1984), p. 5. However, our formulation—in terms of the values of freedom, order, and equality—is quite different.

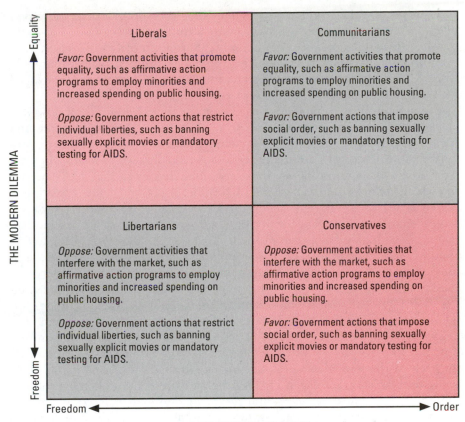

FIGURE 1.2   *Ideologies: A Two-Dimensional Framework*
The four ideological types above are defined by the values they favor in resolving the two major dilemmas of government: how much freedom should be sacrificed in pursuit of order and equality, respectively? Test yourself by thinking about the values that are most important to you. Which box in the figure best represents your combination of values?

Finally, we have the ideological type positioned at the upper right in Figure 1.2. This group values both equality and order more than freedom. Its members support both affirmative action laws and laws that restrict pornography. We will call this new group *communitarians.* The *Oxford English Dictionary* (1989) defines a communitarian as "a member of a community formed to put into practice communistic or socialistic theories." The term is used more narrowly in contemporary politics, to reflect the philosophy of the Communitarian Network, a political movement founded by sociologist Amitai Etzioni.[10] This movement rejects both the liberal-conservative classification and the libertarian argument that "individuals should be left on their own to pursue their choices, rights, and self-interests."[11] Like liberals, Etzioni's communitarians believe that there is a role for government in helping the disadvantaged. Like conservatives, they believe that government should be used to promote moral values—preserving the family through more stringent divorce laws, and limiting the dissemination of pornography, for example.[12] However, the Communitarian Network is not dedicated to big government. According to its platform, "The government should step in only to the extent that other social subsystems fail, rather than seek to replace them."[13]

Although it clearly embraces the Communitarian Network's philosophy, our definition of communitarian (small "c") is broader and more in keeping with the dictionary definition. Thus **communitarians** favor government programs that promote both order and equality, in keeping with socialist theory.

By analyzing political ideologies on two dimensions rather than one, we can explain why people can seem to be liberal on one issue (favoring a broader scope of government action) and conservative on another (favoring less government action). The answer hinges on the purpose of a given government action: which value does it promote, order or equality? According to our typology, only libertarians and communitarians are consistent in their attitudes toward the scope of government activity, whatever its purpose. Libertarians value freedom so highly that they oppose most government efforts to enforce either order or equality. Communitarians (in our usage) are inclined to trade off freedom for both order and equality. Liberals and conservatives, on the other hand, favor or oppose government activity depending on its purpose. As you will learn in Chapter 4, large groups of Americans fall into each of the four ideological categories. Because Americans increasingly choose four different resolutions to the original and modern dilemmas of government, the simple labels *liberal* and *conservative* no longer describe contemporary political ideologies as well as they did in the 1930s, 1940s, and 1950s.

The American Governmental Process: Majoritarian or Pluralist?

When, by a vote or 239 to 173, the House of Representatives passed legislation designed to repeal the ban on assault weapons in March 1996, many Americans were mystified. Only a few years earlier, Congress had passed a *ban* on assault weapons (military rifles that can fire in very rapid succession). What may seem most puzzling is that polls consistently show that Americans overwhelmingly support such a ban. Critics of the House vote pointed to the National Rifle Association (NRA), which pushed hard for lifting the assault weapons ban.

The assault ban repeal died in the Senate, however. Seeing little public support for the repeal, Senate Majority Leader Bob Dole quickly indicated that he wouldn't bring the bill up for a vote. The split between the House and the Senate reflects a dilemma that legislators often face: an interest group representing a small minority of the population comes to Congress to ask that it enact or defend some policy that the group's members favor. But what is good for that group may not be what is best for the public at large. Moreover, the majority may not be well mobilized, because it is apathetic about the issue, thus making it enticing for legislators to earn the gratitude of the interest group's followers, who are watching closely to see what Congress will do on that particular policy. Is it democratic for policymakers to favor an intense minority at the expense of a less-committed majority?

To this point, our discussion of political ideologies has centered on conflicting views about the values government should pursue. We now examine how government should decide what to do. In particular, we set forth criteria for judging whether or not a government's decision-making process is democratic.

The Theory of Democratic Government

Americans have a simple answer to the question "Who should govern?" It is "The people." Unfortunately, this answer is too simple. It fails to define who *the people* are. Should we include young children? Recent immigrants? Illegal aliens? This answer also fails to tell us how the people should do the governing. Should they be assembled in a stadium? Vote by mail? Choose others to govern for them? We need to take a closer look at what "government by the people" really means.

The word *democracy* originated in Greek writings around the fifth century B.C.; *demos* referred to the common people, the masses; *kratos* meant "power." The ancient Greeks were afraid of democracy—rule by rank and file citizens. That fear is evident in the term *demagogue*. We use that term today to refer to a politician who appeals to and often deceives the masses by manipulating their emotions and prejudices.

Many centuries after the Greeks first defined democracy, the idea still carried the connotation of mob rule. When George Washington was president, opponents of a new political party disparagingly called it a *democratic* party. Today, however, **democracy**—rule by the people—has become the apple pie and motherhood of political discourse. Like *justice* and *decency*, the word *democracy* is used reverently by politicians of all persuasions.

There are two major schools of thought about what constitutes democracy. The first believes democracy is a form of government. It emphasizes the procedures that enable the people to govern—meeting to discuss issues, voting in elections, running for public office. The second sees democracy in the substance of government policies, in freedom of religion and providing for human needs. The procedural approach focuses on how decisions are made; the substantive approach is concerned with *what* government does.

The Procedural View of Democracy   **Procedural democratic theory** sets forth principles that describe how government should make decisions. These principles address three distinct questions:

1. *Who* should participate in decision making?
2. *How much* should each participant's vote count?
3. *How many* votes are needed to reach a decision?

According to procedural democratic theory, all adults within the boundaries of the political community should participate in government decision making. We refer to this principle as **universal participation**. How much should each participant's vote count? According to procedural theory, all votes should be counted equally. This is the principle of **political equality**. Note that universal participation and political equality are two distinct principles. It is not enough for everyone to participate in a decision; all votes must carry equal weight.

Finally, procedural theory prescribes that a group should decide to do what the majority of its participants wants to do. This principle is called **majority rule**. (If participants divide over more than two alternatives and none receives a simple majority, the principle usually defaults to *plurality* rule, in which the group should do what most participants want.)

Direct Versus Indirect Democracy   These three principles—universal participation, political equality, and majority rule—are widely recognized as necessary for democratic decision making. Small, simple societies can meet the principles with a direct, or **participatory democracy**, in which all members of the group meet to make decisions, observing political equality and majority rule. However, in the United States and virtually all other democracies, participatory democracy is rare. Clearly, we cannot all gather at the Capitol in Washington to decide defense policy.

The framers of the Constitution were convinced that participatory democracy on the national level was both impossible and undesirable. Instead, they instituted **representative democracy**. In such a system, citizens participate in government by electing public officials to make government decisions on their behalf.

Within the context of representative democracy, we adhere to the principles of universal participation, political equality, and majority rule to guarantee that elections are democratic. But what happens after the election? The elected representatives might not make the same decisions the people would have made if they had gathered for the same purpose. To account for this possibility in representative government, procedural theory gives us a fourth decision-making principle: **responsiveness**. Elected representatives should follow the general contours of public opinion as complex pieces of legislation are formulated.[14]

By adding responsiveness to deal with the case of indirect democracy, we now have four principles of procedural democracy:

- Universal participation
- Political equality
- Majority rule
- Government responsiveness to public opinion

The Substantive View of Democracy   According to procedural theory, the principle of responsiveness is absolute. The government should do what the majority wants, regardless of what that is. At first this seems a reasonable way to protect the rights of citizens in a representative democracy. But what about the rights of minorities? To limit the government's responsiveness to public opinion, we must look outside procedural democratic theory to substantive democratic

Speak Right Up
At this neighborhood meeting a citizen speaks out regarding airport noise abatement issues.
Such citizen participation in the democratic process occurs throughout the United States. It
may be done directly, as in the town meetings of some small New England villages, or indi-
rectly, as citizens make their views known to elected officials at all levels of government.

theory. **Substantive democratic theory** focuses on the substance of government policies, not on the procedures followed in making those policies. It argues that in a democratic government, certain principles must be embodied in government policies. Substantive theorists would reject a law that requires Bible reading in schools because it would violate a substantive principle, the freedom of religion. The core of our substantive principles of democracy is embedded in the Bill of Rights and other amendments to the Constitution.

In defining the principles that underlie democratic government—and the policies of that government—most substantive theorists agree on a basic criterion: government policies should guarantee civil liberties (freedom of behavior such as freedom of religion and freedom of expression)—and civil rights (powers or privileges that government may not arbitrarily deny to individuals, such as protection against discrimination in employment and housing).

Agreement among substantive theorists breaks down when discussion moves from civil rights to social rights (adequate health care, quality education, decent housing) and economic rights (private property, steady employment). For example, some insist that policies that promote social equality are essential to democratic government.[15] Others restrict the requirements of substantive democracy to those policies that safeguard civil liberties and civil rights.

A theorist's political ideology tends to explain his or her position on what democracy really requires in substantive policies. Conservative theorists have a narrow view of the scope of democratic government and a narrow view of the social and economic rights guaranteed by that government. Liberal theorists believe that a democratic government should guarantee its citizens a much broader spectrum of social and economic rights.

Procedural Democracy Versus Substantive Democracy   The problem with the substantive view of democracy is that it does not provide clear, precise criteria that allow us to determine whether a government is democratic. Substantive theorists are free to promote their pet values—separation of church and state, guaranteed employment, equal rights for women, whatever—under the guise of substantive democracy.

The procedural viewpoint also has a problem. Although it presents specific criteria for democratic government, those criteria can produce undesirable social policies that prey on minorities. This clashes with **minority rights**—the idea that all citizens are entitled to certain rights that cannot be denied by the majority. One way to protect minority rights is to limit the principle of majority rule—by requiring a two-thirds majority or some other extraordinary majority when decisions must be made on certain subjects—or to put the issue in the Constitution, beyond the reach of majority rule.

Clearly, procedural and substantive democracy are not always compatible. In choosing one over the other, we are also choosing to focus on either procedures or policies. As authors of this text, we favor a compromise between the two. On the whole we favor the procedural conception of democracy because it more closely approaches the classical definition of democracy—"government by the people." And procedural democracy is founded on clear, well-established rules for decision making. But the theory has a serious drawback: It allows a democratic government to enact policies that can violate the substantive principles of democracy. Thus it is best that pure procedural democracy be diluted so that minority rights and civil liberties are guaranteed as part of the structure of government.

Institutional Models of Democracy

Some democratic theorists favor institutions that tie government decisions closely to the desires of the majority of citizens. If most citizens want laws against the sale of pornography, then the government should outlaw pornography. If citizens want more money spent on defense and less on social welfare (or vice versa), the government should act accordingly. For these theorists, the essence of democratic government is majority rule and responsiveness.

Other theorists place less importance on these principles. They do not believe in relying heavily on mass opinion; instead, they favor institutions that allow groups of citizens to defend their interests in the public policy-making process.

Both schools hold a procedural view of democracy, but they differ in how they interpret "government by the people." We can summarize these theoretical positions using two alternative models of democracy. As a model, each is a hypothetical plan, a blueprint, for achieving democratic government through institutional mechanisms. The majoritarian model values participation by the people in general; the pluralist model values participation by the people in groups.

The Majoritarian Model of Democracy The **majoritarian model of democracy** relies on our intuitive notion of what is fair. It interprets "government by the people" as government by the *majority* of the people. To force the government to respond to public opinion, the majoritarian model depends on several mechanisms that allow the people to participate directly.

The popular election of government officials is the primary mechanism for democratic government in the majoritarian model. Citizens are expected to control their representatives' behavior by choosing wisely in the first place and by re-electing or voting out public officials according to their performance.

Majoritarian theorists also see elections as a means for deciding government policies. An election on a policy issue is called a *referendum*. When a policy question is put on the ballot by the action of citizens circulating petitions and gathering a required minimum number of signatures, it is called an *initiative*. Twenty-one states allow their legislatures to put referenda before the voters and give their citizens the right to place initiatives on the ballot. Five other states make provision for one mechanism or the other.[16]

In the United States no provisions exist for referenda at the federal level. However, Americans strongly favor instituting a system of national referenda.[17] The most fervent advocates of majoritarian democracy would like to see modern technology used to maximize the government's responsiveness to the majority. Some have proposed incorporating public opinion polls or using computers for referenda.[18]

The majoritarian model contends that citizens can control their government if they have adequate mechanisms for popular participation. It also assumes that citizens are knowledgeable about government and politics, that they want to participate in the political process, and that they make rational decisions in voting for their elected representatives.

Critics contend that Americans are not knowledgeable enough for majoritarian democracy to work. They point to research that shows that only 22 percent of a national sample of voters said that they "followed what's going on" in government "most of the time." More (40 percent) said that they followed politics "only now and then" or "hardly at all."[19] Some believe that instead of quick and easy mass voting on public policy, what we need is more deliberation by citizens and their elected representatives. Defenders of majoritarian democracy respond that the American public has coherent and stable opinions on the major policy questions.[20]

An Alternative Model: Pluralist Democracy   For years, political scientists struggled valiantly to reconcile the majoritarian model of democracy with polls that showed a widespread ignorance of politics among the American people. When only a little more than half of the adult population bothers to vote in presidential elections, our form of democracy seems to be government by *some* of the people.

The 1950s saw the evolution of an alternative interpretation of democracy, one tailored to the limited knowledge and participation of the real electorate, not the ideal one. It was based on the concept of *pluralism*—that modern society consists of innumerable groups that share economic, religious, ethnic, or cultural interests. Often people with similar interests organize formal groups. When an organized group seeks to influence government policy, it is called an **interest group**. Many interest groups regularly spend a great deal of time and money trying to influence government policy (see Chapter 7). Among them are the American Hospital Association, the National Association of Manufacturers, the National Education Association (NEA), the National Organization for Women (NOW), and, of course, the NRA.

The **pluralist model of democracy** interprets "government by the people" to mean government by people operating through competing interest groups. According to this model, democracy exists when many (plural) organizations operate separately from the government, press their interests on the government, and even challenge the government.[21] Compared with majoritarian thinking, pluralist theory shifts the focus of democratic government from the mass electorate to organized groups. It changes the criterion for democratic government from responsiveness to mass public opinion to responsiveness to organized groups of citizens.

A decentralized, complex government structure offers the access and openness necessary for pluralist democracy. For pluralists, the ideal system is one that divides government authority among numerous institutions with overlapping authority. Under such a system, competing interest groups have alternative points of access to present and argue their claims.

Our Constitution approaches the pluralist ideal in the way it divides authority among the branches of government. When the National Association for the Advancement of Colored People (NAACP) could not get Congress to outlaw segregated schools in the South, it turned to the federal court system, which did what Congress would not. According to the ideal of pluralist democracy, if all opposing interests are allowed to organize, and if the system can be kept open so that all substantial claims have an opportunity to be heard, the decision will serve the diverse needs of a pluralist society.

The Majoritarian Model Versus the Pluralist Model   In majoritarian democracy, the mass public—not interest groups—controls government actions. The citizenry must be knowledgeable about government and willing to participate in the electoral process. Majoritarian democracy relies on electoral mechanisms that harness the power of the majority to make decisions. Conclusive elections and a centralized structure of government are mechanisms that aid majority rule. Cohesive political parties with well-defined programs also contribute to majoritarian democracy, because they offer voters a clear way to distinguish alternative sets of policies.

Pluralism does not demand much knowledge from citizens in general. It requires specialized knowledge only from groups of citizens, in particular their leaders. In contrast to majoritarian democracy, pluralist democracy seeks to limit majority action so that interest groups can be heard. It relies on strong interest groups and a decentralized government structure—mechanisms that interfere with majority rule, thereby protecting minority interests. We could even say that pluralism allows minorities to rule.

An Undemocratic Model: Elite Theory   If pluralist democracy allows minorities to rule, how does it differ from **elite theory**—the view that a small group of people (a minority) makes most important government decisions? According to elite theory, important government decisions are made by an identifiable and stable minority that shares certain characteristics, usually vast wealth and business connections.[22]

Elite theory appeals to many people, especially those who believe that wealth dominates politics.

According to elite theory, the United States is not a democracy but an oligarchy where government power is in the hands of an elite. Although the voters appear to control the government through elections, elite theorists argue that the powerful few in society manage to define the issues and to constrain the outcomes of government decisions to suit their own interests. Clearly, elite theory describes a government that operates in an undemocratic fashion.

Political scientists have conducted numerous studies designed to test the validity of elite theory. Although not all of those studies have come to the same conclusion, the preponderance of available evidence documenting government decisions on many different issues does not generally support elite theory—at least in the sense that an identifiable ruling elite usually gets its way.[23] Not surprising, elite theorists reject this view. They argue that studies of decisions made on individual issues do not adequately test the influence of the power elite. Rather, they contend that much of the elite's power comes from its ability to keep things off the political agenda. That is, its power derives from its ability to keep people from questioning fundamental assumptions about American capitalism.[24]

Consequently, elite theory remains part of the debate about the nature of American government and is forcefully argued by radical critics of our political system.[25] Although we do not believe that the scholarly evidence supports elite theory, we do recognize that contemporary American pluralism favors some segments of society over others. The poor are chronically unorganized and are not well represented by interest groups. On the other hand, business is better represented than any other sector of the public.[26] Thus, one can endorse pluralist democracy as a more accurate description than elitism in American politics without believing all groups are equally well represented.

Elite Theory Versus Pluralist Theory   The key difference between elite and pluralist theory lies in the durability of the ruling minority. In contrast to elite theory, pluralist theory does not define government conflict in terms of a minority versus the majority; instead, it sees many minorities vying with one another in each policy area. Pluralist democracy makes a virtue of the struggle between competing interests. It argues for government that accommodates this struggle and channels the result into government action. According to pluralist democracy, the public is best served if the government structure provides access for different groups to press their claims in competition with one another. Note that pluralist democracy does not insist that all groups have equal influence on government decisions. In the political struggle, wealthy, well-organized groups have an inherent advantage over poorer, inadequately organized groups. In fact, unorganized segments of the population may not even get their concerns placed on the agenda for government consideration. This is a critical weakness of pluralism. However, pluralists contend that so long as all groups are able to participate vigorously in the decision-making process, the process is democratic.

American Democracy: More Pluralist Than Majoritarian

It is not idle speculation to ask what kind of democracy is practiced in the United States. The answer to this question can help us understand why our government can be called democratic despite a low level of citizen participation in politics and despite government actions that run contrary to public opinion.

Throughout this book, we probe more deeply to determine how well the United States fits the two alternative models of democracy: majoritarian and pluralist. If our answer is not already apparent, it soon will be. We argue that the political system in the United States rates relatively low according to the majoritarian model of democracy, but that it fulfills the pluralist model very well. Yet, the pluralist model is far from a perfect representation of democracy. Its principal drawback is that it favors the well organized, and the poor are the least likely to be members of interest groups. As one advocate of majoritarian democracy once wrote, "The flaw in the pluralist heaven is that the heavenly chorus sings with a strong upper-class accent."[27]

This evaluation of the pluralist nature of American democracy may not mean much to you now. But you will learn that the pluralist model makes the United States look far more democratic than the majoritarian model would. Eventually, you will have to decide the answers to three questions: Is the pluralist model truly an adequate expression of democracy, or is it a perversion of classical ideals designed to portray America as democratic when it is not? Does the majoritarian model result in a "better" type of democracy? If so, could new mechanisms of government be devised to produce a desirable mix of majority rule and minority rights? These questions should play in the back of your mind as you read more about the workings of American government in meeting the challenge of democracy.

Summary

The challenge of democracy lies in making difficult choices—choices that inevitably bring important values into conflict. This chapter has outlined a normative framework for analyzing the policy choices that arise in the pursuit of the purposes of government.

The three major purposes of government are maintaining order, providing public goods, and promoting equality. In pursuing these objectives, every government infringes on individual freedom. But the degree of that infringement depends on the government's (and by extension, its citizens') commitment to order and equality. What we have, then, are two dilemmas. The first—the original dilemma—centers on the conflict between freedom and order. The second—the modern dilemma—focuses on the conflict between freedom and equality.

Some people use political ideologies to help them resolve the conflicts that arise in political decision making. These ideologies define the scope and purpose of government. At opposite extremes of the continuum are totalitarianism, which supports government intervention in every aspect of society, and anarchism, which rejects government entirely. An important step back from totalitarianism is socialism. Democratic socialism, an economic system, favors government ownership of basic industries but preserves civil liberties. Capitalism, another economic system, promotes free enterprise. A significant step short of anarchism is libertarianism, which allows government to protect life and property but little else.

In the United States, the terms *liberal* and *conservative* are used to describe a narrow range toward the center of the political continuum. The usage is probably accurate when the scope of government action is being discussed. That is, liberals support a broader role for government than do conservatives. But it is easier to understand the differences among libertarians, liberals, conservatives, and communitarians and their views on the scope of government if the values of freedom, order, and equality are incorporated into the description of their political ideologies. Libertarians choose freedom over both order and equality. Communitarians are willing to sacrifice freedom for both order and equality. Liberals value freedom more than order and equality more than freedom. Conservatives value order more than freedom and freedom more than equality.

Most scholars believe the United States is a democracy. But what kind of democracy is it? The answer depends on the definition of *democracy*. Some believe democracy is procedural; they define democracy as a form of government in which the people govern through certain institutional mechanisms. Others hold to the substantive theory, claiming a government is democratic if its policies promote civil liberties and rights.

In this book, we emphasize the procedural conception of democracy, distinguishing between direct (participatory) and indirect (representative) democracy. In participatory democracy, all citizens gather to govern themselves according to the principles of universal participation, political equality, and majority rule. In an indirect democracy, the citizens elect representatives to govern for them. If a representative government is elected mostly in accordance with the three principles just listed and is also usually responsive to public opinion, then it qualifies as a democracy.

Procedural democratic theory has produced rival institutional models of democratic government. The classical majoritarian model—which depends on majority votes in elections—assumes that people are knowledgeable about government, that they want to participate in the political process, and that they carefully and rationally choose among candidates. The pluralist model of democracy—which depends on interest group interaction with government—argues that democracy in a complex society requires only that government allow private interests to organize and press their competing claims openly in the political arena.

- Which is better: to live under a government that allows individuals complete freedom to do whatever they please or to live under one that enforces strict law and order?

- Which is better: to allow businesses and private clubs to choose their customers and members or to pass laws that require those businesses and clubs to admit and serve everyone, regardless of race or sex?

- Which is better: a government that is highly responsive to public opinion on all matters or one that responds deliberately to organized groups that argue their cases effectively?

These are enduring questions, and the framers of the Constitution dealt with them, too. Their struggle is the appropriate place to begin our analysis of how these competing models of democracy have animated the debate about the nature of our political process.

Key Terms

government	laissez faire
order	anarchism
communism	liberals
public goods	conservatives
freedom of	communitarians
freedom from	democracy
police power	procedural democratic theory
political equality	universal participation
social equality	political equality
equality of opportunity	majority rule
equality of outcome	participatory democracy
rights	representative democracy
political ideology	responsiveness
totalitarianism	substantive democratic theory
socialism	minority rights
democratic socialism	majoritarian model of democracy
capitalism	interest group
libertarianism	pluralist model of democracy
libertarians	elite theory

Selected Readings

Berry, Jeffrey M., Kent E. Portney, and Ken Thomson. *The Rebirth of Urban Democracy.* Washington, D.C.: Brookings Institution, 1993. An examination of neighborhood government in five American cities. The authors conclude that participatory democracy on the local level is a feasible and desirable alternative.

Clawson, Dan, Alan Neustadtl, and Denise Scott. *Money Talks.* New York: Basic Books, 1992. Using data on campaign contributions, the three authors make an elitist interpretation of the American political process.

Dahl, Robert A. *Democracy and Its Critics.* New Haven, Conn.: Yale University Press, 1989. The nation's leading expert on pluralist theory examines the basic foundations of democracy. Dahl defends democracy against a variety of criticisms that have focused on its shortcomings.

Ebenstein, William, and Edwin Fogelman. *Today's Isms: Communism, Fascism, Capitalism, Socialism.* 10th ed. Englewood Cliffs, N.J.: Prentice-Hall, 1994. This standard source describes the history of the four major "isms" and relates each to developments in contemporary politics. It is concise, informative, and readable.

Etzioni, Amitai. *Rights and the Common Good: The Communitarian Perspective.* New York: St. Martin's Press, 1995. Reprints the Communitarian Network's platform and presents thirty essays on various aspects of the communitarian perspective.

World Wide Web Resources

The World Wide Web (WWW) on the Internet has many sites with information relevant to studying American government and politics. Below are some that are particularly relevant to the ideological typology described in this chapter. The Uniform Resource Locator (URL) needed to find the site on the WWW is given within angle brackets < >. Because these addresses may change over time, you may have to search the WWW by keywords to locate the site.

The Communitarian Network. This site "is a coalition of individuals and organizations who have come together to shore up the moral, social, and political environment. We are a nonsectarian, nonpartisan, nationwide association."
<www.gwu.edu/~ccps/>

Libertarian Student Clubs' WWW Network. This site "is a links and updates page for all the libertarian student clubs using the Web. This includes both student affiliates of the Libertarian Party and other student groups seeking to further the cause of libertarianism."
<www.mit.edu:8001/activities/libertarians/cwn.html>

Lefties on the Web. "This page is for those of us who don't buy into Newt's New Right agenda, and who still believe there's a constructive role for government in America."
<www.tiac.net/users/rafeb/>

The Right Side of the Web. A creation of Jeff Donels, whose home page describes him as "Webmaster, member of the Militia of Northern Virginia AND digeratti wanna-be (even though WiReD hates me)," this site contains a melange of material dealing with conservative causes.
<www.rtside.com>

Impact On Line. This is an on-line public interest organization that seeks to "plug you into the existing conduits for making positive change." In addition to providing access to other public interest groups (both conservative and liberal), you can learn about current issues and volunteer opportunities in your community and you can exchange views with other concerned citizens.

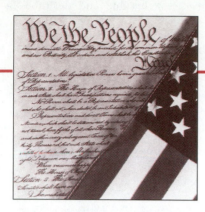

2

The Constitution

The midnight burglars made a small mistake. They left a piece of tape over the latch they had tripped to enter the Watergate office and apartment complex in Washington, D.C. But a security guard discovered their tampering and called the police, who surprised the burglars in the offices of the Democratic National Committee at 2:30 A.M. The arrests of five men in the early hours of June 17, 1972, triggered a constitutional struggle that eventually involved the president of the United States, the Congress, and the Supreme Court.

The Watergate story unfolded completely only after the landslide reelection of Richard Nixon in November 1972. The five burglars and two men closely connected with the president answered in court for the break-in. The Senate launched its own investigation.

After a stunned nation learned that the president had secretly tape-recorded all of his conversations in the White House, the Senate committee asked for the tapes. Nixon refused, citing the separation of powers between the legislative and the executive branches and claiming that "executive privilege" allowed him to withhold information from Congress.

Nixon also resisted subpoenas demanding the White House tapes. Eventually, the special prosecutor appointed by the attorney general to investigate Watergate brought indictments against Nixon's closest aides. Nixon himself was named as an unindicted co-conspirator. Both the special prosecutor and the defendants wanted the White House tapes, but Nixon continued to resist. Finally, on July 24, 1974, the Supreme Court ruled that the president had to hand over the tapes. At almost the same time, the House Judiciary Committee voted to recommend to the full House that Nixon be impeached.

Faced with the collapse of his support and likely impeachment by the full House, Nixon resigned the presidency on August 9, 1974. A month later, acting within his constitutional powers, President Gerald Ford granted private citizen Richard Nixon an unconditional pardon for all crimes that he may have committed. Others were not so fortunate. Three members of the Nixon cabinet (two attorneys general and a secretary of commerce) were convicted and sentenced for their crimes in the Watergate affair.

The Watergate affair posed one of the most serious challenges to the constitutional order of modern American government. The incident ultimately developed into a struggle over the rule of law, between the president on the one hand and Congress and the courts on the other. In the end, the constitutional principle separating power among the executive, legislative, and judicial branches prevented the president from controlling the Watergate investigation. The principle of checks and balances allowed Congress to threaten Nixon with impeachment. The belief that Nixon had violated the Constitution finally prompted members of both political parties to support impeachment.

Nixon resigned the presidency a little more than a year and a half into his second term. In some countries, an irregular change in government leadership provides an opportunity for a palace coup, an armed revolution, or a military dictatorship. But here, significantly, there was no political violence after Nixon's resignation; in fact, none was expected. Constitutional order in the United States had been put to a test, and it passed with high honors.

This chapter poses some questions about the Constitution. How did it evolve? What form did it take? What values does it reflect? How can it be altered? And which model of democracy—majoritarian or pluralist—does it fit best?

The Revolutionary Roots of the Constitution

The Constitution is just 4,300 words long. But those 4,300 words define the basic structure of our national government. A comprehensive document, it divides the government into three branches and describes the powers of those branches, their relationships, and the interaction between the government and the governed. The Constitution makes itself the supreme law of the land and binds every government official to support it.

Most Americans revere the Constitution as political "scripture." To charge that a political action is unconstitutional is akin to claiming that it is unholy. And so the Constitution has taken on a symbolic value that has strengthened its authority as the basis of American government. Strong belief in the Constitution has led many politicians to abandon party for principle when constitutional issues are at stake.

The U.S. Constitution, written in 1787 for an agricultural society huddled along the coast of a wild new land, now guides the political life of a massive urban society in the nuclear age. To fully understand the reasons for the stability of the Constitution—and of the political system it created—we must first look at its historical roots, roots that lie in colonial America.

Freedom in Colonial America

Although they were British subjects, the American colonists in the eighteenth century enjoyed a degree of freedom denied most people in the world. In contrast to Europe, where ancient custom and the relics of feudalism restricted private property, compelled support for established religion, and restricted access to trades and professions, Americans were relatively free of such controls. Also, in America, colonists enjoyed almost complete freedom of speech, press, and assembly.[1]

By 1763, Britain and the colonies had reached a compromise between imperial control and colonial self-government. America's foreign affairs and overseas trade were controlled by the king and Parliament, the British legislature; the rest was left to home rule. But the cost of administering the colonies was substantial. Because Americans benefited the most, contended their English countrymen, Americans should bear that cost.

The Road to Revolution

The British believed that taxing the colonies was the obvious way to meet the costs of administering the colonies. The colonists did not agree. They especially did not want to be taxed by a distant government in which they had no representation. During the decade preceding the outbreak of hostilities in 1775, this issue was to convert increasing numbers of colonists from loyal British subjects seeking the rights of Englishmen to revolutionaries seeking the end of British rule over the American colonies.

On the night of December 16, 1773, a group of colonists reacted to a British duty on tea by organizing the Boston Tea Party. A mob boarded three ships and emptied 342 chests of that valuable substance into Boston Harbor.

In an attempt to reassert British control over its recalcitrant colonists, Parliament passed the Coercive (or "Intolerable") Acts (1774). One act imposed a blockade on Boston until the tea was paid for; another gave royal governors the power to quarter British soldiers in private homes. Now the taxation issue was secondary; more important was the conflict between British demands for order and American demands for liberty. The Virginia and Massachusetts assemblies summoned a continental congress, an assembly that would speak and act for the people of all the colonies.

The First Continental Congress met in Philadelphia in September 1774. The objective of the assembly was to restore harmony between Great Britain and the American colonies. A leader, called the president, was elected. (The terms *president* and *congress* in American government trace their origins to the First Continental Congress.) In October 1774, the delegates adopted a statement of rights and principles; many of these later found their way into the Declaration of Independence and the Constitution. For example, the congress claimed a right "to life, liberty, and property" and a right "peaceably to assemble, consider of their grievances, and petition the king." Then the congress adjourned, planning to reconvene in May 1775.

Revolutionary Action

By early 1775, however, a movement that the colonists themselves were calling a revolution had already begun. Colonists in Massachusetts were fighting the British at Concord and Lexington. Delegates to the Second Continental Congress, meeting in May, faced a dilemma: Should they prepare for war, or should they try to reconcile with Britain? As conditions deteriorated, the Second Continental Congress remained in session, to serve as the government of the colony-states.

Uniquely American Protest
Americans protested the Tea Act (1773) by holding the Boston Tea Party (see background, left) and by using a unique form of painful punishment—tarring and feathering—on the tax collector (see Stamp Act upside-down on the Liberty Tree). An early treatise on the subject offered the following instructions: "First, strip a person naked, then heat the tar until it is thin, and pour upon the naked flesh, or rub it over with a tar brush. After which, sprinkle decently upon the tar, whilst it is yet warm, as many feathers as will stick to it."

On June 7, 1776, the Virginia delegation called on the Continental Congress to resolve "that these United Colonies are, and of right ought to be, free and Independent States, that they are absolved from all allegiance to the British Crown, and that all political connection between them and the State of Great Britain is, and ought to be, totally dissolved." A committee of five men was appointed to prepare a proclamation expressing the colonies' reasons for declaring independence.

The Declaration of Independence

Thomas Jefferson, a young farmer and lawyer from Virginia, drafted the proclamation. Jefferson's document, the **Declaration of Independence**, expressed simply, clearly, and rationally the arguments in support of separation from Great Britain.

The principles underlying the declaration were rooted in the writings of the English philosopher John Locke and had been expressed many times by speakers in congress and in the colonial assemblies. Locke argued that people have

God-given, or natural, rights that are inalienable—that is, they cannot be taken away by any government. According to Locke, all legitimate political authority exists to preserve these natural rights and is based on the consent of those who are governed. The idea of consent is derived from **social contract theory**, which states that the people agree to establish rulers for certain purposes but they have the right to resist or remove rulers who violate those purposes.[2]

Jefferson used similar arguments in the Declaration of Independence. His simple yet impassioned statement of faith in democracy reverberates to this day: "We hold these truths to be self-evident, that all men are created equal, that they are endowed by their Creator with certain unalienable rights, that among these are life, liberty and the pursuit of happiness."

The First Continental Congress had declared in 1774 that the colonists were entitled to "life, liberty, and property." Jefferson reformulated the objectives as "life, liberty, and the pursuit of happiness." Furthermore, he continued:

> That to secure these rights, Governments are instituted among Men, deriving their just powers from the consent of the governed. That whenever any Form of Government becomes destructive of these ends, it is the Right of the People to alter or to abolish it, and to institute new Government, laying its foundation on such Principles and organizing its Powers in such form, as to them shall seem most likely to effect their Safety and Happiness.

He went on to list the many deliberate acts of the king that had exceeded the legitimate role of government. Finally, Jefferson declared that the colonies were "Free and Independent States," with no political connection to Great Britain.

The major premise of the Declaration of Independence is that the people have a right to revolt if they determine that their government is denying them their legitimate rights. The long list of the king's actions was evidence of such denial. So the people had the right to rebel, to form a new government. On July 2, 1776, the Second Continental Congress finally voted for independence. The vote was by state, and the motion carried 11 to 0. (Rhode Island was not present, and the New York delegation, lacking instructions, did not cast its "yea" vote until July 15.) Two days later, the Declaration of Independence was approved with few changes.

The War of Independence lasted far longer than anyone expected. It began in a moment of confusion, when a shot rang out as British soldiers approached the town of Lexington on the way to Concord, Massachusetts, on April 19, 1775. The end came six and a half years later with Lord Cornwallis's surrender of his six-thousand-man army at Yorktown, Virginia, on October 19, 1781. It was a costly war: More died and were wounded in relation to the population than in any other conflict except the Civil War.[3]

From Revolution to Confederation

By declaring their independence from England, the colonies left themselves without any real central government. So the revolutionaries proclaimed the creation of a republic. Strictly speaking, a **republic** is a government without a monarch, but the term had come to mean a government based on the consent of the governed, whose power is exercised by representatives who are responsible to them. A republic need not be a democracy, and this was fine with the founders; at that time democracy was associated with mob rule and instability (see Chapter 1). The revolutionaries were less concerned with determining who would control their new government than with limiting the powers of that government. They had revolted in the name of liberty, and now they wanted a government with sharply defined powers. To make sure they got one, they meant to define its structure and powers in writing.

The Articles of Confederation

Barely a week after the Declaration of Independence was signed, the Second Continental Congress received a committee report entitled "Articles of Confederation and Perpetual Union." A **confederation** is a loose association of independent states that agree to cooperate on specified matters. In a confederation, the states retain their sovereignty, which means that each has supreme power within its borders. The central government is weak; it can only coordinate, not control, the actions of its sovereign states.

The **Articles of Confederation**, the compact among the thirteen original colonies that established the United States, was finally adopted on November 15, 1777. The Articles jealously guarded state sovereignty; their provisions clearly reflected the delegates' fears of a strong central government. Under the Articles, each state, regardless of its size, had one vote in the congress. Votes on financing the war and other important issues required the consent of at least nine of the thirteen states. The common danger—Britain—had forced the young republic to function under the Articles, but this first try at a government was inadequate to the task. The delegates had succeeded in crafting a national government that was largely powerless.

The Articles failed for at least four reasons: First, they did not give the national government the power to tax. As a result, the congress had to plead for money from the states to pay for the war and to carry on the affairs of the new nation. Second, the Articles made no provision for an independent leadership position to direct the government (the president was merely the presiding officer of the congress). The omission was deliberate—the colonists feared the reestablishment of a monarchy—but it left the nation without a leader. Third, the Articles did not allow the national government to regulate interstate and foreign commerce. (When John Adams proposed that the confederation enter into a commercial treaty with Britain after the war, he was asked, "Would you like one treaty or thirteen, Mr. Adams?").[4] Finally, the Articles could not be amended without the unanimous agreement of the congress and the assent of all the state legislatures; thus, each state had the power to veto any changes to the confederation.

The goal of the delegates who drew up the Articles of Confederation was to retain power in the states. This was consistent with republicanism, which viewed the remote power of a national government as a danger to liberty. In this sense alone, the Articles were a grand success. They completely hobbled the infant government.

Disorder Under the Confederation

Once the Revolution had ended and independence was a reality, it became clear that the national government had neither the economic nor the military power to function. Freed from wartime austerity, Americans rushed to purchase goods from abroad. Debt mounted and, for many, bankruptcy followed.

The problem was particularly severe in Massachusetts, where high interest rates and high state taxes were forcing farmers into bankruptcy. In 1786 and 1787, farmers under the leadership of Daniel Shays, a revolutionary war veteran, carried out a series of insurrections to prevent the foreclosure of their farms by creditors. With the congress unable to secure funds from the states to help out, the governor of Massachusetts eventually called out the militia and restored order.[5] Shays' Rebellion demonstrated the impotence of the confederation and the urgent need to suppress insurrection and maintain domestic order.

From Confederation to Constitution

Order, the original purpose of government, was breaking down under the Articles of Confederation. The "league of friendship" envisioned in the Articles was not enough to hold the nation together in peacetime.

In 1786, Virginia invited the states to attend a convention at Annapolis to explore revisions to the Articles of Confederation. Although only five states sent delegates, they seized the opportunity to call for another meeting in Philadelphia the next year. The congress agreed to the convention but limited its mission to "the sole and express purpose of revising the Articles of Confederation."

Shays' Rebellion lent a sense of urgency to the task before the Philadelphia convention. The congress's inability to confront the rebellion was evidence that a stronger national government was necessary to preserve order and property—to protect the states from internal as well as external dangers. "While the Declaration was directed against an excess of authority," remarked Supreme Court Justice Robert H. Jackson some 150 years later, "the Constitution [that followed the Articles of Confederation] was directed against anarchy."[6]

The Constitutional Convention officially opened on May 25, 1787. Although its delegates were authorized only to "revise" the Articles of Confederation, within the first week of debate, Edmund Randolph of Virginia had presented a long list of changes, suggested by fellow Virginian James Madison, that would replace the weak confederation of states with a powerful national government. The delegates unanimously agreed to debate Randolph's proposal, which was called the **Virginia Plan**. Almost immediately, then, they rejected the idea of amending the Articles of Confederation, working instead to create an entirely new constitution.

The Virginia Plan

The Virginia Plan dominated the convention's deliberations for the rest of the summer making several important proposals for a strong central government:

- That the powers of the government be divided among three separate branches: a **legislative branch**, for making laws; an **executive branch**, for enforcing laws; and a **judicial branch**, for interpreting laws.

- That the legislature consist of two houses. The first would be chosen by the people; the second by the members of the first house from among persons nominated by the state legislatures.

- That each state's representation in the legislature be in proportion to taxes paid to the national government, or in proportion to its free population.

- That an executive of unspecified size be selected by the legislature and serve for a single term.

- That the national judiciary include one or more supreme courts and other lower courts, with judges appointed for life by the legislature.

- That the executive and a number of national judges serve as a council of revision, to approve or veto (disapprove) legislative acts. Their veto could be overridden, however, by a vote of both houses of the legislature.

- That the range of powers of all three branches be far greater than that assigned the national government by the Articles of Confederation and include the power of the legislature to override state laws.

By proposing a powerful national legislature that could override state laws, the Virginia Plan clearly advocated a new form of government. It was a mixed structure, with more authority over the states and new authority over the people.

Madison was a monumental force in the ensuing debate on the proposals. However, the constitution that emerged from the convention bore only partial resemblance to the document Madison wanted to create. He endorsed seventy-one specific proposals but he ended up on the losing side on forty of them.[7] And the parts of the Virginia Plan that were ultimately adopted in the Constitution were not adopted without challenge. Conflict revolved primarily around the basis of representation in the legislature, the method of choosing legislators, and the structure of the executive branch.

The New Jersey Plan

When in 1787 it appeared that much of the Virginia Plan would be approved by the big states, the small states united in opposition. William Paterson of

New Jersey introduced an alternative set of resolutions, written to preserve the spirit of the Articles of Confederation by amending rather than replacing them. The **New Jersey Plan** included the following proposals:

- That a single-chamber legislature have the power to raise revenue and regulate commerce.
- That the states have equal representation in the legislature and choose the members of that body.
- That a multiperson executive be elected by the legislature, with powers similar to those listed in the Virginia Plan but without the right to veto legislation.
- That a supreme judiciary be created with a very limited jurisdiction. (There was no provision for a system of national courts.)
- That the acts of the legislature be binding on the states; that is, be regarded as the "supreme law of the respective states," with force used to compel obedience.

The New Jersey Plan was defeated in the first major convention vote, 7–3. However, the small states had enough support to force a compromise on the issue of representation in the legislature.

The Great Compromise

The Virginia Plan's provision for a two-chamber legislature was never seriously challenged, but the idea of representation according to population stirred up heated debate. The small states demanded equal representation for all states.

A committee was created to resolve the deadlock. It consisted of one delegate from each state, chosen by secret ballot. After working through the Independence Day recess, the committee reported reaching the **Great Compromise** (sometimes called the Connecticut Compromise). Representation in the House of Representatives would be apportioned according to the population of each state. Initially, there would be fifty-six members. Revenue-raising acts would originate in the House. Most important, the states would be represented equally in the Senate, with two senators each. Senators would be selected by their state legislatures, not directly by the people.

The delegates accepted the Great Compromise. The smaller states got their equal representation; the larger states, their proportional representation. The small states might dominate the Senate, and the big states might control the House, but because all legislation had to be approved by both chambers, neither group would be able to dominate the other.

Compromise on the Presidency

Contention replaced compromise when the delegates turned to the executive branch. They did agree on a one-person executive—a president—but they disagreed on how the executive would be selected and what the term of office would be. The delegates distrusted the people's judgment; some feared that popular election would arouse public passions. Consequently, the delegates rejected the idea. At the same time, representatives of the small states feared that election by the legislature would allow the larger states to control the executive.

Once again they compromised, creating the *electoral college*. This cumbersome system consists of a group of electors who are chosen for the sole purpose of selecting the president and vice president. Each state legislature would choose a number of electors equal to the number of its representatives in Congress. Each elector would then vote for two people. The candidate with the most votes would become president, provided that the number of votes constituted a majority; the person with the next greatest number of votes would become vice president. (This procedure was changed in 1804 by the Twelfth Amendment, which mandates separate votes for each office.) If no candidate won a majority, then the House of Representatives would choose a president, with each state casting one vote.

The electoral college compromise eliminated the fear of a popular vote for president. At the same time, it satisfied the small states. If the electoral college failed to produce a president—which the delegates expected would happen—an election by the House would give every state the same voice in the selection process.

Finally, the delegates agreed that the president's term of office should be four years and that the president should be eligible for reelection.

The delegates also realized that removing a president from office would be a very serious political matter. For that reason, they involved the other two branches of government in the process. The House alone was empowered to charge a president with "Treason, Bribery, or other high Crimes and Misdemeanors," by a majority vote. The Senate was given the sole power to try such impeachments. It could convict, and thus remove, a president only by a two-thirds vote. And the chief justice of the United States was required to preside over the Senate trial.

The Final Product

Once the delegates resolved their major disagreements, they dispatched the remaining issues relatively quickly. A committee was appointed to draft a constitution. The Preamble, which was the last section to be drafted, begins with a phrase that would have been impossible to write when the convention opened. This single sentence contains four elements that form the foundation of the American political tradition.[8]

- *It creates a people:* "We the People of the United States" was a dramatic departure from a loose confederation of states.

- *It explains the reason for the Constitution:* "in Order to form a more perfect Union" was an indirect way of saying that the first effort, under the Articles of Confederation, had been inadequate.

- *It articulates goals:* "[to] establish Justice, insure domestic Tranquility, provide for the common defence, promote the general Welfare, and secure the

Blessings of Liberty to ourselves and our posterity"—in other words, the government exists to promote order and freedom.

- *It fashions a government:* "do ordain and establish this Constitution for the United States of America."

The Basic Principles

In creating the Constitution, the founders relied on four political principles that together established a revolutionary new political order. These principles were republicanism, federalism, separation of powers, and checks and balances.

Republicanism   **Republicanism** is a form of government in which power resides in the people and is exercised by their elected representatives. The framers were determined to avoid aristocracy (rule by a hereditary class), monarchy (rule by one), and direct democracy (rule by the people). A republic was both new and daring: no people had ever been governed by a republic on so vast a scale. Indeed, the framers themselves were far from sure that their government could be sustained. After the convention had ended, Benjamin Franklin was asked what sort of government the new nation would have. "A republic," he replied, "if you can keep it."

Federalism   **Federalism** is the division of power between a central government and regional units. Citizens are thus subject to two different bodies of law. It stands between two competing government schemes. On the one side is unitary government, in which all power is vested in a central government. On the other side stands confederation, a loose union with powerful states. The Constitution embodied a division of power, but conferred substantial powers on a national government at the expense of the states.

According to the Constitution, the powers vested in the national and state governments are derived from the people, who remain the ultimate sovereign. National and state governments can exercise their powers over persons and property within their own spheres of authority. But, at the same time, by participating in the electoral process or by amending their governing charters, the people can restrain both the national and the state governments if necessary to preserve liberty.

The Constitution lists the powers of the national government and the powers denied to the states. All other powers remain with the states. However, the Constitution does not clearly describe the spheres of authority within which these powers can be exercised. As we will discuss in Chapter 3, limits on the exercise of power by the national government and the states have evolved as a result of political and military conflict; moreover, the limits have proved changeable.

Separation of Powers   **Separation of powers** is the assignment of the lawmaking, law-enforcing, and law-interpreting functions of government to independent legislative, executive, and judicial branches. Nationally, the lawmaking power resides in Congress; the law-enforcing power resides in the presidency;

and the law-interpreting power resides in the courts. Service in one branch prohibits simultaneous service in the others. Separation of powers safeguards liberty by ensuring that all government power does not fall into the hands of a single person or group of people. But the framers' concern with protecting the liberty of the people did not extend to the election process. The Constitution constrained majority rule by limiting the direct influence of the people on that process (see Figure 2.1). In theory, separation of powers means that one branch cannot exercise the powers of the other branches. In practice, however, the separation is far from complete. One scholar has suggested that what we have instead is "separate institutions sharing powers."[9]

Checks and Balances   The constitutional system of **checks and balances** is a means of giving each branch of government some scrutiny of and control over the other branches. The framers reasoned that checks and balances would prevent one branch from ignoring or overpowering the others.

Separation of powers and checks and balances are two distinct principles, but both are necessary to ensure that one branch does not dominate the government. Separation of powers divides government responsibilities among the legislative, executive, and judicial branches; checks and balances prevent the exclusive exercise of those powers by any one of the three branches. For example, only Congress can enact laws. But the president (through the power of the veto) can cancel them, and the courts (by finding a law in violation of the Constitution) can nullify them. And the process goes on. In a "check on a check," Congress can override a president's veto by an extraordinary (two-thirds) majority in each chamber; and it is empowered to propose amendments to the Constitution, counteracting the courts' power to find a national law invalid. Figure 2.2 depicts the relationship between separation of powers and checks and balances.

The Articles of the Constitution

In addition to the Preamble, the Constitution includes seven articles. The first three establish the separate branches of government and specify their internal operations and powers. The remaining four define the relationships among the states, explain the process of amendment, declare the supremacy of national law, and explain the procedure for ratifying the Constitution.

Article I: The Legislative Article   In structuring their new government, the framers began with the legislative branch because they thought lawmaking was the most important function of a republican government. Article I is the most detailed and therefore the longest of all the articles. It defines the bicameral (two-chamber) character of the Congress and describes the internal operating procedures of the House of Representatives and the Senate. Section 8 of Article I expresses the principle of **enumerated powers**, which means that Congress can exercise only the powers that the Constitution assigns to it. Eighteen powers are enumerated; the first seventeen are specific powers (for example, the power to regulate interstate commerce).

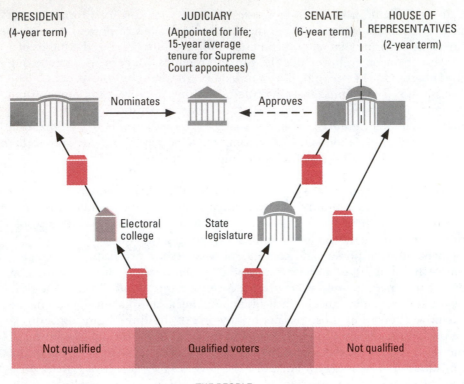

PRESIDENT
(4-year term)

JUDICIARY
(Appointed for life;
15-year average
tenure for Supreme
Court appointees)

SENATE
(6-year term)

HOUSE OF
REPRESENTATIVES
(2-year term)

Nominates

Approves

Electoral
college

State
legislature

Not qualified

Qualified voters

Not qualified

THE PEOPLE

 Ballot
box

FIGURE 2.1   ***The Constitution and the Electoral Process***
The framers were afraid of majority rule, and that fear is reflected in the electoral process for
national office described in the Constitution. The people, speaking through the voters, partic-
ipated directly only in the choice of their representatives in the House. The president and
senators were elected indirectly, through the electoral college and state legislatures. (Direct
election of senators did not become law until 1913, when the Seventeenth Amendment was
ratified.) Judicial appointments are, and always have been, far removed from representative
links to the people. Judges are nominated by the president and approved by the Senate.

The last clause in Section 8, known as the **necessary and proper clause** (or
the elastic clause), gives Congress the means to execute the enumerated powers (see the Appendix). This clause is the basis of Congress's **implied
powers**—those powers that Congress must have in order to execute its enumerated powers. For example, the power to levy and collect taxes (Clause 1)
and the power to coin money and regulate its value (Clause 5), when joined
with the necessary and proper clause (Clause 18), imply that Congress has the
power to charter a bank. Otherwise, the national government would have no
means of managing the money it collects through its power to tax. Implied

BRANCHES OF GOVERNMENT

	The legislature can:	The executive can:	The judiciary can:
Legislative	• Make laws	• Veto legislation • Recommend legislation	• Review legislative acts
Executive	• Confirm executive appointments (Senate) • Override executive veto • Reject foreign treaties	• Enforce laws	• Review executive acts • Issue injunctions
Judicial	• Impeach • Create or eliminate courts	• Grant pardons • Nominate judges	• Interpret laws

POWERS OF GOVERNMENT

FIGURE 2.2 *Separation of Powers and Checks and Balances*
Separation of powers is the assignment of lawmaking, law-enforcing, and law-interpreting functions to the legislative, executive, and judicial branches. The phenomenon is illustrated by the diagonal from upper left to lower right in the figure. Checks and balances give each branch some power over the other branches. For example, the executive branch possesses some legislative power, and the legislative branch possesses some executive power. These checks and balances are listed outside the diagonal.

powers clearly expand the enumerated powers conferred on Congress by the Constitution.

Article II: The Executive Article   Article II sets the president's term of office, the procedure for electing a president through the electoral college, the qualifications for becoming president, and the president's duties and powers. The last include acting as commander in chief of the military; making treaties (which must be ratified by a two-thirds vote in the Senate); and appointing government officers, diplomats, and judges (again, with the advice and consent of the Senate).

The president also has legislative powers—part of the constitutional system of checks and balances. For example, the Constitution requires that the president periodically inform the Congress of the "State of the Union" and of the policies and programs that the executive branch intends to advocate in the coming year. Today this is done annually, in the president's State of the Union address. Under special circumstances, the president can also convene or adjourn Congress. Additionally, the duty to "take Care that the Laws be faithfully executed" in Section 3 has provided presidents with a reservoir of power.

Article III: The Judicial Article   The third article was left purposely vague. The Constitution established the Supreme Court as the highest court in the land. But beyond that, the framers were unable to agree on the need for a national judiciary, or its size, its composition, or the procedures it should follow. They left these issues to the Congress, which resolved them by creating a system of federal, that is, national, courts separate from the state courts.

Unless they are impeached, federal judges serve for life. They are appointed to indefinite terms "during good Behavior," and their salaries cannot be lowered while they hold office. These stipulations reinforce the separation of powers; they see to it that judges are independent of the other branches, that they do not have to fear retribution for their exercise of judicial power.

Congress exercises a potential check on the judicial branch through its power to create (and eliminate) lower federal courts. Congress can also restrict the power of the federal courts to decide cases. And, as we have noted, the president appoints—with the advice and consent of the Senate—the justices of the Supreme Court and the judges of the lower federal courts.

Article III does not explicitly give the courts the power of **judicial review**, the authority to invalidate congressional or presidential actions. That power has been inferred from the logic, structure, and theory of the Constitution.

The Remaining Articles   The remaining four articles of the Constitution cover a lot of ground. Article IV requires that the judicial acts, and criminal warrants of each state be honored in all other states, and it forbids discrimination against citizens of one state by another state. This provision promotes equality; it keeps the states from treating outsiders differently from their own citizens. The origin of this clause can be traced to the Articles of Confederation.

Article IV also allows the addition of new states and stipulates that the national government will protect the states against foreign invasion and domestic violence.

Article V specifies the methods for amending (changing) the Constitution. We will have more to say about this shortly.

An important component of Article VI is the **supremacy clause**, which asserts that, when they conflict with state or local laws, the Constitution, national laws, and treaties take precedence. The stipulation is vital to the operation of federalism. In keeping with the supremacy clause, Article VI also requires that all national and state officials, elected or appointed, take an oath to support the Constitution. The article also mandates that religion cannot be a prerequisite for holding government office.

Finally, Article VII describes the ratification process, stipulating that approval by conventions in nine states would be necessary for the Constitution to take effect.

The Framers' Motives

What forces motivated the framers? Surely economic issues were important, but they were not the major issues. The single most important factor leading to the Constitutional Convention was the inability of the national or state governments to maintain order under the loose structure of the Articles of Confederation. Certainly order involved the protection of property, but the framers had a broader view of property than their portfolios of government securities. They wanted to protect their homes, their families, and their means of livelihood from impending anarchy.

Although they disagreed bitterly on the structure and mechanics of the national government, the framers agreed on the most vital issues. For example, three of the most crucial features of the Constitution—the power to tax, the necessary and proper clause, and the supremacy clause—were approved unanimously without debate. Indeed, the motivation to create order was so strong, the framers were willing to draft clauses that protected the most undemocratic of all institutions—slavery.

The Slavery Issue

The institution of slavery was well ingrained in American life at the time of the Constitutional Convention, and slavery helped shape the Constitution, although it is mentioned nowhere by name in it. It is doubtful, in fact, that there would have been a Constitution if the delegates had had to resolve the slavery issue.

The question of representation in the House of Representatives brought the issue close to the surface of the debate at the Constitutional Convention, and it led to the Great Compromise. Representation in the House was to be based on population. But who counted in the "population"? Eventually, the delegates agreed unanimously that in apportioning representation in the House and in assessing direct taxes, the population of each state was to be determined by adding "the whole Number of free Persons" and "three fifths of all other Persons" (Article I, Section 2). The phrase "all other Persons" is, of course, a substitute for "slaves."

The three-fifths clause gave states with large slave populations (the South) greater representation in Congress than states with small slave populations (the North). The compromise left the South with 47 percent of the House seats, a sizable minority, but in all likelihood a losing one on slavery issues.[10] The overrepresentation resulting from the South's large slave populations translated into greater influence in selecting the president as well, because the electoral was based on the size of the states' congressional delegations. The three-fifths clause also undertaxed states with large slave populations.

All Were Not Created Equal
This 1845 photograph of Isaac Jefferson, who had been one of Thomas Jefferson's slaves at Monticello, reminds us that the framers of the Constitution did not extend freedom and equality to all. Slavery was widely accepted as a social norm in the eighteenth century.

Another issue centered around the slave trade. Several southern delegates were uncompromising in their defense of the slave trade, while other delegates favored prohibition. The delegates compromised, agreeing that the slave trade could not be ended before twenty years had elapsed (Article I, Section 9). Finally, the delegates agreed, without serious challenge, that fugitive slaves be returned to their masters (Article IV, Section 2).

In addressing these points, the framers in essence condoned slavery. Clearly, slavery existed in stark opposition to the idea that "All men are created equal," and though many slaveholders, including Jefferson and Madison, agonized over it, few made serious efforts to free their own slaves. Most Americans seemed indifferent to slavery. Nonetheless, the eradication of slavery proceeded gradually in certain states. By 1787, Connecticut, Massachusetts, New Jersey, New York, Pennsylvania, Rhode Island, and Vermont abolished slavery or provided for gradual emancipation. This slow but perceptible shift on the slavery issue in many states masked a volcanic force capable of destroying the Constitutional Convention and the Union.

Selling the Constitution

On September 17, 1787, nearly four months after the Constitutional Convention opened, the delegates convened for the last time, to sign the final version of their handiwork. Because several delegates were unwilling to sign the document, the last paragraph was craftily worded to give the impression of unanimity: "Done in Convention by the Unanimous Consent of the States present." However, before it could take effect, the Constitution had to be ratified by a minimum of nine state conventions. In each, support was far from "unanimous."

The proponents of the new charter, who wanted a strong national government, called themselves Federalists. The opponents of the Constitution were quickly dubbed Antifederalists. They claimed, however, that they were true federalists because they wanted to protect the states from the tyranny of a strong national government. The viewpoints of the two groups formed the bases of the first American political parties.

The *Federalist* Papers

Beginning in October 1787, an exceptional series of eighty-five newspaper articles defending the Constitution appeared under the title *The Federalist: A Commentary on the Constitution of the United States.* The essays bore the pen name "Publius" and were written primarily by James Madison and Alexander Hamilton, with some assistance from John Jay. Logically and calmly, Publius argued in favor of ratification. Reprinted extensively during the ratification battle, The *Federalist* papers remain the best single commentary we have on the meaning of the Constitution and the political theory it embodies.

Not to be outdone, the Antifederalists offered their own intellectual basis for rejecting the Constitution. In several essays, the most influential authored under the pseudonyms "Brutus" and "Federal Farmer," they attacked the centralization of power in a strong national government, claiming it would obliterate the states, violate the social contract of the Declaration of Independence, and destroy liberty in the process. They defended the status quo, maintaining that the Articles of Confederation established true federal principles.[11]

Of all the *Federalist* papers, the most magnificent and most frequently cited is *Federalist* No. 10, which was written by James Madison. He argued that the proposed constitution was designed "to break and control the violence of faction": "By a faction," Madison wrote, "I understand a number of citizens, whether amounting to a majority or minority of the whole, who are united and actuated by some common impulse of passion, or of interest, adverse to the rights of other citizens, or to the permanent and aggregate interests of the community."

Madison was discussing what we described in Chapter 1 as *pluralism*. What Madison called factions are today called interest groups or even political parties. According to Madison, "The most common and durable source of factions has been the various and unequal distribution of property." Madison was concerned not with reducing inequalities of wealth (which he took for granted) but with controlling the seemingly inevitable conflict that stems from them. The Constitution, he argued, was well constructed for this purpose.

Through the mechanism of representation, wrote Madison, the Constitution would prevent a "tyranny of the majority" (mob rule). The government would not be controlled directly by the people, but would be governed indirectly, by their elected representatives. And those representatives would have the intelligence and the understanding to serve the larger interests of the nation. Moreover, the federal system would require that majorities form first within each state, then organize for effective action at the national level. This and the vastness of the country would make it unlikely that a majority would form that would "invade the rights of other citizens."

The purpose of *Federalist* No. 10 was to demonstrate that the proposed government was not likely to be ruled by any faction. Contrary to conventional wisdom, Madison argued, the key to controlling the evils of faction is to have a large republic—the larger, the better. The more diverse the society, the less likely it is that an unjust majority can form. Madison certainly had no intention of creating a majoritarian democracy; his view of popular government was much more consistent with the model of pluralist democracy discussed in Chapter 1.

Madison pressed his argument from a different angle in *Federalist* No. 51. Asserting that "ambition must be made to counteract ambition," he argued that the separation of powers and checks and balances would control tyranny from any source. If power is distributed equally across the three branches, then each branch has the capacity to counteract the other. In Madison's words, "usurpations are guarded against by a division of the government into distinct and separate departments." Because legislative power tends to predominate in republican governments, legislative authority is divided between the Senate and the House of Representatives, which have different methods of selection and terms of office. Additional protection comes through federalism, which divides power "between two distinct governments"—national and state—and subdivides "the portion allotted to each . . . among distinct and separate departments."

The Antifederalists wanted additional separation of powers and additional checks and balances, which, they maintained, would eliminate the threat of tyranny entirely. The Federalists believed that this would make decisive national action virtually impossible. But to ensure ratification, they agreed to a compromise.

A Concession: The Bill of Rights

Despite the eloquence of the Federalist papers, many prominent citizens, including Thomas Jefferson, were unhappy that the Constitution did not list basic civil liberties—the individual freedoms guaranteed to citizens. The omission of a bill of rights was the chief obstacle to the adoption of the Constitution by the states. The colonists had just rebelled against the British government to preserve their basic freedoms; why didn't the proposed Constitution spell out those freedoms?

The answer was rooted in logic, not politics. Because the national government was limited to those powers that were granted to it and because no power was granted to abridge the people's liberties, then a list of guaranteed freedoms was not necessary. In *Federalist* No. 84, Hamilton went even further, arguing that the addition of a bill of rights would be dangerous. Because it is not possible to list all prohibited powers, wrote Hamilton, any attempt to provide a partial list would make the remaining areas vulnerable to government abuse.

But logic was no match for fear. Many states agreed to ratify the Constitution only after Washington suggested that a list of guarantees be added through the amendment process. Well in excess of one hundred amendments were proposed by the states. These were eventually narrowed down to twelve, which were approved by Congress and sent to the states. Ten of them became part of the Constitution in 1791, after securing the approval of the required three-fourths of the states. Collectively, these ten amendments are known as the **Bill of Rights**. They restrain the national government from tampering with fundamental rights and civil liberties and emphasize the limited character of the national government's power (see Table 2.1).

Ratification

The Constitution officially took effect upon its ratification by the ninth state, New Hampshire, on June 21, 1788. However, the success of the new government was not ensured until July 1788, by which time the Constitution was ratified by the key states of Virginia and New York after lengthy debate.

The reflection and deliberation that attended the creation and ratification of the Constitution signaled to the world that a new government could be launched peacefully. The French observer Alexis de Tocqueville (1805–1859) later wrote:

> That which is new in the history of societies is to see a great people, warned by its lawgivers that the wheels of government are stopping, turn its attention on itself without haste or fear, sound the depth of the ill, and then wait for two years to find the remedy at leisure, and then finally, when the remedy has been indicated, submit to it voluntarily without its costing humanity a single tear or drop of blood.[12]

Constitutional Change

The founders realized that the Constitution would have to be changed from time to time. To this end, they specified a formal amendment process—a process that was used almost immediately to add the Bill of Rights. With the passage of time, the Constitution also has been altered through judicial interpretation and changes in political practice.

TABLE 2.1 The Bill of Rights
The first ten amendments to the Constitution are known as the Bill of Rights. The following is a list of those amendments, grouped conceptually. For the actual order and wording of the Bill of Rights, see the Appendix.

Guarantees	Amendment
Guarantees for Participation in the Political Process	
No government abridgement of speech or press; no government abridgement of peaceable assembly; no government abridgement of petitioning government for redress.	1
Guarantees Respecting Personal Beliefs	
No government establishment of religion; no government prohibition of free religious exercise.	1
Guarantees of Personal Privacy	
Owners' consent necessary to quarter troops in private homes in peacetime; quartering during war must be lawful.	3
Government cannot engage in unreasonable searches and seizures; warrants to search and seize require probable cause.	4
No compulsion to testify against oneself in criminal cases.	5
Guarantees Against Government's Overreaching	
Serious crimes require a grand jury indictment; no repeated prosecution for the same offense; no loss of life, liberty, or property without due process; no taking of property for public use without just compensation.	5
Criminal defendants will have a speedy public trial by impartial local jury; defendants are informed of accusation; defendants may confront witnesses against them; defendants may use judicial process to obtain favorable witnesses; defendants may have legal assistance for their defense.	6
Civil lawsuits can be tried by juries if controversy exceeds $20; in jury trials, fact-finding is a jury function.	7
No excessive bail; no excessive fines; no cruel and unusual punishment.	8
Other Guarantees	
The people have the right to bear arms.	2
No government trespass on unspecified fundamental rights.	9
The states or the people retain all powers not delegated to the national government or denied to the states.	10

The Formal Amendment Process

The amendment process has two stages, proposal and ratification; both are necessary for an amendment to become part of the Constitution. The Constitution provides two alternative methods for completing each stage (see Figure 2.3). Amendments can be proposed by a two-thirds vote in both

Roll Out the Barrels

*The Eighteenth Amendment, which was ratified by the states in 1919, banned the manufac-
ture, sale, or transportation of alcoholic beverages. The amendment was spurred by moral
and social reform groups, such as the Women's Christian Temperance Union, founded by
Evanston, Illinois, resident Frances Willard in 1874. The amendment proved to be an utter
failure. People continued to drink, but their alcohol came from illegal sources.*

the House of Representatives and the Senate, or by a national convention,
summoned by Congress at the request of two-thirds of the state legislatures.
All constitutional amendments to date have been proposed by the first
method.

A proposed amendment can be ratified by a vote of the legislatures of
three-fourths of the states, or by a vote of constitutional conventions held in
three-fourths of the states. Congress chooses the method of ratification. It has
used the state convention method only once, for the Twenty-first Amendment,
which repealed the Eighteenth (Prohibition).

Note that the amendment process requires the exercise of **extraordinary
majorities** (two-thirds and three-fourths). The framers purposely made it difficult to propose and ratify amendments. They wanted only the most significant
issues to lead to constitutional change.

Calling a national convention to propose an amendment has never been
tried. Certainly the method raises several thorny questions, the most significant
of which concerns what limits, if any, there are on the business of the convention. Would a national convention, called to consider a particular amendment,
be within its bounds to rewrite the Constitution? No one really knows.

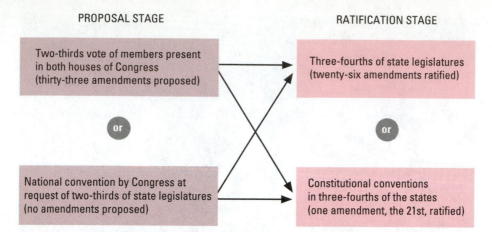

PROPOSAL STAGE   **RATIFICATION STAGE**

FIGURE 2.3   Amending the Constitution
There are two stages in amending the Constitution: proposal and ratification. Congress has no control over the proposal stage, but it prescribes the ratification method. Once a state has ratified an amendment, it cannot retract its action. However, a state may reject an amendment and then reconsider its decision.

Most of the Constitution's twenty-seven amendments were adopted to help keep it abreast of changes in political thinking. The first ten amendments (the Bill of Rights) were the price of ratification, but they have been fundamental to our system of government. The last seventeen amendments fall into three main categories: they make public policy; they correct deficiencies in the government's structure; or they promote equality (see Table 2.2).

Since 1787, about ten thousand constitutional amendments have been introduced; only a fraction have passed through the proposal stage. However, once an amendment has been voted by the Congress, chances of ratification are high. Only six amendments submitted to the states have failed to be ratified.

Interpretation by the Courts

In *Marbury v. Madison* (1803), the Supreme Court declared that the courts have the power to nullify government acts when they conflict with the Constitution. (We will elaborate on judicial review in Chapter 11.) The exercise of judicial review forces the courts to interpret the Constitution. In a way, this makes a lot of sense. The judiciary is the law-interpreting branch of the government; as the supreme law of the land, the Constitution is fair game for judicial interpretation. Judicial Review is the courts' main check on the other branches of government. But in interpreting the Constitution, the courts cannot help but give new meaning to its provisions. This is why judicial interpretation is a principal form of constitutional change.

TABLE 2.2 **Constitutional Amendments: 11 Through 27**

No.	Proposed	Ratified	Intent	Subject
11	1794	1795	G	Prohibits an individual from suing a state in federal court without the state's consent.
12	1803	1804	G	Requires the electoral college to vote separately for president and vice president.
13	1865	1865	E	Prohibits slavery.
14	1866	1868	E	Gives citizenship to all persons born or naturalized in the United States (including former slaves); prevents states from depriving any person of "life, liberty, or property, without due process of law," and declares that no state shall deprive any person of "the equal protection of the laws."
15	1869	1870	E	Guarantees that citizens' right to vote cannot be denied "on account of race, color, or previous condition of servitude."
16	1909	1913	E	Gives Congress the power to collect an income tax.
17	1912	1913	E	Provides for popular election of senators, who were formerly elected by state legislatures.
18	1917	1919	P	Prohibits the making and selling of intoxicating liquors.
19	1919	1920	E	Guarantees that citizens' right to vote cannot be denied "on account of sex."
20	1932	1933	G	Changes the presidential inauguration from March 4 to January 20 and sets January 3 for the opening date of Congress.
21	1933	1933	P	Repeals the Eighteenth Amendment.
22	1947	1951	G	Limits a president to two terms.
23	1960	1961	E	Gives citizens of Washington, D.C., the right to vote for president.
24	1962	1964	E	Prohibits charging citizens a poll tax to vote in presidential or congressional elections.
25	1965	1967	G	Provides for succession in event of death, removal from office, incapacity, or resignation of the president or vice president.
26	1971	1971	E	Lowers the voting age to eighteen.
27	1989	1992	G	Bars immediate pay increases to members of Congress.

P Amendments legislating public policy
G Amendments correcting perceived deficiencies in government structure
E Amendments advancing equality

Political Practice

The Constitution is silent on many issues. It says nothing about political parties or the president's cabinet, for example, yet both have exercised considerable influence in American politics. Some constitutional provisions have fallen out of use. The electors in the electoral college, for example, were supposed to exercise their own judgment in voting for president and vice president. Today the electors function simply as a rubber stamp, validating the outcome of election contests in their states.

Meanwhile, political practice has altered the distribution of power without changes in the Constitution. The framers intended Congress to be the strongest branch of government. But the president has come to overshadow Congress. Presidents like Abraham Lincoln and Franklin Roosevelt used their powers imaginatively to respond to national crises. And their actions paved the way for future presidents to further enlarge the powers of the office.

An Evaluation of the Constitution

The U.S. Constitution is one of the world's most praised political documents. It is the oldest written national constitution and one of the most widely copied, sometimes word for word. It is also one of the shortest. The brevity of the Constitution may be one of its greatest strengths. The framers simply laid out a structural framework for government; they did not describe relationships and powers in detail. For example, the Constitution gives Congress the power to regulate "Commerce . . . among the several States," but does not define interstate commerce. Such general wording allows interpretation in keeping with contemporary political, social, and technological developments.

The generality of the U.S. Constitution stands in stark contrast to the specificity of most state constitutions. The constitution of California, for example, provides that "fruit and nut-bearing trees under the age of four years from the time of planting in orchard form and grapevines under the age of three years from the time of planting in vineyard form . . . shall be exempt from taxation" (Article XIII, Section 12). Because they are so specific, most state constitutions are much longer than the U.S. Constitution.

Freedom, Order, and Equality in the Constitution

The revolutionaries constructed a new form of government—a *federal* government—that was strong enough to maintain order but not so strong that it could dominate the states or infringe on individual freedoms. In short, the Constitution provided a judicious balance between order and freedom. It paid virtually no attention to equality.

Consider social equality. The Constitution never mentioned *slavery*—a controversial issue even then. As we have seen, the Constitution implicitly condones slavery in the wording of several articles. Not until the ratification of the Thirteenth Amendment in 1865 was slavery prohibited.

The Constitution was designed long before social equality was ever thought of as an objective of government. In fact, in *Federalist* No. 10, Madison held that protection of the "diversities in the faculties of men from which the rights of property originate" is "the first object of government."

Over a century later, the Constitution was changed to incorporate a key device for the promotion of social equality—the income tax. The Sixteenth Amendment (1913) gave Congress the power to collect an income tax; it was proposed and ratified to replace a law that had been declared unconstitutional in an 1895 court case. The income tax had long been seen as a means of putting into effect the concept of *progressive taxation*, in which the tax rate increases with income. The Sixteenth Amendment gave progressive taxation a constitutional basis.[13] Progressive taxation later helped promote social equality through the redistribution of income—that is, higher income people are taxed at higher rates to help fund social programs that benefit low-income people.

Social equality itself has never been, and is not now, a prime *constitutional* value. The Constitution has been much more effective in securing order and freedom. Nor did the Constitution take a stand on political equality. It left voting qualifications to the states, specifying only that people who could vote for "the most numerous Branch of the State Legislature" could also vote for representatives to Congress (Article I, Section 2). Most states at that time allowed only taxpaying or property-owning white males to vote. Such inequalities have been rectified by several amendments.

The Constitution and Models of Democracy

Think back to our discussion of the models of democracy in Chapter 1. Which model does the Constitution fit: the pluralist or majoritarian? Actually, it is hard to imagine a government framework better suited to the pluralist model of democracy than the Constitution of the United States. It is also hard to imagine a document more at odds with the majoritarian model. Consider Madison's claim, in *Federalist* No. 10, that government inevitably involves conflicting factions. This concept coincides perfectly with pluralist theory (see Chapter 1). Then recall his description in *Federalist* No. 51 of the Constitution's ability to guard against the concentration of power in the majority through separation of powers and checks and balances. This concept— avoiding a single center of government power that might fall under majority control—also fits perfectly with pluralist democracy.

The delegates to the Constitutional Convention intended to create a republic, a government based on majority consent; they did not intend to create a democracy, which rests on majority rule. They succeeded admirably in creating that republic. In doing so, they also produced a government that developed into a democracy—but a particular type of democracy. The framers neither wanted nor got a democracy that fit the majoritarian model. They may have wanted and they certainly did create, a government that conforms to the pluralist model.

Summary

The U.S. Constitution is more than a historic document, an antique curiosity. Although over two hundred years old, it still governs the politics of a mighty modern nation. It still has the power to force from office a president who won re-election by a landslide. It still has the power to see the country through government crises.

The Constitution was the end product of a revolutionary movement aimed at preserving existing liberties. That movement began with the Declaration of Independence, which proclaimed that everyone is entitled to certain rights (among them, life, liberty, and the pursuit of happiness) and that government exists for the good of its citizens. When government denies those rights, the people have the right to rebel.

War with Britain was only part of the process of independence. Some form of government was needed to replace the British monarchy. The Americans chose a republic and defined the structure of that republic in the Articles of Confederation. The Articles were a failure, however. Although they guaranteed the states the independence they coveted, they left the central government too weak to deal with disorder and insurrection.

The Constitution was the second attempt at limited government. It replaced a loose union of powerful states with a strong, but still limited national government, incorporating four political principles: republicanism, federalism, separation of powers, and checks and balances. Republicanism is a form of government in which power resides in the people and is exercised by their elected representatives. Federalism is a division of power between the national government and the states. The federalism of the Constitution conferred substantial powers on the national government at the expense of the states. Separation of powers is a further division of the power of the national government into legislative (lawmaking), executive (law-enforcing), and judiciary (law-interpreting) branches. Finally, the Constitution established a system of checks and balances, giving each branch some scrutiny of and control over the others.

When work began on ratification, a major stumbling block proved to be the failure of the Constitution to list the individual liberties the Americans had fought to protect. With the promise to add a bill of rights, the Constitution was ratified. The subsequent ten amendments guaranteed participation in the political process, respect for personal beliefs, and personal privacy. They also contained guarantees against government overreaching in criminal prosecutions. Over the years the Constitution has evolved through the formal amendment process, through the exercise of judicial review, and through political practice.

The Constitution was designed to strike a balance between order and freedom. It was not designed to promote equality; in fact, it had to be amended to redress inequality. The framers had compromised on many issues, including slavery, to ensure the creation of a new and workable government. The framers had not set out to create a democracy. Faith in government by the people was virtually nonexistent two centuries ago. Nevertheless, they produced a democratic form of government. That government, with its separation of powers and checks and balances, is remarkably well suited to the pluralist model of democracy. Simple majority rule, which lies at the heart of the majoritarian model, was precisely what the framers wanted to avoid.

The framers also wanted balance between the powers of the national government and the states. The exact balance was a touchy issue, skirted by the delegates at the Constitutional Convention. Some seventy years later, a civil war was fought over that balance of power. That war and countless political battles before and after it have demonstrated that the national government dominates the state governments in our political system. In the next chapter, we look at how a loose confederation of states has evolved into a "more perfect Union."

Key Terms

Declaration of Independence
social contract theory
republic
confederation
Articles of Confederation
Virginia Plan
legislative branch
executive branch
judicial branch
New Jersey Plan
Great Compromise

republicanism
federalism
separation of powers
checks and balances
enumerated powers
necessary and proper clause
implied powers
judicial review
supremacy clause
Bill of Rights
extraordinary majorities

Selected Readings

Becker, Carl. *The Declaration of Independence: A Study in the History of Political Ideas.* New York: Alfred A. Knopf, 1942. A classic study of the theory and politics of the Declaration of Independence.

Bowen, Catherine Drinker. *Miracle at Philadelphia.* Boston: Atlantic–Little, Brown, 1966. An absorbing, well-written account of the events surrounding the Constitutional Convention.

Kammen, Michael. *A Machine That Would Go of Itself: The Constitution in American Culture.* New York: Alfred A. Knopf, 1986. A remarkable examination of the Constitution's cultural influence. The author argues that Americans' reverence for the Constitution is inconsistent with their ignorance of its content and meaning.

Rakove, Jack N. *Original Meanings: Politics and Ideas in the Making of the Constitution.* New York: Alfred A. Knopf, 1996. The meaning, intention, and understanding of the U.S. Constitution from a historian's perspective.

Wood, Gordon S. *The Radicalism of the American Revolution.* New York: Alfred A. Knopf, 1992. Wood argues that the Revolution was not a conservative defense of American rights but a radical revolution that produced a free and democratic society far beyond what was envisioned by the founders.

World Wide Web Resources

The Charters of Freedom. View America's founding documents at the National Archives' virtual exhibit hall. Good graphics, especially of items never exhibited in public.
<www.nara.gov/exhall/charters/charters.html>

Comparing the World's Constitutions. English text and background materials for the world's constitutions. This site contains cross-references for quick comparison of constitutional provisions.
<www.uni-wuerzburg.de/law/index.html>
and mirrored at
<www.law.cornell.edu/law/index.html>

Federalism

The locals called it "our Blood Border." It was a stretch of flat country due east of Beaumont, Texas, down Interstate 10 to the Louisiana state line, where eighteen-year-olds could still drink legally. White crosses dotted the highway alongside the westbound lanes. In 1993, eighty accidents marked by death or injury involved underage drinkers. The crosses were grim reminders of where Texas teenagers, driving home from bars across the Louisiana border, died. Eighteen-year-olds could still drink alcoholic beverages in Louisiana, despite the fact that the minimum drinking age is twenty-one everywhere else in the country. In July 1996, the Louisiana Supreme Court brought the state in line with the rest of the nation.[1]

Our federal system of government explains both Louisiana's lonely stand and the drive toward uniformity. The Constitution divides power between the national and state governments. With only one sobering exception (Prohibition under the Eighteenth Amendment), regulating liquor sales and setting the minimum drinking age have always been the responsibilities of state governments. But over the years, the national government has found ways to extend its influence into areas that are well beyond those originally defined in the Constitution.

Back in 1981, twenty-nine states and the District of Columbia allowed people under twenty-one to purchase and consume some forms of alcoholic beverages. In 1984, however, an action taken in Washington, D.C., marked the beginning of the end of legalized drinking for those under twenty-one. What happened? Did Congress establish a national minimum drinking age? No, at least not directly. Congress simply added a provision to a highway bill. Under that provision, states would lose 5 percent of their federal highway funds in 1986 and 10 percent every year thereafter if they allowed the purchase or consumption of alcohol by those younger than twenty-one. States would have to change their own laws or risk losing federal funds. This was a roundabout method to achieve a national objective. If the national government wanted to set twenty-one as a national drinking age, why not act directly and pass legislation to do so? The plain fact is that the national government lacks the power to act directly in this area.

The national government became concerned about the drinking age because Mothers Against Drunk Driving (MADD) and other interest groups fought hard to increase public awareness of the dangers of driving drunk. These groups argued that a uniform drinking age of twenty-one would reduce highway fatalities. However, campaigning for change on a state-by-state basis would be slow and might even be dangerous. So long as some states allowed teenagers to drink, young people would be able to drive across state lines in order to drink legally. The borders between states would become bloody borders—as the border remained in east Texas—strewn with victims of teenage drinking and driving.

Supporters of the legislation believed that the national government's responsibility to maintain order justified intervention. The lives and safety of people were at stake. Opponents of the plan argued that it constituted age discrimination and infringed on states' rights. They claimed the act was an unwarranted extension of national power, that it limited the freedom of the states and of their citizens.

President Reagan, who had campaigned on a pledge to reduce the size and scope of the national government, strongly opposed replacing state standards with national ones. When confronted with this issue, which pitted order against freedom and national standards against state standards, he first opposed the bill; later, he changed his position. At the signing ceremony, he said:

> This problem is bigger than the individual states. It's a grave national problem and it touches all our lives. With the problem so clear cut and the proven solution at hand we have no misgiving about this judicious use of federal power. I'm convinced that it will help persuade state legislators to act in the national interest.[2]

Several states took the matter to court, hoping to have the provision declared unconstitutional under the Tenth and the Twenty-first Amendments. In June 1987, the Supreme Court reached a decision in *South Dakota v. Dole*. The justices conceded that direct congressional control of the drinking age in the states would be unconstitutional. Nevertheless, the Constitution does not bar the indirect achievement of such objectives. The seven-justice majority argued that far from being an infringement on states' rights, the law was a "relatively mild encouragement to the states to enact higher minimum drinking ages than they otherwise would choose."[3]

These events show how much the role of the national government has changed since the Constitution was adopted. In the early part of the nineteenth century, presidents routinely vetoed bills authorizing roads, canals, and other interstate improvements because they believed these kinds of projects exceeded the constitutional authority of the national government. Eventually, the national government used its authority over interstate commerce to justify creating a role for itself in building roads. Witness the forty-three-thousand mile interstate highway system.

The Highway Act of 1984 (and its successor, the 1986 National Minimum Drinking Age Act) shows how national and state governments can interact. Congress did not challenge the constitutional power of the states to regulate the minimum drinking age (under the Twenty-first Amendment), but it used its own powers to tax and spend (Article I, Section 8, clause 1) to encourage the states to implement a national standard. Lawmakers in Washington, D.C., believed that few states would pass up highway funds to retain the power to set a minimum drinking age, and they were right.

An important element of federalism was at work here: the respective sovereignty of national and state governments. (Sovereignty is the quality of being supreme in power or authority.) Congress acknowledged the sovereignty of the states by not legislating a national drinking age. And the states were willing to barter their sovereignty in this area in exchange for needed revenues. As long as this remains true, there are few areas where national power cannot reach.

Sovereignty also affects political leadership. A governor may not be the political equal of a president, but governors have their own sovereignty, apart from the national government. Consequently, presidents rarely command governors; they negotiate, even plead.

In this chapter, we examine American federalism in theory and in practice. Is the division of power between nation and states a matter of constitutional principle or practical politics? How does the balance of power between nation and states relate to the conflicts between freedom and order, and between freedom and equality? Does federalism reflect the pluralist or the majoritarian model of democracy?

Theories of Federalism

The delegates who met in Philadelphia in 1787 tackled the problem of making one nation out of thirteen independent states by inventing a new political form—federal government—which combined features of a confederacy with features of unitary government (see Chapter 2). Under the principle of **federalism**, two or more governments exercise power and authority over the same people and the same territory. For example, the governments of the United States and Pennsylvania share certain powers (the power to tax, for instance), but other powers belong exclusively to one or the other. As James Madison wrote in *Federalist* 10, "The federal Constitution forms a happy combination . . . the great and aggregate interests being referred to the national, and the local and particular to state governments." So the power to coin money belongs to the national government; but the power to grant divorces remains a state prerogative. By contrast, authority over state militia may sometimes belong to the national government and sometimes to the states. The history of American federalism reveals that it has not always been easy to draw a line between what is "great and aggregate" and what is "local and particular."*

Nevertheless, federalism offered a solution to citizens' fears that they would be ruled by majorities from different regions and different interests and

---

*The phrase Americans use to refer to their central government—federal government—muddies the waters even more. Technically speaking, we have a federal system of government which includes both national and state governments. To avoid confusion from here on, we use the term *national government* rather than *federal government* when we are talking about the central government.

values. Federalism also provided a new political model. A leading scholar of federalism estimated in 1990 that 40 percent of the world's population lives under a formal federal constitution, while another 30 percent lives in polities that apply federal principles or practices without formal constitutional acknowledgment of their federalism.[4]

Representations of American Federalism

The history of American federalism is full of attempts to capture its true meaning in an adjective or metaphor. By one reckoning, scholars have generated nearly five hundred ways to describe federalism.[5] Let us concentrate on two such representations: dual federalism and cooperative federalism.

Dual Federalism

The term **dual federalism** sums up a theory about the proper relationship between the national government and the states. This theory has four essential parts. First, the national government rules by enumerated powers only. Second, the national government has a limited set of constitutional purposes. Third, each government unit—nation and state—is sovereign within its sphere. And fourth, the relationship between nation and states is best characterized by tension rather than cooperation.[6]

Dual federalism portrays the states as powerful components of the federal system—in some ways, the equals of the national government. Under dual federalism, the functions and responsibilities of the national and state governments are theoretically different and practically separate from each other. Dual federalism sees the Constitution as a compact among sovereign states. Of primary importance in dual federalism are **states' rights**, a concept that reserves to the states all rights not specifically conferred on the national government by the Constitution. Claims of states' rights often come from opponents of a national government policy. Their argument is that the people have not delegated the power to make such policy, and thus the power remains in the states or the people. Proponents of states' rights believe that the powers of the national government should be interpreted narrowly. They insist that, despite the elastic clause, which gives Congress the **implied powers** needed to execute its enumerated powers (see Chapter 2), the activities of Congress should be confined to the enumerated powers only. They support their view by quoting the Tenth Amendment: "The powers not delegated to the United States by the Constitution, nor prohibited by it to the States, are reserved to the states respectively, or to the people."

Political scientists use a metaphor to describe dual federalism. They call it *layer-cake-federalism;* the powers and functions of national and state governments are as separate as the layers of a cake (see Figure 3.1). Each government is supreme in its own "layer," its own sphere of action; the two layers are distinct; and the dimensions of each layer are fixed by the Constitution.

Dual Federalism:
The Layer-Cake Metaphor

*Citizens cutting into the
political system will find clear
differences between state
and national powers,
functions, and responsibilities.*

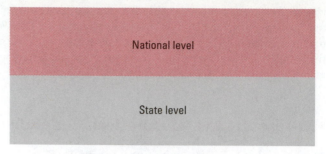

Cooperative Federalism:
The Marble-Cake Metaphor

*Citizens cutting into the
political system at any point
will find national and state
powers, functions, and
responsibilities mixed and
mingled.*

FIGURE 3.1 *Metaphors for Federalism*
The two views of federalism can be represented graphically.

Dual federalism has been challenged on historical and other grounds. Some critics argue that if the national government is really a creation of the states, it is a creation of only thirteen states, those that ratified the Constitution. The other thirty-seven states were admitted after the national government came into being and were created by that government out of land it had acquired. Another challenge has to do with the ratification process. Remember, special conventions in the original thirteen states, not the states' legislatures, ratified the Constitution. Ratification, then, was an act of the people, not the states. Moreover, the Preamble to the Constitution begins "We the people of the United States," not "We the States." The question of just where the people fit into the federal system is not handled well by dual federalism.

Cooperative Federalism

Cooperative federalism, a phrase coined in the 1930s, is a different theory of the relationship between national and state governments. It acknowledges the increasing overlap in state and national functions and rejects the idea of separate spheres, or layers, for the states and the national government. Cooperative federalism includes three elements. First, national and state agencies typically undertake governmental functions jointly, rather than exclusively. Second, nation and states routinely share power. And, third, power is not concentrated at any government level, or in any agency; this fragmentation of responsibilities gives people and groups access to many centers of influence.

The bakery metaphor used to describe this kind of federalism is a *marble cake*. The national and state governments do not act in separate spheres; they are intermingled. Their functions are mixed in the American federal system. Critical to cooperative federalism is an expansive view of the Constitution's supremacy clause (Article VI), which specifically subordinates state law to national law and charges every judge with disregarding state laws that are inconsistent with the Constitution, national laws, and treaties.

In contrast to dual federalism, cooperative federalism blurs the distinction between national and state powers. Some scholars argue that the layer-cake metaphor has never accurately described the American political structure.[7] The national and state governments have many common objectives and have often cooperated to achieve them. In the nineteenth century, for example, cooperation not separation, made it possible to develop transportation systems, such as canals, and to establish state land-grant colleges.

A critical difference between the theories of dual and cooperative federalism is the way they interpret two sections of the Constitution that set out the terms of the relationship between the national and state governments. Article I, Section 8 lists the enumerated powers of Congress, then concludes with the **elastic clause**, which gives Congress the power to "make all Laws which shall be necessary and proper for carrying into Execution the foregoing Powers." The Tenth Amendment, reserves for the states or the people "powers" not given to the national government or denied to the states by the Constitution. Dual federalism postulates an inflexible elastic clause and a capacious Tenth Amendment. Cooperative federalism postulates suppleness in the elastic clause and confines the Tenth Amendment to a self-evident, obvious truth.

In their efforts to limit the scope of the national government, conservatives have given much credence to the layer-cake metaphor. In contrast, liberals, believing that one of the functions of the national government is to bring about equality, have argued that the marble-cake metaphor is more desirable.

Conservatives continue to argue that different states have different problems and resources, and that returning control to state governments would thus actually promote diversity. States would be free to experiment with alternative ways to meet their problems.

Conservatives also maintain that the national government is too remote, too tied to special interests, and not responsive to the public at large. The national government overregulates and tries to promote too much uniformity. Moreover, the size and complexity of the federal system lead to waste and inefficiency. States, on the other hand, are closer to the people and better able to respond to specific local needs. If state governments were revitalized, individuals might believe that they could have a greater influence on decision making. The quality of political participation would improve. Furthermore, conservatives believe that shifting power to the states would help them achieve other parts of their political agenda. States would work harder to keep taxes down; they would not be willing to spend a lot of money on social welfare programs; and they would be less likely to pass stiff laws regulating businesses. The 1994

Compared with What? 3.1

The Perpetually Fragmenting Federation of Canada

Federalism tolerates the centrifugal forces (such as different languages and religions) that can sunder a nation and provides the centripetal forces that bind it (such as the powers to raise an army and control a national economy). But federalism is no guarantee that the forces of unity will always overcome those of disunity. Consider the example of Canada.

Canada is a federation of ten provinces. But the Canadian province of Quebec is different. Eighty percent of its population is French speaking; almost half speak little or no English. (The vast majority of Canadians outside Quebec speak only English.) Quebec has its own holidays, its own music videos, its own literature. By law, all signs must be in French. English is scarcely tolerated.

For decades, Canadians have struggled with the challenge of assimilating yet differentiating Quebec. When Canada drafted a new constitution in 1982, Quebec refused to sign it. Quebecers conditioned their union with the other provinces on a constitutional amendment that would recognize Quebec as a "distinct society" within the country. The amendment had to be approved by all ten provinces. It failed when two provinces refused to ratify the Quebec agreement by the June 1990 deadline.

In October 1992, Canadians rejected another constitutional solution to the Quebec question. The reforms aimed at recognizing Quebec's special status, electing the national senate, and providing self-government for native peoples. Québecois rejected the reforms because they did not go far enough; other provinces rejected the reforms because they went too far.

Repeated threats of secession reached a crescendo in October 1995 when Quebec's voters confronted the latest referendum on independence. The vote was the closest ever: 50.6 percent against independence and 49.4 percent in favor of it. Separatist leaders, taking hope from the substantial movement toward independence, planned for yet another referendum (or *neverendum,* a term coined by some English Canadian wags).

(continued)

"Republican Revolution" brought a chorus of new conservative voices to Congress calling for a return of power to the states.

What conservatives hope for, liberals fear. They remember that the states' rights model allowed political and social inequalities, and that it supported racism. Blacks and city dwellers were often left virtually unrepresented by white state legislators who disproportionately served rural interests. Liberals believe the states remain unwilling to protect the rights or provide for the needs of their citizens, whether those citizens are consumers seeking protection from business interests, defendants requiring guarantees of due process of law, or poor people seeking a minimum standard of living.

These ideological conceptions of federalism reveal a simple truth. Federalism is not something written or implied in the Constitution; the

Compared with What? 3.1 (continued)

Canadians appeared doomed to endure continued wrangling over the structure of their nation. There is no assurance that they will be able to accommodate Quebec's determined demand for greater autonomy and official recognition of its distinctiveness. Perhaps this perpetual conflict has come to define Canada. While many would say that Canada would not be Canada without Quebec, many might also say that Canada would not be Canada without this perpetual conflict over Quebec's status.

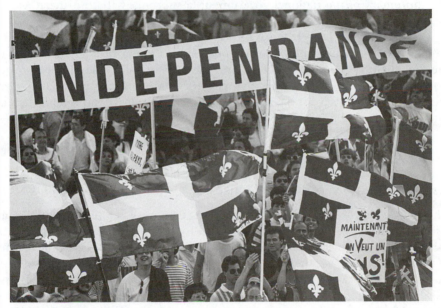

Quebec Demonstration

Sources: Robert C. Vipond, "Seeing Canada Through the Referendum: Still a House Divided," *Publius* 23 (Summer 1993), p. 39; Clyde H. Farnsworth, "For Quebec, the Neverendum," *New York Times*, 5 November 1995, sect. 4, p. 3.

Constitution is only the starting point in the debate. As one scholar observed, "To understand the condition of federalism, one needs to comprehend the functioning of the whole polity."[8]

The Dynamics of Federalism

Although the Constitution defines a kind of federalism, the actual balance of power between nation and states has always been more a matter of politics than of formal theory. A discussion of federalism, then, must do more than simply list the powers the Constitution assigns the different levels of government. The balance of power has shifted substantially since President Madison agonized over the proper role the national government should play in funding roads. Today, that government has assumed functions never dreamed of in the nineteenth century.

Why has power shifted so dramatically from the states to the national government? The answer lies in historical circumstances, not debates over constitutional theory. By far the greatest test of states' rights came when several southern states attempted to secede from the union. The threat of secession challenged the supremacy of the national government, a supremacy that northern armies established militarily in the nation's greatest bloodbath, the Civil War.

Some changes in the balance of power were the product of constitutional amendments—for example, the due process and equal protection clauses of the Fourteenth Amendment (1868) and the Seventeenth Amendment's provision for the direct election of senators (1913). Most of the national government's power, however, has come to it through legislation and judicial interpretation. Let us examine these tools of political change.

Legislation and the Elastic Clause

The elastic clause of the Constitution gives Congress the power to make all laws that are "necessary and proper" to carry out its responsibilities. By using this power in combination with its enumerated powers, Congress has been able to increase the scope of the national government tremendously during the past two centuries. Change has often come in times of crisis and national emergency—the Civil War, the Great Depression, the world wars. The role of the national government has grown as it has responded to needs and demands that state and local governments were unwilling or unable to meet.

Legislation is one of the prods the national government has used to achieve goals at the state level. The Voting Rights Act of 1965 is a good example. Section 2 of Article I of the Constitution gives the states the power to specify qualifications for voting. But the Fifteenth Amendment (1870) provides that no person should be denied the right to vote "on account of race, color, or previous condition of servitude." Before the Voting Rights Act, states could not specifically deny blacks the right to vote, but they could require that voters pass literacy tests or pay poll taxes, requirements that virtually disenfranchised blacks in many states. The Voting Rights Act was designed to correct this political inequality (see Chapter 12).

The act gives officials of the national government the power to decide whether individuals are qualified to vote in all elections, including primaries and national, state, and local elections. The constitutional authority for the act rests on the second section of the Fifteenth Amendment, which gives Congress the power to enforce the amendment through "appropriate legislation."

Judicial Interpretation

The Voting Rights Act was not a unanimous hit. Its critics adopted the language of dual federalism and insisted that the Constitution gives the states the power to determine voter qualifications. Its supporters claimed that the Fifteenth Amendment guarantee of voting rights takes precedence over states' rights and gives the national government new responsibilities.

The conflict was ultimately resolved by the Supreme Court, the umpire of the federal system. The Court settles disputes over the powers of the national and state governments by deciding whether the actions of either are unconstitutional (see Chapter 11). In the nineteenth and early twentieth centuries, the Supreme Court often decided in favor of the states. Then for nearly sixty years, from 1937 to 1995, the Court almost always supported the national government in contests involving the balance of power between nation and states. Today, a conservative majority on the Court has started to tip the balance back to the states.

Due Process and Reapportionment   During Chief Justice Earl Warren's tenure (1953–1969), the Court used the Fourteenth Amendment to make the states subject to various provisions of the Bill of Rights, shifting power from the states to the national government. The Supreme Court has set minimum due process standards for criminal cases that the states have to meet. The standards provide equality before the law for individuals who are suspected of crimes, but critics argue that they hamper state governments in trying to maintain order.

A series of Supreme Court decisions concerning reapportionment—redrawing the boundaries of electoral districts—also eroded the power of the states in the early 1960s.[9] Until that time, states had set the boundaries of voting districts, but some had failed to adjust those boundaries to reflect shifts in population. As a result, small numbers of rural voters in certain areas were electing as many representatives as were large numbers of urban voters. The Court established a new standard of one person, one vote, which meant that voting districts must be apportioned on the basis of population to satisfy the equal protection clause of the Fourteenth Amendment. The new standard forced the states to redraw their districts and reapportion their legislatures.

In the due process and reapportionment cases, the Supreme Court was protecting individual rights and in the process championing political equality. But the Supreme Court is also part of the national government. When it defends the rights of an individual against a state, it also substitutes a national standard for the state standard that previously governed that relationship.

The Commerce Clause: Engine of National Power   The growth of national power has been advanced by the Supreme Court's interpretation of the Constitution's **commerce clause**. The third clause of Article I, Section 8, states that "Congress shall have Power . . . To regulate Commerce . . . among the several States." The Court's interpretation of the clause has varied through the years, but since the middle of the Great Depression, it has generally given Congress wide latitude to exercise legislative power by regulating interstate commerce. However, a shift toward the states occurred in 1995, when the Supreme Court rediscovered constitutional limits on Congress that had been dead and buried for nearly sixty years. The Court's 5–4 ruling in *United States v. Lopez* held that Congress exceeded its authority under the commerce clause when it enacted a law in 1990 banning the possession of a gun in or near a school. A conservative majority, headed by Chief Justice William H. Rehnquist, concluded that having a gun in a school zone "has nothing to do with 'commerce' or any sort of economic enterprise, however broadly one might define those terms." Whether the ruling will have wide or narrow consequences depends on its subsequent application and interpretation. At a minimum, however, the Court is still the umpire of the federal system.

The Eleventh Amendment: The Umpire Strikes Back   In 1996, the umpire made another dramatic call curtailing congressional power in favor of the states. In a bitterly fought 5–4 ruling, the same five-justice majority bolstered state power by sharply curtailing the authority of Congress to subject states to lawsuits in federal courts. The ruling came in an obscure suit arising from a Seminole Indian tribe's dispute with Florida officials.[10]

A 1988 federal law allowed Indian tribes to sue a state in federal court if the state failed to negotiate in good faith over allowing gambling operations on tribal lands. Many federal laws have provisions that allow people hurt by state violations of such federal laws to sue in federal court. However, the Eleventh Amendment bars such courts from hearing cases in which a state is sued by citizens of another state or country.

The significance of the decision extends far beyond the particular facts; it affects whether individuals or groups can use the federal courts to force states to abide by a variety of national laws. In the majority opinion, the chief justice asserted that "the states, although a union, maintain certain attributes of sovereignty," including immunity from lawsuits.

1997 Supreme Court Decisions: Strike Two   In another series of decisions in 1997, the Court further chipped away at congressional power and bolstered the authority of the states. In *Idaho v. Coeur d'Alene Tribe* the Court again pointed out that the Eleventh Amendment provides states with a "sovereign immunity from suit" in federal courts except under very limited circumstances.[11] In *Boerne v. Flores* the Catholic Archbishop of San Antonio sought protection from local zoning ordinances asserting that such restrictions were made illegal by a 1993 federal law, the Religious Freedom Restoration Act (RFRA) (see Chapter 12). The Court ruled that the RFRA was unconstitutional because it contradicted an earlier Supreme Court decision which held that religious beliefs did not shield someone from compliance with a law prohibiting conduct a state was free to regulate. Writing for the majority Justice Kennedy wrote "When the political branches of the government act against the background of a judicial interpretation of the Constitution already issued, it must be understood that the court will treat its precedents with the respect due them . . . and contrary expectations must be disappointed."[12] Two days later, in *Printz v. United States,* the Court also struck down provisions of the Brady Handgun Prevention Act that required state law enforcement officers to conduct background checks on gun purchasers. In a 5–4 decision the Court held that the federal government could not require state officials to "minister or enforce a federal regulatory program.[13]

Grants-in-Aid

Since the 1960s, the national government's use of financial incentives has rivaled its use of legislation and judicial interpretation as a means of shaping relationships between national and state governments. The principal method the national government uses to make money available to the states is grants-in-aid.

A **grant-in-aid** is money paid by one level of government to another level of government, to be spent for a specific purpose. Most grants-in-aid come with standards or requirements prescribed by Congress. Many are awarded on a matching basis; that is, a recipient must make some contribution of its own, which is then matched by the national government. Grants-in-aid take two general forms: categorical grants and block grants.

Categorical grants target specific purposes, and restrictions on their use typically leave the recipient relatively little discretion. Recipients today include state governments, local governments, and public and private nonprofit organizations. There are two kinds of categorical grants: formula grants and project grants. As their name implies, **formula grants** are distributed according to a particular formula, which specifies who is eligible for the grant and how much each eligible applicant will receive. The formulas may weigh such factors as state per capita income, number of school-age children, urban population, and number of families below the poverty line. Most grants, however, are **project grants**—grants awarded on the basis of competitive applications. Recent grants have focused on health (substance abuse and HIV-AIDS programs); natural resources and the environment (asbestos, and toxic pollution); and education, training, and employment (for the disabled, the homeless, and the aged).

In contrast to categorical grants, **block grants** are awarded for broad, general purposes. They allow recipient governments considerable freedom in deciding how to allocate money to individual programs. While a categorical grant might be given to promote a very specific activity—say, ethnic heritage studies—a block grant might be earmarked for elementary, secondary, and vocational education. The state or local government receiving the block grant would then choose the specific educational programs to fund with it.

Grants-in-aid are a method of redistributing income. Money is collected by the national government from citizens of all fifty states, then allocated to other citizens, supposedly for worthwhile social purposes. Many grants have worked to remove gross inequalities among states and their citizens. But the formulas used to redistribute this income are not impartial; they are highly political, established through a process of congressional horse trading. Whatever its form or purpose, grant money comes with strings attached. Some strings are there to ensure that the money is used for the purpose for which it was given; other regulations are designed to evaluate how well the grant is working. Still others are designed to achieve some broad national goal, a goal that is not always closely related to the specific purpose of the grant. For example, as noted earlier, the Highway Act of 1984 reduced the amount of money available to states that allowed those under age twenty-one to drink. The lure of financial aid has proved to be a powerful incentive for states to relinquish the freedom to set their own standards and to accept those set by the national government.

The Developing Concept of Federalism

Federalism scholars have noted that each generation faced with new problems has had to work out its own version of federalism. Succeeding generations have used judicial and congressional power in varying degrees to shift the balance of power back and forth between the national and state governments.

McCulloch v. Maryland

Early in the nineteenth century, the nationalist interpretation of federalism triumphed over states' rights. In 1819, under Chief Justice John Marshall, the Supreme Court expanded the role of the national government in *McCulloch v. Maryland*. The Court was asked to rule whether Congress had the power to establish a national bank and, if so, whether states had the power to tax that bank. In a unanimous opinion written by Marshall, the Court conceded that Congress had only the powers conferred on it by the Constitution, which nowhere mentioned banks. However, Article I granted to Congress the authority to enact all laws "necessary and proper" to the execution of Congress's enumerated powers. Marshall gave a broad interpretation to this elastic clause: "Let the end be legitimate, let it be within the scope of the constitution, and all means which are appropriate, which are plainly adapted to that end, which are not prohibited, but consistent with the letter and spirit of the constitution, are constitutional."

The Court clearly agreed that Congress had the power to charter a bank. But did the states (in this case, Maryland) have the power to tax the bank? Arguing that "the power to tax involves the power to destroy," Marshall insisted that states could not tax the national government because the powers of the national government came not from the states but from the people.[14] Marshall was embracing cooperative federalism.

States' Rights and Dual Federalism

Many people assume that the Civil War was fought over slavery. It was not. The real issue was the character of the federal union, of federalism itself. At the time of the Civil War, economic and cultural differences between the Northern and Southern states were considerable. With the Southern economy based on labor-intensive agriculture, Southerners supported both low tariffs on imported goods and slavery. Northerners, to protect their manufacturing economy, wanted high tariffs. When they sought national legislation that threatened Southern interests, Southerners invoked states' rights. They even

Made in the U.S.A.
Young boys working in a Georgia cotton mill around the turn of the century. The Supreme Court decided in 1918 that Congress had no power to limit child labor. According to the Court, that power belonged to the states, which resisted imposing limits for fear such legislation would drive businesses to other (less restrictive) states.

introduced the theory of **nullification,** the idea that a state could declare a particular action of the national government null and void. The Civil War rendered the idea of nullification null and void, but it did not settle the balance between national and state power.

The New Deal and Its Consequences

The problems of the Great Depression proved too extensive for either state governments or private businesses to handle. So the national government assumed a heavy share of responsibility for providing relief and pursuing economic recovery. Under the New Deal—President Franklin D. Roosevelt's response to the Depression—Congress enacted various emergency relief programs to stimulate economic activity and help the unemployed. Many measures required the cooperation of national and state governments. Through the regulations it attached to funds, the national government extended its power and control over the states.[15]

At first, the Supreme Court's view of the Depression was different from that of the other branches of the national government. In the Court's opinion, the whole structure of federalism was threatened when collections of local troubles were treated as one national problem.

In 1937, however, with no change in personnel, the Court began to alter its course. The Court upheld major New Deal measures. Perhaps the Court had studied the 1936 election returns and was responding to the country's endorsement of the use of national policies to address national problems. Or perhaps the Court sought to defuse the President's threat to enlarge the Court with justices sympathetic to his views. In any event, the Court gave up its effort to set a rigid boundary between national and state power.

Some call the New Deal era revolutionary. There is no doubt that the period was critical in reshaping federalism in the United States. But perhaps the most significant change was in the way Americans thought about their problems and the role of the national government in solving them. Difficulties that at one time had been seen as personal or local problems were now national problems, requiring national solutions. The general welfare, broadly defined, became a legitimate concern of the national government.

In other respects, however, the New Deal was not very revolutionary. For example, Congress did not claim any new powers to address the nation's economic problems. Congress simply used its constitutional powers to suit the circumstances.

The Civil Rights Revolution and the War on Poverty

During the 1950s and 1960s, the national government assumed the task of promoting social equality by combating racism and poverty (see Chapter 12). Both racism and poverty seemed impossible to solve at the state level.

Matters of race relations had generally been left to the states, which more or less ignored them despite the constitutional amendments passed after the Civil War. When in 1896 the Supreme Court found no constitutional objection to a state policy of providing "separate but equal" facilities for whites and blacks,* states were free to do as much—or as little—as they pleased about racial inequality.

In 1954, however, in *Brown v. Board of Education*, the Supreme Court decided that racially separate but objectively equal public schools were inherently unequal.[16] The decision put the national government in the position of ordering the desegregation of public schools. As the civil rights movement focused increasing attention on the problems of discrimination, Congress passed a momentous piece of legislation: the Civil Rights Act of 1964. Through this act, the national government made use of the commerce clause as a vital constitutional lever allowing Congress to outlaw racial discrimination in arenas of state regulation, employment, and public accommodations. The act sharply limited invidiously discriminatory practices that had a substantial effect on interstate commerce. The civil rights revolution established the national government as the principal guarantor of political and social equality.

In the 1960s, President Lyndon Johnson's War on Poverty generated an enormous amount of social legislation and a massive increase in the scope of

---

*In *Plessey v. Ferguson* (163 U.S. 537 [1896]), the Supreme Court upheld state-imposed racial segregation, ruling that separate facilities for blacks and whites could be maintained as long as they were "equal" (see Chapter 12).

the national government. In an attempt to provide equality of opportunity and improve the quality of life throughout the United States, the national government adopted a vast array of social legislation accompanied by monetary inducements. Programs ranged from increased aid to higher education, to aid to elementary and secondary schools, to food stamps and employment-training projects.

Johnson's recipe for marble-cake federalism included some new ingredients. Before 1960, nearly all intergovernmental assistance (that is, aid from one level of government to another) had flowed from the national government to state governments. But the War on Poverty frequently bypassed state government by offering direct aid to local governments and even to community groups.

As the expansion of the national government became more widely accepted, the focus of the debate over federalism changed. National, state, and local governments were no longer separate and distinct; they interacted. The growth of government programs created a federal system that critics describe as overloaded and out of control. The Advisory Commission on Intergovernmental Relations (ACIR), a group created by Congress to monitor the federal system, concluded in 1980 that, since the 1960s, relations between national and state governments had become "more pervasive, more intrusive, more unmanageable, more ineffective, more costly and, above all, more unaccountable."[17]

From New Federalism to New Age Federalism

In 1969, Richard Nixon advocated giving more power to state and local governments. Nixon wanted to decentralize national policies. He called this the *New Federalism*. Today, Bill Clinton proposes that the national government act as guru, guiding and encouraging states to experiment with vexing problems. We call this *New-Age Federalism*.

An Evolving Federalism

Nixon's New Federalism called for combining and reformulating categorical grants into block grants. The shift had dramatic implications for federalism. Block grants were seen as a way to redress the imbalance of power between Washington and the states and localities. New Federalism was nothing more than dual federalism in modern dress.

The perception that the federal system was bloated and out of control began to take hold. In 1976, Jimmy Carter campaigned for president as an outsider who promised to reduce the size and cost of the national government. And he did have some success. As Figure 3.2 shows, after 1978 national government aid to states and localities actually did begin to drop and then level off.

When Ronald Reagan took office in 1981 he promised a "new New Federalism" that would restore a proper constitutional relationship between the federal, state, and local governments. The national government, he said, treated "elected state and local officials as if they were nothing more than ad-ministrative agents for federal authority."[18] Reagan's commitment to reduce both taxes and government spending meant he could not offer the incentive of new funding to make his version of New Federalism palatable. He did resur-rect an element of Nixon's New Federalism, however, in his use of block grants. State officials were enthusiastic about the prospect of having greater control over grant money; they were less enthusiastic when they realized that the amounts they received would be cut by approximately 25 percent. The share of state and local bills footed by the national government continued to fall (see Figure 3.2). In the mid-1970s, the national government contributed about 25 percent of state and local government spending. By 1990, its contri-bution had declined to below 20 percent. Bill Clinton's election to the presi-dency, coupled with Democratic control of Congress, affected spending patterns. By 1995, the national government's contribution to the states had edged back up to 22 percent.[19] The 1994 Republican congressional victory spelled stalemate for increased spending, however, especially when it implied greater control over the states.

Despite what some may say, money isn't everything. The national govern-ment's declining contributions to state coffers in the 1980s and the increased use of block grants in the 1990s did not necessarily imply reduced control over the states. Congress found other ways to restrict the states or require certain state actions, without spending money.

Preemption: The Instrument of Federalism

Before 1965, increased national power and diminished state power followed from the growth in categorical grant-in-aid programs—with their attached conditions—emanating from Washington, D.C. Since 1965, Congress has used its centralizing power in new fields and in novel ways.[20]

Preemption is the power of Congress to enact laws that have the national gov-ernment assume total or partial responsibility for a state government function. When the national government shoulders a new government function, it restricts the discretionary power of the states. For example, under the Age Discrimination in Employment Act of 1967, the national government stripped the states of their power to establish a compulsory retirement age for their employees.

Mandates and Restraints   Congressional preemption statutes infringe on state powers in two ways, through mandates and restraints. A **mandate** is a require-ment that a state undertake an activity or provide a service in keeping with minimum national standards. For example, in 1990, Congress mandated Medicaid coverage for all poor children. As a result, state Medicaid and wel-fare costs are expected to increase by about 66 percent from 1995 to 1999. To pay for these mandates, state officials face stark choices: shift scarce resources by reducing or eliminating programs or raise taxes.[21]

In contrast, a **restraint** forbids state government from exercising a certain power. Consider bus regulation, for example. To ensure bus service to small and remote communities, in the past, some states would condition the is-

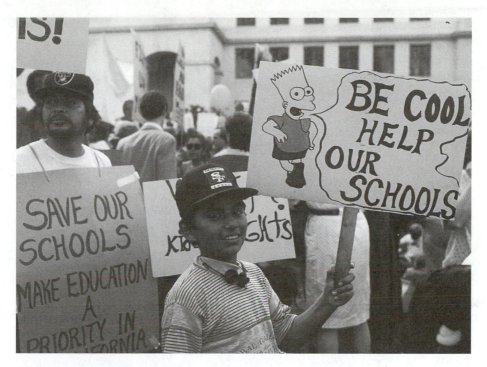

Bart Says, "Pay Up, Dudes!"
Californians urge their state legislators to provide more support for California's school sys-
tem. In 1980, the national government shouldered more than 11 percent of public education
costs. By 1991, that contribution had declined to approximately 8 percent. Because a 1
percent reduction in school aid equals nearly $3 billion, state governments are really feeling
the pinch.

suance of bus franchises on bus operators agreeing to serve such communities, even if the routes lost money. But in 1982, Congress passed the Bus Regulatory Reform Act, which forbade the states from imposing such conditions. Many states now provide subsidies to bus operators to ensure service to out-of-the-way areas.

Whether preemption takes the form of mandates or restraints, the result is additional costs for state and local government, and interference with a fundamental government task: setting priorities. Furthermore, the national government is not obliged to pay for the costs it imposes. As preemption grew in the 1980s, the national government reduced spending in the form of grants to the states, and the states had to pick up the tab.

Constraining Unfunded Mandates   State and local government officials have long voiced strong objections to the national government's practice of imposing requirements on the states without providing the financial support needed to satisfy them. By 1992, more than 170 congressional acts had established partially or wholly unfunded mandates.[22] One of the early results of the

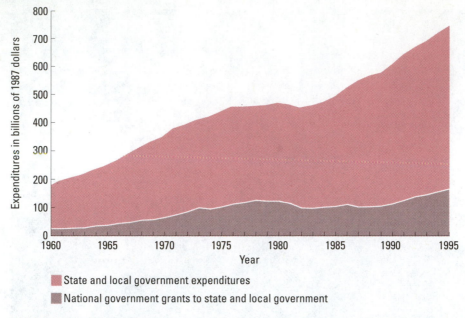

State and local government expenditures
National government grants to state and local government

FIGURE 3.2   The National Government's Contribution to State and Local Governments *In 1960, the national government contributed less than 15 percent of total state and local spending. By 1978, the national government had nearly doubled its contribution to state and local government spending. By 1988, the national government's contribution had declined to about 18 percent. As the national government's spending remained static or declined, state and local government spending accelerated, especially for Medicaid, welfare, prisons, and education. (The slopes of the two figures here indicate the pace of spending change.) (Source:* The Budget for FY 1997: Historical Tables *(Washington, D.C.: U.S. Government Printing Office, 1996), Table 15.2, p. 257.)*

Republican-led 104th Congress was the Unfunded Mandates Relief Act of 1995. The legislation requires the Congressional Budget Office to prepare cost estimates of any proposed national legislation that would impose more than $50 million a year in costs on state and local governments or more than $100 million a year in costs on private business. It also requires a cost analysis of the impact of agency regulations.

Other Governments in the Federal System

We have concentrated in this chapter on the roles the national and state governments play in shaping the federal system. Although the Constitution explicitly recognizes just national and state governments, the American federal system has spawned a multitude of local governments as well. A 1992 census counted nearly eighty-seven thousand.[23]

Types of Local Governments

Americans are citizens of both nation and state but they also come under the jurisdiction of various local government units. These units include **municipal governments**, the governments of cities and towns. Municipalities, in turn, are located in (or may contain or share boundaries with) counties, which are administered by **county governments**. (Sixteen states further divide counties into townships.) Most Americans also live in a **school district**, which is responsible for administering local elementary and secondary educational programs. They also may be served by one or more **special districts**, government units created to perform particular functions, typically when those functions—such as fire protection and water purification and distribution—are best performed across jurisdictional boundaries. All these local governments are created by state governments, either in their constitutions or through legislation

So Many Governments: Advantages and Disadvantages

In theory, at least, one benefit of localizing government is that it brings government closer to the people; it gives them an opportunity to participate in the political process, to have a direct impact on policy. From this perspective, overlapping governments appear compatible with a majoritarian view of democracy.

The reality is somewhat different, however. Studies have shown that people are much less likely to vote in local elections than national elections. In fact, voter turnout in local contests tends to be very low, even though the impact of individual votes is much greater. Furthermore, the fragmentation of powers, functions, and responsibilities among national, state, and local governments makes government as a whole seem complicated and hence incomprehensible and inaccessible to ordinary people. In addition, most people have little time to devote to public affairs. These factors tend to discourage individual citizens from pursuing politics and, in turn, enhance the influence of organized groups, which have the resources—time, money, and know-how—to sway policymaking (see Chapter 7). Instead of bringing government closer to the people and reinforcing majoritarian democracy, then, the system's enormous complexity tends to encourage pluralism.

One potential benefit of having many governments is that they enable the country to experiment with new policies on a small scale. New programs or solutions to problems can be tested in one city or state or in a few cities or states. Successful programs can then be adopted by other cities or states or by the nation as a whole. For this reason, states are sometimes called the "laboratories of democracy."

The large number of governments also makes it possible for government to respond to the diversity of conditions that prevails in different parts of the country. States and cities differ enormously in population, size, economic resources, climate, and other characteristics. Smaller political units are better able to respond to particular local conditions and can generally do so more quickly than larger units. On the other hand, smaller units may not be able to muster the economic resources to meet some challenges. Consequently, throughout American history, the national government has used its funds to equalize disparities in wealth and development among states.

Contemporary Federalism and the Dilemmas of Democracy

To what extent were conservative hopes and liberal fears realized as federalism developed from the 1980s to the 1990s? Neither were fully realized under the various renditions of federalism. Federalism of the Reagan-Bush variety was used as a tool for cutting the national budget by offering less money to the states. Contrary to the expectations of conservatives and liberals alike, however, states approved tax increases to pay for social services and education. In an era when Washington was less willing to enforce antitrust legislation, civil rights laws, or affirmative action plans, state governments were more likely to do so. At a time when a conservative national government put little emphasis on the value of equality, state governments did more to embrace it.[24]

Conservatives thought that the value of freedom would be emphasized if more matters were left to the states. Traditionally, state governments were relatively small and lacking the wherewithal to limit large corporate interests, for example. But since the 1970s, state governments have become "big governments" themselves. They are better able to tackle problems, and they are not afraid to use their power to promote equality.

To the surprise of liberals, who had originally looked to the national government to protect individuals by setting reasonable minimum standards for product safety, welfare payments, and employee benefits, states are now willing to set higher standards than the national government.

When Clinton came to the White House, liberals were delighted. His conservative predecessors, Reagan and Bush, had sought to reinstate layer-cake federalism and dismantle the national government's welfare-state efforts to promote social and political equality. But Clinton's experience as a governor has created a strange brew when joined with the Democrat's liberal social welfare policies. Thus far, no coherent theory of federalism has emerged.[25]

Federalism and Pluralism

Our federal system of government was designed to allay citizens' fears that they might be ruled by a majority in a distant region and with whom they did not necessarily agree or share interests. By recognizing the legitimacy of the states as political divisions, the federal system also recognized the importance of diversity. The existence and cultivation of diverse interests are hallmarks of pluralism.

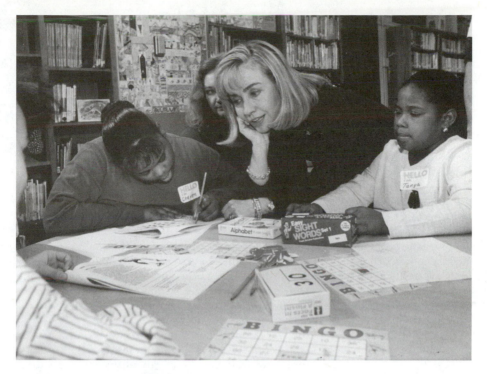

The First Lady Goes to School
In our federal system, education remains primarily a state responsibility. However, the national government has increased its involvement dramatically since the 1960s when, as a part of President Lyndon Johnson's War on Poverty, the national government provided massive assistance in an effort to promote greater equality of opportunity. In this picture First Lady Hillary Rodham Clinton meets children at a New York public school to symbolize the continuing interest of the national government in education.

Each of the two competing theories of federalism supports pluralism but in somewhat different ways. Dual federalism aims to decentralize government, to shift power to the states. It recognizes the importance of local rather than national standards and applauds the diversity of those standards. The variety allows the people, if not a direct voice in policymaking, at least a choice of policies under which to live.

In contrast, cooperative federalism is perfectly willing to override local standards for a national standard in the interests of promoting equality. Yet this view of federalism also supports pluralist democracy. It is highly responsive to all manner of group pressures, including pressure at one level from groups unsuccessful at other levels. By blurring the lines of national and state responsibility, this kind of federalism encourages petitioners to try their luck at whichever level of government offers them the best chance of success.

Summary

The government framework outlined in the Constitution was the product of political compromise, an acknowledgment of the original thirteen states' fear of a powerful central government. The division of powers sketched in the Constitution was supposed to turn over "great and aggregate" matters to the national government, leaving "local and particular" concerns to the states. The Constitution does not explain, however, what is great and aggregate and what is local and particular.

Federalism comes in many varieties. Two stand out because they capture valuable differences between the original and modern vision of a federal government. Dual, or layer-cake, federalism wants to retain power in the states and to keep the levels of government separate. Cooperative, or marble-cake, federalism emphasizes the power of the national government and sees national and state governments working together to solve national problems. In its own way, each view supports the pluralist model of democracy.

Over the years, the national government has used both its enumerated and its implied powers to become involved in virtually every area of human activity. The tools of political change include direct legislation, judicial interpretation, and grants-in-aid to states and localities. In the absence of financial incentives, the national government has used its preemptive power, imposing mandates and restraints on the states without necessarily footing the cost.

As its influence grew, so did the national government. Major events, such as the Civil War and the Great Depression, mark major shifts in its growth in size and power. To alter its course, conservatives offered New Federalism and argued for cutting back on the size of the national government, reducing federal spending, and turning programs over to the states in order to solve the problem of unwieldy government. Liberals worried that in their haste to decentralize and cut back, conservatives would turn over important responsibilities to states that were unwilling or unable to assume them. Rather than being too responsive, government would be unresponsive. But neither happened in the 1980s. Congressional preemption forced states to meet national standards with or without financial inducements. The states proved ready to tackle some major problems. More than this, they were willing to fund many programs that promoted equality.

The debate over federalism has started to shift in the conservative direction as a result of two forces: the Republican congressional victory in 1994 and the formation of a slender but solid conservative majority in the Supreme Court. One truth emerges from this overview of federalism: the balance of power between the national and state governments will be settled by political means, not by theory.

Key Terms

federalism	grant-in-aid
dual federalism	categorical grant
states' rights	formula grant
implied powers	project grant
cooperative federalism	block grant
elastic clause	nullification
commerce clause	preemption

mandate
restraint
municipal government

county government
school district
special district

Selected Reading

Beer, Samuel H. *To Make a Nation: The Rediscovery of American Federalism.* Cambridge, Mass.: Harvard University Press, 1993. A historical examination of federalism and nationalism in American political philosophy.

Dye, Thomas R. *American Federalism: Competition Among Governments.* Lexington, Mass.: Lexington Books, 1990. Presents a theory of competitive federalism that encourages rivalry among states and local governments, to offer citizens the best array of public services at the lowest cost.

Peterson, Paul E. *The Price of Federalism.* Washington, D.C.: Brookings/A Twentieth Century Fund Book, 1995. Peterson argues that development projects such as roads and buildings are best left to state and local government and that redistributive policies such as welfare and social security are best left to the national government.

Rivlin, Alice. *Reviving the American Dream: The Economy, the States, and the Federal Government.* Washington, D.C.: Brookings Institution, 1992. A lucid examination of economic performance and government performance, resting on a re-examination of the division of responsibilities between the nation and the states.

Zimmerman, Joseph F. *Contemporary American Federalism: The Growth of National Power.* New York: Praeger, 1992. Argues that the expansion of preemption power has altered the allocation of power between nation and states.

World Wide Web Resources

The states have their own organization called The Council for State Government. One of its missions is to promote the sovereignty of the states and their role in the American federal system.

<www.csg.org>

Everything you always wanted to know about the states but were afraid to ask can be found at State- Search. This is a service of the National Association of State Information Resource Executives. It is designed to serve as a topical clearinghouse of state government information on the Internet.

<www.nasire.org>

If you want to be present for the Supreme Court oral arguments in all the leading federalism cases decided after 1955 and cited in this chapter, point your browser to "OYEZ. OYEZ. OYEZ.: A Supreme Court WWW Resource." You can listen from your computer using RealAudio.

<oyez.at.nwu.edu/cases/subject-index.html>

4

Public Opinion, Political Socialization, and the Media

Fridays are different in Saudi Arabia. After prayers, criminals are paraded in the streets, then punished publicly. Murderers are beheaded; adulterers are flogged; and thieves have their hands chopped off. The Saudi government wants its citizens to get the message: Crime will not be tolerated. Moreover, what constitutes a crime in Saudi Arabia may not be a crime in the United States. Members of the U.S. armed forces sent there in 1990 during the Persian Gulf crisis learned this as their mail from home was opened to keep out alcohol and sexually oriented magazines, both of which are illegal. It is also illegal for a woman to drive a car there. Saudi Arabia, which claims the lowest crime rate in the world, is a country that greatly values order.

In contrast, the United States has one of the highest crime rates in the world. Its homicide rate, for example, is three to ten times that of most other Western countries. Although no one is proud of this record, our government would never consider beheading, flogging, or dismembering as a means of lowering the crime rate. First, the Eighth Amendment to the Constitution forbids "cruel and unusual punishment." Second, the public would not tolerate such punishment.

However, the public definitely is not squeamish about applying the death penalty (capital punishment) for certain crimes. The Gallup organization has polled the nation on this issue for fifty years. Except in 1966, most respondents have consistently supported the death penalty for murder. In fact, public support for capital punishment has increased dramatically since the late 1960s. In 1995, 77 percent of all respondents were in favor of the death penalty for murder, while only 13 percent opposed it.[1]

Government has been defined as the legitimate use of force to control human behavior. During most of American history, government execution of people who threaten the social order was legal. In colonial times, capital punishment was imposed not just for murder but also for antisocial behavior— denying the "true" God, cursing one's parents, committing adultery, practicing witchcraft, or being a rebellious child, for example.[2] In the late

1700s, some writers, editors, and clergy argued for abolishing the death sentence. The campaign intensified in the 1840s, and again in 1890, when New York State adopted a new "scientific" technique, electrocution, as the instrument of death. By 1917, twelve states had passed laws against capital punishment. But the outbreak of World War I fed the public's fear of foreigners and radicals, leading to renewed support for the death penalty. Reacting to this shift in public opinion, four states restored it.

The security needs of World War II and postwar fears of Soviet communism fueled continued support for capital punishment. After the anticommunist hysteria subsided in the late 1950s, public opposition to the death penalty increased. But public opinion was neither strong enough nor stable enough to force state legislatures to outlaw the death penalty. In keeping with the pluralist model of democracy, efforts to abolish the death penalty shifted from the legislative arena to the courts.

The opponents argued that the death penalty is cruel and unusual punishment, and is therefore unconstitutional. Certainly the public in the 1780s did not consider capital punishment either cruel or unusual. But nearly two hundred years later, opponents contended that execution by the state had become cruel and unusual by contemporary standards. Their argument had some effect on public opinion; in 1966, a plurality of respondents opposed the death penalty for the first (and only) time since the Gallup Organization began polling the public on the question.

The states responded to this shift in public opinion by reducing the number of executions, until they stopped completely in 1968 in anticipation of a Supreme Court decision. By then, however, public opinion had again reversed in favor of capital punishment. Nevertheless, in 1972, the Court ruled in a 5–4 vote that the death penalty as imposed by existing state laws was unconstitutional.[3] The decision was not well received in many states, and thirty-five state legislatures passed new laws to get around the ruling. Meanwhile, as the nation's homicide rate increased, public approval of the death penalty jumped almost 10 points and continued climbing.

In 1976, the Supreme Court changed its position and upheld three new state laws that let judges consider the defendant's record and the nature of the crime in deciding whether to impose a sentence of death.[4] The Court also rejected the argument that punishment by death itself violates the Constitution, and it noted that public opinion favors the death penalty. Through the end of the 1970s, however, only three criminals were executed. Eventually, the states began to heed public concern about the crime rate. In 1995 alone, fifty-six murderers were executed.[5]

The history of public thinking on the death penalty reveals several characteristics of public opinion:

1. *The public's attitudes toward a given government policy can vary over time, often dramatically.* Opinions about capital punishment tend to fluctuate with threats to the social order. The public is more likely to favor capital punishment in times of war and when fear of foreign subversion and crime rates are high.

2. *Public opinion places boundaries on allowable types of public policy.* Chopping off a thief's hand is not acceptable to the American public (and surely not to courts interpreting the Constitution), but electrocuting a murderer is.

3. *If asked by pollsters, citizens are willing to register opinions on matters outside their expertise.* People clearly believe execution by lethal injection is more humane than electrocution, asphyxiation in the gas chamber, or hanging. But how can the public know enough about execution to make these judgments?

4. *Governments tend to respond to public opinion.* State laws for and against capital punishment have reflected swings in the public mood. The Supreme Court's 1972 decision against capital punishment came when public opinion on the death penalty was sharply divided; the Court's approval of capital punishment in 1976 coincided with a rise in public approval of the death penalty.

5. *The government sometimes does not do what the people want.* Although public opinion overwhelmingly favors the death penalty for murder, there were only fifty-six executions in 1995.

The last two conclusions bear on our discussion of the majoritarian and pluralist models of democracy discussed in Chapter 1. Here we probe more deeply into the nature, shape, depth, and formation of public opinion in a democratic government. What is the place of public opinion in a democracy? How do people acquire their opinions? What are the major lines of division in public opinion? How do individuals' ideology and knowledge affect their opinions? What is the relationship between public opinion and ideology?

Public Opinion and the Models of Democracy

Public opinion is simply the collective attitudes of the citizens on a given issue or question. Opinion polling, which involves interviewing a sample of citizens to estimate public opinion as a whole, is such a common feature of contemporary life that we often forget it is a modern invention, dating only from the 1930s (see Figure 4.1). In fact, survey methodology did not develop into a powerful research tool until the advent of computers in the 1950s.

Before polling became an accepted part of the American scene, politicians, journalists, and everyone else could argue about what the people wanted, but no one really knew. Today, sampling methods and opinion polling have altered the debate about the majoritarian and pluralist models of democracy. Now that we know how often government policy runs against majority opinion, it becomes harder to defend the U.S. government as democratic under the majoritarian model. Even at a time when Americans overwhelmingly favored the death penalty for murderers, the Supreme Court decided that existing state laws applying capital punishment were unconstitutional. Even after the Court approved new state laws as constitutional, relatively few murderers were actually executed.

The two models of democracy make different assumptions about public opinion. The majoritarian model assumes that a majority of the people hold

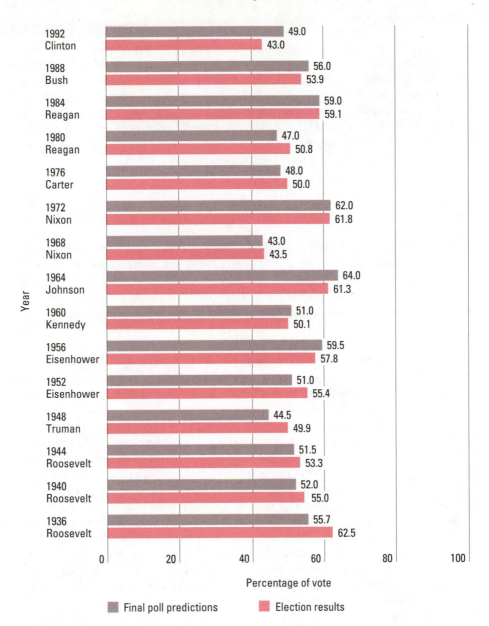

Year

Year		
1992 Clinton	49.0	43.0
1988 Bush	56.0	53.9
1984 Reagan	59.0	59.1
1980 Reagan	47.0	50.8
1976 Carter	48.0	50.0
1972 Nixon	62.0	61.8
1968 Nixon	43.0	43.5
1964 Johnson	64.0	61.3
1960 Kennedy	51.0	50.1
1956 Eisenhower	59.5	57.8
1952 Eisenhower	51.0	55.4
1948 Truman	44.5	49.9
1944 Roosevelt	51.5	53.3
1940 Roosevelt	52.0	55.0
1936 Roosevelt	55.7	62.5

Percentage of vote

■ Final poll predictions   ■ Election results

FIGURE 4.1   Gallup Poll Accuracy
One of the nation's oldest polls was started by George Gallup in the 1930s. The accuracy of
the Gallup Poll in predicting presidential elections over nearly fifty years is charted here.
Although not always on the mark, its predictions have been fairly close to election results.
The poll was most notably wrong in 1948, when it predicted that Thomas Dewey, the
Republican candidate, would defeat the Democratic incumbent, Harry Truman, underesti-
mating Truman's vote by 5.4 percentage points. In 1996, the Gallup Poll predicted that
Bill Clinton would win 52 percent of the popular vote and he received 49 percent, which
was within the poll's three-point margin of error. (Source: Gallup Report, November 1992.
Used by permission of The Gallup Poll.)

clear, consistent opinions on government policy. The pluralist model assumes that the public is often uninformed and ambivalent about specific issues, and opinion polls frequently support that claim. What are the bases of public opinion? What principles, if any, do people use to organize their beliefs and attitudes about politics? Exactly how do individuals form their political opinions? We will look for answers to these questions in this chapter. In later chapters, we assess the effect of public opinion on government policies. The results should help you make up your own mind about the viability of the majoritarian and pluralist models in a functioning democracy.

Political Socialization

Public opinion is grounded in political values. People acquire their values through **political socialization**, a complex process through which individuals become aware of politics, learn political facts, and form political values. Think for a moment about your political socialization. What is your earliest memory of a president? When did you first learn about political parties? If you identify with a party, how did you decide to do so? If you do not, why don't you? Who was the first liberal you ever met? The first conservative? Obviously, the paths to political awareness, knowledge, and values differ among individuals, but most people are exposed to the same influences, or agents of socialization, especially in childhood through young adulthood. These influences are family, school, community, peers, and—of course—television.

Political socialization continues throughout life. As parental and school influences wane in adulthood, peer groups (neighbors, coworkers, club members) assume a greater importance in promoting political awareness and in developing political opinions.[6] Because adults usually learn about political events from the mass media—newspapers, magazines, television, and radio—the media emerge as socialization agents. The role of television is especially important.[7]

Regardless of how people learn about politics, as they grow older, they gain perspective on government. They are apt to measure new candidates (and new ideas) against the old ones they remember. Their values also may change. Finally, political learning comes simply through exposure and familiarity. One example is the simple act of voting, which people do with increasing regularity as they grow older.

Social Groups and Political Values

No two people are influenced by precisely the same socialization agents in precisely the same way. Still, people with similar backgrounds do share learning experiences; this means they tend to develop similar political opinions. In this section, we examine the ties between people's social backgrounds and their political values. In the process, we will examine the ties between background and values by looking at responses to two questions posed by the 1992

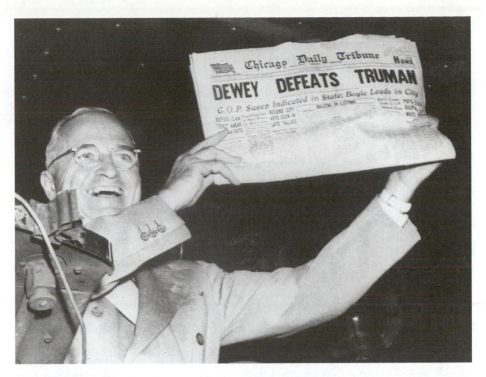

Stop the Presses! Oops, Too Late . . .
As the 1948 election drew near, few people gave President Harry Truman a chance to defeat his Republican opponent, Thomas E. Dewey. Polling was still new, and virtually all the early polls showed Dewey far ahead. Most organizations simply stopped polling weeks before the election. The Chicago Daily Tribune *believed the polls and proclaimed Dewey's victory before the votes were counted. Here, the victorious Truman triumphantly displays the most embarrassing headline in American politics. Later, it was revealed that the few polls taken closer to election day showed Truman catching up to Dewey. Clearly, polls estimate the vote only at the time they are taken.*

National Election Study administered by the University of Michigan's Center for Political Studies.

The first question deals with abortion. The interviewer said,

There has been some discussion about abortion during recent years. Which opinion on this page best agrees with your view? You can just tell me the number of the opinion you choose:

1. By law, abortion should never be permitted. [10 percent agreed.]

2. The law should permit abortion only in case of rape, incest, or when the woman's life is in danger. [28 percent]

3. The law should permit abortion for reasons other than rape, incest, or danger to the woman's life, but only after the need for the abortion has been clearly established. [14 percent]

4. By law, a woman should be able to obtain an abortion as a matter of personal choice. [47 percent][8]

Those who chose the last category most clearly valued individual freedom over order imposed by government. Moreover, evidence shows the pro-choice respondents also have concerns about broader issues of social order, such as the role of women and the legitimacy of alternative lifestyles.[9]

The second question pertained to the role of government in guaranteeing employment:

Some people feel the government in Washington should see to it that every person has a job and a good standard of living. Suppose that these people are at one end of the scale. . . . Others think the government should just let each person get ahead on his own. Suppose these people were at the other end. . . . Where would you put yourself on this scale, or haven't you thought much about this?

Excluding those people who "haven't thought much" about this question, 30 percent of the respondents wanted government to provide every person with a living and 22 percent were undecided. That left 48 percent who wanted the government to leave people alone to "get ahead" on their own. These respondents, who opposed government efforts to promote equality, apparently valued freedom over equality.

Overall, the responses to each of these questions were divided approximately equally. Somewhat less than half the respondents (47 percent) felt that government should not set restrictions on abortion and nearly half (48 percent) thought the government should not guarantee everyone a job and a good standard of living. However, sharp differences in attitudes emerged for both issues when the respondents were grouped by socioeconomic factors—education, income, region, race, religion, and sex. The differences are shown in Figure 4.2 as positive and negative deviations from the national averages for each question. Bars that extend to the right identify groups that are more likely than most Americans to sacrifice freedom for a given value of government, either equality or order. Next, we examine the opinion patterns more closely for each socioeconomic group.

Education

Education increases people's awareness and understanding of political issues. Higher education also promotes tolerance of unpopular opinions and behavior and invites citizens to see issues in terms of civil rights and liberties. This result is clearly shown in the left-hand column of Figure 4.2, which shows that people with more education are more likely to view abortion as a matter of a woman's choice.[10] When confronted with a choice between personal freedom and social order, college-educated individuals tend to choose freedom.

With regard to the role of government in reducing income inequality, the right-hand column in Figure 4.2 shows that people with more education also tend to favor freedom over equality. The higher their level of education, the

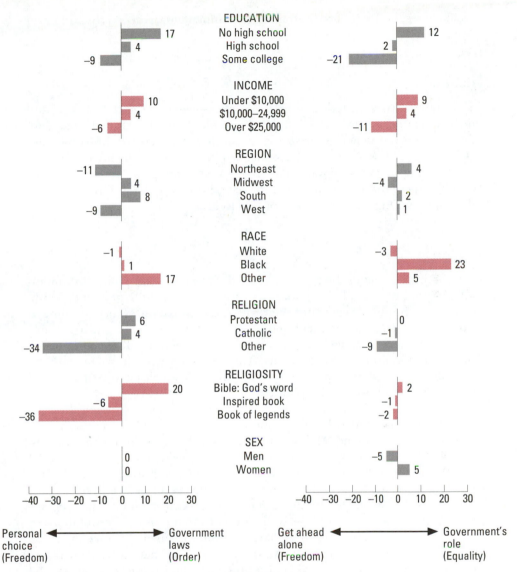

FIGURE 4.2 ***Group Deviations from National Opinion on Two Questions***
Two questions—one on abortion (representing the dilemma of freedom versus order) and the other on the government's role in guaranteeing employment (freedom versus equality)—were asked of a national sample in 1992. Public opinion for the nation as a whole was sharply divided on each question. These two graphs show how respondents in several social groups deviated from overall public opinion. The longer the bars next to each group, the more its respondents deviated from the expression of opinion for the entire sample. Bars that extend to the left show group opinions that deviate toward freedom. Bars that extend to the right show deviations away from freedom, toward order or equality. (Source: Data from 1992 National Election Study, copyright © Center for Political Studies, University of Michigan. Reprinted with permission.)

less likely respondents were to support government-guaranteed jobs and living standards.

Income

In many countries, differences in social class—based on social background and occupation—divide people in their politics.[11] In the United States, we have avoided the uglier aspects of class conflict, but here wealth sometimes substitutes for class. As Figure 4.2 shows, wealth is consistently linked to opinions favoring a limited government role in promoting order and equality. Wealth and education have a similar impact on opinion: the groups with more education and higher income opt for freedom.

Region

Early in our country's history, regional differences were politically important—important enough to spark a civil war between the North and South. For nearly a hundred years after the Civil War, regional differences continued to affect American politics. The moneyed Northeast was thought to control the purse strings of capitalism. The Midwest was long regarded as the stronghold of isolationism in foreign affairs. The South was virtually a one-party region, almost completely Democratic. And the individualistic West pioneered its own mixture of progressive politics.

In the past, differences in wealth fed cultural differences between these regions. In recent decades, however, the movement of people and wealth away from the Northeast and Midwest to the Sunbelt states in the South and Southwest has equalized the per capita income of the regions. One product of this equalization is that the "solid South" is no longer solidly Democratic. In fact, the South has tended to vote for Republican candidates for president since 1968.

Figure 4.2 shows more striking differences between the four major regions of the United States on social issues than on economic issues. Respondents in the Northeast and West were more likely to support personal choice than residents of the South. People in the Midwest were somewhat more likely to oppose government efforts to equalize income than were people in the Northeast. Despite these differences, regional effects on public opinion are weaker than the effects of most other socioeconomic factors.

The "Old" and "New" Ethnicity: European Origin and Race

In the early twentieth century, the major ethnic groups in America were immigrants from Ireland, Italy, Germany, Poland, and other European countries, who came to the United States in waves during the late 1800s and early 1900s. They found themselves in a strange land, usually without money and unable to speak the language. Moreover, their religious backgrounds—mainly Catholic and Jewish—differed from that of the predominantly Protestant earlier set-tlers. Local politicians saw the newcomers, who were concentrated in urban areas in the Northeast and Midwest, as a new source of votes and soon mobilized them politically. These urban ethnics and their descendants became part of the great coalition of Democratic voters that President Franklin Roosevelt forged in the 1930s. And for years after, the European ethnics supported liberal candidates and causes more strongly than the original Anglo-Saxon immigrants.[12] More recent studies of public opinion show the differences are disappearing.[13] But if this **"old" ethnicity**, based on European origin, is giving way to assimilation, a **"new" ethnicity**, based on race, is taking its place.

With the rise of black consciousness and the grassroots civil rights movement in the late 1950s and 1960s, blacks secured genuine voting rights in the South and exercised those rights more vigorously in the North. Although they represented only about 12 percent of the total population, blacks made up sizable voting blocs in southern states and northern cities. Like the European ethnics before them, American blacks were courted for their votes; at long last, their opinions were politically important.

Blacks constitute the largest racial minority in American politics but not the only significant one. Asians, American Indians (Native Americans), and other nonwhites account for another 5 percent of the population. People of Latin American origin are often called Latinos. If they speak Spanish, they are also known as Hispanics. Hispanics make up about 10 percent of the nation's population, but they constitute as much as 26 percent of the population in California and Texas, and 38 percent in New Mexico.[14] Although they are politically strong in some communities, Hispanics have lagged behind blacks in mobilizing across the nation. However, Hispanics are being wooed by non-Hispanic candidates and are increasingly running for public office themselves.

Blacks and members of other minorities display similar political attitudes on questions pertaining to equality. The reasons are twofold.[15] First, racial minorities (excepting second-generation Asians) tend to have low **socioeconomic status**, a combination of education, occupation, status, and income. Second, all racial minorities have been targets of racial prejudice and discrimination and have benefited from government actions in support of equality. The right-hand column in Figure 4.2 clearly shows the effects of race on the freedom-equality issue. Blacks strongly favored government action to improve economic opportunity; other minorities also favored government action but to a lesser degree. On the abortion issue, however, blacks differed little from whites, whereas other minorities favored government restrictions.

Religion

Since the last major wave of European immigration in the 1930s and 1940s, the religious makeup of the United States has remained fairly stable. Today, almost 65 percent of the population are Protestant, about 25 percent are Catholic, only about 2 percent are Jewish, and about 10 percent denied any religious affiliation or choose some other faith.[16] For many years, analysts found strong and consistent differences in the opinions of Protestants, Catholics, and Jews.[17] Protestants were more conservative than Catholics, and Catholics tended to be more conservative than Jews.

Some such differences have remained, especially on the questions of freedom versus order (e.g., such as the abortion question), but they are less marked than one might expect. Protestants oppose personal choice on abortion slightly more than Catholics. Nonreligious persons and non-Christians are much more likely to favor personal choice on abortion and are somewhat less inclined toward favoring government job guarantees.

Even greater differences emerge when respondents were classified by their "religiosity," which was measured by their attitude toward the Bible. As Figure 4.2 indicates, religiosity has little effect on attitudes toward economic equality but a powerful influence on attitudes toward social order. Political opinions in the United States do differ sharply according to religious beliefs.

Gender

Differences in sex, which has become known as *gender* in American politics, are often related to political opinions, primarily on the issue of freedom versus equality. As shown in the right-hand column of Figure 4.2, women are more likely to favor government actions to promote equality. However, men and women usually differ less on issues of freedom versus order. Even on the abortion issue, women and men are equally likely to favor personal choice over government restrictions (see the column on the left of Figure 4.2. Still, on many issues of government policy, the "gender gap" in American politics is noticeable, with women more supportive than men of government spending for social programs.

From Values to Ideology

We have just seen that differences in groups' responses on two survey questions reflect those groups' value choices between freedom and order and between freedom and equality. But to what degree do people's opinions on specific issues reflect explicit political ideology (the set of values and beliefs that they hold about the purpose and scope of government)? Political scientists generally agree that ideology influences public opinion on specific issues; they have much less consensus on the extent to which people explicitly think in ideological terms.[18] They also agree that the public's ideological thinking cannot be categorized adequately in conventional liberal-conservative terms.[19]

The Degree of Ideological Thinking in Public Opinion

In an early but important study of public opinion, respondents were asked to describe the parties and candidates in the 1956 election.[20] Only about 12 percent of the sample volunteered responses that contained ideological terms (such as *liberal, conservative,* and *capitalism*). Most respondents (42 percent) evaluated the parties and candidates in terms of "benefits to groups" (farmers, workers, or businesspeople, for example). Others (24 percent) spoke more generally about "the nature of the times" (for example, inflation, unemployment, and the threat of war). Finally, a good portion of the sample (22 percent) gave answers that contained no classifiable issue content.

Subsequent research found somewhat greater ideological awareness within the electorate, especially during the 1964 presidential contest between Lyndon Johnson, a Democrat and ardent liberal, and Barry Goldwater, a Republican who was then considered an archconservative.[21] But more recent research has questioned whether American voters have really changed in their ideological thinking.[22] The tendency to respond to questions by using ideological terms increased with increasing education, which helps people understand political issues and relate them to one another. People's personal political socialization can lead them to think ideologically.

The Quality of Ideological Thinking in Public Opinion

What people's ideological self-placement means in the 1990s is not clear. At one time, the liberal-conservative continuum represented a single dimension: attitudes toward the scope of government activity. Liberals were in favor of more government action to provide public goods, and conservatives were in favor of less. The simple distinction is not as useful today. Many people who call themselves liberals no longer favor government activism in general, and many self-styled conservatives no longer oppose it in principle. As a result, many people have difficulty deciding whether they are liberal or conservative.

Studies of the public's ideological thinking find that two themes run through people's minds when asked to describe liberals and conservatives. People associate liberals with change and conservatives with tradition. This theme corresponds to the distinction between liberals and conservatives on the exercise of freedom and the maintenance of order.[23]

The other theme has to do with equality. The conflict between freedom and equality was at the heart of President Roosevelt's New Deal economic policies (social security, minimum wage legislation, farm price supports) in the 1930s. The policies expanded the interventionist role of the national government in order to promote greater economic equality, and attitudes toward government intervention in the economy served to distinguish liberals from conservatives for decades afterward.[24] Attitudes toward government interventionism still underlie opinions about domestic economic policies.[25] Liberals support intervention to promote their ideas of economic equality; conservatives favor less government intervention and more individual freedom in economic activities.

In Chapter 1, we proposed an alternative ideological classification based on people's relative evaluations of freedom, order, and equality. We described liberals as people who believe that government should promote equality, even if some freedom is lost in the process, but who oppose surrendering freedom to government-imposed order. Conservatives do not oppose equality in and of itself, but put a higher value on freedom than equality when the two conflict.

Yet conservatives are not above restricting freedom when threatened with the loss of order. So both groups value freedom, but one is more willing to trade freedom for equality, and the other is more inclined to trade freedom for order. If you have trouble thinking about these tradeoffs on a single dimension, you are in good company. The liberal-conservative continuum presented to survey respondents takes a two-dimensional concept and squeezes it into a one-dimensional format.[26]

Ideological Types in the United States

Our ideological typology in Chapter 1 (see Figure 1.2) classifies people as liberals if they favor freedom over order and equality over freedom. Conversely, conservatives favor freedom over equality and order over freedom. Libertarians favor freedom over both equality and order—the opposite of communitarians. By cross-tabulating people's answers to the two questions from the 1992 National Election Study about freedom versus order (abortion) and freedom versus equality (government job guarantees), we can classify respondents according to their ideological tendencies. As shown in Figure 4.3, responses of people to the two questions are virtually unrelated to each other. This finding indicates that people do not decide about government activity according to a one-dimensional ideological standard. Figure 4.3 also classifies the sample according to the two dimensions in our ideological typology. Using only two issues to classify people in an ideological framework leaves substantial room for error. Still, if the typology is worthwhile, the results should be meaningful, and they are.

It is striking that the ideological tendencies of the respondents in the 1992 sample depicted in Figure 4.3 are divided almost equally among the four categories of the typology. The sample suggests that more than three-quarters of the electorate favor government action to promote order, increase equality, or both.

The ideological tendencies illustrate important differences among different social groups. Communitarians are prominent among minorities and among people with little education and low income, groups that tend to look favorably on the benefits of government in general. Libertarians are concentrated among people with more education and with higher income, who tend to be suspicious of government interference in their lives. People in the southern states tend to be communitarians, those in the Midwest tend to be conservatives, and those in the Northeast are inclined to be liberals. Men are more likely to be conservative or libertarian than women, who tend to be liberal or communitarian.[27]

This more refined analysis of political ideology explains why even Americans who pay close attention to politics find it difficult to locate themselves on the liberal-conservative continuum. Their problem is that they are liberal on some issues and conservative on others. Forced to choose along just one dimension, they opt for the middle category, moderate. However, our analysis also indicates that many people who classify themselves as liberals or

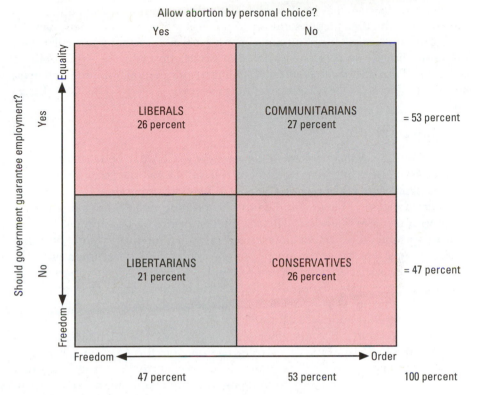

Allow abortion by personal choice?

FIGURE 4.3   *Respondents Classified by Ideological Tendencies*
Two survey questions presented choices between freedom and order and between freedom and equality by asking respondents whether abortion should be a matter of personal choice or of government regulation, and whether government should guarantee people a job and a good standard of living or people should get ahead on their own. (The questions are given verbatim on pages 85 and 86.) People's responses to the questions showed no correlation, demonstrating that these value choices cannot be explained by a simple liberal-conservative continuum. Instead, their responses can be more usefully analyzed according to four different ideological types. (The one-point difference in the percentage of responses for the "Should government guarantee employment?" question from that given on page 86 is the result of losing a few cases when the questions were cross-tabulated.) (*Source:* 1992 National Election Study, *Center for Political Studies, University of Michigan.*)

conservatives do fit these two categories in our typology. There is value, then, in the liberal-conservative distinction, as long as we understand its limitations.

The Process of Forming Political Opinions

We have seen that people acquire political values through the socialization process and that different social groups develop different sets of political values.

We also have learned that some people, but only a minority, think about politics ideologically, holding a consistent set of political attitudes and beliefs. Now let us look at how people form opinions on any particular issue. In particular, how do those who are not ideologues—in other words, most citizens—form political opinions? Four factors—self-interest, political information, opinion schemas, and political leadership—play a part in the process.

Self-Interest

The **self-interest principle** states that people choose what benefits them personally.[28] The principle plays an obvious role in how people form opinions on government economic policies. Taxpayers tend to prefer low taxes to high taxes; farmers tend to favor candidates who promise them more support over those who promise them less. The self-interest principle also applies, but less clearly, to some government policies outside of economics. Members of minority groups tend to see more personal advantage in government policies that promote social equality than do members of majority groups; teenage males are more likely to oppose compulsory military service than are older people of either sex. Group leaders often cue group members, telling them what they should support or oppose.[29]

When a person is not directly affected by a government policy, the self-interest principle plays little or no role. Then people form opinions based on their underlying values.[30] When moral issues are not in question and when people do not benefit directly from a policy, many people have trouble relating to the policy and forming an opinion about it. This tends to be true of the whole subject of foreign policy. Here, many people have no opinion, or their opinions are not firmly held and are apt to change quite easily, given almost any new information.

Political Information

In the United States today, the level of education is high, and media coverage of national and international events is extensive. Yet the average American displays an astonishing lack of political knowledge.[31]

But Americans do not let lack of knowledge stop them from expressing their opinions. They readily offer opinions on issues ranging from capital punishment to nuclear power to the government's handling of the economy. When opinions are based on little knowledge, however, they change easily in the face of new information. The result is a high degree of instability in public opinion poll findings, depending on how questions are worded and on recent events that bear on the issue at hand.

The most recent study of political knowledge was undertaken by Delli Carpini and Keeter.[32] In addition to conducting their own specialized surveys, they collected from existing surveys approximately 3,700 individual items that measured some type of factual knowledge about public affairs. They concluded that enough of the public is "reasonably well informed about politics . . . to meet high standards of good citizenship." They found, "Many of the basic institutions and procedures of government are known to half or more of the public, as are the relative positions of the parties on many major issues."[33] Their analysis also found, however, that political knowledge is not randomly distributed within our society. "In particular, women, African Americans, the poor, and the young tend to be substantially less knowledgeable about politics than are men, whites, the affluent, and older citizens."[34] Education is the strongest single predictor of political knowledge.

Researchers have not found any meaningful relationship between political sophistication and self-placement on the liberal-conservative scale. That is, people with equal knowledge about public affairs and levels of conceptualization are as likely to call themselves liberals as conservatives.[35] Equal levels of political understanding, then, may produce quite different political views as a result of individuals' unique patterns of political socialization.

Opinion Schemas

Even people who do not approach politics from the perspective of a full-blown ideology interpret political issues in terms of some preexisting mental structure. Psychologists refer to the packet of preexisting beliefs that people apply to specific issues as an **opinion schema**—a network of organized knowledge and beliefs that guides the processing of information on a particular subject.[36] The schema concept gives us a more flexible tool for analyzing public opinion than the more rigid concept of ideology. Opinion schemas can pertain to any political figure and to any subject—race, economics, or international relations, for example.[37]

Still, the more encompassing concept of ideology is hard to escape. Researchers have found that people's personal schemas tend to be organized in ways that parallel broader ideological categories. In other words, a conservative's opinion schema about Bill Clinton may not differ factually from a liberal's, but it will differ considerably in its evaluation of those facts.[38]

Some scholars argue that most citizens, in their attempt to make sense out of politics, pay less attention to the policies pursued by government than to their leaders' "style" in approaching political problems—for instance, whether they are seen as tough, compassionate, honest, or hardworking.[39] In this way citizens can relate the complexities of politics to their own personal experiences.

Political Leadership

Public opinion on specific issues is molded by political leaders, journalists, and policy experts. Because of the attention given to the presidency by the media, presidents are uniquely positioned to shape popular attitudes. Consider Ronald Reagan and the issue of nuclear disarmament. In late 1987, President Reagan and Mikhail Gorbachev signed a treaty banning intermediate-range nuclear forces (INFs) from Europe and the Soviet Union. Soon afterward, a national survey found that 82 percent of the sample approved the treaty while 18 percent opposed it. As might be expected, those hard-liners who viewed the

Soviet Union as highly threatening ("hard-liners") were least enthusiastic about the INF treaty. Respondents were then asked to agree or disagree with this statement: "President Reagan is well known for his anticommunism, so if he thinks this is a good deal, it must be." Analysis of the responses showed that those hard-liners who agreed with the statement were nearly twice as likely to approve the treaty as those who were unmoved by his involvement. The researcher concluded that "a highly conciliatory move by a president known for long-standing opposition to just such an action" can override expected sources of opposition among the public.[40]

The ability of political leaders to affect public opinion has been enhanced enormously by the growth of the broadcast media, especially television.[41] The majoritarian model of democracy assumes that government officials respond to public opinion; but the evidence is substantial that this causal sequence is reversed, that public opinion responds instead to the actions of government officials.[42] If this is true, how much potential is there for public opinion to be manipulated by political leaders through the mass media?

The Media in America

"We never talk anymore" is a common lament of couples who are not getting along very well. In politics, too, citizens and their government need to communicate in order to get along well. *Communication* is the process of transmitting information from one individual or group to another. *Mass communication* is the process by which information is transmitted to large, heterogeneous, widely dispersed audiences. The term **mass media** refers to the means for communicating to these audiences. The mass media are commonly divided into two types. *Print media* (newspapers, magazines) communicate information through the publication of written words and pictures. *Broadcast media* (radio, television) communicate information electronically through sounds and images. Modern politics also utilize the *fax* (facsimile images sent by telephone) and computers linked over the *Internet*. We refer to these as *group media,* and we consider them separately below.

Our focus here is on the role of the media in promoting communication from government to its citizens and from citizens to their government. In totalitarian governments, information flows more freely in one direction (from government to people) than the other. In democratic governments, information must flow freely in both directions; a democratic government can respond to public opinion only if its citizens can make their opinions known. Moreover, the electorate can hold government officials accountable for their actions only if voters know what their government has done, is doing, and plans to do. Because the mass media (and increasingly the group media) provide the major channels for this two-way flow of information, they have the dual capability of reflecting and shaping our political views.

The media are not the only means of communication between citizens and government. Agents of socialization (especially schools) function as "linkage mechanisms" that promote such communication. In the next three chapters, we will discuss other major mechanisms for communication: voting, political parties, campaigning in elections, and interest groups.

Modern Forms of Group Media

The revolution in electronics during the last quarter of the twentieth century produced two new technologies—the fax and the Internet—that have been readily adapted to politics. Neither are "mass" media that communicate with the general public, however. They are called **group media**—communications technologies used primarily within groups of people with common interests.

Facsimile Transmissions   The fax machine has become standard communications equipment in practical politics. Campaign managers routinely communicate with campaign workers and media representatives via fax, and it is a major medium for communication among political officeholders in Washington.[43] Interest groups frequently rely on automated fax messages concerning issues before Congress—as many as ten thousand a night—sent automatically by computers to sympathizers across the country.[44] Increasingly, recipients of these faxes respond by faxing fervent messages of opposition or support to their congressional representatives, simulating a ground swell of public opinion—despite the fact that only 8 percent of U.S. homes had fax machines in 1995 (see High-Tech Lobbying, Chapter 7).[45]

The Internet   What we today call the Internet began in 1969 when, with support from the U.S. Defense Department's Advanced Research Projects Agency, computers at four universities were linked to form ARPANET. In its early years, the Internet was used mainly to transmit messages, known as electronic mail, or *e-mail*, among researchers. In 1991, a group of European physicists devised a standardized system for encoding and transmitting a wide range of materials, including graphics and photographs, over the Internet, and the World Wide Web (WWW) was born. Today there are many thousands of Web sites and millions of WWW users.

Like the fax, the Internet was soon utilized in political life. By 1995, there was enough political material on the Internet to fill a 375-page book, *Politics on the Net*.[46] Recently, the Internet has been proposed as a systematic means of registering citizens' opinions or votes. However, only 21 percent of respondents in a 1996 national survey said that they ever used a computer at work, school, or home to connect with other computers on the Internet, and only 3 percent ever obtained information on the presidential campaign from the Internet.[47] Of course, these percentages will grow over time.

Private Ownership of the Media

In the United States, people take private ownership of the media for granted. In other Western democratic countries, the print media (both newspapers and magazines) are privately owned, but the broadcast media often are not. Private ownership of both the print and broadcast media gives the news industry in America more political freedom than any other in the world, but it also makes the media more dependent on advertising revenues. To make a profit, the news operations of the mass media in America must appeal to the audiences they serve.

The primary criterion of a story's **newsworthiness** is usually its audience appeal, which is judged according to its potential impact on readers or listeners; its degree of sensationalism (exemplified by violence, conflict, disaster, or scandal), its treatment of familiar people or life situations; its treatment of familiar people or life situations, its close-to-home character; and its timeliness.[48]

Media owners can make more money either by increasing their audiences or by acquiring additional publications or stations. There is a decided trend toward concentrated ownership of the media, increasing the risk that a few major owners could control the news flow to promote their own political interests. In fact, the number of *independent newspapers* has declined as newspaper chains (owners of two or more newspapers in different cities) have acquired more newspapers. Only about four hundred dailies are still independent, and many of these papers are too small and unprofitable to invite acquisition.

As with newspapers, chains sometimes own television stations in different cities, and ownership sometimes extends across different media. When it acquired CBS in 1995, Westinghouse owned TV stations in fourteen major cities and thirty-nine radio stations. In 1996, Westinghouse extended its media empire by purchasing Infinity Broadcasting, giving Westinghouse a total of eighty-three AM and FM stations, many in the nation's largest markets.[49] Some people fear the concentration of media under a single owner, and government has addressed those fears by regulating media ownership, as well as other aspects of media operation.

Government Regulation of the Media

Although most of the mass media in the United States are privately owned, they do not operate free of government regulation. The broadcast media, however, operate under more regulations than the print media.

The Federal Communications Act of 1934 created the **Federal Communications Commission** (FCC) to regulate the broadcast and telephone industries. The FCC has five members (no more than three from the same political party) nominated by the president for terms of five years. The commissioners can be removed from office only through impeachment and conviction. Consequently, the FCC is considered an independent regulatory commission: It is insulated from political control by either the president or Congress. (We discuss independent regulatory commissions in Chapter 10.) Today, the FCC is charged with regulating interstate and international communications by radio, television, telephone, telegraph, cable, and satellite.

For six decades—as technological change made television commonplace and brought the invention of computers, fax machines, and satellite transmissions—the communications industry was regulated under the basic framework of the 1934 law that created the FCC. Pressured by businesses that wanted to exploit new electronic technologies, Congress, in a bipartisan effort, swept away most existing regulations in the Telecommunications Act of 1996.

The 1996 law relaxed or scrapped limitations on media ownership. For example, broadcasters were previously limited to owning only twelve TV stations and forty radio stations. Now there are no limits on the number of TV stations one company may own, just so long as their coverage doesn't extend beyond 35 percent of the market nationwide. The law set no national limits for radio ownership, and it relaxed local limits. In addition, it lifted rate regulations for cable systems, allowed cross-ownership of cable and telephone companies, and allowed local and long-distance telephone companies to compete with one another and to sell television services. Although even those who wrote the law could not predict its long-range effect, the law quickly spurred even greater concentration of media ownership.

The First Amendment to the Constitution prohibits Congress from abridging the freedom of the press. Over time, *the press* has come to mean all the mass media, and the courts have decided many cases that define how far freedom of the press extends under the law. The most important of these cases are often quite complex.

Usually the courts strike down government attempts to restrain the press from publishing or broadcasting the information, reports, or opinions it finds newsworthy. One notable exception concerns strategic information during wartime; the courts have supported censorship of information such as the sailing schedules of troop ships or the planned movements of troops in battle. Otherwise, they have recognized a strong constitutional case against press censorship.

Because the broadcast media are licensed to use the public airwaves, they are subject to additional regulation, beyond that applied to the print media, of the content of their news coverage. The basis for the FCC's regulation of content lies in its charge to ensure that radio (and, later, television) stations would "serve the public interest, convenience, and necessity." With its **equal opportunities rule**, the FCC requires any broadcast station that gives or sells time to a candidate for public office to make an equal amount of time available under the same conditions to all other candidates for that office. The **reasonable access rule** required that stations make their facilities available for the expression of conflicting views or issues from all responsible elements in the community.

Political Effects of the Media

In this section we discuss how the media cover political affairs, and examine where citizens acquire their political knowledge. We also look at what people learn from the media, and probe the media's effects on public opinion, the political agenda, and political socialization.

Covering National Politics

Washington has by far the biggest press corps of any city in the world—over 6,000 accredited reporters: 2,100 from newspapers, 2,000 from periodicals, and 2,200 from radio and television.[50] However, only about seventy-five "regular" journalists are in the White House press corps.[51] As recently as the Truman administration, reporters enjoyed informal personal relationships with the president. Today, the media's relationship with the president is mediated primarily through the Office of the Press Secretary.

White House correspondents rely heavily on information they receive from the president's staff, each piece carefully crafted in an attempt to control the news report. The most frequent form is the news release—a prepared text distributed to reporters in the hope that they will use it verbatim. A daily news briefing at 11:30 A.M. enables reporters to question the press secretary about news releases. A news conference involves questioning high-level officials in the executive branch—including the president on occasion. News conferences appear to be freewheeling, but officials tend to carefully rehearse precise answers to anticipated questions.

Occasionally, information is given "on background," meaning the information can be quoted but reporters cannot identify the source. A vague reference—"a senior official says"—is all right. Information disclosed "off the record" cannot even be printed. Journalists who violate these well-known rules risk losing their welcome at the White House.

Most reporters in the Washington press corps are accredited to sit in the House and Senate press galleries, but only about four hundred cover Congress exclusively.[52] Most news about Congress comes from innumerable press releases issued by its 535 members and from an unending supply of congressional reports.

Congress banned microphones and cameras from its chambers until 1979, when the House permitted live coverage, though it insisted on controlling the shots being televised. To share in the exposure, the Senate began television coverage in 1986. C-SPAN (the Cable Satellite Public Affairs Network) coverage of Congress has become important to professionals in government and politics in Washington. Even members of the Washington press corps watch C-SPAN.

In addition to these recognized sources of news, selected reporters occasionally benefit from leaks of information released by officials who are guaranteed anonymity. Officials may leak news to interfere with others' political plans or to float ideas ("trial balloons") past the public and other political leaders to gauge their reactions. At times, one carefully placed leak can turn into a gusher of media coverage through the practice of "pack journalism"—the tendency of journalists to adopt similar viewpoints toward the news simply because they hang around together, exchanging information and defining the day's news with one another.

Where the Public Gets Its News

Virtually all citizens rely on the mass media for their political news. Until the early 1960s, most people reported getting more of that news from newspapers than from any other source. Television nudged out newspapers as the public's major source of news in the early 1960s. By the mid-1990s, nearly three-fourths of the public cited television as their news source, compared with about two-fifths who named newspapers (some named both). Not only is television the public's most important source of news, but those polled rated television news as more trustworthy than newspaper news by a margin of 2 to 1.[53] But recent studies have found that fewer adults are regularly watching television news, particularly nightly network news (only 42 percent in 1996 versus 60 percent in 1993).[54]

As one would expect, level of education is strongly related to news attentiveness. So is age. One major study found that nearly half of the "news sophisticates," who read specialized opinion magazine and listen to news programs on public radio and public television, are college graduates. Also, nearly half of those news sophisticates are age fifty or older.[55] Among other factors, race bears no relationship to news attentiveness,[56] but sex has a decided effect, with news sophisticates more likely to be male (56 percent) and nonusers to be female (60 percent).

What People Remember and Know

If, as surveys indicate, 84 percent of the public read or hear the news each day, and if nearly 75 percent regularly watch the news on television, how much political information do they absorb? By all accounts, not much. When a national sample was asked in the summer of 1992 (an election year) which party controlled the House of Representatives, fewer than half correctly identified the Democrats, but when asked to name the television show that Vice President Dan Quayle had criticized for glamorizing unwed motherhood, several years before, two-thirds correctly said "Murphy Brown."[57]

Those who are more attentive to news answer more political knowledge questions correctly than those who are less attentive—as expected. Given the enormous improvements in television news coverage and the increasing reliance of the public on TV for news, we might also expect the public to know more than it did twenty years ago.[58] Unfortunately, that is not so. Similar surveys in 1967 and in 1987 asked respondents to name their state governor, representative in the House, and head of the local school district. Only 9 percent failed to name a single official in 1967 compared with 17 percent in 1987. The author of this study attributed the lower performance in 1987 to greater reliance on television for news.[59]

Numerous studies have found that those who rely on television for their news score lower on tests of knowledge about public affairs than those who rely on print media.[60] Among media researchers, this finding has led to the **television hypothesis**—the belief that television is to blame for the low level of citizen's knowledge about public affairs.[61] However, recent research questioned the hypothesis and found that "television was more successful in communicating information about topics that were of low salience [significance] to the audience, while print media were superior in conveying information about topics that had high salience."[62]

Influencing Public Opinion

Americans overwhelmingly believe that the media exert a strong influence on their political institutions, and almost nine out of ten Americans believe that the media strongly influence public opinion.[63] However, measuring the extent

Compared with What? 4.1

Live (and Sometimes Colored): Election News on Television in Three Countries

Compared with television reporters in Britain and Germany, reporters in the United States are more likely to color campaign news through commentary before and after reporting a story. This finding comes from a cross-national study of television coverage of elections in the United States and Britain in 1992 and in Germany in 1990. Stories about the candidates' activities were coded by researchers according to reporters' comments in statements that preceded or followed film of the candidates' appearance. The comments were coded as "deflating," "straight or neutral," "mixed," or "reinforcing." Nearly one-quarter of all U.S. reporters' comments were deflating—nearly three times the incidence in Britain and more than ten times that in Germany. In fact, only about half the comments in the United States were straight or neutral, compared with more than two-thirds in Britain and nearly all in Germany.

Source: These data were calculated from Table 7 in Holli A. Semetko, "American Election News in Comparative Perspective," paper presented at the annual meeting of the American Political Science Association, Washington, D.C., September 1993.

of media influence on public opinion is difficult.[64] Because few of us learn about political events except through the media, it could be argued that the media create public opinion simply by reporting events. Consider the dismantling of the Berlin Wall in 1989. Surely the photographs of joyous Berliners demolishing that symbol of oppression affected American public opinion about the reunification of Germany.

Studies of opinion change have found television coverage of particular events to have systematic, and in some cases dramatic, effects. In 1993, for example, Vice President Al Gore and Ross Perot held a "debate" about the North American Free Trade Agreement (NAFTA) on CNN's "Larry King Live." Contrary to Perot, Gore argued that NAFTA would create more jobs than it might cost. *USA Today* polled viewers before and after the debate and found those who favored NAFTA grew from 34 to 57 percent, with the main vote coming from the "undecideds."[65] Many commentators claimed that Gore's strong showing helped NAFTA pass Congress and become law.

Documenting general effects of media on opinions about general issues in the news is difficult. One study analyzed polls on eighty issues in foreign and domestic affairs at two points in time. For nearly half of these issues, public opinion changed over time by about six percentage points. The researchers compared these changes with policy positions taken by ten different sources of information composed of commentators on television network news, including the president; members of the president's party; members of the opposition party; and members of interest groups. The authors found the news commentators to have the most dramatic effect—they could link a single commentary for or against an issue to a significant corresponding change in opinion (more than four percentage points).[66]

Setting the Political Agenda

Despite the media's potential for influencing public opinion, most scholars believe that the media's greatest impact on politics is found in their power to set the **political agenda**—a list of issues that people identify as needing government attention. Those who set the political agenda define which issues government decision makers should discuss and debate.

The mass media in the United States have traditionally played an important role in defining the political agenda. Television, which brings pictures and sound into virtually every home, has an enormous potential for setting the political agenda. As a careful study designed to isolate and examine television's effects on public opinion concluded, "By attending to some problems and ignoring others, television news shapes the American public's political priorities."[67] Indeed, the further the viewer is removed from public affairs, "the stronger the agenda-setting power of television news."[68]

One study found varying correlations between media coverage and what the public sees as "the most important problem facing this country today," depending on the type of event. Public opinion was especially responsive to media coverage of recurring problems such as inflation and unemployment.[69]

The media's ability to influence public opinion by defining "the news" makes politicians eager to influence media coverage. Politicians attempt to affect not only public opinion but the opinions of other political leaders.[70] The president receives a daily digest of news and opinion from many sources. In a curious sense, the mass media have become a network for communicating among attentive elites, all trying to influence one another or to assess others' weaknesses and strengths. Suppose the White House is under pressure on some policy matter and is asked to send a representative to appear for fifteen minutes of intensive questioning on the "Newshour with Jim Lehrer." The White House might comply as much to influence the thinking of other insiders (who faithfully watch the program) as to influence opinions among the relatively few news sophisticates in the public who watch public television.

Socialization

The mass media act as important agents of political socialization.[71] Young people who rarely follow the news by choice, nevertheless acquire political values through the entertainment function of the broadcast media. Years ago, children learned from radio programs; now they learn from television. What children learned from radio was quite different from what they are learning now, however. In the golden days of radio, youngsters listening to popular radio dramas heard repeatedly that "crime does not pay." The message never varied: criminals are bad; the police are good; criminals get caught and are severely punished for their crimes.

Television today does not portray the criminal justice system in the same way, even in police dramas. Consider programs such as "Homicide" and "The X-Files," which have portrayed police and FBI agents as killers. Other series, such as "Law and Order" and even "NYPD Blue" sometimes portray a tainted criminal justice system and institutionalized corruption.[72] Certainly, one cannot easily argue that television's entertainment programs help prepare law-abiding citizens.

So the media play contradictory roles in the process of political socialization. On one hand, they promote popular support for government by joining in the celebration of national holidays, heroes' birthdays, political anniversaries, and civic accomplishments. On the other hand, the media erode public confidence by publicizing citizens' grievances, airing investigative reports of agency malfeasance, and even showing dramas about crooked cops.[73]

Evaluating the Media in Government

Are the media fair or biased in reporting the news? What contributions do the media make to democratic government? What effects do they have on freedom, order, and equality?

Is Reporting Biased?

News reports are presented as objective reality, yet critics of modern journalism contend that news is filtered through the ideological biases of the owners and editors (the gatekeepers) and of the reporters themselves.

Fraternizing with the Enemy?
Although the news media and the government are sometimes viewed as adversaries, as this photo shows, they are also often very "close." In this picture, newsmen swarm around Bill Clinton in an effort to be the first to gain some new bit of information which will immediately be conveyed to the public.

The argument that news is politically biased has two sides. On one hand, news reporters are criticized for tilting their stories in a liberal direction, promoting social equality and undercutting social order. On the other hand, wealthy and conservative media owners are suspected of preserving inequalities and reinforcing the existing order by serving a relentless round of entertainment that numbs the public's capacity for critical analysis.

Although the picture is far from clear, available evidence seems to confirm the charge of liberal leanings among reporters in the major news media. Studies of the voting behavior of hundreds of reporters and broadcasters show that they voted overwhelmingly for Democratic candidates in presidential elections from 1964 through 1980.[74] Moreover, a 1992 survey of 1,400 journalists found that 44 percent called themselves Democrats, versus 16 percent who were Republicans.[75] But, do reporters' personal opinions color news coverage?

A study of television coverage during the summer of the 1992 presidential campaign found that the candidates alternated in the spotlight before Labor Day. In the weeks before and during the Democratic convention, Clinton had 454 minutes on network news shows to Bush's 400. But between the Republican convention and Labor Day, Bush drew about 2.6 minutes per newscast versus Clinton's 1.6.[76] Of course, reporters can "spin" the news so that coverage is good or bad. When Bush chose Texas to announce that he would sell fighter jets to Taiwan to save jobs, ABC's Brit Hume reported that Bush was adjusting foreign policy to help his campaign in his home state. After Labor Day, the Times Mirror Center for Media & Public Affairs analyzed all interviews about the candidates on the ABC, CBS, and NBC evening news broadcasts. It classified 69 percent of the comments about Bush as negative, compared with 63 percent about Clinton, and only 54 percent about Perot.[77]

To some extent, working journalists in the national and local media are at odds with their own editors, who tend to be more conservative and tend to tone down reporters' liberal leanings.[78]

If media owners and their editors are indeed conservative supporters of the status quo, we might expect them to support officeholders over challengers in elections, regardless of party. However, the evidence tends in the other direction. Let's compare 1980 (when Jimmy Carter, a liberal Democrat, was president and Ronald Reagan, a conservative Republican was his challenger) with 1984 (when President Reagan faced Walter Mondale, a liberal Democrat). A comparison of television news in 1980 and 1984 found more negative coverage of the incumbent president both times.[79] The researcher concluded that virtually no *continuing* ideological or partisan bias existed on the evening television news. Instead, what was seen as ideological or partisan bias in 1980 and 1984 was actually a bias against presidential *incumbents* and *front-runners* for the presidency.[80] According to this reasoning, if journalists have any pronounced bias, it is against office-holding politicians. When an incumbent runs for reelection, journalists may feel a special responsibility to counteract his or her advantage by putting the opposite partisan spin on the news.[81]

Contributions to Democracy

As noted earlier, in a democracy, communication must move in two directions: from government to citizens and from citizens to government. In fact, political communication in the United States seldom goes directly from government to citizens without passing through the media. The point is important because, as just discussed, news reporters tend to be highly critical of politicians; they consider it their job to search for inaccuracies in fact and weaknesses in argument. Some observers have characterized the news media and the government as adversaries—each mistrusting the other, locked in competition for popular favor while trying to get the record straight. To the extent that this is true, the media serve both the majoritarian and the pluralist models of democracy well by improving the quality of information transmitted to the people about their government.

The mass media transmit information in the opposite direction by reporting citizens' reactions to political events and government actions. The press has traditionally reflected public opinion (and often created it) in the process of defining the news and suggesting courses of government action. But the media's role in reflecting public opinion has become much more refined in the information age. After commercial polls (such as the Gallup and Roper polls) were established in the 1930s, newspapers began to report reliable readings of public opinion. By the 1970s, some news organizations acquired their own survey research divisions. Occasionally, print and electronic media have joined forces to conduct major national surveys. For example, the well-respected *New York Times*/CBS News Poll conducts surveys that are first aired on the "CBS Evening News," and then analyzed at length in the *Times*.

Although polls sometimes create opinions just by asking questions, their net effect has been to generate more accurate knowledge of public opinion and to report that knowledge back to the public. Although widespread knowledge of public opinion does not guarantee government responsiveness to popular demands, such knowledge is necessary if government is to function according to the majoritarian model of democracy.

Effects on Freedom, Order, and Equality

The media in the United States have played an important role in advancing equality, especially racial equality. Throughout the civil rights movement of the 1950s and 1960s, the media gave national coverage to conflict in the South, as black children tried to attend white schools or civil rights workers were beaten and even killed in the effort to register black voters. Partly because of this media coverage, civil rights moved up on the political agenda, and coalitions were formed in Congress to pass new laws promoting racial equality. Women's rights have also been advanced by the media, which have reported instances of blatant sexual discrimination exposed by groups working for sexual equality. In general, the mass media offer spokespersons for any disadvantaged group an opportunity to state their case before a national audience and to work for a place on the political agenda.

Although the media are willing to encourage government action to promote equality at the cost of some personal freedom, they resist government's attempts to infringe on freedom of the press to promote order. The media, far more than the public, believe freedom of the press is sacrosanct. For example, 98 percent of 2,703 journalists surveyed by the *Los Angeles Times* opposed allowing a government official to prevent the publication of a story the government claims to be inaccurate, compared with only 50 percent of the public. Whereas a majority of the public believes that certain types of news should never be published—exit polls saying who will win an election, secret documents dealing with national security issues, the names of CIA spies, photographs that invade people's privacy—journalists are more reluctant to draw the line anywhere.[82]

To protect their freedom, the media operate as an interest group along pluralist lines. They have an interest in being able to report whatever they wish, whenever they wish, which certainly erodes the government's efforts to maintain order. Three examples illustrate this point.

- The media's sensational coverage of terrorist activities gives terrorists exactly what they want, making it more difficult to reduce terrorist threats to order.
- The portrayal of brutal killings and rapes on television, often under the guise of entertainment, has produced "copycat" crimes, those admittedly committed "as seen on TV."
- The national publicity given to claims of syringes found in cans of Pepsi Cola in 1993 prompted similar tampering with other products.[83] Publicity given to the burning of black churches in 1996 raised fears of "copycat" arson.

Freedom of the press is a noble value and one that has been important to our democratic government. But we should not ignore the fact that we sometimes pay a price for pursuing it without qualification.

Summary

Public opinion does not rule in America. On most issues, it merely sets general boundaries for government policy. People form their values through the process of political socialization. The most important socialization agents in childhood and young adulthood are family, school, community, and peers. Members of the same social group tend to experience similar socialization processes and thus to adopt similar values. People in different social groups, that hold different values, often express vastly different opinions. Differences in education, race, and religion tend to produce sharper divisions of opinion today on questions of order and equality than do differences in income, region, or ethnicity.

Most people do not think about politics in ideological terms. When asked to do so by pollsters, however, they readily classify themselves along a liberal-conservative continuum. Many respondents choose the middle category, moderate, because the choice is safe. Others choose it because they have liberal views on some issues and conservative views on others. Their political orientation is better captured by a two-dimensional framework that analyzes ideology according to the values of order and equality. Responses to the survey questions we used to establish our ideological typology divide the American electorate almost equally as liberals, conservatives, libertarians, and communitarians. The quarter of the public that gave liberal responses—favoring government action to promote equality but not to impose order—was matched by an equal portion who gave the opposite, conservative responses. Similarly, the somewhat larger group of communitarians, who wanted government to impose both order and equality, was opposed by a smaller group of libertarians, who wanted government to do neither.

In addition to ideological orientation, many other factors enter the process of forming political opinions. When individuals stand to benefit or suffer from proposed government policies, they usually base their opinions of these policies on self-interest. When citizens lack information on which to base their opinions, they usually respond anyway, which leads to substantial fluctuations in poll results, depending on how questions are worded and on intervening events. The various factors that impinge on the process of forming political opinions can be mapped out within an opinion schema, a network of beliefs and attitudes about a particular topic. The schema image helps us visualize the complex process of forming opinions. This process is not completely idiosyncratic, however: people tend to organize their schemas according to broader ideological thinking. In the absence of information, respondents are particularly susceptible to cues of support or opposition from political leaders, communicated through the mass media.

Sometimes the public shows clear and settled opinions on government policy, conforming to the majoritarian model. However, public opinion is often not firmly grounded in knowledge and may be unstable on given issues. Moreover, powerful groups often divide on what they want government to do. This lack of consensus leaves politicians with a great deal of latitude in enacting specific policies, a finding that conforms to the pluralist model. Of course, politicians' actions are under close scrutiny by journalists reporting in the mass media.

The mass media transmit information to large, heterogeneous, and widely dispersed audiences through print and broadcasts. The main function of the mass media is entertainment, but the media also perform the political functions of reporting news, interpreting news, influencing citizens' opinions, setting the political agenda, and socializing citizens about politics.

The mass media in the United States are privately owned and in business to make money, which they do mainly by selling space or air time to advertisers. Both print and electronic media determine which events are newsworthy, largely on the basis of audience appeal.

The broadcast media operate under technical, ownership, and content regulations imposed by the government, which tend to promote the equal treatment of political contests on radio and television more than in newspapers and news magazines.

Washington, D.C., hosts the biggest press corps in the world, but only a portion of those correspondents concentrate on the presidency. Because Congress is a more decentralized institution, it is covered in a more decentralized manner. All professional journalists recognize rules for citing sources that guide their reporting. What actually gets reported in the media depends on the media's gatekeepers, the publishers and editors.

Although Americans today get more news from television than from newspapers, newspapers usually do a more thorough job of informing the public about politics. Despite heavy exposure to news in the print and electronic media, the ability of most people to retain much political information is shockingly low. The problem appears to be not with the media's ability to supply quality news coverage, but with the lack of demand for it by the public. The media's most important effect on public opinion is in setting the country's political agenda. The role of the news media may be more important for affecting interactions among attentive policy elites than in influencing public opinion. The media play more subtle, contradictory roles in political socialization, both promoting and undermining certain political and cultural values. Reporters from the national media tend to be more liberal than the public, as judged by their tendency to vote for Democratic candidates and by their own self-descriptions. However, if the media systematically demonstrate pronounced bias in their news reporting, it tends to work against incumbents and front-runners, regardless of their party, rather than a bias in favor of liberal Democrats.

From the standpoint of majoritarian democracy, one of the most important effects of the media is to facilitate communication from the people to the government through the reporting of public opinion polls. The media zealously defend the freedom of the press, even to the point of encouraging disorder by granting extensive publicity to violent protests, terrorist acts, and other threats to order.

Key Terms

public opinion
political socialization
"old" ethnicity
"new" ethnicity
socioeconomic status
self-interest principle
opinion schema
mass media

group media
newsworthiness
Federal Communications Commission
  (FCC)
equal opportunities rule
reasonable access rule
television hypothesis
political agenda

Selected Readings

Ansolabehere, Stephen, Roy Behr, and Shanto Iyengar. *The Media Game: American Politics in the Television Age.* New York: Macmillan, 1993. A recent text on the media's influence in politics that explores how the media can filter, alter, distort, or even ignore what politicians have to say.

Delli Carpini, Michael X., and Scott Keeter. *What Americans Know About Politics and Why It Matters.* New Haven, Conn.: Yale University Press, 1996. A comprehensive review and analysis of the public's responses to thousands of factual questions about political processes and institutions, public figures, political parties and groups, and public policies.

Kerbel, Matthew Robert. *Remote and Controlled: Media Politics in a Cynical Age.* Boulder, Colo.: Westview Press, 1995. A historical account of political journalism coverage that draws lessons for today.

Page, Benjamin I. *Who Deliberates: Mass Media in Modern Democracy.* Chicago: University of Chicago Press, 1996. Thoughtfully discusses and analyzes how the public "deliberates" through three specific case studies: the war with Iraq, the Los Angeles riots, and the failed nomination of Zoe Baird for Attorney General.

Stimson, James A. *Public Opinion in America: Mood, Cycles, and Swings.* Boulder, Colo.: Westview Press, 1992. The result of a massive study of more than one thousand survey questions from 1956 to 1989, this book charts the drift of public opinion from liberal in the 1950s to conservative at the end of the 1970s and back toward liberal in the 1980s.

Traugott, Michael W., and Paul J. Lavrakas. *The Voter's Guide to Election Polls.* Chatham, N.J.: Chatham House, 1996. A guide for evaluating election polls, including sampling, interviewing, questionnaires, and data analysis. Done in a question-and-answer format.

World Wide Web Resources

Pew Research Center for The People & The Press. "We are an independent opinion research group that studies attitudes toward the press, politics, and public policy issues. We are best known for regular national surveys that measure public attentiveness to major news stories, and for our polling that charts trends in values and fundamental political and social attitudes."

The Gallup Organization World Wide Web Server. George Gallup founded his polling organization in the United States in the 1930s, and the Gallup Poll is now an international institution. This site permits searching the *Gallup Newsletter Archives* for press releases of past surveys. You can also retrieve some results from the latest political polls.

<www.gallup.com/index.html>

Roper Center for Public Opinion Research. Located at the University of Connecticut, this center was founded by Elmo Roper, a contemporary of George Gallup. This site offers a powerful question-retrieval system, but you will need access to the Lexis/Nexis subscription service to use it. Some colleges subscribe to that service.

<www.lib.uconn.edu/RoperCenter/>

ABC News Reports. This site offers some text files to view, but most of its news reports require the Real-Audio player so that you can listen to contemporary news, old news, Peter Jennings's commentary, and more. The software can be downloaded from the site and installed on your computer.

<www.prognet.com/contentp/abc.html>

CNN Interactive. According to Scott Woelfel, editor in chief of CNN Interactive, "Our site will be rich with images, both still and moving. And the experience is made all the richer by the audio clips which we use to help tell the story as often as we can."

PBS Online. This site provides a gateway to various PBS progams, including a button to the "Online NewsHour," a page based on the comprehensive television evening news program hosted by Jim Lehrer. The page also covers stories in depth, usually involving interviews with key actors in politics.

Wall Street Journal Interactive. The *Journal* is the nation's largest-selling newspaper. Unlike the other sites mentioned here, this one requires a subscription. But if you like the *Journal*, you may find it worthwhile.

New York Times on the Web. Many people consider the nationally distributed *Times* to be as liberal as the *Wall Street Journal* is conservative. You don't have to subscribe, but you do have to register to use this service.

5

Participation and Voting

They seemed like ordinary folks. That's how their suburban neighbors regarded the ten men and two women arrested in Phoenix, Arizona, on July 1, 1996. One worked in a doughnut shop. Another worked for the telephone company. Others painted houses or sold office equipment.[1] One had even run for political office (unsuccessfully). But to the arresting federal agents, they were the Viper Militia, a small, secret paramilitary organization charged with plotting to destroy several public buildings. Indeed, the agents found the suspects' homes stocked with an arsenal of weapons—in addition to the 140 guns, there were hand grenades, rocket launchers, gas masks, silencers, and homemade bombs.[2]

Although it may represent the more extreme paramilitary groups in the United States today, the Viper Militia is but one of hundreds of active militia groups that operate throughout the nation. They communicate through group media: newsletters, faxes, and the Internet.[3] One of the most prominent antimilitia sites on the World Wide Web, "The Militia Watchdog," lists scores of militia sites, including home pages for movements in ten states.[4]

Is involvement in a militia a form of political participation, or is it simply a form of recreation—playing war games in the woods? No doubt, some people are attracted to militias for fun and fellowship, but the militia movement also has a distinct political cast. It views the federal government as a threat to personal freedom. Militia members also see conspiracies against freedom coming from the United Nations, the Council of Foreign Relations (an academically oriented institution that publishes *Foreign Affairs*, a respected journal on international politics), and the Trilateral Commission (a group consisting of business, labor, academic, and media leaders from America, Europe, and Japan). These conspiracies are referenced in a militia movement Web site called "Restoring America." The militia movement is deadly serious in its pledges to defend its view of freedom. Its exaltation of weapons is apparent in the "Minuteman Prayer," seen on a militia Web site:

> God grant me the serenity to accept the things I cannot change; the courage to change the things I can; and the superior firepower to make the difference.[5]

Although most people think of political participation primarily in terms of voting, there are other forms of political activity that are more robust than voting. Have militia members exceeded the boundaries of political participation, or are they simply defending freedom, in the tradition of the minutemen of the American Revolution? How politically active are Americans in general? How do they compare with citizens of other countries? How much and what kind of participation is necessary to sustain the pluralist and majoritarian models of democracy?

In this chapter, we try to answer these and other important questions about popular participation in government. We begin by studying participation in democratic government, distinguishing between conventional and unconventional participation. Then we evaluate the nature and extent of both types of participation in American politics. Next, we study the expansion of voting rights and voting as the major mechanism for mass participation in politics. Finally, we will examine the extent to which the various forms of political participation serve the values of freedom, equality, and order and the majoritarian and pluralist models of democracy.

Democracy and Political Participation

Government ought to be run by the people. That is the democratic ideal in a nutshell. But how much and what kind of citizen participation are necessary for democratic government? Champions of direct democracy believe that if citizens do not participate directly in government affairs, making government decisions among themselves, they should give up all pretense of living in a democracy. More practical observers contend that people can govern indirectly through their elected representatives. And they maintain that choosing leaders through elections—formal procedures for voting—is the only workable approach to democracy in a large, complex nation.

Elections are a necessary condition of democracy, but they do not guarantee democratic government. Before the collapse of communism, the former Soviet Union regularly held elections in which more than 90 percent of the electorate turned out to vote, but it certainly did not function as a democracy, because there was only one party. Both the majoritarian and pluralist models of democracy rely on voting to varying degrees, but both models expect citizens to participate in politics in other ways. For example, they expect citizens to discuss politics, to form interest groups, to contact public officials, to campaign for political parties, to run for office, and even to protest government decisions.

We define **political participation** as "those actions of private citizens by which they seek to influence or to support government and politics."[6] This definition embraces both conventional and unconventional forms of political participation. **Conventional participation** is relatively routine behavior that uses the established institutions of representative government, especially campaigning for candidates and voting in elections. **Unconventional participation** is relatively uncommon behavior that challenges or defies established institu-

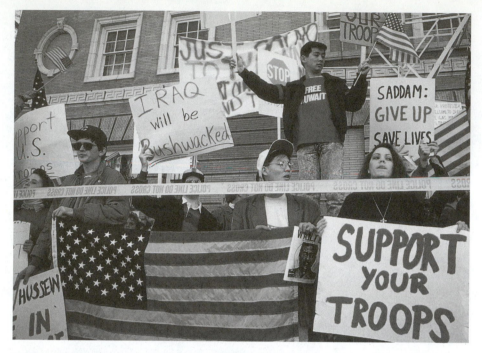

No Blood for Oil . . . No Tolerance for Tyranny
Although the onset of the 1991 military action in the Persian Gulf provoked some antiwar demonstrations on campuses, unlike their predecessors during the Vietnam War, protesters did not draw broad support from American citizens. On some campuses more students participated in rallies that supported the military effort than rallies that opposed it.

tions or the dominant culture (and thus is personally stressful to participants and their opponents).

Voting and writing letters to public officials are examples of conventional political participation; staging sit-down strikes in public buildings and chanting slogans outside officials' windows are examples of unconventional participation. Certainly training with the militia is unconventional; the question is whether the activity is political or not. Experts contend that group participation is often a politicizing experience, developing skills in the individual that transfer to politics.[7] Political demonstrations can be conventional (carrying signs outside an abortion clinic) or unconventional (linking arms to prevent entrance). Various forms of unconventional participation are used by powerless groups to gain political benefits while still working within the system.[8] Militia groups, however, blatantly reject the system. Voting and other methods of conventional participation are important to democratic government. So are unconventional forms of participation. Let us look at both kinds of political participation in the United States.

L.A. Riots, 1992
At the extremes of unconventional political behavior are activities in which individuals with a group consciousness protest political actions through personal violence and the destruction of property. In at least some respects the 1992 riots in Los Angeles can be viewed as such behavior. In this photo two L.A. residents view the immediate results of that violence. Its long-term political results are yet to be determined.

Unconventional Participation

On Sunday, March 7, 1965, a group of about six hundred people attempted to march fifty miles from Selma, Alabama, to the state capital at Montgomery. The marchers were demonstrating in favor of voting rights for blacks. (At the time, Selma had fewer than five hundred registered black voters, out of fifteen thousand who were eligible.)[9] Alabama Governor George Wallace declared the march illegal and sent state troopers to stop it. The two groups met at the Edmund Pettus Bridge over the Alabama River at the edge of Selma. The peaceful marchers were disrupted and beaten by state troopers and deputy sheriffs—some on horseback—using clubs, bullwhips, and tear gas. The day became known as Bloody Sunday.

The march from Selma was a form of unconventional political participation. Marching fifty miles in a political protest is certainly not common; moreover, the march challenged the existing institutions that prevented blacks from participating conventionally—voting in elections—for many decades. In contrast to some later demonstrations against the Vietnam War, this civil rights march posed no threat of violence. The brutal response to the marchers helped the rest of the nation understand the seriousness of the civil rights problem in the South. Unconventional participation is stressful and occasionally violent, but sometimes it is worth the risk.

Support for Unconventional Participation

Unconventional political participation has a long history in the United States. The Boston Tea Party of 1773 was only the first in a long line of violent protests against British rule that eventually led to revolution. Yet, we know less about unconventional political participation than about conventional participation. The reasons are twofold: first, since it is easier to collect data on conventional practices, they are studied more frequently. Second, political scientists are biased toward institutionalized, or conventional, politics. In fact, some basic works on political participation explicitly exclude any behavior that is "outside the system."[10] One major study of unconventional political action asked people whether they had engaged in or approved of ten types of political participation outside of voting.[11] As shown in Figure 5.1, of the five activities, only signing petitions was clearly regarded as conventional, in the sense that the behavior was widely practiced.

The conventionality of two other forms of behavior—lawful demonstrations and boycotts—was questionable. The other two political activities listed in Figure 5.1 are clearly unconventional. In fact, when political activities interfere with people's daily lives (occupying buildings, for example), disapproval is nearly universal. Americans usually disapprove of unconventional political behavior. When protesters demonstrating against the Vietnam War disrupted the 1968 Democratic national convention in Chicago, they were clubbed by the city's police. Although the national television audience saw graphic footage of the confrontations, most viewers condemned the demonstrators, not the police.

The Effectiveness of Unconventional Participation

Vociferous antiabortion protests discouraged many doctors from performing abortions, but they have not led to outlawing abortions. Does unconventional participation ever work (even when it provokes violence)? Yes. Antiwar protesters helped convince President Lyndon Johnson not to seek reelection in 1968, and they heightened public concern over U.S. participation in the Vietnam War.

The unconventional activities of civil rights workers also produced notable successes. Dr. Martin Luther King, Jr., led the 1955 Montgomery bus boycott that sparked the civil rights movement. He used **direct action** to challenge specific cases of discrimination, assembling crowds to confront businesses and local governments, and demanding equal treatment in public accommodations and government.

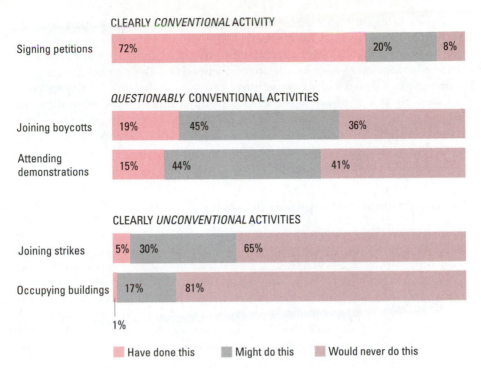

CLEARLY *CONVENTIONAL* ACTIVITY

Signing petitions — 72% | 20% | 8%

QUESTIONABLY CONVENTIONAL ACTIVITIES

Joining boycotts — 19% | 45% | 36%

Attending demonstrations — 15% | 44% | 41%

CLEARLY *UNCONVENTIONAL* ACTIVITIES

Joining strikes — 5% | 30% | 65%

Occupying buildings — 17% | 81%

1%

■ Have done this   ■ Might do this   ■ Would never do this

FIGURE 5.1   What Americans Think Is Unconventional Political Behavior
A survey presented Americans with five different forms of political participation outside the electoral process and asked whether they "have done," "might do," or "never do" any of them. The respondents disapproved of two forms overwhelmingly. Only signing petitions was widely done and rarely ruled out. Even attending demonstrations (a right guaranteed in the Constitution) was disapproved of by 44 percent of the respondents. Boycotting products was less objectionable and more widely practiced. According to this test, attending demonstrations and boycotting products are only marginally conventional forms of political participation. Joining strikes and occupying buildings are clearly unconventional activities for most Americans. (Source: 1990–91 World Values Survey. Data for the United States are available from the Inter-University Consortium for Political and Social Research. The weighted sample size was 1,837.)

Denied the usual opportunities for conventional political participation, members of minorities used unconventional politics to pressure Congress to pass a series of civil rights laws in 1957, 1960, 1964, and 1968—each one in some way extending federal protection against discrimination by reason of race, color, religion, or national origin. (The 1964 act also prohibited discrimination in employment on the basis of sex.)

In addition, the Voting Rights Act of 1965 put state electoral procedures under federal supervision, increasing the registration of black voters and the rate of black voter turnout (especially in the South). The civil rights movement shows that social change can occur, even when it is violently opposed at first. Although direct political action and the politics of confrontation can work, using them takes a special kind of commitment. Studies show that direct action appeals most to those who both (1) distrust the political system and (2) have a strong sense of political efficacy—the feeling that they can do something to affect political decisions.[12] Whether this combination of attitudes produces behavior that challenges the system depends on the extent of organized group activity.[13] The decision to use unconventional behavior also depends on the extent to which individuals develop a group consciousness—identification with their group and an awareness of its position in society, its objectives, and its intended course of action.[14] These characteristics were present among blacks and young people in the mid-1960s and are strongly present today among blacks and to a lesser degree among women.

Unconventional Participation in America

Although most Americans may disapprove of using certain forms of participation to protest government policies, U.S. citizens are about as likely to take direct action in politics as citizens in European democracies. Surveys in Britain, Germany, and France in 1981 found that Americans claim to have participated as much or more than British, German, and French citizens in unconventional actions, such as demonstrations, boycotts, strikes, and occupying buildings.[15] Contrary to the popular view that Americans are apathetic about politics, they are more likely to engage in political protests of various sorts than citizens in other democratic countries.[16]

Is something wrong with our political system if citizens resort to unconventional—and widely disapproved—methods of political participation? To answer this question, we must first learn how much Americans use conventional methods of participation.

Conventional Participation

A practical test of the democratic nature of any government is whether citizens can affect its policies by acting through its institutions—meeting with public officials, supporting candidates, voting in elections. Citizens should not have to risk their life and property to participate in politics, and they should not have to take direct action to force the government to hear their views. The objective of democratic institutions is to make political participation conventional—to allow ordinary citizens to engage in relatively routine, nonthreatening behavior to get the government to heed their opinions, interests, and needs.

In a democracy, for a group to gather at a statehouse or city hall to dramatize its position on an issue—say a tax increase—is not unusual. Such a demonstration is a form of conventional participation. The group is not powerless, and its members are not risking their personal safety. But violence can erupt between opposing groups. Circumstances, then, often determine whether organized protest is or is not conventional. Conventional political behaviors fall into two major categories: actions that show support for government policies and those that try to change or *influence* policies.

Supportive Behavior

Supportive behaviors are actions that express allegiance to country and government. When we recite the Pledge of Allegiance or fly the American flag on holidays, we are showing support for the country and, by implication, its political system. Such ceremonial activities usually demand little initiative on the part of the citizen. The simple act of turning out to vote is in itself a show of support for the political system. Other supportive behaviors—serving as an election judge in a nonpartisan election or organizing a holiday parade—demand greater initiative.

At times, people's perception of patriotism moves them across the line from conventional to unconventional behavior. In their eagerness to support the American system, they break up a meeting or disrupt a rally of a group they believe is radical or somehow "un-American." Radical groups may threaten the political system with wrenching change, but superpatriots pose their own threat. Their misguided excess of allegiance denies nonviolent means of dissent to others. [17]

Influencing Behavior

Citizens use **influencing behaviors** to modify or even reverse government policy to serve political interests. Some forms of influencing behavior seek particular benefits from government; other forms have broad policy objectives.

Particular Benefits   Some citizens try to influence government to obtain benefits for themselves, their immediate families, or close friends. Serving one's self-interest through the voting process is certainly acceptable to democratic theory. Each individual has only one vote, and no single voter can wangle particular benefits from government through voting unless a majority of the voters agree.

Political actions that require considerable knowledge and initiative are another story. Individuals or small groups who influence government officials to advance their self-interest may secretly benefit without others knowing. Those who quietly obtain particular benefits from government pose a serious challenge to a democracy. Pluralist theory holds that groups ought to be able to make government respond to their special problems and needs. On the other hand, majoritarian theory holds that government should not do what a majority does not want it to do. A majority of citizens might very well not want the government to do what any particular person or group seeks—if it is costly to other citizens.

What might individual citizens or groups ask of their government, and how might they go about asking for it? Some citizens ask for special services from their local government. Such requests may range from contacting the city forestry department to remove a dead tree in front of a house to calling the county animal control center to deal with a vicious dog in the neighborhood. Studies of such "contacting" behavior find that it tends not to be empirically related to other forms of political activity. Contacting behavior is related to socioeconomic status: People of higher socioeconomic status are more likely to contact public officials.[18] Americans demand much more of their local government than of the national government. Although many people value self-reliance and individualism in national politics, most people expect local government to solve a wide range of social problems. A study of residents of Kansas City, Missouri, found that more than 90 percent thought it was the city's responsibility to provide services in thirteen areas, including maintaining parks, setting standards for new home construction, demolishing vacant and unsafe buildings, ensuring that property owners clean up trash and weeds, and providing bus service. The researcher noted that "it is difficult to imagine a set of federal government activities about which there would [be] more consensus."[19] Citizens can also mobilize against a project. The 1980s saw the emergence of the "not-in-my-back-yard," or NIMBY, phenomenon, as citizens pressured local officials to stop undesired projects from being located near their homes.

Finally, contributing money to a candidate's campaign is another form of influencing behavior. Here, too, the objective can be particular or broad benefits. Several points emerge from this review of "particularized" forms of political participation. First, approaching government to serve one's particular interests is consistent with democratic theory, because it encourages input from an active citizenry. Second, particularized contact may be a form of participation unto itself, not necessarily related to other forms of participation. Third, such participation tends to be used more by citizens who are advantaged in terms of knowledge and resources. Fourth, particularized participation may serve private interests to the detriment of the majority.

Broad Policy Objectives   We come now to what many scholars have in mind when they talk about political participation: activities that influence the selection of government personnel and policies. Here, too, we find behaviors that require little initiative (such as voting) and high initiative (attending political meetings, persuading others how to vote). In the next section, we focus on elections as a mechanism for participation. For now, we simply note that voting to influence policy is usually a low-initiative activity. As we discuss later, it actually requires more initiative to *register* to vote in the United States than to cast a vote on election day.

Other types of participation to affect broad policies require high initiative. Running for office requires the most (see Chapter 6). Some high-initiative activities, such as attending party meetings and working in campaigns, are associated with the electoral process; others, such as attending legislative hearings and writing letters to Congress, are not. Studies of citizen contacts in the United States show that about two-thirds deal with broad social issues and only one-third are for private gain.[20]

Few people realize that using the court system is a form of political participation, a way for citizens to press for their rights in a democratic society. Although most people use the courts to serve their particular interests, some also use them, as we discuss shortly, to meet broad objectives. Going to court demands high personal initiative.[21] It also requires knowledge of the law or the financial resources to afford a lawyer.

People use the courts for both personal benefit and broad policy objectives. A person or group can bring **class-action suits** on behalf of other people in similar circumstances. Lawyers for the National Association for the Advancement of Colored People pioneered this form of litigation in the famous school desegregation case *Brown v. Board of Education* (1954).[22] They succeeded in getting the Supreme Court to outlaw segregation in public schools, not just for Linda Brown, who brought the suit in Topeka, Kansas, but for all others "similarly situated"—that is, for all other black students who wanted to attend desegregated schools. This form of participation has proved to be effective for organized groups, especially those who have been unable to gain their objectives through Congress or the executive branch.

Individual citizens can also try to influence policies at the national level by direct participation in the legislative process. One way is to attend congressional hearings, which are open to the public and occasionally held outside Washington. To facilitate citizen involvement, national government agencies are required to publish all proposed and approved regulations in the daily *Federal Register* and to make government documents available to citizens on request.

Conventional Participation in America

How often do Americans contact government officials and engage in other forms of conventional political participation, compared with citizens in other countries? The most common political behavior reported in a study of five countries was voting to choose candidates. Americans are less likely to vote than citizens in the other four countries studied. On the other hand, Americans are as likely (or substantially more likely) to engage in all other forms of conventional political participation. As we have seen, the same pattern holds true for unconventional behaviors. Americans, then, are more apt to engage in nearly all forms of unconventional and conventional political participation, except voting.

Other researchers have noted this paradox and written: "If, for example, we concentrate our attention on national elections we will find that the United States is the least participatory of [all] five nations." But looking at the other indicators, they found that "political apathy, by a wide margin, is lowest in the United States. Interestingly, the high levels of overall involvement reflect a rather balanced contribution of both ... conventional and unconventional politics."[23] Clearly, low voter turnout in the United States constitutes a puzzle, to which we will return.

Participating Through Voting

The heart of democratic government lies in the electoral process. Whether a country holds elections—and if so, what kind—constitutes the critical difference between democratic and nondemocratic government. Elections institutionalize mass participation in democratic government according to the three normative principles of procedural democracy discussed in Chapter 1: Electoral rules specify *who* is allowed to vote, *how much* each person's vote counts, and *how many* votes are needed to win.

The Fights for Women's Suffrage . . . and Against It
Young people and minorities are not the only groups that have resorted to unconventional
means of political participation. In the late 1800s and early 1900s, women marched and
demonstrated for equal voting rights, sometimes encountering strong opposition. Their gath-
erings were occasionally disrupted by men—and other women—who opposed extending the
right to vote to women.

Again, elections are formal procedures for making group decisions. *Voting*
is the act individuals engage in when they choose among alternatives in an
election. **Suffrage** and the **franchise** both mean the right to vote. By formaliz-
ing political participation through rules for suffrage and for counting ballots,
electoral systems allow large numbers of people, who individually have little
political power, to wield great power. Electoral systems decide collectively who
governs and, in some instances, what government should do. The simple fact
of holding elections is less important than the specific rules and circumstances
that govern voting. According to democratic theory, everyone should be able

to vote. In practice, however, no nation grants universal suffrage. All countries have age requirements for voting, and all disqualify some inhabitants on various grounds: lack of citizenship, criminal record, mental incompetence, and so forth. What is the record of enfranchisement in the United States?

Expansion of Suffrage

The United States was the first country to provide for general elections of representatives through "mass" suffrage, but the franchise was far from universal. When the Constitution was framed, the idea of full adult suffrage was too radical to consider seriously. Instead, the framers left the issue of enfranchisement to the states, stipulating only that individuals who could vote for "the most numerous Branch of the State Legislature" could also vote for their representatives to the U.S. Congress (Article I, Section 2).

Initially, most states established taxpaying or property-holding requirements for voting. Virginia, for example, required ownership of twenty-five acres of settled land or five hundred acres of unsettled land. The original thirteen states began to lift such kinds of requirements after 1800. Expansion of the franchise accelerated after 1815, with the admission of new "western" states (Indiana, Illinois, Alabama), where land was more plentiful and widely owned. By the 1850s, the states had eliminated virtually all taxpaying and property-holding requirements, thus allowing the working class—at least its white male members—to vote. Extending the vote to blacks and women took more time.

The Enfranchisement of Blacks The Fifteenth Amendment, adopted shortly after the Civil War, prohibited the states from denying the right to vote "on account of race, color, or previous condition of servitude." However, the states of the old Confederacy worked around the amendment by reestablishing old voting requirements (poll taxes, literacy tests) that worked primarily against blacks. Because the amendment said nothing about voting rights in private organizations, these states denied blacks the right to vote in the "private" Democratic *primary* elections held to choose the party's candidates for the general election. Because the Democratic party came to dominate politics in the South, the "white primary" effectively disenfranchised blacks despite the Fifteenth Amendment. Finally, in many areas of the South, the threat of violence kept blacks from the polls.

The extension of full voting rights to blacks came in two phases, separated by twenty years. In 1944, the Supreme Court decided in *Smith v. Allwright* that laws preventing blacks from voting in primary elections were unconstitutional, holding that party primaries are part of the continuous process of electing public officials.[24] The Voting Rights Act of 1965, which followed Selma's Bloody Sunday by less than five months, suspended discriminatory voting tests. It also authorized federal registrars to register voters in seven southern states, where less than half of the voting-age population had registered to vote in the 1964 election. For good measure, in 1966 the Supreme Court ruled in *Harper v. Virginia State Board of Elections* that state poll taxes are unconstitutional.[25]

Although long in coming, these actions by the national government to enforce political equality within the states dramatically increased the registration of southern blacks.

The Enfranchisement of Women   Women also had to fight long and hard to win the right to vote. Until 1869, women could not vote anywhere—in the United States or in the world.[26] Women began to organize to obtain suffrage in the mid-1800s. Known then as *suffragettes** the early feminists initially had a limited effect on politics. Their first major victory did not come until 1869, when Wyoming, while still a territory, granted women the right to vote. No state followed suit until 1893, when Colorado enfranchised women.

Between 1896 and 1918, twelve other states gave women the vote. Most of these states were in the West, where pioneer women often departed from traditional women's roles. Nationally, the women's suffrage movement intensified, often resorting to unconventional political behaviors (marches, demonstrations), which occasionally invited violent attacks from men and even other women. In 1919, Congress finally passed the Nineteenth Amendment, which prohibits states from denying the right to vote "on account of sex." The amendment was ratified in 1920, in time for the November election.

Evaluating the Expansion of Suffrage in America   The last major expansion of suffrage in the United States took place in 1971, when the Twenty-sixth Amendment lowered the voting age to eighteen. For most of its history, the United States has been far from the democratic ideal of universal suffrage. However, compared with other countries, the United States looks pretty democratic.[27] Women did not gain the vote on equal terms with men until 1921 in Norway; 1922 in the Netherlands; 1944 in France; 1946 in Italy, Japan, and Venezuela; 1948 in Belgium; and 1971 in Switzerland. Comparing the enfranchisement of minority racial groups is difficult because most other democratic nations do not have a comparable racial makeup. We should note, however, that the indigenous Maori population in New Zealand won suffrage in 1867, but the aborigines in Australia were not fully enfranchised until 1961. And, of course, in South Africa, blacks were not allowed to vote freely in elections until 1994. With regard to voting age, nineteen of twenty-seven countries that allow free elections also have a minimum voting age of eighteen. None has a lower age.

Voting on Policies

Disenfranchised groups have struggled to gain voting rights because of the political power that comes with suffrage. Belief in the ability of ordinary citizens to make political decisions and to control government through the power of the ballot box was strongest in the United States during the Progressive era, which began around 1900 and lasted until about 1925.

---

*The term *suffragist* applied to a person of either sex who advocated extending the vote to women, while *suffragette* was reserved primarily for women who did so militantly.

Progressivism was a philosophy of political reform that trusted the goodness and wisdom of individual citizens and distrusted "special interests" (railroads, corporations) and political institutions (traditional political parties, legislatures). Such attitudes have resurfaced among the followers of H. Ross Perot and others who appeal to this populist outlook.

The leaders of the progressive movement were prominent politicians (former president Theodore Roosevelt, Senator Robert La Follette of Wisconsin) and eminent scholars (historian Frederick Jackson Turner, philosopher John Dewey). Not content to vote for candidates chosen by party leaders, the Progressives championed the **direct primary**—a preliminary election, run by the state governments, in which the voters chose the party's candidates for the general election. Wanting a mechanism to remove elected candidates from office, the Progressives backed the **recall**—a special election initiated by a petition signed by a specified number of voters.

The Progressives also championed the power of the masses to propose and pass laws, approximating the citizen participation in policymaking that is the hallmark of direct democracy. They developed two voting mechanisms for policymaking that are still in use:

- A **referendum** is a direct vote by the people on either a proposed law or on an amendment to a state constitution. The measures subject to popular vote are known as *propositions*. About twenty-five states permit popular referenda on laws, and all but Alabama require a referendum for a constitutional amendment. Most referenda are placed on the ballot by legislatures, not voters.

- The **initiative** is a procedure by which voters can propose an issue to be decided by the legislature or by the people in a referendum. The procedure involves gathering a specified number of signatures from registered voters (usually 5 to 10 percent of the total in the state), then submitting the petition to a designated state agency. About twenty states currently provide for some form of voter initiative.

One scholar estimates that there have been more than 17,000 referenda since 1898 and more than 2,300 between 1968 and 1978 alone.[28] Over 350 propositions have appeared on state ballots in general elections during the 1990s, although relatively few (usually fewer than fifty) got there by means of initiatives.[29]

What conclusion can we draw about the Progressives' legacy of mechanisms for direct participation in government? One scholar who studied the use of the initiative and referendum paints an unimpressive picture. He notes that an expensive "industry" developed in the 1980s that makes money circulating petitions, then managing the large sums of money needed to run a campaign to approve (or defeat) a referendum.[30] The money required to mount a statewide campaign has increased the involvement of special interest groups in referendum politics. Moreover, most voters confess they do not know enough about most ballot propositions to vote intelligently on them. Another major study concluded that direct democracy devices "worked better at the state and local levels than most people realize," but also proposed fourteen safeguards "to ensure that they serve the larger and longer-term public interest" at the state and local levels.[31] Noting that the United States was one of the few democracies that do not permit a national referendum, the study nevertheless opposed adopting the initiative and the referendum at the national level.[32]

Clearly, citizens can exercise great power over government policy through the mechanisms of the initiative and referendum. What is not clear is whether these forms of direct democracy improve on the policies made by representatives elected for that purpose.

Voting for Candidates

We have saved for last the most visible form of political participation: voting to choose candidates for public office. Voting for candidates serves democratic government in two ways. First, citizens can choose the candidates they think will best serve their interests. Second, voting allows the people to reelect the officials they guessed right about and to kick out those they guessed wrong about. We look at the factors that underlie voting choice in Chapter 6. Here, we examine Americans' reliance on the electoral process.

In national politics, voters seem content to elect just two executive officers—the president and vice president—and to trust the president to appoint a cabinet to round out his administration. But at the state and local levels, voters insist on selecting all kinds of officials. Every state elects a governor (and forty-two elect a lieutenant governor). Forty elect an attorney general; thirty-five, a treasurer and a secretary of state; twenty-three, an auditor. The list goes on, down through the superintendent of education, secretary of agriculture, controller, board of education, and public utilities commissioners.[33] Elected county officials commonly include commissioners, a sheriff, a treasurer, a clerk, a superintendent of schools, and a judge (often several). At the local level, voters elect all but about 600 of 15,300 school boards across the nation.[34] Instead of trusting state and local chief executives to appoint lesser administrators (as we do for more important offices at the national level), we expect voters to choose intelligently among scores of candidates they meet for the first time on a complex ballot in the polling booth.

In the American version of democracy, the laws recognize no limit to voters' ability to make informed choices among candidates and thus to control government through voting. The reasoning seems to be that elections are good; therefore, more elections are better, and the most elections are best. By this thinking, the United States clearly has the best and most democratic government in the world because it is the undisputed champion at holding elections. The author of a study that compared elections in the United States with elections in twenty-six other democracies concluded:

> No country can approach the United States in the frequency and variety of elections, and thus in the amount of electoral participation to which its citizens have a right. No other country elects its lower house as often as every two years, or its president as frequently as every four years. No other country popularly elects its state governors and town mayors; no other has as wide a variety of nonrepresentative offices (judges, sheriffs, attorneys general, city treasurers, and so on) subject to election.... The average

American is entitled to do far more electing—probably by a factor of three or four—than the citizen of any other democracy. [35]

However, we learn from Compared with What? 5.1 that the United States ranks at the bottom of twenty-seven countries in voter turnout! How do we square low voter turnout with Americans' devotion to elections as an instrument of democratic government? To complicate matters further, how do we square low voter turnout with the findings we mentioned earlier, which establish the United States as the leader among five Western democratic nations in both conventional and unconventional political participation, except for voting? Americans seem to participate at high levels in everything except elections.

Explaining Political Participation

As you have seen, political participation can be unconventional or conventional, can require little or much initiative, and can serve to support the government or influence its decisions. This section examines some factors that affect the more obvious forms of political participation, with particular emphasis on voting. Our first task is to determine how much variation there is in patterns of participation within the United States over time.

Patterns of Participation over Time

Have Americans become more politically apathetic in the 1990s than they were in the 1960s? The answer lies in Figure 5.2, which plots several measures of participation from 1952 through 1992. The graph shows a steady pattern of participation over the years (with upward spurts in 1992 because Ross Perot's candidacy added a new dimension to the presidential race). Otherwise, participation varied little across time in the percentage of citizens who worked for candidates, attended party meetings, and tried to persuade people how to vote. In fact, interest in election campaigns tended to increase even before 1992. *The only line that shows a downward trend is voting in elections.* The plot has thickened. Not only is voter turnout low in the United States compared with that in other countries, but turnout has basically declined over time. Moreover, while voting has decreased, other forms of participation have remained stable or even increased. What is going on? Who votes? Who does not? Why? And does it really matter?

The Standard Socioeconomic Explanation

Researchers have found that socioeconomic status is a good indicator of most types of conventional political participation. People with more education, higher incomes, and white-collar or professional occupations tend to be more aware of the impact of politics on their lives, to know what can be done to influence government actions, and to have the necessary resources (time and money) to take action. So they are more likely to participate in politics than

Compared with What? 5.1

Voter Turnout in Democratic Nations, 1975–1995

Americans participate as much as or more than citizens of other nations in all forms of conventional political behavior except voting. Voter turnout in American presidential elections ranks at the bottom of voting rates for twenty-seven countries with competitive elections. As discussed in the text, the facts are correct, but the comparison is not as damning as it appears.

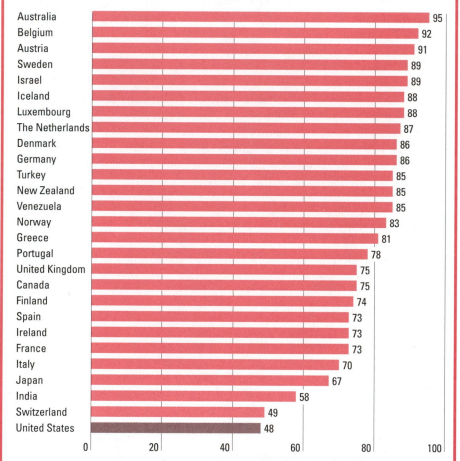

Percentage of voter turnout in democratic nations

Source: Inter-Parliamentary Union, *Chronicle of Parliamentary Elections and Developments* (Geneva: Switzerland, Vols. X-XXIX (1975–1995); U.S. Bureau of the Census, Current Population Reports, P20-453 and P20-466, *Voting and Registration in the Election of 1990 [and 1992]* (Washington, D.C.: U.S. Government Printing Office, 1991 [and 1993]), pp. viii, 10. The U.S. data are for all elections from 1976 to 1992, both presidential and nonpresidential election years. (Compared with What? 5.1 shows the percent of respondents who *said* they voted, which is usually higher than the actual voting turnout in this figure.)

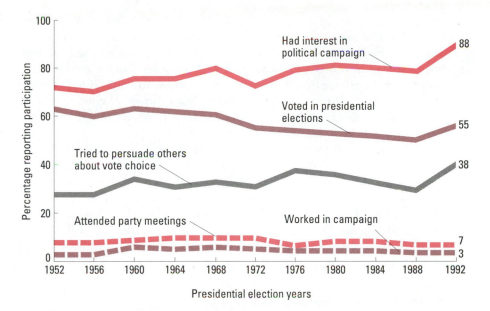

FIGURE 5.2   *Electoral Participation in the United States over Time*

Participation patterns from five decades show that in the 1980s Americans participated in election campaigns about as much or more than they did in the 1950s on every indicator except voting. The turnout rate dropped more than ten percentage points from 1952 to 1988. The turnout for 1992 was 55 percent, a sharp rise. The decline before 1992 runs counter to the rise in educational level, a puzzle that is discussed in the text. (Source: Reprinted by permission of the publishers from American National Election Studies Data Sourcebook, 1952–1978, *Warren Miller and Edward J. Schneider, eds. (Cambridge, Mass.: Harvard University Press). Copyright © 1980 by the President and Fellows of Harvard College. Data after 1978 comes from subsequent National Election Studies.)*

are people of lower socioeconomic status. This relationship between socioeconomic status and conventional political involvement is called the **standard socioeconomic model** of participation.[36]

Unconventional political behavior is less clearly related to socioeconomic status. Studies of unconventional participation in other countries have found that protest behavior is related to low socioeconomic status and especially to youth.[37] However, scattered studies of unconventional participation in the United States have found that protesters (especially blacks) are often higher in socioeconomic status than those who do not join in protests.[38]

Obviously, socioeconomic status does not account for all the differences in the ways people choose to participate in politics, even for conventional participation. Another important variable is age. As just noted, young people are more likely to take part in political protests, but they are less likely to participate in conventional politics. Voting rates tend to increase as people grow older until about age sixty-five, when physical infirmities begin to lower rates again.[39]

Two other variables—race and gender—have been related to participation in the past, but as times have changed, so have those relationships. Blacks, who had very low participation rates in the 1950s, now participate at rates comparable to whites', when differences in socioeconomic status are taken into account.[40] Women also exhibited low participation rates in the past, but gender differences in political participation have virtually disappeared.[41] (The one exception is in attempting to persuade others how to vote, which women are less likely to do than men.)[42] Recent research on the social context of voting behavior has shown that married men and women are more likely to vote than those of either sex living without a spouse.[43]

Of all the social and economic variables, education is the strongest single factor in explaining most types of conventional political participation.[44] The strong link between education and electoral participation raises questions about low voter turnout in the United States both over time and relative to other democracies. The fact is that the proportion of individuals with college degrees is greater in the United States than in other countries. Moreover, that proportion has been increasing steadily. Why, then, is voter turnout in elections so low? And why has it dropped over time?

Low Voter Turnout in America

Voting is a low-initiative form of participation that can satisfy all three motives for political participation—showing allegiance to the nation, obtaining particularized benefits, and influencing broad policy. How then do we explain the decline in voter turnout in the United States?

The Decline in Voting over Time   The graph of voter turnout in Figure 5.3 shows that the sharpest drop (five percentage points) occurred between the 1968 and 1972 elections. It was during this period (in 1971, actually) that Congress proposed and the states ratified the Twenty-sixth Amendment, which expanded the electorate by lowering the voting age from twenty-one to eighteen. Because people younger than twenty-one are much less likely to vote, their eligibility actually reduced the overall national turnout rate (the percentage of those eligible to vote who actually vote). Some observers estimate that the enfranchisement of eighteen-year-olds accounts for about one or two percentage points in the total decline in turnout since 1952, but that still leaves more than ten percentage points to be explained.[45]

Why has voter turnout declined since 1968, while the level of education has increased? Many researchers have tried to solve this puzzle.[46] Some attribute most of the decline to changes in voters' attitudes toward politics. One major factor is the growing belief that government is not responsive to citizens and that voting does no good. Another is a change in attitude toward political parties, along with a decline in the extent and strength of party identification.[47]

U.S. Turnout Versus Turnout in Other Countries   Scholars cite two factors to explain the low voter turnout in the United States compared with that in other countries. First are the differences in voting laws and administrative machin-

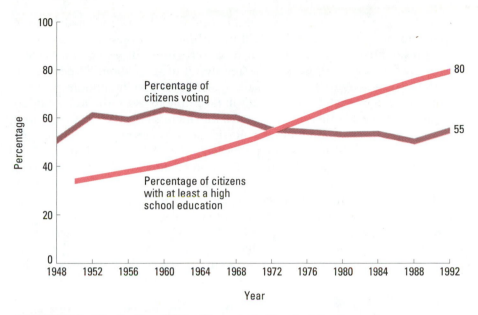

FIGURE 5.3   *The Decline of Voter Turnout: An Unsolved Puzzle*
Level of education is one of the strongest predictors of a person's likelihood of voting in the
United States, and the percentage of citizens older than twenty-five with a high school educa-
tion or more has grown steadily since the end of World War II. Nevertheless, the overall rate
of voter turnout has gone down almost steadily in presidential elections since 1960, except
for the spurt in 1992 inspired by Ross Perot's campaign. The phenomenon is recognized as
an unsolved puzzle in American voting behavior. (Sources: "Percentage voting" data up to 1988
come from Michael Nelson, ed., Congressional Quarterly's Guide to the Presidency *(Washington,*
D.C.: Congressional Quarterly, Inc., 1989), p. 170; voter turnout for 1992 and "percentage of citizens
with at least a high school education" come from U.S. Bureau of the Census, Statistical Abstract of
the United States, 1993 *(Washington, D.C.: U.S. Government Printing Office, 1993), pp. 284*
and 153.)

ery.[48] In a few countries, voting is compulsory, and, obviously, turnout is extremely high. But other methods can encourage voting—declaring election
days to be public holidays, providing a two-day voting period, making it easy to
cast absentee ballots. The United States does none of these things.

Furthermore, nearly every other democratic country places the burden of
registration on the government rather than on the individual voter. This is important. Voting in the United States is a two-stage process, and the first stage
(going to the proper officials to register) requires more initiative than the second stage (going to the polling booth to cast a ballot). In most American
states, the registration process is separated from the voting process in terms of
both time (usually voters have to register weeks in advance of the election) and
geography (often voters have to register at the county courthouse, not the
polling place). Moreover, registration procedures often have been obscure,

requiring potential voters to call around to find out what to do. Furthermore, people who move (and roughly one-third of the U.S. population moves between presidential elections) have had to reregister. If we compute voter turnout on the basis of those who are registered to vote, about 87 percent of Americans vote—a figure that moves the United States to the middle (but not the top) of all democratic nations.[49] It will take time to assess the impact upon registration of the so-called motor-voter law, which, since 1995, has required states to allow citizens to register by mail (similar to renewing drivers' licenses) and at certain agencies that provide public assistance.[50] However, initial indications were not encouraging. A Federal Election Commission study comparing voter registration and turnout for the 1992 and 1996 elections found that, although voter registration was indeed higher in 1996, voter turnout declined from 55 percent to 49 percent of those eligible to vote.[51]

The second factor usually cited to explain low turnout in American elections is the lack of political parties that mobilize the vote of particular social groups, especially lower-income and less-educated people. American parties do make an effort to get out the vote, but neither party is as closely linked to specific groups as are parties in many other countries, where certain parties work hand in hand with ethnic, occupational, or religious groups. Research shows that strong party-group links can significantly increase turnout.[52]

To these explanations for low voter turnout in the United States—the traditional burden of registration and the lack of strong party-group links—we add another. Although the act of voting requires low initiative, the process of learning about the scores of candidates on the ballot in American elections requires a great deal of initiative. Some people undoubtedly fail to vote simply because they feel inadequate to the task of deciding among candidates for the many offices on the ballot in U.S. elections.

Teachers, newspaper columnists, and public affairs groups tend to worry a great deal about low voter turnout in the United States, suggesting that it signifies some sort of political sickness—or at least that it gives us a bad mark for democracy. Others are less concerned.[53] One scholar argues:

> Turnout rates do not indicate the amount of electing—the frequency of occasion, the range of offices and decisions, the "value" of the vote—to which a country's citizens are entitled.... Thus, although the turnout rate in the United States is below that of most other democracies, American citizens do not necessarily do less voting than other citizens; most probably, they do more.[54]

Participation and Freedom, Equality, and Order

As we have seen, Americans do participate in government in a variety of ways, and to a reasonable extent, compared with citizens of other countries. What is the relationship of political participation to the values of freedom, equality, and order?

America's Largest Civil Rights Demonstration
On August 28, 1963, more than 200,000 blacks and whites participated in a march on Washington, D.C., to rally for jobs and freedom. Martin Luther King, Jr., one of the march's leaders, delivered his electrifying "I Have a Dream" speech from the steps of the Lincoln Memorial. The demonstrators pressed for legislation ensuring full civil rights for blacks, and their leaders were welcomed at the White House by President John F. Kennedy.

Participation and Freedom

From the standpoint of normative theory, the relationship between participation and freedom is clear. Individuals should be free to participate in government and politics in the way they want and as much as they want. And they should be free not to participate as well. Ideally, all barriers to participation (such as restrictive voting registration and limitations on campaign expenditures) should be abolished—as should any schemes for compulsory voting. In theory, freedom to participate also means that individuals should be able to use their wealth, connections, knowledge, organizational power (including sheer numbers in organized protests), or any other resource to influence government decisions, provided they do so legally. Of all these resources, the individual vote may be the weakest—and the least important—means of exerting political influence. Obviously, then, freedom as a value in political participation favors those with the resources to advance their own political self-interest.

Participation and Equality

The relationship between participation and equality is also clear. Each citizen's ability to influence government should be equal to that of every other citizen, so that differences in personal resources do not work against the poor or otherwise disadvantaged. Elections, then, serve the ideal of equality better than any other means of political participation. Formal rules for counting ballots—in particular, one person, one vote—cancel differences in resources among individuals.

At the same time, groups of people who have few resources individually can combine their votes to wield political power. Various European ethnic groups exercised this type of power in the late nineteenth and early twentieth centuries, when their votes won them entry to the sociopolitical system and allowed them to share in its benefits (see Chapter 4). More recently, blacks, Hispanics, homosexuals, and the disabled have used their voting power to gain political recognition. However, minorities often have had to use unconventional forms of participation to win the right to vote. As two major scholars of political participation put it, "Protest is the great equalizer, the political action that weights intensity as well as sheer numbers."[55]

Participation and Order

The relationship between participation and order is complicated. Some types of participation (pledging allegiance, voting) promote order and so are encouraged by those who value order; other types promote disorder and so are discouraged. Many citizens—men and women alike—even resisted giving women the right to vote for fear of upsetting the social order by altering the traditional roles of men and women.

Both conventional and unconventional participation can lead to the ouster of government officials, but the regime—the political system itself—is threatened more by unconventional participation. To maintain order, the government has a stake in converting unconventional participation to conventional participation whenever possible. Think about the student unrest on college campuses during the Vietnam War when thousands of protesting students stopped traffic, occupied buildings, destroyed property, and behaved in other unconventional ways. Confronted by such civil strife and disorder, Congress took action. On March 23, 1971, it enacted and sent to the states the proposed Twenty-sixth Amendment, lowering the voting age to eighteen. Three-quarters of the state legislatures had to ratify the amendment before it became part of the Constitution. Astonishingly, thirty-eight states (the required number) complied by July 1, establishing a new speed record for ratification.[56] As one observer argued, the right to vote was extended to eighteen-year-olds not because young people demanded it but because "public officials believed suffrage expansion to be a means of institutionalizing youths' participation in politics, which would, in turn, curb disorder."[57]

Participation and the Models of Democracy

Ostensibly, elections are institutional mechanisms that implement democracy by allowing citizens to choose among candidates or issues. But elections also serve several other important purposes:[58]

- Elections socialize political activity. They transform what might otherwise consist of sporadic citizen-initiated acts into a routine public function. That is, the opportunity to vote for change encourages citizens to refrain from demonstrating in the streets. This helps preserve government stability by containing and channeling away potentially disruptive or dangerous forms of mass political activity.

- Elections institutionalize access to political power. They allow ordinary citizens to run for political office or to play an important role in selecting political leaders. Working to elect a candidate encourages the campaign worker to identify problems or propose solutions to the newly elected official.

- Elections bolster the state's power and authority. The opportunity to participate in elections helps convince citizens that the government is responsive to their needs and wants, which reinforces its legitimacy.

Participation and Majoritarianism

Although the majoritarian model assumes that government responsiveness to popular demands comes through mass participation in politics, majoritarianism views participation rather narrowly. It favors conventional, institutionalized behavior—primarily, voting in elections. Because majoritarianism relies on counting votes to determine what the majority wants, its bias toward equality in political participation is strong. Clearly, better-educated, wealthier citizens are more likely to participate in elections, and get-out-the-vote campaigns cannot counter this distinct bias.[59] Because it favors collective decisions formalized through elections, majoritarianism has little place for motivated, resourceful individuals to exercise private influence over government actions.

Majoritarianism also limits individual freedom in another way: its focus on voting as the major means of mass participation narrows the scope of conventional political behavior by defining which political actions are "orderly" and acceptable. By favoring equality and order in political participation, majoritarianism goes hand in hand with the ideological orientation of communitarianism (see Chapter 1).

Participation and Pluralism

Resourceful citizens who want the government's help with problems find a haven in the pluralist model of democracy. A decentralized and organizationally complex form of government allows many points of access and accommodates various forms of conventional participation in addition to voting. For example, wealthy people and well-funded groups can afford to hire lobbyists to press their interests in Congress. In one view of pluralist democracy, citizens are free to ply and wheedle public officials to further their own selfish visions of the public good. From another viewpoint, pluralism offers citizens the opportunity to be treated as individuals when dealing with the government, to influence policymaking in special circumstances, and to fulfill (insofar as possible in representative government) their social potential through participation in community affairs.

Summary

To have "government by the people," the people must participate in politics. Conventional forms of participation—contacting officials and voting in elections—come most quickly to mind. However, citizens can also participate in politics in unconventional ways—staging sit-down strikes in public buildings, blocking traffic, and so on. Most citizens disapprove of most forms of unconventional political behavior. Yet, blacks and women used unconventional tactics to win important political and legal rights, including the right to vote.

People are motivated to participate in politics for various reasons: to show support for their country, to obtain particularized benefits for themselves or their friends, or to influence broad public policy. Their political actions may demand either little political knowledge or personal initiative, or a great deal of both.

The press often paints an unflattering picture of political participation in America. Clearly, the proportion of the electorate that votes in general elections in the United States has dropped and is far below that in other nations. When compared with other nations on a broad range of conventional and unconventional political behavior, however, the United States tends to show as much or more citizen participation in politics. Voter turnout in the United States suffers by comparison with that of other nations because of differences in voter registration requirements. We also lack institutions (especially strong political parties) that increase voter registration and help bring those of lower socioeconomic status to the polls. People's tendency to participate in politics is strongly related to their socioeconomic status. Education, one component of socioeconomic status, is the single strongest predictor of conventional political participation in the United States. Because of the strong effect of socioeconomic status, the political system is potentially biased toward the interests of higher-status people. Pluralist democracy, which provides many avenues for resourceful citizens to influence government decisions, tends to increase this bias. Majoritarian democracy, which relies heavily on elections and the concept of one person, one vote, offers citizens without great personal resources the opportunity to influence government decisions through elections.

Elections also serve to legitimize government simply by involving the masses in government through voting. Whether voting means anything depends on the nature of voters' choices in elections. The range of choices available is a function of the nation's political parties, the topic of the next chapter.

Key Terms

political participation
conventional participation
unconventional participation
direct action
supportive behavior
influencing behavior
class-action suit
suffrage

franchise
progressivism
direct primary
recall
referendum
initiative
standard socioeconomic model

Selected Readings

Conway, M. Margaret. *Political Participation in the United States.* 2d. ed. Washington, D.C.: Congressional Quarterly Press, 1991. An excellent review of survey data on conventional political participation.

Craig, Stephen C. *The Malevolent Leaders: Popular Discontent in America.* Boulder, Colo.: Westview Press, 1993. This book uses in-depth interviews with citizens and members of Congress to look at the rise of popular discontent with and disengagement from politics.

Dalton, Russell J. *Citizen Politics in Western Democracies,* 2d ed. Chatham, N.J.: Chatham House, 1996. Studies public opinion and behavior in the United States, Britain, Germany (west and east), and France. Two chapters compare conventional citizen action and protest politics in these countries.

Grofman, Bernard, and Chandler Davidson, eds. *Controversies in Minority Voting: The Voting Rights Act in Perspective.* Washington, D.C.: Brookings Institution, 1992. Reviews the aims and accomplishments of the 1965 law that enforced voting rights for blacks in the South and some of its unintended consequences.

Teixeira, Ruy A. *The Disappearing American Voter.* Washington, D.C.: Brookings Institution, 1992. An empirical analysis of why many people do not vote, how that affects politics, and reflections on what can be done about it.

World Wide Web Resources

The National Political Index offers information on thirty-two means of accessing government, including contacting federal elected officials, contacting state and local officials, creating state initiatives and referenda, tracking congressional legislation, and so on.

"The mission of the *California Voter Foundation* is to shape a more informed and engaged California electorate. Use our online voter resources to get substantive information on candidates and measures." More states will undoubtedly follow this model.
<www.webcom.com/cvf/>

Project Vote Smart is a nonpartisan, nonprofit political information system founded by former presidents Ford and Carter. It includes voting returns, candidate information, campaign finance records, and so on.
<www.vote-smart.org>

6

Political Parties, Campaigns, and Elections

Like many other citizens in early 1992, H. Ross Perot was unhappy with the presidential candidates of the two major parties. Unlike most other citizens, Perot was a billionaire businessman. He could do much more than complain—and he did. In February 1992, Perot announced on national television that he was an independent candidate for president. Perot's announcement struck a chord with people who were disenchanted with both President George Bush and his Democratic challenger, Bill Clinton. By mid-September, Perot's name had made the ballot in every state—thanks to the thousands of citizens who donated their time and to the millions of dollars donated by Perot.

Perot's campaign advertised heavily on national television, and it produced impressive results. Ross Perot—a man with virtually no government experience who had never before run for public office and had no party backing—won nearly 19 percent of the popular vote. That was more than any candidate from outside the two major parties had won in a presidential election since 1912. Nevertheless, he failed to carry a single state and thus failed to win any votes in the electoral college. Although Bill Clinton won only 43 percent of the popular vote, he won the presidency by taking 370 electoral votes out of 535.

In 1996, both Bill Clinton and Bob Dole—the two major candidates for president—pondered the same question: Would Perot run again? In September 1995, Perot announced on the CNN talk show, "Larry King Live" that he would create a new political party for independent voters fed up with the two-party system. With Perot's financial backing, an effort was quickly launched to get the Reform Party, as it was known, on the ballot in all fifty states for the 1996 presidential election. As expected, Perot was nominated as the party's candidate.

On paper, the Reform Party's chances looked good. Nearly 60 percent of a 1995 sample had agreed that "we should have a third major political party in this country in addition to the Democrats and Republicans," and a March 1996 survey had estimated that 20 percent of registered voters would prefer some independent or third-party candidate to either Clinton or Dole.[1] Nevertheless, most political analysts predicted that the Reform Party was doomed to fail in 1996. It could only play the role of "spoiler"—as many thought Perot had done in 1992.

The Populist Billionaire
H. Ross Perot promised to buy the presidency for the American people, and he made a valiant effort. Perot spent over $60 million and won nearly 20 percent of the popular vote, but he failed to carry a single state and won no electoral votes. Nevertheless, he profoundly affected the 1992 presidential campaign and the election outcome. His hard-hitting attacks on President Bush complemented Clinton's campaign, and Perot's snappy style played well on television and helped raise voting turnout to 55 percent, the highest level since 1972.

Political analysts discounted the Reform Party's chances because the structure and dynamics of U.S. politics work strongly *against* any third party and *for* the operation of a two-party system. Indeed, the Democratic and Republican parties have dominated national and state politics in the United States for more than 125 years. Their domination is more complete than that of any pair of parties in any other democratic government. Although all democracies have some form of multiparty politics, few have a stable two-party system—Britain and New Zealand being the most notable exceptions.

Why do we have any political parties? What functions do they perform? How did we become a nation of Democrats and Republicans? Do these parties truly differ in their platforms and behavior? Are parties really necessary for democratic government, or do they just get in the way of citizens and their government? In this chapter, we will answer these questions by examining political parties, perhaps the most misunderstood element of American politics.

And what of the election campaigns conducted by the two major parties? In this chapter, we also consider how those campaigns have changed over time, how candidates get nominated in the United States, what factors are important in election campaigns, and why voters choose one candidate over another. In addition, we address these important questions: Do election campaigns function more to inform or to confuse voters? How important is money in conducting a winning election campaign? What are the roles of party identification, issues, and candidate attributes in influencing voters' choices and thus election outcomes? How do campaigns, elections, and parties fit into the majoritarian and pluralist models of democracy?

Political Parties and Their Functions

According to democratic theory, the primary means by which citizens control their government is voting in free elections. Most Americans agree that voting is important: Of those surveyed after the 1992 presidential campaign, 87 percent felt that elections made the government "pay attention to what the people think."[2] Americans are not nearly as supportive of the role played by political parties in elections, however. When asked whether Perot should run for president in 1996 as "head of a third party which would also run candidates in state and local races" or "by himself as an independent candidate," 60 percent of a national sample favored his running without a party.[3]

On the other hand, Americans are quick to condemn as "undemocratic" countries that do not hold elections contested by political parties. In truth, Americans have a love-hate relationship with political parties. They believe that parties are necessary for democratic government; at the same time, they think parties are somehow "obstructionist" and not to be trusted. This distrust is particularly strong among younger voters. To better appreciate the role of political parties in democratic government, we must understand exactly what parties are and what they do.

What Is a Political Party?

A **political party** is an organization that sponsors candidates for political office *under the organization's name.* The italicized part of this definition is important. True political parties select individuals to run for public office through a formal **nomination** process, which designates them as the parties' official candidates. This activity distinguishes the Democratic and Republican parties from interest groups. The AFL-CIO and the National Association of Manufacturers are interest groups. They often support candidates in various ways, but they do not nominate them to run as their avowed representatives. If they did, they would be transformed into political parties. In short, the sponsoring of candidates designated as representatives of the organization is what defines an organization as a party.

Most democratic theorists agree that a modern nation-state cannot practice democracy without at least two political parties that regularly contest elections. In fact, the link between democracy and political parties is so close that many people define *democratic government* in terms of competitive party politics.

Party Functions

Parties contribute to democratic government through the functions they perform for the **political system**—the set of interrelated institutions that links people with government. Four of the most important party functions are nominating candidates for election to public office, structuring the voting choice in elections, proposing alternative government programs, and coordinating the actions of government officials.

Nominating Candidates   Without political parties, voters would confront a bewildering array of self-nominated candidates, each seeking votes on the basis of personal friendships, celebrity status, or name. Parties can provide a form of quality control for their nominees through the process of peer review. Party insiders, the nominees' peers, usually know the strengths and faults of potential candidates much better than average voters, and thus can judge their suitability for representing the party.

In nominating candidates, parties often do more than pass judgment on potential office seekers; sometimes they go so far as to recruit talented individuals to become party candidates. In this way, parties help not only to ensure a minimum level of quality among candidates who run for office but also to raise the quality of those candidates.

Structuring the Voting Choice   Political parties also help democratic government by structuring the voting choice—reducing the number of candidates on the ballot to those who have a realistic chance of winning. Established parties—those with experience in contesting elections—acquire a following of loyal voters who guarantee the party's candidates a predictable base of votes. The ability of established parties to mobilize their supporters has the effect of discouraging nonparty candidates from running for office and of discouraging new parties from forming. Consequently, the realistic choice is between candidates offered by the major parties, reducing the amount of new information that voters need in order to make a rational decision.

Proposing Alternative Government Programs   Parties also help voters choose candidates by proposing alternative programs of government action—the general policies their candidates will pursue if they gain office. Even if voters know nothing about the qualities of the parties' candidates, they can vote rationally for candidates of the party that has policies they favor. The specific policies advocated vary from candidate to candidate and from election to election. However, candidates of the same party tend to favor policies that fit their party's underlying political philosophy, or ideology.

In many countries, parties' names—such as "Conservative" and "Socialist" —reflect their political stance. The Democrats and Republicans have issue-neutral names, but many minor parties in the United States have used their names to advertise their policies: the Prohibition Party, the Socialist party, and even the Reform Party. The neutrality of the two major parties' names suggests that their policies are similar. This is not true. As we shall see, they regularly adopt very different policies in their platforms.

Coordinating the Actions of Government Officials   Finally, party organizations help coordinate the actions of public officials. A government based on the sep-aration of powers, such as that of the United States, divides responsibilities for making public policy. The president and the leaders of the House and Senate are not required to cooperate with one another. Political party organizations are the major means for bridging the separate powers to produce coordinated policies that can govern the country effectively.

A History of U.S. Party Politics

The two major U.S. parties are among the oldest in the world. In fact, the Democratic party, founded in 1828 but with roots reaching back into the late 1700s, has a strong claim to being the oldest party in existence. Its closest rival is the British Conservative party, formed in 1832, two decades before the Republican party was organized, in 1854. Several generations of citizens have supported the Democratic and Republican parties. They have become institu-tionalized in our political process.

The Emergence of the Party System

Today we think of party activities as normal, even essential, to American poli-tics. It was not always so. The Constitution makes no mention of political par-ties, and none existed when the Constitution was written in 1787. It was common then to refer to groups pursuing some common political interest as *factions*. Although factions were seen as inevitable in politics, they were also considered dangerous. One argument for adopting the Constitution—pro-posed in *Federalist* No. 10 (see Chapter 2)—was that its federal system would prevent factional influences from controlling the government.

The debate over ratification of the Constitution produced two factions. Those who backed the Constitution were loosely known as *federalists*, their op-ponents, as *antifederalists*. At this stage, the groups could not be called parties because they did not sponsor candidates for election. We can classify Washington as a federalist because he supported the Constitution, but he was not a factional leader and actually opposed factional politics. During Wash-ington's administration, however, the political cleavage sharpened between those who favored a stronger national government and those who wanted a less powerful, more decentralized national government.

The first group, led by Alexander Hamilton, proclaimed themselves Federalists. The second group, led by Thomas Jefferson, called themselves Republicans.* Disheartened by the political split in his administration, Washington spoke out against "the baneful effects" of parties in his farewell address in 1796. Nevertheless, parties already existed in the political system. For the most part, two major political parties have competed for political power from that time to the present.

The Present Party System: Democrats and Republicans

By 1820, the Federalists were no more. In 1828, the Democratic Republican party split in two. One wing, led by Andrew Jackson, became the Democratic party; the other later joined forces with several minor parties and formed the Whig party, which lasted for two decades.

In the early 1850s, antislavery forces (including Whigs and antislavery Democrats) began to organize. They formed a new party, the Republican party, to oppose the extension of slavery into the Kansas and Nebraska territories. It is this party, founded in 1854, that continues as today's Republican party. In 1860, the Republicans nominated Abraham Lincoln and successfully confronted a Democratic party that was deeply divided over the slavery issue.

The election of 1860 is considered the first of three critical elections under the current party system.[4] A **critical election** is marked by a sharp change in the existing patterns of party loyalties among groups of voters. Moreover, this change in voting patterns, which is called an **electoral realignment**, lasts through several subsequent elections.[5] When one party in a two-party system *regularly* enjoys support from most of the voters, it is called the *majority party*; the other is called the *minority party*.

The 1860 election divided the country between the northern states, which mainly voted Republican, and the southern states, which were overwhelmingly Democratic. The victory of the North over the South in the Civil War cemented Democratic loyalties in the South, particularly following the withdrawal of federal troops after the 1876 election. For forty years, from 1880 to 1920, no Republican presidential candidate won even one of the eleven states of the Confederacy.

A second critical election, in 1896, transformed the Republican party into a true majority party when, in opposition to the Democrats' inflationary free silver platform, a link was forged between the Republican party and business. Voters in the heavily populated Northeast and Midwest surged toward the Republican party—many of them permanently.

A third critical election occurred in 1932 when Franklin Delano Roosevelt led the Democratic party to majority party status by uniting Southern Democrats, Northern urban workers, middle-class liberals, Catholics, Jews, and white ethnic minorities in the "Roosevelt coalition." (The relatively few blacks

---

*Although they used the same name, they were not Republicans as we know them today. Indeed, Jefferson's followers were later known as Democratic Republicans, and in 1828, a wing of that party became the Democratic party.

who voted at that time tended to remain loyal to the Republicans—the "party of Lincoln.") Democrats have held control of both houses of Congress in most sessions from 1933 through 1994. In 1994, Republicans gained control of Congress for the first time in forty years. They retained control after the 1996 elections—the first time that Republicans have taken both houses in successive elections since Herbert Hoover's presidency.

Signs are strong that the coalition of Democratic voters forged by Roosevelt in the 1930s has cracked. Certainly the South is no longer solid for the Democrats. Since 1952, in fact, it has voted more consistently for Republican presidential candidates than for Democrats. The party system in the United States may not be undergoing another realignment; rather, we may be in a period of **electoral dealignment**, in which party loyalties have become less important to voters as they cast their ballots. We examine the influence of party loyalty on voting later in this chapter.

The American Two-Party System

The critical election of 1860 established the Democratic and Republican parties as the major parties in our **two-party system**. In a two-party system, most voters are so loyal to one or the other of the major parties that independent candidates or candidates from a third party—which means any minor party—have little chance of winning office. Third-party candidates tend to be most successful at the local or state level. Since the present two-party system was established, relatively few minor-party candidates have won election to the U.S. House; very few have won election to the Senate; and none have won the presidency. However, we should not ignore the special contributions of certain minor parties, among them the Anti-Masonic Party, the Populists, and the Progressives of 1912. In this section, we study the fortunes of minor or third parties in American politics. We also will look at why we have only two major parties, explain how federalism helps the parties survive, and describe voters' loyalty to the two major parties today.

Minor Parties in America

Minor parties have always figured in party politics in America. Most true minor parties in our political history have been of four types:[6]

- *Bolter parties* are formed from factions that have split off from one of the major parties. Six times in thirty-two presidential elections since the Civil War, disgruntled leaders have "bolted the ticket" and challenged their former parties. Bolter parties have occasionally won significant proportions of the vote. However, with the exception of Teddy Roosevelt's Progressive Party in 1912 and the possible exception of George Wallace's American Independent Party in 1968, bolter parties have not affected the outcome of presidential elections.

- *Farmer-labor parties* represent farmers and urban workers who believe that they, the working class, are not getting their share of society's wealth. The People's Party, founded in 1892 and nicknamed the "Populist Party," was a prime example of a farmer-labor party. The Populists won 8.5 percent of the vote in 1892 and also became the first third party since 1860 to win any electoral votes. Flushed by success, it endorsed William Jennings Bryan, the Democratic candidate, in 1896. When he lost, the party quickly faded. Farm and labor groups revived many Populist ideas in the Progressive Party in 1924. The party died in 1925.

- *Parties of ideological protest* go further than farmer-labor parties in criticizing the established system. These parties reject prevailing doctrines and propose radically different principles, often favoring more government activism. The Socialist Party has been the most successful party of ideological protest. Even at its high point in 1912, however, it garnered only 6 percent of the vote, and Socialist candidates for president have never won a single state. In recent years, the sound of ideological protest has been heard more from rightist parties, arguing for the radical disengagement of government from society. Such is the program of the Libertarian Party, which stresses freedom over order and equality. The party has run candidates for president in every election since 1972, but it has never won more than 1 percent of votes cast.

- *Single-issue parties* are formed to promote one principle, not a general philosophy of government. The Free Soil Party of the 1840s and 1850s worked to abolish slavery. The Prohibition Party, the most durable example of a single-issue party, opposed the consumption of alcoholic beverages. The party has run candidates in every presidential election since 1884.

Third parties, then, have been formed primarily to express discontent with the choices offered by the major parties and to work for their own objectives within the electoral system.[7] Certainly the Reform Party reflects discontent with existing politics, but otherwise it resists classification. Of the nine principles presented by the Reform Party in 1996, six dealt with government reforms, and only three vaguely addressed substantive policies.[8] Perhaps the Reform Party foreshadows a new type of party, one created from the top by a dynamic leader through a well-funded, mass media–dependent appeal for support from citizens previously uninvolved in partisan politics.[9]

How have minor parties fared historically? As vote getters, they have not performed well. However, bolter parties have twice won more than 10 percent of the vote. More significantly, the Republican Party originated in 1854 as a single-issue third party opposed to slavery in the nation's new territories; in its first election, in 1856, the party came in second, displacing the Whigs. (Undoubtedly, the Republican exception to the rule has inspired the formation of other hopeful third parties.)

As policy advocates, minor parties have a slightly better record. At times, they have had a real effect on the policies adopted by the major parties. Women's suffrage, the graduated income tax, and the direct election of senators all originated in third parties.[10]

Most important, minor parties function as safety valves. They allow those who are unhappy with the status quo to express their discontent within the system, to contribute to the political dialogue. Surely this was the function of Perot's candidacy and of the Reform Party. If minor parties and independent candidates indicate discontent, what should we make of the scores of parties that have sponsored candidates in recent congressional elections or of the several minor parties (Libertarian, Reform, U.S. Taxpayers, Green, Natural Law) that held conventions in the summer of 1996? Not much. The number of third parties that contest elections is much less important than the total number of votes they receive. Despite the presence of numerous minor parties in every presidential election, the two major parties usually collect over 99 percent of the vote. In 1996, Perot took only 8.5 percent of the popular vote, and all the other sixteen independent and minor party candidates won less than two percent. Of course the two major parties captured all of the electoral votes.

Why a Two-Party System?

The history of party politics in the United States is essentially the story of two parties that have alternating control of the government. With relatively few exceptions, Americans conduct elections at all levels within the two-party system. This pattern is unusual in democratic countries, where multiparty systems are more common. Why does the United States have only two major parties? The two most convincing answers to this question stem from the electoral system in the United States and the process of political socialization here.

In the typical U.S. election, two or more candidates contest each office, and the winner is the single candidate who collects the most votes, whether those votes constitute a majority or not. When the two principles of *single winners* chosen by a *simple plurality* of votes govern the election of members of a legislature, the system (despite its reliance on pluralities rather than majorities) is known as **majority representation**. Think about how American states choose representatives to Congress. A state entitled to ten representatives, is divided into ten congressional districts; each district elects one representative. Majority representation of voters through single-member districts is also a feature of most state legislatures.

Alternatively, a legislature might be chosen through a system of **proportional representation**, which awards legislative seats to a party in proportion to the total number of votes it wins in an election. Under this system, the state might have a single statewide election for all ten seats, with each party presenting a list of ten candidates. Voters could vote for the entire party list they preferred, and the party's candidates would be elected from the top of each list, according to the proportion of votes won by the party. Thus, if a party got 30 percent of the vote in this example, its first three candidates would be elected.

Although this form of election may seem strange, many democratic countries (for example, The Netherlands, Israel, and Denmark) use it. Proportional representation tends to produce (or perpetuate) several parties, because each can win enough seats nationwide to wield some influence in the legislature. In contrast, our system of elections forces interest groups of all sorts to work within the two major parties, for only one candidate in each race stands a chance to be elected under plurality voting. Therefore, the system tends to produce only two parties.

The rules of our electoral system may explain why only two parties tend to form in specific election districts, but why do the same two parties

Federalism at Work
In November 1993, Republican candidate Christine Todd Whitman was elected governor of New Jersey, defeating the Democratic incumbent, Jim Florio. Only one year earlier, New Jersey had voted for Clinton for president in 1992. Whitman's victory demonstrates the federal structure of the party system: one party may win executive office at the national level, while another party wins executive office at the state level. Before the 1994 election, approximately 60 percent of the nation's governors were Democratic; after the election, 60 percent were Republican.

(Democratic and Republican) operate within every state? The contest for the presidency is the key to this question. A candidate can win a presidential election only by amassing a majority of electoral votes from across the entire nation. Presidential candidates try to win votes under the same party label in each state in order to pool their electoral votes in the electoral college. The presidency is a big enough political prize to induce parties to harbor uncomfortable coalitions of voters (southern white Protestants allied with northern Jews and blacks in the Democratic party, for example) just to win the electoral vote and the presidential election.

The American electoral system may force U.S. politics into a two-party mold, but why must the same two parties reappear from election to election? Why do the Democrats and Republicans persist? This is where political socialization comes into play. These two parties persist simply because they have persisted. After more than one hundred years of political socialization, the two parties today have such a head start in structuring the vote that they discourage challenges from new parties.

The Federal Basis of the Party System

Focusing on contests for the presidency is a convenient and informative way to study the history of American parties, but it also oversimplifies party politics to the point of distortion. Even during its darkest defeats for the presidency, a party can still claim many victories for state offices. Victories outside the arena of presidential politics give each party a base of support that keeps its machinery oiled and running for the next contest.[11]

Reagan's victory in 1980, his 1984 landslide, and Bush's convincing win in 1988 might have suggested that the Democrats were doomed to extinction in presidential politics. Perhaps in an earlier time, when the existing parties were not so well institutionalized, that would have been so. However, the Democratic party not only remained alive but thrived in our federal system. The separation of state politics from national trends affords each party a chance to lick its wounds after a presidential election debacle and return to campaign optimistically in the next election, as the Republicans did so successfully in the 1994 congressional elections after losing the presidency in 1992.

Party Identification in America

The concept of **party identification** is one of the most important in political science. It signifies a voter's sense of psychological attachment to a party, which is not the same thing as voting for the party in any given election. Scholars measure party identification simply by asking, "Do you usually think of yourself as a Republican, a Democrat, an independent, or what?"[12] Voting is a behavior; identification is a state of mind. For example, millions of southerners voted for Eisenhower for president in 1952 and 1956 but continued to consider themselves Democrats. The proportions of self-identified Republicans, Democrats, and independents (no party attachment) in the electorate since 1952 are shown in Figure 6.1. Three significant points stand out.

- The number of Republicans and Democrats combined far exceeds the proportion of independents in every year.

- The number of Democrats consistently exceeds that of Republicans.

- The number of Democrats has shrunk over time, to the benefit of both Republicans and independents, and the three groups are now almost equal in size.

Although party identification predisposes citizens to vote for their favorite party, other factors may cause voters to choose the opposition candidate. If they vote against their party often enough, they may rethink their party identification and eventually switch. Apparently, this rethinking has gone on in the minds of many southern Democrats over time. In 1952, about 70 percent of white southerners thought of themselves as Democrats, and fewer than 20 per-

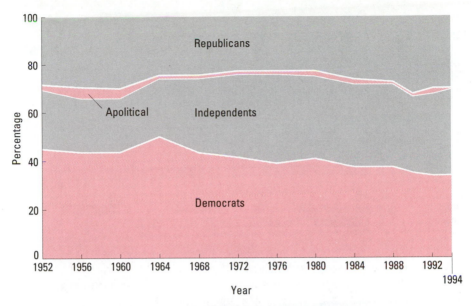

FIGURE 6.1   *Distribution of Party Identification, 1952–1994*
In every presidential election since 1952, voters across the nation have been asked, "Generally speaking, do you usually think of yourself as a Republican, a Democrat, an independent, or what?" Most voters think of themselves as either Republicans or Democrats, but the proportion of those who think of themselves as independents has increased over time. The size of the Democratic party's majority has also shrunk. Nevertheless, most Americans today still identify with one of the two major parties, and Democrats still outnumber Republicans. (Source: National Election Studies Guide to Public Opinion and Electoral Behavior, obtained at <www.umich.edu/~nes/nesguide/toptables/tab2a_1.htm>.)

cent thought of themselves as Republicans. By 1992, white southerners were only 34 percent Democratic—30 percent Republican, and 36 percent independent. Much of the nationwide growth in the proportion of Republicans and independents (and the parallel drop in the number of Democrats) stems from changes in party preferences among white southerners and from the migration of northerners, which translated into substantial gains in the number of registered Republicans by 1996.[13]

Who are the self-identified Democrats and Republicans in the electorate? Figure 6.2 shows party identification by various social groups in 1992. The effects of socioeconomic factors are clear. People who have lower incomes and less education are more likely to think of themselves as Democrats than as Republicans. But the cultural factors of religion and race produce even sharper differences between the parties. Jews are strongly Democratic compared with other religious groups, and African Americans are also overwhelmingly Democratic. Finally, American politics has a gender gap: Women tend to be more Democratic than men.

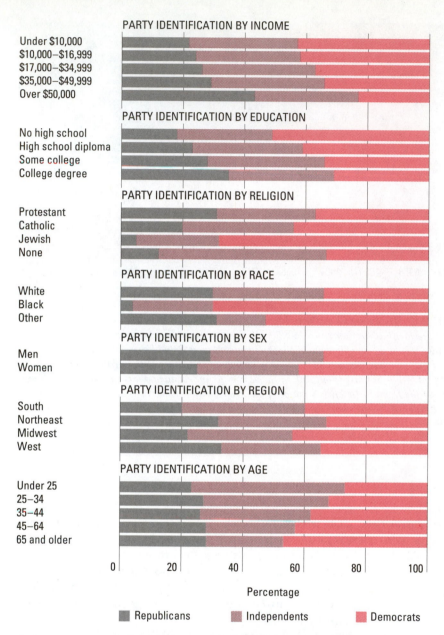

FIGURE 6.2   **Party Identification by Social Groups**
*Respondents to a 1992 survey were grouped by seven different socioeconomic criteria—
income, education, religion, race, sex, region, and age—and analyzed according to their
self-descriptions as Democrats, independents, or Republicans. Region was found to have the
least effect on party identification; religion and race had the greatest effects. (Source: 1992
National Election Study, Center for Political Studies, University of Michigan.)*

The influence of region on party identification has changed over time. Because of the high proportion of blacks in the South, it is still the most heavily Democratic region, followed closely by the Northeast. The Midwest and West have proportionately more Republicans. Despite the erosion of Democratic strength in the South, we still see elements of Roosevelt's old Democratic coalition in the socioeconomic groups. Perhaps the major change in that coalition has been the replacement of white European ethnic groups by blacks, attracted by the Democrats' backing of civil rights legislation in the 1960s.

Studies show that about half the citizens in the United States adopt their parents' party. But it often takes time for party identification to develop. The youngest group of voters is most likely to be independent, but they have also identified increasingly with Republicans, ever since the Reagan years (see Politics in a Changing America 6.1). The oldest group shows the greatest partisan commitment, reflecting the fact that citizens become more interested in politics as they mature. Also, the youngest age group is most evenly divided between the parties. Some analysts believe this ratio of party identification among today's young voters will persist as they age, contributing to further erosion of the Democratic majority and perhaps greater electoral dealignment.

Americans tend to find their political niche and stay there.[14] The enduring party loyalty of American voters tends to structure the vote even before an election is held, even before the candidates are chosen. Later we will examine the extent to which party identification determines voting choice. But first, we will look to see whether the Democratic and Republican parties have any significant differences.

Party Ideology and Organization

George Wallace, a disgruntled Democrat who ran for president in 1968 on the American Independent Party ticket, complained that "there isn't a dime's worth of difference" between the Democrats and Republicans. Humorist Will Rogers said, "I am not a member of any organized political party—I am a Democrat." Wallace's comment was made in disgust; Rogers's in jest. Wallace was wrong; Rogers was close to being right. Here we will dispel the myth that the parties do not differ significantly on issues and explain how they are organized to coordinate the activities of party candidates and officials in government.

Differences in Party Ideology

George Wallace notwithstanding, there is more than a dime's worth of difference between the two parties. In fact, the difference amounts to many billions of dollars, the cost of the different government programs supported by each party. Democrats are more disposed to government spending to advance social welfare (and hence to promote equality) than are Republicans. And social welfare programs cost money, a lot of money. Republicans, on the other hand, are not averse to spending billions of dollars for the projects they consider

Politics in a Changing America 6.1

The Changing Relationship Between Age and Party Identification

The relationship between age and party identification has changed dramatically during the past forty years. We can visualize this change by comparing Gallup surveys taken in 1952 and 1992. Both graphs show the percentage of Democratic identifiers minus the percentage of Republican identifiers for seventeen different four-year age groupings—ranging from eighteen- to twenty-one-year-olds to those eighty-two years of age and older. In 1952, the percentage of Democratic identifiers exceeded Republican identifiers by about fifteen points or more among younger and middle-aged voters, while the older age groups had far more Republicans than Democrats. By 1992, this pattern had reversed, with younger voters more likely to be Republicans and older voters (those who were young in 1952) retaining their Democratic sentiments. Note also that the overall relationship between age and party identification was substantially weaker in 1992 than in 1952.

(continued)

important, among them, national defense. Ronald Reagan portrayed the Democrats as big spenders, but the defense buildup during just his first administration alone cost the country over $1 trillion—more precisely, $1,007,900,000,000.[15] The differences in spending patterns reflect some real philosophical differences between the parties.

Voters and Activists   One way to examine the differences is to compare party voters with party activists. When such a comparison was done in 1996, it was found that 16 percent of those who identified themselves as Democrats described themselves as conservatives, compared with 55 percent of those who identified themselves as Republicans. The ideological gap between the parties is even larger among party activists. Only 3 percent of the delegates to the 1996 Democratic convention considered themselves conservatives, compared with 79 percent of the delegates to the Republican convention.[16]

Platforms: Freedom, Order, and Equality   For another test of party philosophy, we can look at the **party platforms**—the statements of policies—adopted in party conventions. Although many people feel that party platforms don't matter very much, several scholars have demonstrated, using different approaches, that winning parties tend to carry out much of their platforms when in office.[17] Party platforms also matter a great deal to the parties' convention delegates. The wording of a platform plank often means the difference between victory and defeat for factions within a party.

The platforms adopted by the Democratic and Republican conventions in 1996 were strikingly different in style and substance. As befits a conservative party, the 1996 Republican platform called for "moral clarity in our culture"

Politics in a Changing America 6.1 (continued)

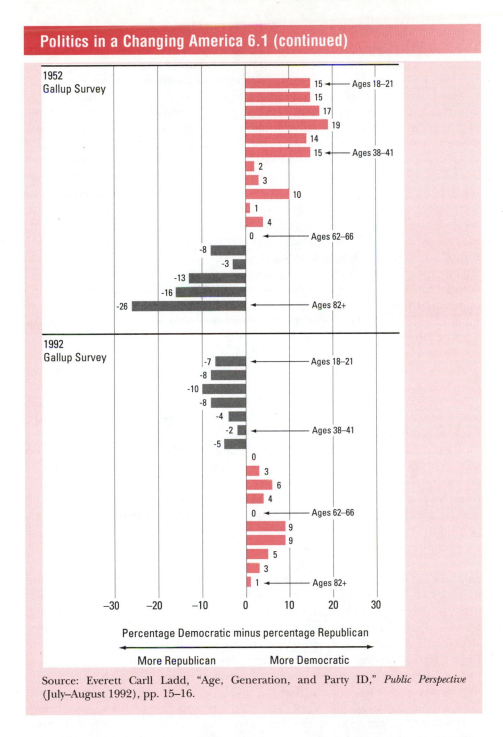

Source: Everett Carll Ladd, "Age, Generation, and Party ID," *Public Perspective* (July–August 1992), pp. 15–16.

and "free market capitalism." The platform also called for several amendments to the Constitution in addition to the human life amendment. It advocated amendments that would guarantee a balanced budget, limit terms for members of Congress, deny automatic citizenship to children born in the United States to illegal immigrants, protect against defiling the flag, and ensure the rights of victims to obtain compensation from criminals.

The 1996 Democratic platform reflected Bill Clinton's move toward the political center as it echoed this proclamation about "the end of the era of big government." Nevertheless, the Democrats proceeded to promise greater government protection of the environment, more national guidance and assistance to schools, and new initiatives for job training.

The differences between the two 1996 party platforms emerged more clearly in their specific proposals. In contrast to the Republicans, the Democrats supported "the right of every woman to choose" between birth and abortion. The Democrats favored "the assault weapons ban," whereas the Republicans defended "the constitutional right to keep and bear arms." Democrats advocated more funding for public education; Republicans proposed diverting funds to tuition subsidies for private schools. Democrats pledged "to end discrimination against gay men and lesbians"; Republicans affirmed that "homosexuality is incompatible with military service." As for medical care, the Democratic party committed itself to ensuring that "Americans have access to affordable high-quality health care," while the Republicans urged that health care providers be allowed "to respond to consumer demand through consumer choice."

These statements of values clearly distinguish the two parties on the values of freedom, order, and equality that underlie the dilemmas of government discussed in Chapter 1. According to our ideological typology, the Republicans' 1996 platform positions on abortion, homosexual rights, education, and medical care place their party firmly in the conservative category, whereas the Democrats' platform puts their party squarely into the liberal category.

The platform of the Reform Party available at the time of its convention was only 550 words. Here is the entire statement for one of its nine planks, *Creating a New Tax System:* "The new tax system must be fair; the new tax system must be paperless; the new tax system must raise the money to pay the bills; and [it must] require that any future tax increases under the new system be approved by the people in the next federal election in order to impose discipline on spending." The main "issue" of the Reform Party was really Ross Perot.

Different but Similar   The Democrats and the Republicans have very different ideological orientations. Yet many observers claim that the parties are really quite similar in ideology compared to the different parties of other countries. Specifically, both support capitalism; that is, both reject government ownership of the means of production (see Chapter 1). A study of Democratic and Republican positions on four economic issues—ownership of the means of production, role in economic planning, redistribution of wealth, and providing for social welfare—found that Republicans consistently oppose increased government activity. Comparing these findings with data on party positions in thirteen other democracies, the researchers found about as much difference between the American parties as is usual within two-party systems. However, both American parties tend to be more conservative on economic matters than parties in other two-party systems. In most multiparty systems, the presence of strong socialist and antisocialist parties ensures a much greater range of ideological choice than we find in our system, despite genuine differences between the Democrats and Republicans.[18]

National Party Organization

American parties parallel our federal system: They have separate national and state organizations (and virtually separate local organizations, in many cases). At the national level, each major party has four main organizational components:

- *National convention.* Every four years, each party assembles thousands of delegates from the states and U.S. territories (such as Puerto Rico and Guam) in a **national convention** for the purpose of nominating a candidate for president. This presidential nominating convention is also the supreme governing body of the party. It determines party policy through the platform, formulates rules to govern party operations, and designates a national committee, which is empowered to govern the party until the next convention.

- *National committee.* The **national committee,** which governs each party between conventions, is composed of party officials representing the states and territories, including the chairpersons of their party organizations. In 1996, the Republican National Committee (RNC) had about 150 members. The Democratic National Committee (DNC) had approximately 400 elected and appointed members.[19] The chairperson of each national committee is chosen by the party's presidential nominee, then duly elected by the committee. If the nominee loses the election, the national committee usually replaces the nominee's chairperson.

- *Congressional party conferences.* At the beginning of each session of Congress, the Republicans and Democrats in each chamber hold separate **party conferences** (the House Democrats call theirs a caucus) to select their party leaders and to decide committee assignments. The party conferences deal only with congressional matters and have no structural relationship to each other and no relationship to the national committee.

- *Congressional campaign committees.* Democrats and Republicans in the House and Senate also maintain separate **congressional campaign committees**, each of which raises its own funds to support its candidates in congressional elections. The separation of these organizations from the national committee tells us that the national party structure is loose; the national committee seldom gets involved with the election of any individual member of Congress. Moreover, even the congressional campaign organizations merely supplement the funds that senators and representatives raise on their own to win reelection.

It is tempting to think of the national party chairperson sitting at the top of a hierarchical party organization that not only controls its members in Congress but also issues orders to the state committees and on down to the local level. Few ideas could be more wrong.[20] The national committee has virtually no voice in congressional activity, and it exercises very little direction of and even less control over state and local campaigns. The main role of a national committee is to support its candidate's personal campaign staff, in the effort to win.

For many years, the role of the national committees was essentially limited to planning for the next party convention. The committee would select the site, issue the call to state parties to attend, plan the program, and so on. In the 1970s, however, the roles of the DNC and RNC began to expand—but in different ways.

In response to street rioting during the 1968 Democratic convention, the Democrats created a special commission to introduce party reforms. The McGovern-Fraser Commission formulated guidelines for the selection of delegates to the 1972 Democratic convention. Included in these guidelines was the requirement that state parties take "affirmative action"—that is, see to it that their delegations included women, blacks, and young people "in reasonable relationship to the group's presence in the population of the state."[21]

Never before had a national party committee imposed these kinds of rules on a state party organization, but it worked. Although the party has since reduced its emphasis on quotas, the gains by women and blacks have held up fairly well. The representation of young people, however, has declined substantially.

While the Democrats were busy with *procedural* reforms, the Republicans were making *organizational* reforms.[22] Republicans were not inclined to impose quotas on state parties through their national committee. Instead, the RNC strengthened its fund-raising, research, and service roles. Republicans acquired their own building and their own computer, and in 1976 they hired the first full-time chairperson of either national party. As RNC chairman, William Brock expanded the party's staff, launched new publications, held seminars, conducted election analyses, and advised candidates—things that national party committees in other countries had been doing for years.

The vast difference between the Democratic and Republican approaches to reforming the national committees shows in the funds raised by the DNC and RNC during election campaigns. During Brock's tenure as chairman of the RNC, the Republicans raised three to four times as much money as the Democrats. Although the margin has narrowed, Republican party fund-raising efforts are still superior. From January 1, 1995, through June 30, 1996, the Republicans' national, senatorial, and congressional committees raised $180 million, compared with $102 million raised by the comparable Democratic committees.[23] Also, the Republicans received more of their funds in small contributions (less than $100), mainly through direct-mail solicitation, than the Democrats. In short, the RNC has been raising far more money than the DNC, from many more citizens, as part of its long-term commitment to improving its organizational services. Its efforts have also made a difference at the state and local levels.

State and Local Party Organizations

At one time, both major parties were firmly anchored by strong state and local party organizations. Big-city party organizations, such as the Democrats' Tammany Hall in New York City and the Cook County Central Committee in Chicago, were called *party machines*. A **party machine** was a centralized organi-

zation that dominated local politics by controlling elections—sometimes by illegal means, often by providing jobs and social services to urban workers in return for their votes. These patronage and social service functions of party
machines were undercut when the government expanded its social services. As
a result, most local party organizations lost their ability to deliver votes and
thus to determine the outcome of elections.

The individual state and local organizations of both parties vary widely in
strength, but recent research has found that "neither the Republican nor
Democratic party has a distinct advantage with regard to direct campaign activities."[24] Whereas once both the RNC and the DNC were dependent for their
funding on "quotas" paid by state parties, now the funds flow the other way. In
addition to money, state parties also receive candidate training, poll data and
research, and campaigning instruction.[25]

Decentralized but Growing Stronger

The absence of centralized power has always been the most distinguishing
characteristic of American political parties. Moreover, the rise in the proportion of citizens who style themselves as independents suggests that our already
weak parties are in further decline.[26] But there is evidence that our political
parties, *as organizations*, are enjoying a period of resurgence. Both parties' national committees have never been better funded or more active in grassroots
campaign activities.[27] And more votes in Congress are being decided along
party lines. In fact, a specialist in congressional politics has concluded, "When
compared to its predecessors of the last half-century, the current majority
party leadership is more involved and more decisive in organizing the party
and the chamber, setting the policy agenda, shaping legislation, and determining legislative outcomes."[28]

The Model of Responsible Party Government

According to the majoritarian model of democracy, parties are essential to
making the government responsive to public opinion. In fact, the ideal role of
parties in majoritarian democracy has been formalized in the four principles
of **responsible party government**: [29]

1. Parties should present clear and coherent programs to voters.
2. Voters should choose candidates according to the party programs.
3. The winning party should carry out its program once in office.
4. Voters should hold the governing party responsible at the next election for
   executing its program.

How well do these principles describe American politics? You've learned
that the Democratic and Republican platforms are different and that they are
much more ideologically consistent than many people believe. So the first
principle is being met fairly well. To a lesser extent, so is the third principle:

once parties gain power, they usually do what they said they would do. From the standpoint of democratic theory, the real question lies in principles 2 and 4: do voters really pay attention to party platforms and policies when they cast their ballots? And, if so, do voters hold the governing party responsible at the next election for delivering, or failing to deliver, on its pledges? To answer these questions, we must consider in greater detail the parties' role in nominating candidates and structuring the voters' choice in elections. At the conclusion of this chapter we will return to evaluating the role of political parties in democratic government.

The Evolution of Campaigning

An **election campaign** is an organized effort to persuade voters to choose one candidate over others competing for the same office. An effective campaign requires sufficient resources to acquire and analyze information about voters' interests, to develop a strategy and matching tactics for appealing to these interests, to deliver the candidate's message to the voters, and to get them to cast their ballots.[30]

In the past, political parties conducted all phases of the election campaign. Today, however, candidates seldom rely much on political parties. How do candidates plan their campaign strategy and tactics now? By hiring political consultants to devise clever "soundbites" (brief, catchy phrases) that catch voters' attention on television, not by consulting party headquarters. How do candidates deliver their messages to voters? By conducting media campaigns, not by counting on party regulars to canvass the neighborhoods.

Increasingly, election campaigns have evolved from being party-centered to being candidate-centered.[31] Whereas the parties virtually ran election campaigns in the past, now they exist mainly to support candidate-centered campaigns by providing services or funds to their candidates. Nevertheless, we will see that the party label is usually a candidate's prime attribute at election time.

Perhaps the most important change in American elections is that candidates don't campaign just to get elected anymore. It is now necessary to campaign for *nomination* as well. Party organizations once controlled that function. For most important offices today, however, candidates are no longer nominated *by* the party organization but *within* the party. That is, party leaders seldom choose candidates themselves; they organize and supervise the election process by which party *voters* choose the candidates. Because almost all aspiring candidates must first win a primary election to gain their party's nomination, those who would campaign for election must first campaign for nomination.

Nominations

The distinguishing feature of the nomination process in American party politics is that it usually involves an election by party voters. Virtually no other political parties in the world nominate candidates to the national legislature through party elections.[32] In more than half the world's parties, local party leaders choose legislative candidates, and their national party organization must usually approve those choices. In fact, in more than one-third of the world's parties, the national organization itself selects the candidates.

Democrats and Republicans nominate their candidates for national and state offices in varying ways across the country because each state is entitled to make its own laws governing the nomination process. (This is significant in itself, for political parties in most other countries are largely free of laws stating how they must select their candidates.) We can classify their nomination practices by the types of party elections held and the level of office sought.

Nomination for Congress and State Offices

In the United States, most aspiring candidates for major offices are nominated through a **primary election**, a preliminary election conducted within the party to select its candidates. Forty-three states use primary elections alone to nominate candidates for all state and national offices, and primaries figure in the nomination process in all the other states.[33] The nomination process, then, is highly decentralized, resting on the decisions of thousands, perhaps millions, of the party rank and file who participate in primary elections.

States hold different types of primary elections for state and congressional offices. The most common type (used by about forty states) is the **closed primary**, in which voters must declare their party affiliation before they are given the primary ballot, which lists the party's potential nominees. A few states use the **open primary**, in which voters may choose either party's ballot, listing that party's potential nominees to take into the polling booth. Four states use variations of the **blanket primary**, in which voters receive one or more ballots listing all parties' potential nominees for each office and can mark their ballots for any candidate, but only one for each office. The top vote-getter from each party advances to the general election.

Nomination for President

The decentralized nature of American parties is readily apparent in candidates' campaigns for the parties' nomination for president. Delegates attending the parties' national conventions held the summer before the presidential election in November nominate presidential candidates. In the past, delegates chose their party's nominee right at the convention, sometimes after repeated balloting over several candidates who divided the vote and kept anyone from getting the majority needed to win the nomination. However, the last time that either party needed more than one ballot to nominate its presidential candidate was in 1952, when the Democrats took three ballots to nominate Adlai E. Stevenson. Since 1972, both parties' nominating conventions have simply ratified the results of the complex process for selecting the convention delegates.

Selecting Convention Delegates   No national legislation specifies how state parties must select delegates to their national conventions. Instead, state legislatures have enacted a bewildering variety of procedures, which often differ for Democrats and Republicans in the same state. The most important distinction in delegate selection is between the presidential primary and the local caucus.

A **presidential primary** is a special primary held to select delegates to attend the party's national nominating convention. In *presidential preference primaries* (used in all Democratic primaries and in thirty-five Republican primaries in 1996), party supporters vote directly for the person they favor as their party's nominee for president, and the primary candidates win delegates according to a variety of formulas. In all Democratic primaries, candidates who win at least 15 percent of the vote divide the delegates from that state in proportion to the percentage they won. In almost half the Republican primaries, the winning candidate takes all the states' convention delegates. In *delegate selection primaries* (used only by Republicans in six states in 1996), party voters directly elect convention delegates, who may or may not have declared for a presidential candidate.[34]

The **local caucus** method of delegate selection has several stages. It begins with local meetings, or caucuses, of party supporters to choose delegates to attend a larger subsequent meeting, usually at the county level. Most delegates selected in the local caucuses openly back one of the presidential candidates. The county meetings, in turn, select delegates to a higher level. The process culminates in a state convention, which actually selects the delegates to the national convention. Eighteen states used the caucus process in 1996 (a few states combine caucuses with primaries), and Democrats used caucuses more than Republicans did.[35]

Primary elections were first used to select delegates to nominating conventions in 1912. Now parties in about forty states rely on presidential primaries, which generate more than 80 percent of the delegates.

Campaigning for the Nomination   The process of nominating party candidates for president is a complex, drawn-out affair that has no parallel in any other nation. Would-be presidents announce their candidacy and begin campaigning many months before the first convention delegates are selected. Soon after one election ends, prospective candidates quietly begin lining up political and financial support for their likely race nearly four years later. By historical accident, two small states—Iowa and New Hampshire—have become the testing ground of candidates' popularity with party voters. Accordingly, each basks in the media spotlight once every four years.

The Iowa caucuses and the New Hampshire primary have served different functions in the presidential nominating process.[36] The contest in Iowa has traditionally tended to winnow out candidates who are rejected by the party faithful. The New Hampshire primary, held one week later, tests the Iowa front-runners' appeal to ordinary party voters, which foreshadows their likely strength in the general election.

Over 35 million citizens voted in presidential primaries in 1996, and about half a million participated in party caucuses. Requiring prospective presidential candidates to campaign before many millions of party voters in primaries and hundreds of thousands of party activists in caucus states has several consequences:

- The uncertainty of the nomination process attracts a half-dozen or so plausible candidates, especially when the party does not have a president seeking re-election.

- Candidates favored by most party identifiers usually win their party's nomination. There have been only two exceptions to this rule since 1936, when poll data first became available: Adlai E. Stevenson in 1952 and George McGovern in 1972.[37] Both were Democrats; both lost impressively in the general election.

- Candidates who win the nomination do so largely on their own and owe little or nothing to the national party organization, which usually does not promote a candidate. In fact, Jimmy Carter won the nomination in 1976 against a field of nationally prominent Democrats, although he was a party outsider with few strong connections in the national party leadership.

Elections

By national law, all seats in the House of Representatives and one-third of the seats in the Senate are filled in a **general election** held in early November in even-numbered years. Every state takes advantage of the national election to also fill some of nearly five hundred thousand state and local offices across the country, which makes the election even more "general." When the president is chosen every fourth year, the election year is identified as a *presidential election.* The intervening years are known as *congressional, midterm,* or *off-year elections.*

Presidential Elections

In contrast to almost all other offices in the United States, the presidency does not go automatically to the candidate who wins the most votes. Instead, a two-stage procedure specified in the Constitution decides elections for president; it requires selection of the president by a group (college) of electors representing the states.

The Electoral College   Voters choose the president only indirectly; they actually vote for a slate of little-known electors (their names are usually not even on the ballot) pledged to one of the candidates. Occasionally, electors break their pledges when they cast their written ballots at their state capitols in December. (This happened as recently as 1988.)[38] But usually the electors are faithful. The fundamental principle of the electoral college is that the outcome of the popular vote determines the outcome of the electoral vote. Whether a candidate wins a state by five or five hundred thousand votes, he or she wins all that state's electoral votes.*

In the electoral college, each state is accorded one vote for each of its senators (100 votes total) and representatives (435 votes total), adding up to 535 votes. In addition, the Twenty-third Amendment to the Constitution awarded three electoral votes to the District of Columbia, even though it elects no voting members of Congress. So the total number of electoral votes is 538, and a candidate needs a majority of 270 electoral votes to win the presidency.**

The most troubling aspect of the electoral college is the possibility that despite winning a plurality or even a majority of popular votes, a candidate could lose the election in the electoral college. This could happen if one candidate wins certain states by very wide margins, while the other candidate wins other states by slim margins. Indeed, it has happened in three elections, most recently in 1888.

Abolish the Electoral College? Reformers argue that it is simply wrong to have a system that allows a candidate who receives the most popular votes to lose the election. They favor a purely majoritarian means of choosing the president, direct election by popular vote. Defenders of the electoral college point out that this system, warts and all, has been a stable one. It might be riskier to replace it with a new arrangement that could alter our party system or the way presidential campaigns are conducted. Also, some scholars argue that the electoral college's tendency to magnify the winner's victory margin increases the legitimacy of the president-elect. In any case, recent proposals for fundamental reform have not come close to adoption.

Congressional Elections

The candidates for the presidency are listed at the top of the ballot in a presidential election, followed by the candidates for other national offices and for state and local offices. Voters are said to vote a **straight ticket** when they choose the same party's candidates for all the offices. A voter who chooses candidates from different parties is said to vote a **split ticket**. About half of all voters admit to splitting their tickets, and the proportion of voters who chose a presidential candidate from one party and a congressional candidate from the other has increased from about 13 percent in 1952 to 25 percent in 1992.[39] A common pattern in the 1970s and 1980s was to elect a Republican as president but send mostly Democrats to Congress, producing divided government (see

---

*The two exceptions are Maine and Nebraska, where two and three of the states' electoral votes, respectively, are awarded by congressional district. The presidential candidate who carries each district wins a single electoral vote and the statewide winner gets two votes.

**If no candidate receives a majority when the electoral college votes, the election is thrown into the House of Representatives. The House votes by state, with each state casting one vote. The candidates of the House election are the top three finishers in the general election. A presidential election has gone to the House only twice in American history, in 1800 and in 1824, before a stable two-party system had developed.

Chapter 9). This pattern was reversed in the 1994 election, when voters elected a Republican Congress to face a Democratic president.

Republicans have regularly complained that inequitable districts drawn by Democrat-dominated state legislatures denied them their fair share of seats. For example, the Republicans won 46 percent of the congressional vote in 1992, but they won only 40 percent of the seats.[40] Despite the Republicans' complaint, election specialists point out that this is the inevitable consequence of **first-past-the-post** elections—a British term for elections conducted in single-member districts that award victory to the candidate with the most votes. In all such elections around the world, the party that wins the most votes tends to win more seats than projected by its percentage of the vote. (The same process operates in the electoral college, which, as discussed, generally awards the winner a larger majority in the electoral vote than was won in popular votes.*)

Campaigns

Barbara Salmore and Stephen Salmore have developed an analytical framework that emphasizes the political context of an election campaign, the financial resources available for conducting the campaign, and the strategies and tactics that underlie the dissemination of information about the candidate.

The Political Context

The two most important structural factors that face each candidate planning a campaign are the office the candidate is seeking and whether he or she is the *incumbent* (the current officeholder, running for reelection) or the *challenger* (who seeks to replace the incumbent). Alternatively, the candidate can be running in an **open election**, which lacks an incumbent as a result of resignation or death. Incumbents usually enjoy great advantages over challengers, especially in elections to Congress.

Every candidate organizing a campaign must also examine the characteristics of the district, including its physical size and the sociological makeup of its electorate. In general, the bigger and more populous the district and the more diverse the electorate, the more complicated and costly the campaign.

The party preference of the electorate is an important factor in the context of a campaign. It is easier for candidates to get elected when their party matches the electorate's preference, in part because raising the money needed to conduct a winning campaign is easier. Finally, significant political issues—such as economic recession, personal scandals, and war—not only affect a campaign but can dominate it and even negate such positive factors as incumbency and the normal inclinations of the electorate.

---

*If you have trouble understanding this phenomenon, think of a basketball team that scores, on average, 51 percent of the total points scored in all games that it plays. Such a team usually wins far more than just 51 percent of its games, for it tends to win the close ones.

Political Campaigning: The Inside Story
Actually, it's not all that exciting. Conducting a successful campaign usually involves a careful statistical analysis of voting trends and various social and economic characteristics of the electorate. The sign in Republican strategist Karl Rove's office in Austin, Texas, says a lot: These days, computers may be everything.

Financing

Former House Speaker Thomas ("Tip") O'Neill once said, "As it is now, there are four parts to any campaign. The candidate, the issues of the candidate, the campaign organization, and the money to run the campaign with. Without money you can forget the other three."[41] Money will buy the best campaign managers, equipment, transportation, research, and consultants—making the quality of the organization only a function of money.[42] Although the equation is not quite as strong, when party sources promise ample campaign funds, good candidates become available.

Campaign financing is now heavily regulated by national and state governments, and regulations vary according to the level of the office—national, state, or local. Even at the national level, differences in financing laws for presidential and congressional elections are significant.

Regulating Campaign Financing In 1971, during the period of party reform, Congress passed the Federal Election Campaign Act (FECA), which imposed stringent new rules for full reporting of campaign contributions and expenditures. FECA has been amended several times since 1971, and usually strengthened. A 1974 amendment created the **Federal Election Commission** (FEC) to implement the law. The FEC now enforces limits on financial contributions to national campaigns and requires full disclosure of campaign spending. The FEC also administers the public financing of presidential campaigns, which began with the 1976 election.

Financing Presidential Campaigns   In 1974, a new campaign finance law made public funds available to presidential primary and general election candidates under certain conditions. Candidates for each party's nomination for president can qualify for federal funding by raising $5,000 (in private contributions no greater than $250 each) in each of twenty states. The FEC then matches these contributions up to one-half of a preset spending limit for the primary election campaign. Originally, under the 1974 law, the FEC limited spending in presidential primary elections to $10 million. But by 1996, cost-of-living provisions had raised the limit to $30.9 million (plus $6.2 million for fund-raising activities).

The presidential nominees of the Democratic and Republican parties receive twice the primary election limit in public funds for the general election campaign ($61.8 million in 1996) provided that they spend only the public funds. Every major candidate since 1976 has accepted public funding. Ross Perot won enough votes in his personally financed 1992 run for president to qualify for $29.2 million in public funds for 1996.

Public funds go directly to each candidate's campaign committee, not to either party. But the FEC also limits what the national committees can spend on behalf of the nominees. In 1996, that limit was $12 million.[43] And the FEC limits the amount individuals ($1,000) and organizations ($5,000) can contribute to presidential candidates during the nomination phase and to House and Senate candidates for the primary and general elections. Individuals or organizations are not limited, however, in the amount of *expenses* they can incur to promote candidates of their choice.*

Public funding has had several effects on campaign financing. Obviously, it has limited campaign expenditures. Also, it has helped equalize the amounts spent by major candidates in general elections. And it has strengthened the trend toward "personalized" presidential campaigns because federal funds are given to the candidate, not to the party organization. Finally, public funding has forced candidates to spend a great deal of time seeking $1,000 contributions—a limit that has not changed since 1974, despite the inflation that has more than doubled the FEC's spending limits. In the 1980s, however, both parties began to exploit a loophole in the law that allowed them to raise a virtually unlimited amount of "soft money," funds to be spent for the entire ticket on party mailings, voter registration, and get-out-the-vote campaigns. The national committees channel soft money to state and local party commit-

---

*The distinction between contributions and expenses hinges on whether funds are spent as part of a coordinated campaign (a contribution) or spent independently of the candidate's campaign (an expense). The 1974 amendment to the FECA established limits on both campaign contributions and independent expenditures by interested citizens. In *Buckley v. Valeo* (1976), the Supreme Court struck down the limits on citizens' expenditures as an infringement on the freedom of speech, protected under the First Amendment.

tees for registration drives and other activities that are not exclusively devoted to the presidential candidates but nonetheless help them.[44] The net effect of these "coordinated campaigns" is to enhance the role of both the national and state parties in presidential campaigns.

You might think that a party's presidential campaign would be closely co-ordinated with the campaigns of its candidates for Congress. But remember that campaign funds go to the presidential candidate, not the party, and that the national party organization does not run the presidential campaign. Presidential candidates may join congressional candidates in public appear-ances for mutual benefit, but presidential campaigns are usually isolated—fi-nancially and otherwise—from congressional campaigns. Both parties spoke piously about rewriting campaign finance laws in the 104th Congress, but leg-islators could not agree on how to reform a system observers said was "in shambles" two decades after the 1974 campaign reform legislation.[45] However, reform efforts continued in the 105th Congress.

Strategies and Tactics

In an election campaign, strategy is the broad approach used to persuade citi-zens to vote for the candidate, and tactics determine the content of the mes-sages and the way they are delivered. Three basic strategies, which campaigns may blend in different mixes, are (1) a party-centered strategy, which relies heavily on voters' partisan identification as well as on the party's organization to provide the resources necessary to wage the campaign; (2) an issue-oriented strategy, which seeks support from groups that feel strongly about various poli-cies; and (3) an image-oriented strategy, which depends on the candidate's perceived personal qualities, such as experience, leadership ability, integrity, independence, trustworthiness, and the like.[46]

The campaign strategy must be tailored to the political context of the elec-tion. Research suggests that a party-centered strategy is more suited to voters with little political knowledge.[47] How do candidates learn what the electorate knows and thinks about politics, and how can they use this information? Candidates today usually turn to pollsters and political consultants, of whom there are hundreds.[48] Professional campaign managers can use information from such sources to settle on a strategy that mixes party affiliation, issues, and images in its messages. In major campaigns, the mass media disseminates these messages to voters via news coverage and advertising.[49]

Making the News   Campaigns value news coverage by the media for two rea-sons: The coverage is free, and it seems objective to the audience. If news sto-ries do nothing more than report the candidate's name, that is important, for name recognition by itself often wins elections. Getting free news coverage is yet another advantage that incumbents enjoy over challengers, for incumbents can command attention simply by announcing political decisions.

Advertising the Candidate   In all elections, the first objective of paid advertising is name recognition. The next is to promote the candidates by extolling their virtues. Finally, campaign advertising can have a negative objective, to attack one's opponent. But name recognition is the most important. Studies show that many voters cannot recall the names of their U.S. senators or representatives, but they can recognize their names on a list—as on a ballot. Researchers attribute the high reelection rate for members of Congress mainly to high name recognition (see Chapter 8).

At one time, candidates for national office relied heavily on newspaper advertising; today, they overwhelmingly use the electronic media.[50] After his nomination in 1996, Dole budgeted $45 million of his $62 million in public funds on television to overcome Clinton's lead in the polls.[51]

Using New Media   A major development in campaigning emerged in 1992; the strategic use of new media, including talk shows, entertainment shows, and Perot's half-hour "infomercials." Bill Clinton started the trend in January by appearing on "60 Minutes" to respond to Gennifer Flowers's claim of infidelity. In February, Ross Perot launched his campaign with an appearance on "Larry King Live." Most observers have concluded that these soft-format programs (watched by many people) represent an alternative form of campaigning that provides viewers with important information on candidates' character and policies.

Clinton's successful use of the new media in 1992, including a segment on MTV, guaranteed that candidates would again use it in 1996. Sure enough, even seventy-year-old Bob Dole appeared on MTV. But the hottest new media in 1996 was the Internet. Not only did the major and minor parties put up their own home pages, but so did the presidential candidates—including several just seeking the Republican nomination. The Internet, only in its infancy, is already in politics.

Explaining Voting Choice

Why do people choose one candidate over another? That is not easy to determine, but there are ways to approach the question. Individual voting choices may be viewed as products of both long-term and short-term forces. Long-term forces operate throughout a series of elections, predisposing voters to choose certain types of candidates. Short-term forces are associated with particular elections; they arise from a combination of the candidates and the issues of the time. Party identification is by far the most important long-term force affecting U.S. elections. The most important short-term forces are candidate attributes and their policy positions.

Despite frequent comments in the media about the decline of partisanship in voting behavior, party identification continues to have a substantial effect on the presidential vote, as Figure 6.3 shows. Typically, the winner holds nearly all the voters who identify with his party. The loser holds most of his fellow Democrats or Republicans, but some percentage defects to the winner, a product of short-term forces—the candidates' attributes and the issues—surrounding the election. The winner usually gets most of the independents, who split disproportionately for him, also because of short-term forces.

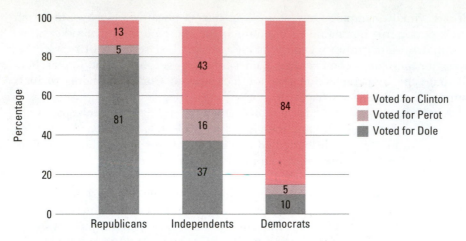

FIGURE 6.3   *Effect of Party Identification on the Vote, 1996*
The 1996 election showed that party identification still plays a key role in voting behavior—even with an independent candidate in the contest. The chart shows the results of exit polls of thousands of voters as they left hundreds of polling places across the nation on Election Day. Voters were asked what party they identified with and how they voted for president. Those who identified with one of the two parties voted strongly for their party's candidate, whereas independent voters divided roughly evenly between Clinton and Dole and were three times more likely to vote for Perot. (Source: "National Exit Poll Results for Presidential Race," distributed by PoliticsNow *on the Internet, November 6, 1996.)*

Candidates' attributes are especially important to voters who lack good information about a candidate's past performance and policy stands—which means most of us. Without such information, voters search for clues about the candidates to try to predict their behavior in office.[52] Some fall back on their personal beliefs about religion, gender, and race in making political judgments. Such stereotypic thinking accounts for the patterns of opposition and support met by a Catholic candidate for president (John Kennedy), and a woman candidate for vice president (Geraldine Ferraro).

Voters who choose between candidates on the basis of their policies are voting on the issues. Unfortunately for democratic theory, most studies of presidential elections show that issues are less important than either party identification or the candidate's attributes when people cast their ballots. Only in 1972, when voters perceived George McGovern as too liberal for their tastes, did issue voting exceed party identification in importance.[53]

Although party voting has declined somewhat since the 1950s, the relationship between voters' positions on the issues and their party identification is clearer today. The more closely party identification is aligned with ideological orientation, the more sense it makes to vote by party. In the absence of detailed information about candidates' positions on the issues, party labels are a handy indicator of those positions.[54]

If party identification is both the most important factor in the voting decision and also resistant to short-term changes, there are definite limits to the capacity of a campaign to influence the outcome of elections.[55] In a close election, however, just changing a few votes means the difference between victory and defeat, so a campaign can be decisive even if it has little overall effect. But, the capacity of image makers and campaign consultants to influence the outcome of presidential elections is minimized because they regularly offset one another by working on both sides. In 1996, both major presidential candidates hired professional campaign consultants and advertising firms.

Campaigns, Elections, and Parties

Election campaigns today tend to be highly personalized, candidate-centered, and conducted outside the control of party organizations. The increased use of electronic media, especially television, has encouraged candidates to personalize their campaign messages; at the same time, the decline of party identification has decreased the power of party-related appeals. Although the party affiliations of the candidates and the party identifications of the voters jointly explain a good deal of electoral behavior, party organizations are not central to elections in America, and this has implications for democratic government.

Parties and the Majoritarian Model

According to the majoritarian model of democracy, parties link people with their government by making government responsive to public opinion. The Republican and Democratic parties follow the model in that they formulate different platforms and tend to pursue their announced policies when in office. The weak links in this model of responsible party government have been those that connect candidates to voters through campaigns and elections.

You have not read much about the role of the party platform in nominating candidates, in conducting campaigns, or in explaining voters' choices. Certainly, a presidential candidate who wins enough convention delegates through the primaries will be comfortable with any platform that her or his delegates adopt. But House and Senate nominations are rarely fought over the party platform. And usually, thoughts about party platforms are virtually absent from campaigning and from voters' minds when they cast their ballots.

The Republicans' "Contract with America" was an exception to the rule that party platforms do not matter in elections and in governing. It consisted of ten major proposals that Republican candidates for the House of Representatives promised to bring to a vote if elected to power in the November election. The Contract with America became a significant factor in the 1994 election campaign and an even larger part of the Republicans' legislative agenda in the 104th Congress, for they not only won control of the House but also control of the Senate in what was called the "Republican Revolution."

The Republicans delivered by bringing all ten proposals to a vote in the House within one hundred days. As detailed in Chapter 8 (especially Table 8.1), several points in the Contract even became law. In early 1995, it appeared that the Republicans were following the script of responsible party government and accordingly that they would run on the Contract with America in the 1996 election. But later in the 104th Congress, some Republicans (especially in the Senate) failed to follow parts of the script, as the public turned against some of their proposals. Before the year ended, Republicans stopped talking about the Contract with America. In fact, when Speaker Newt Gingrich addressed the GOP convention in August 1996, he did not mention it once, thus seemingly ending this short experiment with responsible party government.[56]

Parties and the Pluralist Model

The way parties in the United States operate is more in keeping with the pluralist model of democracy than the majoritarian model. Our parties are not the basic mechanism through which citizens control their government; instead, they function as two giant interest groups. The parties' interests lie in electing and reelecting their candidates, in enjoying the benefits of public office. Except in extreme cases, the parties care little about the positions or ideologies favored by their candidates for Congress and statewide offices.

Some scholars believe that stronger parties would strengthen democratic government, even if they could not meet all the requirements of the responsible party model. Our parties already perform valuable functions in structuring the vote along partisan lines and in proposing alternative government policies, but stronger parties might also be able to play a more important role in coordinating government policies after elections. At present, the decentralized nature of the nominating process and of campaigning for office offers many opportunities for organized groups outside the party to identify and back candidates who favor their interests. Although this is in keeping with pluralist theory, it is certain to frustrate majority interests on occasion.

Summary

Political parties perform four important functions in a political system: nominating candidates, structuring the voting choice, proposing alternative government programs, and coordinating the activities of government officials. Political parties have been performing these functions longer in the United States than in any other country. The Democratic party, founded in 1828, is the world's oldest political party. When the Republican party emerged as a major party after the 1856 election, our present two-party system emerged—the oldest party system in the world.

America's two-party system has experienced three critical elections, each of which realigned the electorate for years and affected the party balance in government. The election of 1860 established the Republicans as the major party in the North and the Democrats as the dominant party in the South. The critical election of 1896 strengthened the link between the Republican party and business interests in the heavily populated Northeast and Midwest, and produced a surge in voter support that made the Republicans the majority party nationally for more than three decades. The Great Depression produced conditions that transformed the

Democrats into the majority party in the critical election of 1932. Until the Republicans won both houses in the 1994 election, the Democrats enjoyed almost uninterrupted control of Congress for six decades.

Minor parties have not enjoyed much electoral success in America, although they have contributed ideas to the Democratic and Republican platforms. The two-party system is perpetuated in the United States because of the nature of our electoral system and by the political socialization process, which results in most Americans identifying with either the Democratic or the Republican party. The federal system of government has also helped the Democrats and Republicans survive major national defeats by sustaining them with electoral victories at the state level. The pattern of party identification has been changing in recent years: As more people are becoming independents and Republicans, the number of Democratic identifiers is dropping. Still, Democrats consistently outnumber Republicans, and together the two parties far outnumber independents.

The two major parties differ in their ideological orientations. Democratic identifiers and activists are more likely to describe themselves as liberal; Republican identifiers and activists tend to be conservative. The 1996 Democratic party platform showed a more liberal orientation by stressing equality over freedom; the Republican platform was more conservative, concentrating on freedom but also emphasizing the importance of restoring social order. Organizationally, the Republicans have recently become the stronger party at both the national and state levels, and both parties are showing signs of resurgence. Nevertheless, both parties are still very decentralized compared with parties in other countries.

Campaigning has evolved from a party-centered to a candidate-centered process. The successful candidate for public office usually must campaign first to win the party nomination, then to win the general election. A major factor in the decentralization of American parties is their reliance on primary elections to nominate candidates. Democratic and Republican nominations for president are no longer actually decided in the parties' national conventions but are determined in advance through the complex process of selecting delegates pledged to particular candidates. Although candidates cannot win the nomination unless they have broad support within the party, the winners can legitimately say that they captured the nomination through their own efforts and that they owe little to the party organization.

The need to win a majority of votes in the electoral college structures presidential elections. Although a candidate can win a majority of the popular vote but lose in the electoral college, that has not happened in more than one hundred years. In fact, the electoral college typically magnifies the victory margin of the winning candidate. Since World War II, Republicans have usually won the presidency, while Democrats have usually controlled Congress; such divided government has interfered with party control of government.

In the general election, candidates usually retain the same staffs that helped them win the nomination. The dynamics of campaign financing also force candidates to rely mainly on their own resources or—in the case of presidential elections—on public funds. Party organizations now often contribute money to congressional candidates, but the candidates must raise most of the money themselves. Money is essential in running a modern campaign for major office—for conducting polls and advertising the candidate's name, qualifications, and positions on issues through the media. Candidates seek free news coverage whenever possible, but most must rely on paid advertising to get their messages across. Ironically, voters also get most of their campaign information from advertisements. The trend in recent years has been toward negative advertising.

Voting choice is influenced by party identification, candidates' attributes, and policy positions. Party identification is still the most important long-term factor in shaping the voting decision.

Traditionally, major American political parties have followed the model of responsible party government to the extent that they formulate different platforms and tend to translate their platform positions into government policy if elected to power. However, the way that nominations, campaigns, and elections are conducted in America is out of keeping with the ideals of responsible party government that fit the majoritarian model of democracy. In particular, campaigns and elections do not function to link parties strongly to voters as the model posits. The Republicans' Contract with America, however, fulfilled some features of the responsible party model. American parties are better suited to the pluralist model of democracy, which sees them as major interest groups competing with lesser groups to further their own interests. At least political parties aspire to the noble goal of representing the needs and wants of most of the people. As we see in the next chapter, interest groups do not even pretend as much.

Key Terms

political party	responsible party government
nomination	election campaign
political system	primary election
critical election	closed primary
electoral realignment	open primary
electoral dealignment	blanket primary
majority representation	presidential primary
proportional representation	local caucus
party identification	general election
party platform	straight ticket
national convention	split ticket
national committee	first-past-the-post election
party conference	open election
congressional campaign committee	Federal Election Commission (FEC)
party machine	

Selected Readings

Ansolabehere, Stephen, and Shanto Iyengar. *Going Negative: How Political Advertisements Shrink and Polarize the Electorate.* New York: Free Press, 1995. The subtitle describes the book's thesis, but in addition the book contends that political advertising also conveys useful information to citizens about politics.

Beck, Paul Allen. *Party Politics in America,* 8th ed. New York: HarperCollins, 1996. The eighth edition of a comprehensive textbook on political parties.

Mayer, William G., ed. *In Pursuit of the White House: How We Choose Our Presidential Nominees.* Chatham, N.J.: Chatham House, 1996. A valuable set of studies, with plenty of data, on the nomination process, including the problems facing third-party candidates.

Patterson, Thomas E. *Out of Order.* New York: Knopf, 1993. This study of mass media's influence in presidential elections from 1960 to 1992 argues that media, and particularly television, have replaced parties in choosing presidential candidates, with woeful results.

Schattschneider, E. E. *Party Government.* New York: Holt, 1942. A clear and powerful argument for the central role of political parties in a democracy according to the model of responsible party government; a classic book in political science.

Shea, Daniel M., and John C. Green, eds., *The State of the Parties: The Changing Role of Contemporary American Parties,* 2nd ed. Lanham, Md.: Rowman & Littlefield, 1996. A valuable collection of empirical studies and theoretical analyses of American parties at the national and state levels. The articles document the increased activity of party organizations in election campaigns.

Thurber, James A., and Candice J. Nelson, eds. *Campaigns and Elections: American Style.* Boulder, Colo.: Westview Press, 1995. Written by academics and campaign practitioners, these studies treat campaign strategy, the use of money and media, opinion polls, and—even—ethics.

Wattenberg, Martin P. *The Decline of American Political Parties, 1952–1994.* Cambridge, Mass.: Harvard University Press, 1996. Argues that the American electorate has lessened its attachment to parties because people now believe that candidates, not parties, solve government problems.

World Wide Web Resources

Party Politics. This new international journal is devoted to the study of political parties, party systems, and political organizations in the United States and elsewhere. It publishes studies on the analysis of political parties, including their historical development, structure, policy programs, ideology, and electoral and campaign strategies.
<www.polisci.nwu.edu:8000/>

Democratic National Committee. The DNC home page describes the party's structure, bylaws, platform, and activities.

Republican Main Street. The RNC employs a glitzy "street scene" for the entrance to its home page, which includes the same kinds of information as the Democrats offer but a bit more of everything.

Campaigns & Elections Online. This is the site for the magazine *Campaigns & Elections,* which reports on current campaigns and campaign strategy, methods, products, and so on.

AllPolitics. Time and CNN (both owned by Time-Warner) join forces to cover issues, polls, elections, Congress, and virtually everything else in national politics.

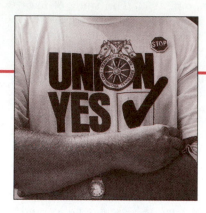

7

Interest Groups

Its death was slow and painful. The cause: a thousand cuts followed by a hemorrhage. Sadly, when the BTU tax was finally buried, no one would claim to be the parent of the proposal. Just about everyone wanted to take credit for the murder though.

The BTU proposal—a tax levied on the amount of heat in an energy source as measured by British thermal units (BTUs)—was part of President Bill Clinton's deficit reduction package introduced at the beginning of his administration in the winter of 1993. Using a combination of spending cuts and tax increases, the deficit reduction proposal was designed to cut the deficit in half within five years.

A broad-based energy tax does not affect everyone the same way. Industries that use a lot of energy are going to pay more. People who live in some areas of the country are going to be affected more because of their dependence on a particular fuel. Interest groups seized on the inequities they saw in the BTU tax and pressed Congress to exempt them. Congress cooperated.

The bill was first taken up in the House, and the farm lobby was fast off the mark in getting the House to reduce the tax on diesel fuel used by tractors. The steel industry got an exemption for metallurgical coal, used in great quantities in their mills. Aluminum producers and chlorine producers argued that because their manufacturing processes use so much energy, they needed a reduction in their BTU tax, too. The administration agreed. Firms that made products for the export market were upset because an energy tax would make their goods more expensive on the world market. The administration promised a rebate on the tax for energy-intensive export products, such as chemicals. The oil lobby got an exemption for fuel used by ships and jets.

By the time the legislation passed the House, interest groups had won so many exemptions that it was hard for most people to understand what the BTU tax still covered. The *New York Times* described the bill as "one of the most exemption-loaded, head-scratchingly complicated, brow-furrowing revenue raisers in history."[1] What was left of the tax came under immediate attack in the Senate. Energy producers, especially oil companies, asked their senators to try to block the tax. With a narrow majority in the Senate, the administration could not afford many defections, because all the Republicans were promising to vote against the bill, no matter what was in it. With the BTU proposal already so badly shredded by all the exemptions, it was hardly worth fighting for. The Clinton administration quickly threw in the towel, promising to introduce another tax instead.[2] The bill that finally passed Congress included a modest increase in the tax on gasoline.

Although Americans tell pollsters that they believe strongly in deficit reduction, the BTU tax was a clear example of pluralism triumphing over majoritarianism. The majority wants the deficit reduced, but no majority favors any particular method of paring down it down. People may grudgingly accept the need for new taxes in any deficit reduction package, but they are not going to demand that their representatives and senators vote for a tax when a specific deficit reduction plan comes before Congress. At the same time, interest groups push hard for exemptions, because their members are intensely upset about some aspect of the tax plan.

In this chapter, we look at the central dynamic of pluralist democracy: the interaction of interest groups and government. In analyzing the process by which interest groups and lobbyists come to speak on behalf of different groups, we focus on a number of questions. How do interest groups form? Who do they represent? What tactics do they use to convince policymakers that their views are best for the nation? Is the interest group system biased to favor certain types of people? If so, what are the consequences?

Interest Groups and the American Political Tradition

An **interest group** is an organized body of individuals who share some political goals and try to influence public policy decisions. Among the most prominent interest groups in the United States are the AFL-CIO (representing labor union members), the American Farm Bureau Federation (representing farmers), the Business Roundtable (representing big business), and Common Cause (representing citizens concerned with reforming government). Interest groups are also called **lobbies**, and their representatives are referred to as **lobbyists**.

Interest Groups: Good or Evil?

A recurring debate in American politics concerns the role of interest groups in a democratic society. Are interest groups a threat to the well-being of the political system, or do they contribute to its proper functioning? Alexis de Tocqueville, a French visitor to the United States in the early nineteenth century, marveled at the array of organizations he found, and later wrote that "Americans of all ages, all conditions, and all dispositions, constantly form associations."[3] Tocqueville was suggesting that the ease with which we form organizations reflects a strong democratic culture.

Yet, other early observers were concerned about the consequences of interest group politics. Writing in the *Federalist* papers, James Madison warned of the dangers of "factions," the major divisions in American society. In *Federalist No. 10*, written in 1787, Madison said that it was inevitable that substantial differences would develop between factions, and that each faction would try to persuade government to adopt policies that favored it at the expense of others.[4]

But Madison argued against trying to suppress factions. He concluded that factions can be eliminated only by removing our freedoms: because "Liberty is to faction what air is to fire."[5] Instead, Madison suggested that relief from the self-interested advocacy of factions should come only through controlling the effects of that advocacy. This relief would be provided by a democratic republic in which government would mediate between opposing factions. The size and diversity of the nation as well as the structure of government would also ensure that even a majority faction could never come to suppress the rights of others.[6]

How we judge interest groups—"good" or "evil"—may depend on how strongly we are committed to freedom or equality (see Chapter 1). A survey of the American public showed that almost two-thirds of those polled regarded lobbying as a threat to American democracy.[7] Yet, as we will demonstrate later, in recent years interest groups have enjoyed unparalleled growth. Apparently, we distrust interest groups as a whole, but we like those that speak on our behalf.

The Roles of Interest Groups

The "evil" side of interest group politics is all too apparent. Each group pushes its own selfish interests, which, despite the group's claims to the contrary, are not always in the best interest of other Americans. The "good" side of interest group advocacy may not be as clear. How do the actions of interest groups benefit our political system?[8]

Representation   Interest groups represent people before their government. Just as a member of Congress represents a particular constituency, so does a lobbyist. A lobbyist for the National Association of Broadcasters, for example, speaks for the interests of radio and television broadcasters when Congress or a government agency is considering a relevant policy decision.

Whatever the political interest—the cement industry, social security, endangered species—it is helpful to have an active lobby operating in Washington. Members of Congress represent a multitude of interests, some of them conflicting, from their own districts and states. Government administrators, too, are pulled in different directions and have their own policy preferences. Interest groups articulate their members' concerns, presenting them directly and forcefully in the political process (see Politics in a Changing America 7.1).

Participation   Interest groups are also vehicles for political participation. They provide a means by which like-minded citizens can pool their resources and channel their energies into collective political action. One farmer fighting against a new pesticide proposal in Congress probably will not get very far, but

Politics in a Changing America 7.1

A Political Voice for Christians

New political movements organized in recent years represent diverse interests and constituencies. What their members have in common, however, is a feeling of being marginalized by our political system. Members share a belief that unless they are highly mobilized and aggressive in pursuing their political objectives, policymakers will ignore their concerns. This is certainly the attitude of fundamentalists—Christians whose religious beliefs are based on a literal interpretation of the Bible.

Fundamentalist Christians believe that modern society has turned away from basic moral principles, leading to serious social problems. In their eyes, liberal and moderate politicians have mistakenly tried to solve these problems with expensive, wasteful, and counterproductive social programs. Christian fundamentalists feel that what is needed instead is a return to strong family values.

Many groups claim to represent fundamentalists in the political arena, but the Christian Coalition plays a central leadership role. Based in Virginia, this conservative group is closely allied with the Reverend Pat Robertson. Robertson, who ran unsuccessfully for the Republican presidential nomination in 1988, is probably best known for his TV show, "The 700 Club," which is shown around the country on the Christian Broadcasting Network. The Christian Coalition has roughly 1.6 million members and an annual budget in excess of $25 million.

Over the years the issues that have most animated the Christian Coalition include abortion, homosexuality, prayer in school, and the decline of the nuclear family. In the past few years, however, Christian Coalition strategist Ralph Reed has led the group in a more secular direction. After the Republicans captured the Congress in the 1994 elections, Reed was in an excellent position to bargain with the House and Senate leadership over the GOP's legislative priorities. Christian Coalition volunteers had fueled many of the newly elected Republicans' campaigns, including distributing 33 million voter guides at churches on the Sunday prior to the election.

Despite the GOP's debt to the Christian Coalition, Reed opted to make the group's highest legislative priority the passage of the House Republicans' "Contract with America." The Christian Coalition spent $1 million on direct mail, ads, and phone calls on behalf of the Contract with America, an extraordinary contribution by any standards. Reed said of all the Contract proposals, the Christian Coalition was most interested in enactment of the $500-per-child tax credit. Although the tax credit has no obvious connection to Christian theology, the Christian Coalition's leadership views it as a critical step in supporting the American family. Reed's strategy seemed oriented toward making the organization appear more mainstream and having the Republicans in Congress regard it as a team player. Still, one wonders if Reed sold the Christian Coalition a bit short. After the House disposed of all the items of the Contract with America, Reed unveiled the Christian Coalition's "Contract with the American Family." This ten-point program

(continued)

Politics in a Changing America 7.1 (continued)

was a one-day story; this second contract quickly sank from sight. All in all, the Christian Coalition didn't get much legislative return on its campaign investment.

Many liberals are antagonistic to the Christian Coalition and other such groups, not simply because they hold competing political views but also because they believe that the Christian right is trying to impose its particular brand of religion on the rest of the country. Yet, in America political activism can also be found in black churches, synagogues, mainline Protestant congregations, and Catholic parishes. Nevertheless, it is the Christian conservatives that are the best organized of all the religious sects in the United States. Also, churches embracing the beliefs of the Christian right are the most rapidly growing denominations in the country. Pentecostals, an evangelical denomination whose followers are generally sympathetic to Christian conservatism, grew in membership from about 1.9 million in 1960 to 9.9 million in 1990, an increase of 423 percent.

What is especially impressive about the Christian Coalition and other groups associated with the religious right is their success in involving rank-and-file citizens in politics and government. Former Senator Nancy Kassebaum of Kansas says of the religious right, "It's a voice that in many ways comes from people who feel that they've never been part of the process." As many Christians who dislike the religious right point out, the Christian Coalition does not speak for all Christians. But for those Christians it does represent, the Christian Coalition is a powerful and passionate advocate.

thousands of farmers united in an organization stand a much better chance of getting policymakers to consider their needs.

Education   As part of their efforts at lobbying and increasing their membership, interest groups help educate their members, the public at large, and government officials.

After Congress proposed significant cutbacks in research money for universities in 1995, the schools and their Washington lobbies swung into action. Members of Congress were told about a study done by the Bank of Boston that demonstrated that three hundred thousand people in Massachusetts were employed by companies utilizing technology and other resources developed by Massachusetts Institute of Technology researchers. The point was clear: Cut research funding, and you will damage your local economy's chance to grow.[9] To gain the attention of the policymakers they are trying to educate, interest groups need to provide them with information that is not easily obtained from other sources.[10]

Agenda Building   In a related role, interest groups bring new issues into the political limelight through a process called **agenda building**. American society has many problem areas, but public officials are not addressing all of them. Through their advocacy, interest groups make the government aware of problems, then try to see to it that something is done to solve them. Women's groups have played a key role in gaining attention for problems—such as unequal pay for women doing similar jobs as men—that were being systematically ignored.[11]

Program Monitoring   Finally, interest groups engage in **program monitoring**. Lobbies follow government programs that are important to their constituents, keeping abreast of developments in Washington and in the communities where the policies are implemented. When a program is not operating as it should, concerned interest groups push administrators to resolve them in ways that promote the group's goals. They draw attention to agency officials' transgressions and even file suit to stop actions they consider unlawful.

Interest groups do, then, play some positive roles in their pursuit of self-interest. But we should not assume that the positive side of interest groups neatly balances the negative. Questions remain about the overall influence of interest groups on public policymaking. Most important are the effects of interest group advocacy being controlled, as Madison believed they should be?

How Interest Groups Form

Do some people form interest groups more easily than others? Are some factions represented while others are not? Pluralists assume that when a political issue arises, interest groups with relevant policy concerns begin to lobby. Policy conflicts are ultimately resolved through bargaining and negotiation between the involved organizations and the government. Unlike Madison, who dwelled on the potential for harm by factions, pluralists believe interest groups are a good thing, that they further democracy by broadening representation within the system.

An important part of pluralism is the belief that new interest groups form as a matter of course when the need arises. David Truman outlines this idea in his classic work *The Governmental Process*.[12] He says that when individuals are threatened by change, they band together in an interest group. For example, if government threatens to regulate a particular industry, the firms that compose that industry will start a trade association to protect their financial well-being. Truman sees a direct cause-and-effect relationship in all of this: Existing groups stand in equilibrium until some type of disturbance (such as falling wages or declining farm prices) forces new groups to form.

Truman's disturbance theory paints an idealized portrait of interest group politics in America. In real life, people do not automatically organize when they are adversely affected by some disturbance. A good example of this "nonorganization" can be found in Herbert Gans's book *The Urban Villagers*.[13] Gans, a sociologist, moved into the West End, a low-income neighborhood in Boston, during the late 1950s. The neighborhood had been targeted for urban redevelopment. This meant that the people living there—primarily poor Italian-Americans who very much liked their neighborhood—would have to move. The people of the West End barely put up a fight to save their neighborhood. They started an organization, but it attracted little support. Residents remained unorganized; soon they were moved and buildings were demolished.

Disturbance theory clearly fails to explain what happened (or didn't happen) in Boston's West End. An adverse condition or change does not automatically mean that an interest group will form. What, then, is the missing ingredient? Political scientist Robert Salisbury says that the quality of interest group leadership may be the crucial factor.[14]

Interest Group Entrepreneurs

Salisbury likens the role of an interest group leader to that of an entrepreneur in the business world. An entrepreneur is someone who starts new enterprises, usually at considerable personal financial risk. Salisbury says that an **interest group entrepreneur** or organizer, succeeds or fails for many of the same reasons a business entrepreneur succeeds or fails. The interest group entrepreneur must have something attractive to "market" in order to convince people to join.[15] Potential members must be persuaded that the benefits of joining outweigh the costs.

The development of the United Farm Workers Union shows the importance of leadership in the formation of an interest group. This union is made up of men and women who pick crops in California and other parts of the country. The pickers are predominantly poor, uneducated Mexican-Americans.

Throughout the twentieth century, various unions tried to organize the pickers. Yet for many reasons—including distrust of union organizers, intimidation by employers, and lack of money to pay union dues—all had failed. Then, in 1962, the late Cesar Chavez, a poor Mexican-American, began to crisscross the central valley of California, talking to workers and planting the idea of a union.

After a strike against grape growers failed in 1965, Chavez changed his tactics of trying to build a stronger union merely by recruiting a larger membership. Copying the civil rights movement, Chavez and his followers marched 250 miles to the state capitol in Sacramento to demand help from the governor. This march and other nonviolent tactics began to draw sympathy from people who had no direct involvement in farming.

With his stature increased by that support, Chavez called for a boycott, and a small but significant number of Americans stopped buying grapes. The growers, who had bitterly fought the union, were finally hurt economically. Under this and other economic pressures, they eventually agreed to recognize and bargain with the United Farm Workers Union.

Who Is Being Organized?

Cesar Chavez is a good example of the importance of leadership in the formation of a new interest group. But another important element is at work in the formation of interest groups. The residents of Boston's West End and the farm workers in California were poor, uneducated or undereducated, and politically inexperienced—factors that made it extremely difficult to organize them into interest groups. If they had been well-to-do, educated, and politically experienced, they probably would have banded together immediately. People who have money, are educated, and know how the system operates are more confident that their actions can make a difference (see Figure 7.1).

Every existing interest group has its own history, but the three variables just discussed can help explain why groups may or may not become fully organized. First, an adverse change or disturbance can contribute to people's awareness that they need political representation. However, this alone does not ensure that an organization will form, and organizations have formed in the absence of a disturbance. Second, the quality of leadership is critical in the organization of interest groups. Finally, the higher the socioeconomic level of potential members, the more likely they are to know the value of interest groups and to participate in politics by joining them.

The question that remains, then, is *how well* are various opposing interests represented. Or, in terms of Madison's premise in *Federalist* No. 10, are the effects of faction—in this case, the advantages of the wealthy and well educated—being controlled? Before we can answer this question, we need to turn our attention to the resources available to interest groups.

Interest Group Resources

The strengths, capabilities, and influence of an interest group depend in large part on its resources. A group's most significant resources are its members, lobbyists, and money, including funds that can be contributed to political candidates. The sheer quantity of a group's resources is important, and so is the wisdom with which its resources are used.

Members

One of the most valuable resources an interest group can have is a large, politically active membership. If a lobbyist is trying to persuade a legislator to support a particular bill, having a large group of members who live in the legislator's home district or state is tremendously helpful. A legislator who has not already taken a firm position on a bill might be swayed by the knowledge that voters back home are kept informed by interest groups of his or her votes on key issues.

Members give an organization not only the political muscle to influence policy but also financial resources. The more money an organization can collect through dues and contributions, the more people it can hire to lobby government officials and monitor the policymaking process. Greater resources also allow the organization to communicate with its members more and to inform them better. And funding helps the group maintain its membership and attract new members.

FIGURE 7.1 **Social Class and Interest Group Membership**

Membership in interest groups is clearly linked to social class. The higher their total family income, the more likely it is that individuals will belong to at least one political interest group. The data here come from a survey of citizens in five American cities (Birmingham, Alabama; Dayton, Ohio; Portland, Oregon; St. Paul, Minnesota; and San Antonio, Texas). (Source: Based on Jeffrey M. Berry, Kent E. Portney, and Ken Thomson, The Rebirth of Urban Democracy *(Washington, D.C.: Brookings Institution, 1993). Used with permission.)*

Maintaining Membership   To keep the members it already has, an organization must persuade them that it is doing a good job in its advocacy. Most lobbies use a newsletter to keep members apprised of developments in government that relate to issues of concern to them and to inform them of the role the organization is playing in protecting their interests.

Business, professional, and labor associations generally have an easier time holding on to members than do citizen groups—groups whose basis of organization is a concern for issues not directly related to their members' jobs. In many companies, corporate membership in a trade group constitutes only a minor business expense. Labor unions are helped in states that require workers to affiliate with the union that is the bargaining agent with their employer. On the other hand, citizen groups base their appeal on members' ideological sentiments. These groups face a difficult challenge: issues can blow hot and cold, and a particularly hot issue one year may not hold the same interest to citizens the next.

Attracting New Members   All membership groups are constantly looking for new members to expand their resources and clout. Groups that rely on ideological appeals have a special problem, because the competition in most policy areas is intense. People concerned about the environment, for example, can join a seemingly infinite number of local, state, and national groups that lobby on environmental issues.

One common method of attracting new members is *direct mail*—letters sent to a selected audience to promote the organization and appeal for contributions. The main drawbacks to direct mail are its expense and low rate of return.

The Free-Rider Problem   The need for aggressive marketing by interest groups suggests that getting people who sympathize with a group's goals actually to support it with their contributions is difficult. Economists call this difficulty the **free-rider problem**, but we might call it, more colloquially, the "let-George-do-it" problem.[16] Funding for public television stations illustrates this dilemma. Only a fraction of those who watch public television contribute on a regular basis. Why? Because the free rider has the same access to public television as the contributor.

The same problem crops up for interest groups. When a lobbying group wins benefits, those benefits are not restricted to the members of the organization. For instance, if the American Business Conference wins a tax concession from Congress for capital expenditures, all businesses that fall within the provisions of the law can take advantage of the tax break. Thus, many business executives might not support their firm's joining the American Business Conference, even though they might benefit from the group's efforts; they prefer instead to let others shoulder the financial burden.

The free-rider problem increases the difficulty of attracting paying members. Nevertheless, millions of Americans contribute to interest groups because they are concerned about an issue or feel a responsibility to help organizations that work on their behalf. Also, many organizations offer membership benefits that have nothing to do with politics or lobbying. Business **trade associations**, for example, are a source of information about industry trends and effective management practices; they organize conventions at which members can learn, socialize, and occasionally find new customers or suppliers.

Lobbyists

Part of the money raised by interest groups is used to pay lobbyists, who represent the organizations before the government. Lobbyists make sure that people in government know what their members want and that their organizations know what the government is doing.[17]

Lobbyists can be full-time employees of their organization or employees of public relations or law firms who are hired on retainer. When hiring a lobbyist, an interest group looks for someone who knows his or her way around Washington. Lobbyists are valued for their experience and their knowledge of how government operates. Often they are people who have served in the legislative or executive branches, people who have first-hand experience with government.

Many lobbyists have law degrees and find their legal backgrounds useful in bargaining and negotiating over laws and regulations. Because of their location, many Washington law firms are drawn into lobbying. Corporations without their own Washington offices rely heavily on law firms to lobby for them before the national government.

The most common image of a lobbyist is that of someone who spends most of his or her time trying to convince a legislator or administrator to back a certain policy. The stereotype of lobbyists also portrays them as people of dubious ethics. However, the lobbyist's primary job is not to trade on favors or campaign contributions but to pass on information to policymakers. Lobbyists provide government officials and their staffs with a constant flow of data that support their organizations' policy goals. Lobbyists also try to build a compelling case for their goals, showing that the "facts" dictate that a particular change be made or avoided. What lobbyists are really trying to do, of course, is to convince policymakers that their data deserve more attention and are more accurate than those presented by other lobbyists.

Political Action Committees

One of the organizational resources that can make a lobbyist's job easier is a **political action committee (PAC)**. PACs pool campaign contributions from group members and donate those funds to candidates for political office. Under federal law, a PAC can give as much as $5,000 to a candidate for Congress for each separate election. A change in campaign finance law in 1974 led to a rapid increase in the number of PACs. The greatest growth came from corporations, most of which had been legally prohibited from operating PACs. There was also rapid growth in the number of nonconnected PACs, largely ideological groups that have no parent lobbying organization and are formed solely for the purpose of raising and channeling campaign funds. (Thus a PAC can be the campaign-wing affiliate of an existing interest group or a wholly independent, unaffiliated group.) (See Figure 7.2.)

Why do interest groups form PACs? The chief executive officer of one manufacturing company said his corporation had a PAC because "the PAC gives you access. It makes you a player."[18] Members of Congress and their staffers generally are eager to meet with representatives of their constituencies, but their time is limited. However, a member of Congress or staffer would find it difficult to turn down a lobbyist's request for a meeting if the PAC of the lobbyist's organization had made a significant campaign contribution in the last election.

Typically, PACs, like most other interest groups, are highly pragmatic organizations; pushing a particular political philosophy takes second place to achieving immediate policy goals. As a group, corporate PACs gave 76.4 percent of their contributions to incumbent members of Congress—many of them liberal and moderate Democrats—during the 1993–1994 election cycle.[19] After the Republicans' capture of Congress in 1994, corporations and other business PACs could target more of their money to conservative Republicans.

The role of PACs in financing congressional campaigns has become the most controversial aspect of interest group politics. Critics charge that members of Congress cannot help but be influenced by the PAC contributions they receive.

Political scientists have not been able to document any consistent link between campaign donations and the way members of Congress vote on the floor of the House and Senate. However, some recent, sophisticated research shows that PACs have an advantage in the committee process and appear to gain influence because of the additional access they receive.[20]

Whatever the research shows, it is clear that the American public sees PACs as a means of securing privileges for those sectors of society with the resources

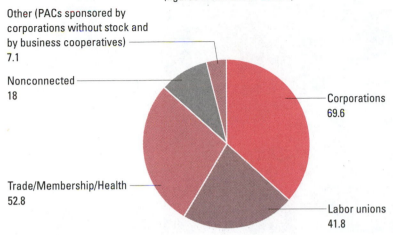

PAC CONTRIBUTIONS, 1993–1994
(figures in millions of dollars)

Other (PACs sponsored by corporations without stock and by business cooperatives) 7.1

Nonconnected 18

Corporations 69.6

Trade/Membership/Health 52.8

Labor unions 41.8

FIGURE 7.2   PACs Americana
Most PAC money comes from corporations, business trade groups, and professional associations. Labor unions contribute significantly as well. A much smaller proportion of all PAC contributions comes from citizen PACs, who form the bulk of the "nonconnected" category. Americans at the lower end of the economic spectrum are left out entirely. As Bob Dole once put it, "There aren't any Poor PACs or Food Stamp PACs or Nutrition PACs or Medicare PACs." (Source: "PAC Activity in 1994 Elections Remains at 1992 Levels," Federal Election Commission, March 31, 1995, p. 3.)

to purchase additional access to Congress. But in a democracy, influence should not be a function of money; some citizens have little to give, yet their interests need to be protected. From this perspective, the issue is political equality.

Strong arguments can be made for retaining PACs. They offer a means for people to participate in the political system. They allow small givers to pool their resources and to fight the feeling that one person cannot make a difference. Finally, PAC defenders also point out that prohibiting PACs would amount to a restriction on the freedom of political expression. (We take up the question of PACs and potential reforms at the end of this chapter.)

Lobbying Tactics

Keep in mind that lobbying extends beyond the legislative branch. Groups can seek help from the courts and administrative agencies as well as from Congress. Moreover, interest groups may have to shift their focus from one branch of government to another. After a bill becomes a law, for example, a group that lobbied for the legislation will probably try to influence the administrative agency responsible for implementing the new law. Some policy decisions are left unresolved by legislation and are settled through regulations.

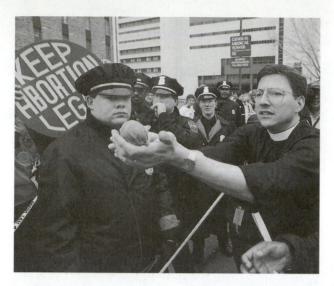

Lobbying to the Extreme
Some interest groups feel that policymakers are generally opposed or indifferent to their cause and that there is little to be gained from conventional lobbying. Instead, they use unusual and even extreme tactics to draw media attention to their side of an issue. In this photo, the Reverend Rob Schenk of Operation Rescue holds up an aborted fetus outside a Buffalo, New York, abortion clinic.

Lobbies want to make sure regulatory decisions are as close to the group's preferences as possible.

We discuss three types of lobbying tactics here: those aimed at policymakers and implemented by interest group representatives (direct lobbying); those that involve group members (grassroots lobbying); and those directed toward the public (information campaigns). We also examine the use of new high-tech lobbying tactics as well as cooperative efforts of interest groups to influence government through coalitions.

Direct Lobbying

Direct lobbying relies on personal contact with policymakers. One survey of Washington lobbyists showed that 98 percent use direct contact with government officials to express their group's views.[21] This interaction takes place when a lobbyist meets with a member of Congress, an agency official, or a staff member. In their meetings, lobbyists usually convey their arguments by providing data about a specific issue. If a lobbyist from, for example, a chamber of commerce meets with a member of Congress about a bill the organization backs, the lobbyist does not say (or even suggest), "Vote for this bill, or our people in the district will vote against you in the next election." Instead, the lobbyist might say, "If this bill is passed, we're going to see hundreds of new jobs created back home." The representative has no trouble at all figuring out that a vote for the bill can help in the next election.

Personal lobbying is a day-in, day-out process. Lobbyists must maintain contact with congressional and agency staffers, constantly providing them with pertinent data. One lobbyist described his strategy in personal meetings with policymakers as rather simple and straightforward: "Providing information is the most effective tool. People begin to rely on you."[22]

A tactic related to direct lobbying is testifying at committee hearings when a bill is before Congress. This tactic allows the interest group to put its views on record and to make them widely known when the hearing testimony is published. Although testifying is one of the most visible parts of lobbying, it is generally considered window dressing. Most lobbyists believe that testimony usually does little by itself to persuade members of Congress.

Another direct but somewhat different approach is legal advocacy. Using this tactic, a group tries to achieve its policy goals through litigation. Claiming some violation of law, a group will file a lawsuit and ask that a judge make a ruling that will benefit the organization. When the Food and Drug Administration (FDA) proposed regulations aimed at reducing smoking by minors, cigarette manufacturers counterattacked with a lawsuit filed in federal court. The tobacco industry believed the FDA had exceeded its authority, and it was concerned the agency would take further steps to restrict smoking.[23]

Grassroots Lobbying

Grassroots lobbying involves an interest group's rank-and-file members and may also include people outside the organization who sympathize with its goals. Grassroots tactics, such as letter-writing campaigns and protests, are often used in conjunction with direct lobbying by Washington representatives. Policymakers are more concerned about what a lobbyist says when they know that constituents are really watching their decisions.

If people in government seem unresponsive to conventional lobbying tactics, a group might resort to some form of political protest. A protest or demonstration, such as picketing or marching, is designed to attract media attention to an issue. The main drawback to protesting is that policymaking is a long-term, incremental process, and a demonstration is only short-lived. It is difficult to sustain anger and activism among group supporters—to keep large numbers of people involved in protest after protest. A notable exception was the civil rights demonstrations of the 1960s, which were sustained over a long period. The protests were a major factor in stirring public opinion, which in turn hastened the passage of the Civil Rights Act of 1964 and the Voting Rights Act of 1965.

Information Campaigns

Interest groups generally feel that public backing adds strength to their lobbying efforts. They believe that they will get that backing if they can only make the public aware of their position and the evidence supporting it. To this end, interest groups launch **information campaigns**, organized efforts to gain public backing by bringing group views to the public's attention. Various means are used. Some are directed at the larger public, others at smaller audiences with longstanding interest in an issue.

Public relations is one information-campaign tactic. A public relations campaign might involve sending speakers to meetings in various parts of the country, producing pamphlets and handouts, or taking out newspaper advertising. During the fight over the Clinton administration's health care reform proposal during 1993 and 1994, the Health Insurance Association of America (HIAA) launched a television ad campaign designed to turn public opinion against the plan. These ads featured a fictional couple named Harry and Louise, who in a series of spots talked conversationally about the plan and pointed out its critical flaws. However, given the costs of televised advertising and the difficulty of truly swaying public opinion through them, it's not surprising that few groups rely on paid TV advertising as their primary weapon in advocacy campaigns.

Sponsoring research is another way interest groups press their cases. When a group believes that evidence has not been fully developed in a certain area, it may commission research on the subject. For example, when the liberal advocacy group, the Environmental Working Group, wanted to try to reduce agriculture-related pollution, it initiated tests of water quality in twenty-nine cities located near concentrations of corn farms. The study received a modest amount of press coverage.[24]

High-Tech Lobbying

In recent years, Washington lobbies have added many high-tech tactics to their arsenals. Using such resources as direct mail, e-mail, faxes, polling, and the World Wide Web, lobbies have tried to find ways to expand their reach and increase their impact. The most conspicuous effect of high-tech lobbying is that it speeds up the political process. Using electronic communication (e-mail, faxes), groups can quickly mobilize their constituents, who will in turn quickly contact policymakers about pending decisions. However, it is important to recognize that electronic lobbying isn't all that different from old-fashioned lobbying. Before the computer, interest groups used to telephone their activists and ask them to write letters to policymakers. That approach may have been a little slower, but it still let those in Washington know what their constituents back home wanted.

Although high-tech lobbying tactics facilitate direct communication between citizens and policymakers, which is to be applauded, there is a down side as well. Technology is expensive, so the introduction of such tactics tends to favor those who are already well represented in the political process.[25]

Coalition Building

A final aspect of lobbying strategy is **coalition building**, in which several organizations band together for the purpose of lobbying. Such joint efforts conserve or make more effective use of the resources of groups with similar views. Most coalitions are informal, ad hoc arrangements that exist only for the purpose of lobbying on a single issue.

Coalitions form most often among groups that work in the same policy area and have similar constituencies, such as environmental groups or feminist groups. Yet, coalitions often extend beyond organizations with similar constituencies and similar outlooks. Some business groups support the same goals as environmental lobbies, because it is in their self-interest. For example, companies that are in the business of cleaning up toxic waste sites have worked with environmental groups.[26]

Is the System Biased?

As we noted in Chapter 1, our political system is more pluralist than majoritarian. Policymaking is determined more by the interaction of groups with government than by elections.

How, then, do we determine whether policy decisions in a pluralist system are fair? There is no precisely agreed-upon formula, but most people would agree with the following two simple notions. First, all significant interests in the population should be adequately represented by lobbying groups. Second, government should listen to the views of all major interests as it develops policy. We should also recognize that elections inject some of the benefits of majoritarianism into our system, because the party that wins an election will have more say in the making of public policy than its opponent.

Membership Patterns

Those who work in business or in a profession, those with a high level of education, and those with high incomes (recall Figure 7.1) are the most likely to belong to interest groups. Even middle-income people are much more likely to join interest groups than those who are poor.

For example, one-third of those receiving veterans' benefits belong to an organization that works to protect and enhance veterans' benefits. Only about 2 percent of recipients of Aid to Families with Dependent Children (AFDC) were members of welfare rights groups.[27] Clearly, a **membership bias** is part of the pattern of who belongs to interest groups: certain types of people are much more likely to belong to interest groups than others.

The Public Interest Movement

Before we reach the conclusion that the interest group system is biased, we should examine another set of data. The actual population of interest groups in Washington surely reflects a class bias in interest group membership, but that bias may be modified in an important way. Some interest groups derive support from sources other than their membership. Thus, although the Center for Budget and Policy Priorities and the Children's Defense Fund have no welfare recipients among their members, they are highly respected Washington lobbies working on the problems of poor people. Poverty groups gain their financial support from philanthropic foundations, government grants, corporations, and wealthy individuals. Such groups have played an important role in influencing policy on poor people's programs. In short, some bias exists in the representation of the poor, but it is not nearly so bad as membership patterns suggest.

Another part of the problem of membership bias has to do with free riders. The interests that are most affected by free riders are broad societal problems, such as the environment and consumer protection, in which literally everyone can be considered as having a stake in the outcome. The greater the number of potential members of a group, the more likely it is that individuals will decide to be free riders, because they believe that plenty of others can offer financial support to the organization.

Environmental and consumer interests have been chronically underrepresented in the Washington interest group community. In the 1960s, however, a strong public interest movement emerged. **Public interest groups** are citizen groups that have no economic self-interest in the policies they pursue.[28] For example, the members of environmental groups fighting for stricter pollution control requirements receive no financial gain from the enactment of environmental protection policies. The benefits to its members are largely ideological and esthetic. In contrast, a corporation fighting the same stringent standards is trying to protect its economic interests. The environmental lobby is a public interest group; the corporation is not.

Today, many public interest groups are important players in Washington politics. Most are environmental and consumer groups, but others work on corporate accountability, good government, poverty, and nutrition. Many conservative public interest groups exist as well, working in areas such as abortion and family values. Overall, the public interest movement has broadened interest group representation in national politics and made the pluralist system more democratic.

Business Mobilization

Because a strong public interest movement has become an integral part of Washington politics, an easy assumption is that the bias in interest group representation in favor of business has been largely overcome. What must be factored in is that business has become increasingly mobilized as well.[29] The 1970s and 1980s saw a vast increase in the number of business lobbies in Washington. Many corporations opened up Washington lobbying offices, and many trade associations headquartered elsewhere either moved to Washington or opened up branch offices there.

This mobilization was partly a reaction to the success of the liberal public interest movement, which business tended to view as hostile to the free-enterprise system. The reaction of business also reflected the expanded scope of the national government. As the Environmental Protection Agency, the Consumer Product Safety Commission, OSHA, and other regulatory agencies were created, many more companies found they were affected by federal regulations.

The health care industry is a case in point. As government regulation has become an increasingly important factor in determining health care profits,

The Tax Lobbyist

Charls Walker is one of the most skilled business lobbyists in Washington. He holds a Ph.D. in economics and was a high-ranking official in the U.S. Treasury Department. Because of Walker's expertise and political skills, many large corporations hire him to lobby Congress on tax policy.

more and more health care trade associations have opened up offices in Washington so that they can make more of an effort to influence the government. In 1981, there were about 250 health care lobbies in Washington. A decade later there were three times that.[30]

The number of organizations is far from a perfect indicator of interest group strength, however. The AFL-CIO, which represents millions of union members, is more influential than a two-person corporate listening post in Washington; nevertheless, as a rough indicator of interest group influence, the data show that business has an advantage in this country's interest group system.

Access

The existence of an interest group makes little difference if the government systematically ignores it. Evidence shows that any particular policymaker or office of government can be highly selective in granting access to interest groups. The ideological compatibility between any given interest group and the policymaker it approaches certainly affects the likelihood that the policymaker will grant the group access and listen to what its lobbyists have to say. However, pluralists are convincing when they argue that the national government has many points of access, and virtually all lobbying organizations can find some part of that government to listen to them. If liberal poverty lobbies are shut out of a conservative White House, liberal members of Congress will work with them. All forms of access are not of equal importance, and some organizations have wider access than others. Nevertheless, American government is generally characterized by the broad access it grants to interest groups.

Reform

In an economic system marked by great differences in income, great differences in the degree to which people are organized are inevitable. Moreover, as Madison foresaw, limiting interest group activity is difficult without limiting fundamental freedoms. The First Amendment guarantees Americans the right to petition their government, and lobbying, at its most basic level, is a form of organized petitioning.

Still, if it is felt that the advantages of some groups are so great that they affect the equality of people's opportunity to be heard in the political system, then restrictions on interest group behavior can be justified on the ground that the disadvantaged must be protected. Pluralist democracy is justified on exactly these grounds: All constituencies must have the opportunity to organize, and the competition between groups as they press their case before policymakers must be fair.

Some critics charge that a system of campaign finance that relies so heavily on PACs undermines our democratic system. It is not merely a matter of wealthy interest groups showering incumbents with donations; members of Congress aggressively solicit donations from PACs. Although observers disagree on whether PAC money actually influences policy outcomes, agreement is widespread that PAC donations give donors better access to members of Congress.

The government has placed some restrictions on interest group campaign donations, however. During the 1970s, Congress put some important reforms into effect. Strong disclosure requirements now exist—the source of all significant contributions to candidates for national office is a matter of public record. Legislation also provides for public financing of presidential campaigns; taxpayer money goes in equal amounts to the presidential nominees of the major parties. In 1995, Congress passed additional modest reforms outside the campaign finance area. Lobbyists are now subject to a strict registration requirement and must file reports every six months listing all their clients, the amount they spent on lobbying activities, and how much they were paid.[31] Another reform banned all gifts from lobbyists to legislators (with the exception of gifts of trivial value).[32]

Reformers have called for public financing of congressional elections to reduce the presumed influence of PACs on Congress. Other proposed approaches include reducing the amounts individual PACs can give; limiting the overall amount of money any one candidate can accept from PACs; reducing the costs of campaigning by subsidizing the costs of commercials, printing, and postage; and giving tax incentives to individuals to contribute to candidates. However, incumbents usually find it easier to raise money from PACs than challengers do, so the incentive to leave the status quo intact is strong. And Republicans and Democrats have sharp, partisan differences over campaign finance reforms, because each party believes that the other is trying to fashion a system that will somehow handicap the opposing party.

Summary

Interest groups play many important roles in our political process. They are a means by which citizens can participate in politics, and they communicate their members' views to those in government. Interest groups differ greatly in the resources at their disposal and in the tactics they use to influence government. The number of interest groups has grown sharply in recent years.[33]

Despite the growth and change in the nature of interest groups, the fundamental problem identified by Madison more than two hundred years ago endures. In a free and open society, groups form to pursue policies that favor them at the expense of the broader national interest. Madison hoped that the solution to the problem would come from the diversity of the population and the structure of our government.

To a certain extent, Madison's expectations have been borne out. The natural differences between groups have prevented a tyranny of any one faction. Yet, the interest group system remains unbalanced, with some segments of society (particularly business, the wealthy, and the educated) considerably better organized than others. The growth of citizen groups has reduced the disparity somewhat, but significant inequalities remain in how well different interests are represented in Washington.

The inequities point to flaws in pluralist theory. There is no mechanism to automatically ensure that interest groups will form to speak for those who need representation. Likewise, when an issue arises and policymakers meet with interest groups that have a stake in the outcome, those groups may not equally represent all the constituencies that the policy changes will affect. The interest group system clearly compromises the principle of political equality stated in the maxim "one person, one vote." Formal political equality is certainly more likely to occur outside interest group politics, in elections between candidates from competing political parties, which better fits the majoritarian model of democracy.

Despite the inequities of the interest group system, little direct effort has been made to restrict interest group activity. Madison's dictum to avoid suppressing political freedoms, even at the expense of permitting interest group activity that promotes the selfish interests of narrow segments of the population, has generally guided public policy. Yet, as the problem of PACs demonstrates, government has had to set some restrictions on interest groups. Permitting PACs to give unlimited amounts to political candidates would undermine confidence in the system. Where to draw the line on PAC activity remains a thorny issue, because there is little consensus on how to balance the conflicting needs of our society. Congress is one institution that must try to balance our diverse country's conflicting interests. In the next chapter, we will see how difficult this part of Congress's job is.

Key Terms

interest group
lobby

lobbyist
agenda building

program monitoring	grassroots lobbying
interest group entrepreneur	information campaign
free-rider problem	coalition building
trade association	membership bias
political action committee (PAC)	public interest group
direct lobbying	

Selected Reading

Berry, Jeffrey M. *The Interest Group Society.* 3d ed. New York: Longman, 1997. An analysis of the growth of interest group politics.

Cigler, Allan J., and Burdett A. Loomis, eds. *Interest Group Politics.* 4th ed. Washington, D.C.: Congressional Quarterly Press, 1995. This reader includes eighteen essays on lobbying groups.

Costain, Anne N. *Inviting Women's Rebellion.* Baltimore: Johns Hopkins University Press, 1992. A careful and original examination of the origins of the women's movement and its development into a political force.

Heinz, John P., Edward O. Laumann, Robert L. Nelson, and Robert H. Salisbury. *The Hollow Core.* Cambridge, Mass.: Harvard University Press, 1993. The best study available of large-scale issue networks in national politics.

Woliver, Laura. *From Outrage to Action.* Urbana: University of Illinois Press, 1993. Four incisive case studies of ad hoc grassroots advocacy groups.

Wright, John R. *Interest Groups and Congress.* Boston: Allyn & Bacon, 1996. An overview of how lobbies and PACs try to influence Congress.

World Wide Web Resources

U.S. Chamber of Commerce. Find out how interest groups function and the services they provide to their membership. The site lists management training information, a video library, and seminars for business—those in business, and those seeking to start a business.

AFL-CIO. Read the organization's policy statements, press releases, and its "Boycott List." Find information on how to organize a union. A dominant feature of this Web site is information about the AFL-CIO's "Standup Campaign"—a campaign to lobby for good jobs, good wages, and worker protection.

The Sierra Club. Find out how public interest groups work. Visitors to this Web page can read the Sierra Club's magazine as well as *The Planet,* a newsletter for environmental activists. Get information on Sierra Club chapters, politics, and the environment. Follow links to other environmental sites on the Internet.

Voters Telecommunications Watch. Track telecommunications policy from a voter/citizen perspective. Find out why voters should be interested in telecommunications policy (regulatory policy, legislation, and so forth). Find out more information on free speech issues and issues of universal access. Use the "Citizen's Guide to the Internet." Help pave the information superhighway.

Congress

Newt Gingrich threw down the gauntlet. "So long as I'm Speaker we're going to spend every day working on decisions that get us to a balanced budget by 2002, period."[1] True to his word, the 104th Congress did work obsessively toward passing a balanced budget amendment to the Constitution. With joyful exuberance, virtually all the Republicans and a minority of Democrats marched into the House of Representatives and passed the amendment by a vote of 300–132.

In the Senate, however, the amendment ran into trouble. Although all the Republican senators but one voted for the amendment, it failed by a single vote to garner the two-thirds majority required of constitutional amendments before they can be sent on to the states. Most Democrats opposed the amendment, and President Clinton worked against its passage. Yet this "defeat" seemed a clear tactical victory for the Republicans. Since the public had expressed support for the amendment by a margin of four to one, the Democrats would shoulder the blame for defeating this popular proposal.

The Republicans pressed on, trying to achieve their goal of a balanced budget by passing appropriations bills that made the necessary spending cuts. (Congress can balance the budget without a constitutional mandate; it simply has to appropriate government spending at a lower rate than the government's income until the deficit is paid off and income equals outflow.) With this strategy, however, came the necessity of specifying which programs to curb. The huge Medicare program, which provides health care to the elderly, was one of the Republicans' targets. Low- and middle-income seniors are a crucial Democratic party constituency, and President Clinton and his congressional allies relentlessly attacked the Republicans for trying to cut medical services to the elderly. Republicans responded that they were merely cutting the *rate of increase* of future Medicare spending. The Democrats had the upper hand, though, because polls demonstrated that two-thirds of the public preferred keeping Medicare from being cut significantly over balancing the federal budget.[2]

Republican congressional leaders entered into negotiations with President Clinton to see if they could come to an agreement for the entire budget. As they became increasingly frustrated with the Democrats because the party wouldn't accede to a balanced budget, the GOP refused on more than one occasion to pass short-term spending bills to keep the whole government running. The public blamed the Republicans for the resulting partial government shutdowns, however, so eventually short-term appropriations bills were passed. Finally, put on the defensive by a public that didn't seem so committed to a balanced budget after all, the Republicans threw in the towel. In the spring of 1996, a spending bill funding the government for the rest of the fiscal year was passed. Gingrich mused, "It may just be that we need one more election."[3] With the mixed results of that election behind them, the president and the Republican congressional leadership tried again to resolve their differences over the budget. On May 2, 1997, a compromise budget agreement was reached. It aimed to achieve a balanced budget by 2002 and to provide $135 billion in tax cuts, but it avoided significant cuts in Medicare or Social Security.[4]

Although the fight was over a highly partisan issue that highlights the different values of the two congressional parties, it also illustrates the continuing tension in American politics between majoritarianism and pluralism. The Republicans certainly believed they had a mandate from a majority of Americans to balance the nation's budget. The Democrats pulled together a coalition of different interests, not only senior citizens but also environmentalists, educators, students, minorities, and others who would be hurt by budget cuts. The defeat of both balanced budget strategies pursued by the Republicans may seem a victory of pluralism over majoritarianism. But what was the true majoritarian position? One majority said it wanted a balanced budget, but another majority said it preferred to protect Medicare.

In this chapter and in Chapters 9, 10, and 11, we emphasize the tension between pluralist and majoritarian visions of democracy. In the pages that follow, we will examine more closely the relationship between members of Congress and their constituents, as well as the forces (such as political parties) that push legislators toward majoritarianism. We'll also focus on Congress's relations with the executive branch and analyze how the legislative process affects public policy. A starting point is to ask how the framers envisioned Congress.

The Origin and Powers of Congress

The framers of the Constitution wanted to keep power from being concentrated in the hands of a few, but they were also concerned with creating a union strong enough to overcome the weaknesses of the government that had operated under the Articles of Confederation. They argued passionately about the structure of the new government. In the end, they produced a legislative body that was as much of an experiment as the new nation's democracy.

The Great Compromise

The U.S. Congress has two separate and powerful chambers: the House of Representatives and the Senate. A bill cannot become law unless it is passed in identical form by both chambers. When drafting the Constitution during the summer of 1787, "the fiercest struggle for power" centered on representation in the legislature.[5] The small states wanted all the states to have equal representation. The more populous states wanted representation based on population; they did not want their power diluted. The Great Compromise broke the deadlock: The small states would receive equal representation in the Senate, but the number of each state's representatives in the House would be based on population, and the House would have the sole right to originate revenue-related legislation.

As the Constitution specifies, each state has two senators, and senators serve six-year terms of office. Terms are staggered, so that one-third of the Senate is elected every two years. When it was ratified, the Constitution directed that senators should be chosen by the state legislatures. However, the Seventeenth Amendment, adopted in 1913, provided for the direct election of senators by popular vote. From the beginning, the people have directly elected members of the House of Representatives. They serve two-year terms, and all House seats are up for election at the same time.

There are 435 members in the House of Representatives. Because each state's representation in the House is in proportion to its population, the Constitution provides for a national census every ten years; population shifts are handled by the **reapportionment** (redistribution) of seats among the states after each census is taken. Since recent population growth has been centered in the Sunbelt, California, Texas, and Florida have gained seats, while the Northeast and Midwest states have lost them. Each representative is elected from a particular congressional district within his or her state, and each district elects only one representative. The districts within a state must be roughly equal in population.

Duties of the House and Senate

Although the Great Compromise provided for considerably different schemes of representation for the House and Senate, the Constitution gives them essentially similar legislative tasks. They share many important powers, among them the powers to declare war, raise an army and navy, borrow and coin money, regulate interstate commerce, create federal courts, establish rules for the naturalization of immigrants, and "make all Laws which shall be necessary and proper for carrying into Execution the foregoing Powers."

Of course, the constitutional duties of the two chambers are different in at least a few important ways. As noted earlier, the House alone has the right to originate revenue bills, a right that apparently was coveted at the Constitutional Convention. In practice, this power is of limited consequence because both the House and Senate must approve all bills—including revenue bills. The House also has the power of **impeachment**, the power formally to charge the president, vice president, or other "civil Officers" of the national government with "Treason, Bribery, or other high Crimes and Misdemeanors." The Senate is empowered to act as a court to try impeachments; a two-thirds majority vote of the senators present is necessary for conviction.

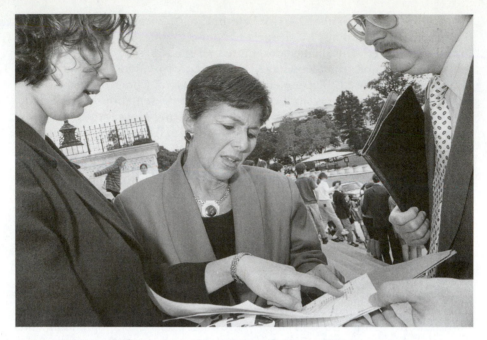

Senator Boxer and Staffers
*The Congress of the United States is, in and of itself, a huge bureaucracy. There are just
535 members of the House and Senate, but there are over 17,000 staffers who work for them.
Another 6,000 staffers work for the General Accounting Office and other congressional
support agencies. Here, Senator Barbara Boxer (D.-Calif.) goes over some instructions with
some of the many staffers who work for her.*

Only one president—Andrew Johnson—has ever been impeached, and in
1868 the Senate came within a single vote of finding him guilty. More recently,
the House Judiciary Committee voted to impeach President Richard Nixon for
his role in the Watergate scandal, but he resigned (in August 1974) before the
full House could vote. A small number of federal judges, however, have been
impeached, convicted, and removed from the bench.

The Constitution gives the Senate the power to approve major presidential
appointments (such as to federal judgeships, ambassadorships, and cabinet
posts) and treaties with foreign nations. The president is empowered to make
treaties, but he must submit them to the Senate for approval by a two-thirds
majority. Because of this requirement, the executive branch generally considers the Senate's sentiments when it negotiates a treaty.[6]

Despite the long list of congressional powers in the Constitution, the question of what powers are appropriate for Congress has generated substantial
controversy. For example, although the Constitution gives Congress the sole
power to declare war, many presidents have initiated military action on their
own. And at times, the courts have found that congressional actions have
usurped the rights of the states.

Electing the Congress

If Americans are not happy with the job Congress is doing, they can use their votes to say so. With a congressional election every two years, the voters have frequent opportunities to express themselves.

The Incumbency Effect

Congressional elections offer voters a chance to show their approval of Congress's performance by reelecting **incumbents** or to demonstrate their disapproval by "throwing the rascals out." The voters seem to do more reelecting than rascal throwing. The reelection rate is astonishingly high; in the majority of elections since 1950, more than 90 percent of all House incumbents have held on to their seats (see Figure 8.1). Most House elections aren't even close; in recent elections most House incumbents have won at least 60 percent of the vote. Senate elections are more competitive, but incumbents still have a high reelection rate.[7]

These findings may seem surprising, since the public does not hold Congress as a whole in particularly high esteem. Two-thirds of the American public tell pollsters that they disapprove of the job Congress is doing.[8] Close to 60 percent believe that at least half of all members of Congress are personally corrupt, a harsh indictment of the institution.[9] Americans strongly support term limits for members of Congress, to limit the number of years a legislator can serve in the House or Senate.[10] Although term limits have been imposed in many states, both in 1995 and 1997 the House voted against a constitutional amendment for term limits on members of Congress. Although Americans feel disdain for Congress, they tend to distinguish the institution as a whole from their own members of Congress. Only 15 percent believe that their own representative is financially corrupt.[11]

Redistricting   One explanation for the incumbency effect centers on redistricting, the way House districts are redrawn by state legislatures after a census-based reapportionment. It is entirely possible for them to draw the new districts to benefit the incumbents of one or both parties. Altering district lines for partisan advantage is commonly called **gerrymandering**.

Name Recognition   Holding office brings with it some important advantages. First, incumbents develop significant name recognition among voters simply by being members of Congress. Congressional press secretaries help the name recognition advantage along through their efforts to get publicity for the activities and speeches of their bosses. The primary focus of such publicity seeking is on the local media back in the district—that's where the votes are.[12] The local press, in turn, is eager to cover what members of Congress are saying about the issues.

Another resource available to members of Congress is the *franking privilege*—the right to send mail free of charge. Mailings work to make constituents aware of their legislators' names, activities, and accomplishments.

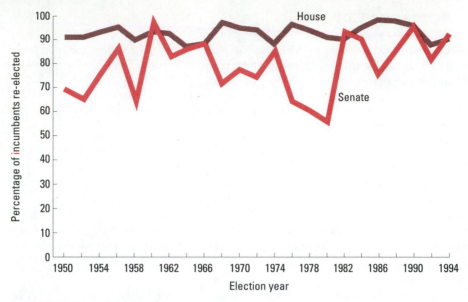

FIGURE 8.1   *Incumbents: Life Is Good*
Despite the public's dissatisfaction with Congress in general, incumbent representatives win reelection at an exceptional rate. Incumbent senators aren't quite as successful but still do well in reelection races. Voters seem to believe that their own representatives and senators don't share the same foibles that they attribute to the other members of Congress. (Source: Norman J. Ornstein, Thomas E. Mann, and Michael J. Malbin, Vital Statistics on Congress, 1995–1996 *(Washington, D.C.: Congressional Quarterly Press, 1996), pp. 60–61.)*

Periodic newsletters, for example, almost always highlight legislators' success at securing funds and projects for their district.

Much of the work performed by the large staffs of members of Congress is **casework**—such services for constituents as tracking down a social security check or directing the owner of a small business to the appropriate federal agency. Constituents who are helped in this way usually remember who assisted them.

Campaign Financing   It should be clear that anyone who wants to challenge an incumbent needs solid financial backing. But here, too, the incumbent has the advantage. Challengers find raising campaign funds difficult because they have to overcome contributors' doubts about whether they can win. PACs show a strong preference for incumbents (see Chapter 7). They tend not to want to risk offending an incumbent by giving money to a long-shot challenger.

Successful Challengers   Clearly the deck is stacked against challengers to incumbents. Yet, some challengers do beat incumbents. How? The opposing party and unsympathetic PACs may target incumbents who seem vulnerable because of age, lack of seniority, a scandal, unfavorable redistricting, or other factors.

Senate challengers have a higher success rate than House challengers in part because they are generally higher quality candidates. Often they are governors or members of the House who enjoy high name recognition and can attract significant campaign funds, because they are regarded as credible candidates.[13]

The broad sweep of national opinion also influences the outcome of House elections. The president's party almost always loses seats in the midterm elections, as voters take out their disappointments with the president on the House candidates of his party. In the 1994 election, negative feelings about government in general and President Clinton in particular fueled a Republican takeover of both the House and the Senate. Thirty-four Democratic House incumbents were defeated, and the Republicans gained fifty-two seats overall to become the majority in the House for the first time since 1952. The incumbents who lost tended to come from districts that were not as strongly Democratic as those where Democratic incumbents survived. Those Democrats who were loyal to President Clinton in their voting on the House floor were also more vulnerable to Republican challengers.[14] (Yet even in that volatile year, 90 percent of all incumbent members of the House who were running won reelection.)[15]

With Speaker Gingrich's unpopularity and President Clinton headed toward a decisive reelection victory, Democrats hoped that they could regain control of the House of Representatives in 1996. Democrats and their allies in the labor movement targeted many of the freshmen Republicans who had loyally supported Gingrich and his Contract with America. Like most congressional elections, however, 1996 was a very good year for incumbents of both political parties. There were around twenty House incumbents who lost, but only a dozen of the seventy Republican House freshmen running for reelection went down to defeat. The Republicans maintained control of both houses of Congress.

Whom Do We Elect?

The people we elect (then reelect) to Congress are not a cross-section of American society. Most members of Congress are professionals—primarily lawyers, businesspeople, and educators.[16] Although nearly a third of the American labor force works in blue-collar jobs, someone currently employed as a blue-collar worker rarely wins a congressional nomination.

Women and minorities have long been underrepresented in elective office. Yet, many women and minorities believe that only members of their own group—people who have experienced what they have experienced—can truly represent their interests. This is a belief in **descriptive representation**, the view that a legislature should resemble the demographic characteristics of the population it represents.[17]

When Congress amended the Voting Rights Act in 1982, it encouraged the states to draw districts that concentrated minorities together so that blacks and Hispanic Americans would have a better chance of being elected to office. Supreme Court decisions also pushed the states to concentrate minorities in

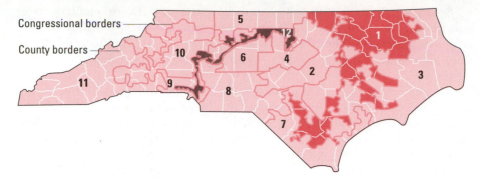

FIGURE 8.2   *"Political Apartheid" or Racial Equality?*
To create districts in which African American candidates were likely to win, the boundaries of two North Carolina congressional districts, 1 and 12, had to weave across the state to incorporate enough neighborhoods with concentrated minority populations. Justice Sandra Day O'Connor called these districts examples of "political apartheid." The Shaw v. Reno *and* Miller v. Johnson *cases are forcing states to redraw the boundaries of some of these oddly shaped districts designed to enhance the representation of minorities in the House of Representatives. (Source: Shaw v. Reno, 509 U.S. 630 (1993).)*

House districts.[18] After the 1990 census, states redrew House boundaries with the intent of creating districts with majority or near-majority minority populations. Some districts were very oddly shaped, snaking through their state to pick up black neighborhoods in various cities but leaving adjacent white neighborhoods to other districts. This effort led to a roughly 50 percent increase in the number of blacks elected to the House. Hispanic representation in the House also increased, from ten to seventeen members, after redistricting created new districts with large concentrations of Hispanic American voters.

In a decision that surprised many, the Supreme Court ruled in 1993 that states' efforts to increase minority representation through **racial gerrymandering** could violate the rights of whites. In *Shaw v. Reno,* the majority ruled in a split decision that a North Carolina district that meandered 160 miles from Durham to Charlotte was an example of "political apartheid" (see Figure 8.2). In effect, the Court ruled that racial gerrymandering segregated blacks from whites instead of creating districts built around contiguous communities.

In a 1995 case, *Miller v. Johnson,* the Supreme Court went even further in restricting the force of the Voting Rights Act. The Court's majority said that the states should not draw district boundaries where race is the "predominant factor."[19] In 1997, the Court reaffirmed its position when it blocked the creation of a majority black district in southwest Georgia that it felt could not be drawn without "engaging in racial gerrymandering."[20] Thus it is not merely the shape of the district that is suspect, but the very intent to draw districts to favor an ethnic or racial group. If equality requires descriptive representation, then the Court's direction to states to move away from racial gerrymandering is a retreat from equality in Congress.

If Congress Looks Different, Will It Act Different?

African Americans were first elected to Congress during the Reconstruction era after the Civil War. After the military occupation of the South ended, the number of African Americans in Congress dwindled to a single representative by the end of the nineteenth century. (Blacks were systematically disenfranchised by southern whites after whites resumed control of their state governments.) George White, the last African American legislator of this period, stood on the floor of the House in 1901 and prophesied of the black man in Congress, "Phoenix-like he will rise up some day and come again."

The phoenix has indeed risen. In the wake of the redistricting after the 1990 census, which created many new districts with a majority of minorities, thirty-nine African Americans won election to the House. The same number won election in the 1994 elections. This is a substantial number of legislators, but does it make any difference? Does descriptive representation bring about more effective representation for a particular sector of society?

Because the sharp increase in African American representation is so recent, there is no definitive answer. Still, early indications are that the Congressional Black Caucus—the organization of African Americans in the House—is gaining leverage in the legislative process. The leader of the Black Caucus, Donald Payne, a Democrat from New Jersey, can bargain with a considerable number of votes when he negotiates with the House leadership. (All but one of the blacks in the House are Democrats.) On issues directly affecting African Americans, the Black Caucus is influential with Democratic presidents, too. President Clinton wanted to nominate John Payton, a District of Columbia government lawyer, as head of the civil rights division of the Justice Department. Members of the Black Caucus objected privately, because Payton refused to commit himself to the racial gerrymandering that has brought more blacks into Congress. Clinton bowed to the Black Caucus's wishes and did not go forward with the nomination.

African Americans have also enhanced their clout by moving up the seniority ladder. Before the Republicans took control of the House in 1994, three blacks chaired House committees and thirteen chaired subcommittees. John Lewis of Georgia serves as chief deputy whip, an important position in the congressional party hierarchy. This leadership cohort of African Americans is in a strong position to initiate policy and advance the interests of their constituents.

The same questions about descriptive representation can be asked about women representatives, who also increased sharply in number in the House. (Progress is also being made in the Senate. When members of the 104th

(continued)

Ironically, none of the South's black representatives were defeated as a result of the Court's rulings.[21] Also, spreading black and Hispanic voters around more districts, rather than concentrating them in a relatively small number of

Politics in a Changing America 8.1 (continued)

Congress took their seats in 1995, there were eight women senators, up from two in 1991.) Although research on women in Congress has been hampered by their low numbers, interesting studies have been done on women in state legislatures.

In many respects, female state legislators act very similarly to male legislators of the same party. In some areas, however, women do operate differently. They are more likely than their male counterparts to introduce bills on issues pertaining to women, children, and the family. They are also likely to make such bills their priorities—the ones they work hardest to get passed. Men and women state legislators are equally successful in getting their priority bills passed, but women's emphasis on these issues means that more such legislation gets passed and signed into law.

Simply put, women bring different concerns to a legislature. Their presence influences the mix of issues on the table and brings new perspectives on how problems may be solved. As one scholar puts it, "Leaving any group out of policy formulation and legitimation necessarily means that the range of ideas is artificially limited."

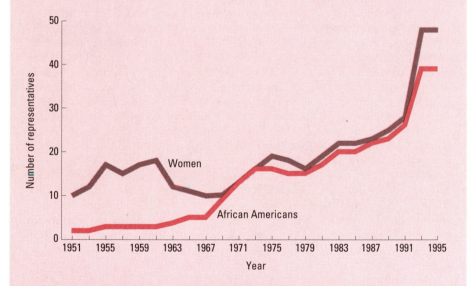

Source: Data for the figure come from Norman J. Ornstein, Thomas E. Mann, and Michael J. Malbin, *Vital Statistics on Congress, 1995–1996* (Washington, D.C.: Congressional Quarterly Press, pp. 38–39.

them, might actually increase their influence. More representatives will have significant numbers of minority voters in their district and will have to consider their views as they contemplate their stand on the issues.

How Issues Get On the Congressional Agenda

The formal legislative process begins when a member of Congress introduces a *bill*, a proposal for a new law. In the House, members drop new bills in the "hopper," a mahogany box near the rostrum where the Speaker presides. Senators give their bills to one of the Senate clerks or introduce them from the floor.[22] But before a bill can be introduced to solve a problem, someone must perceive that a problem exists or that an issue needs to be resolved. In other words, the problem or issue somehow must find its way onto the congressional agenda. *Agenda* actually has two meanings in the vocabulary of political scientists. The first is that of a narrow, formal agenda, such as a calendar of bills to be voted on. The second meaning refers to the broad, imprecise, and unwritten agenda that consists of all the issues an institution is considering. Here we use the term in the second, broader sense.

Many of the issues Congress is working on at any one time seem to have been around forever, yet all issues begin at some point in time. There has always been violence on TV, for example, but for years it was seen as a matter best left to the private sector to solve. Eventually, though, people began to see the problem as a *political* issue. In 1996, Congress passed legislation requiring that new televisions be equipped with a "V chip," an electronic device that will allow parents to lock out all programs they deem unsuitable for their children.

Sometimes a highly visible event focuses national attention on a problem. An explosion in a West Virginia mine in 1989 killed seventy-eight miners; Congress promptly went to work on laws to promote miners' safety.[23] Presidential support can also move an issue onto the agenda quickly. The media attention paid to the president gives him enormous opportunity to draw the nation's attention to problems he believes need some form of governmental action.

Within Congress, party leaders and committee chairs have the opportunity to influence the political agenda. At times, the efforts of an interest group spark an awareness of an issue.

The Dance of Legislation: An Overview

The process of writing bills and getting them passed is relatively simple, in the sense that it follows a series of specific steps. What complicates the process is the many different ways legislation can be treated at each step. Here, we examine the straightforward process by which laws are made. In the next few sections, we discuss some of the complexities of that process.

After a bill is introduced in either house, it is assigned to the committee with jurisdiction over that policy area (see Figure 8.3). A banking bill, for example, would be assigned to the Banking and Finance Services Committee in the House or to the Banking, Housing, and Urban Affairs Committee in the Senate. When a committee actively considers a piece of legislation assigned to it, the bill is usually referred to a specialized subcommittee. The subcommittee may hold hearings, and legislative staffers may do research on the bill. The original bill usually is modified or revised; if passed in some form, it is sent to the full committee. A bill approved by the full committee is reported (that is, sent) to the entire membership of the chamber, where it may be debated, amended, and either passed or defeated.

Bills coming out of House committees go to the Rules Committee before going before the full House membership. The Rules Committee attaches a rule to the bill that governs the coming floor debate, typically specifying the length of the debate and the types of amendments House members may offer. The Senate does not have a comparable committee, although restrictions on the length of floor debate can be reached through unanimous consent agreements (see the "Rules of Procedure" section later in the chapter).

Even if both houses of Congress pass a bill on the same subject, the Senate and House versions are typically different from each other. In that case, a conference committee, composed of legislators from both houses, works out the differences and develops a compromise version. This version goes back to both houses for another floor vote. If both chambers approve the bill, it is then sent to the president for his signature or veto.

When the president signs a bill, it becomes law. If the president **vetoes** (disapproves) the bill, it is sent back to Congress with his reasons for rejecting it. The bill becomes law only if Congress overrides the president's veto by a two-thirds vote in each house. If the president neither signs nor vetoes the bill within ten days (Sundays excepted) of receiving it, the bill becomes law. There is an exception here: if Congress adjourns within the ten days, the president can let the bill die through a **pocket veto**, by not signing it.

In 1996, Congress gave presidents a new tool, the **line item veto**. This gives presidents the authority to strike out different sections of a bill, invalidating particular items but allowing the rest of the bill to become law. Thus, if a president thinks three different projects in an appropriations bill are wasteful "pork barrel," he can cross out the lines in the legislation carrying those projects, vetoing the spending for those parts of the bill only. This new law quickly faced a constitutional challenge and was held to be unconstitutional in an early 1997 federal district court ruling.[24] However, a few months later, without ruling on the merits of the issue, the Supreme Court set aside that ruling and held that the members of Congress who challenged the law had no legal right to do so because they had suffered only "a loss of political power, not loss of any private right, which would make the injury more concrete."[25]

Many scholars believe the law is unconstitutional because the Constitution specifies what a president must do with a bill before him (sign, veto, do neither, or pocket veto it); it says nothing about a president altering bills to make

FIGURE 8.3   *The Legislative Process*
The process by which a bill becomes law is subject to much variation. The diagram on the facing page depicts the typical process a bill might follow. It is important to remember that a bill can fail at any stage because of lack of support.

HOUSE	SENATE

Bill is introduced and assigned to a committee, which refers it to the appropriate . . .

Bill is introduced and assigned to a committee, which refers it to the appropriate . . .

Subcommittee
Subcommittee members study the bill, hold hearings, and debate provisions. If a bill is approved, it goes to the . . .

Subcommittee
Subcommittee members study the bill, hold hearings, and debate provisions. If a bill is approved, it goes to the . . .

Committee
Full committee considers the bill. If the bill is approved in some form, it goes to the . . .

Committee
Full committee considers the bill. If the bill is approved in some form, it goes to the . . .

Rules Committee
Rules Committee issues a rule to govern debate on the floor. Sends it to the . . .

Full House
Full House debates the bill and may amend it. If the bill passes and is in a form different from the Senate version, it must go to a . . .

Full Senate
Full Senate debates the bill and may amend it. If the bill passes and is in a form different from the House version, it must go to a . . .

Conference Committee
Conference committee of senators and representatives meets to reconcile differences between bills. When agreement is reached, a compromise bill is sent back to both the . . .

Full House
House votes on the conference committee bill. If it passes in both houses, it goes to the . . .

Full Senate
Senate votes on the conference committee bill. If it passes in both houses, it goes to the . . .

President
President signs or vetoes the bill. Congress can override a veto by a two-thirds majority vote in both the House and Senate.

them more to his liking. Supporters claim that the line item veto is just another form of legislative delegation of authority to the executive branch and that there are many such perfectly legal delegations already in practice. Whatever the eventual outcome in the Supreme Court, what is remarkable about the line item veto is that Congress has voluntarily given away considerable power to the executive branch. The president now has greater authority to direct spending, greater leverage to bargain with Congress, and greater ability to punish uncooperative members of Congress by deleting the projects that legislators care most about. Nevertheless, Congress passed the statute because it believed that presidents would use the line item veto to control spending and thus reduce the budget deficit. The members of Congress, in essence, said the president could control spending better than they could.[26]

The content of a bill can be changed at any stage of the process, in either house. Lawmaking (and thus policymaking) in Congress has many access points for those who want to influence legislation. This openness tends to fit within the pluralist model of democracy. As a bill moves through the dance of legislation,[27] it is amended again and again, in a search for a consensus that will get it passed and signed into law. The process can be tortuously slow and it is often fruitless. Derailing legislation is much easier than enacting it. The process gives groups frequent opportunities to voice their preferences and, if necessary, thwart their opponents.

Committees: The Workhorses of Congress

Woodrow Wilson once observed that "Congress in session is Congress on public exhibition, whilst Congress in its committee-rooms is Congress at work."[28] The real nuts and bolts of lawmaking goes on in the congressional committees.

The Division of Labor Among Committees

The House and Senate are divided into committees for the same reason that other large organizations are broken into departments or divisions—to develop and use expertise in specific areas. For example, Congressional decisions on weapons systems require a special knowledge that is of little relevance to decisions on reimbursement formulas for health insurance. It makes sense for some members of Congress to spend more time examining defense issues, becoming increasingly expert as they do so, while others concentrate on health matters.

Eventually, all members of Congress have to vote on each bill that emerges from the committees. Those who are not on a particular committee depend on committee members to examine the issues thoroughly, to make compromises as necessary, and to bring forward a sound piece of legislation that has a good chance of being passed. Each member decides individually on the bill's merits. But once it reaches the House or Senate floor, members may get to vote on only a handful of amendments (if any at all) before they must cast their yea or nay for the entire bill.

Standing Committees   There are several different kinds of congressional committees, but the **standing committee** is predominant. Standing committees are permanent committees that specialize in a particular area of legislation—for example, the House Judiciary Committee or the Senate Environment and Public Works Committee. Most of the day-to-day work of drafting legislation takes place in the eighteen standing Senate committees and twenty standing House committees. Typically sixteen to twenty senators serve on each standing Senate committee, and an average of forty-two members serve on each standing committee in the House. The proportions of Democrats and Republicans on a standing committee generally reflect party proportions in the full Senate or House.

With a few exceptions, standing committees are further broken down into subcommittees. The House Agriculture Committee, for example, has five subcommittees, among them one on specialty crops and another on livestock, dairy, and poultry.

Other Congressional Committees

Members of Congress can also serve on joint, select, and conference committees. **Joint committees** are made up of members of both the House and the Senate. Like standing committees, the small number of joint committees are concerned with particular policy areas. The Joint Economic Committee, for instance, analyzes the country's economic policies. Joint committees are much weaker than standing committees because they are almost always restricted from reporting bills to the House or Senate.

A **select committee** is a temporary committee, created for a specific purpose. Congress establishes select committees to deal with special circumstances or with issues that either overlap or fall outside the areas of expertise of standing committees. The Senate committee that investigated the Watergate scandal was a select committee, created for that purpose only.

A **conference committee** is also a temporary committee, created to work out differences between the House and Senate versions of a specific piece of legislation. Its members are appointed from the standing committees or subcommittees from each house that originally handled and reported the legislation. Depending on the nature of the differences and the importance of the legislation, a conference committee may meet for hours or for weeks on end. When the conference committee agrees on a compromise, it reports the bill to both houses, which must then either approve or disapprove the compromise; they cannot amend or change it in any way. Only about 15 to 25 percent of all bills that eventually pass Congress go to a conference committee (although virtually all important or controversial bills do).[29] Committee or subcommittee leaders of both houses reconcile differences in other bills through informal negotiation.

Congressional Expertise and Seniority

Once appointed to a committee, a representative or senator has great incentive to remain on it in order to gain increasing expertise and influence. Influence also grows in a more formal way, with **seniority**, or years of consecutive service on a committee. In their quest for expertise and seniority, members tend to stay on the same committees. However, sometimes they switch places when they are offered the opportunity to move to one of the high-prestige committees (like Ways and Means in the House or Finance in the Senate) or to a committee that handles legislation of vital importance to their constituents.

Within each committee, the senior member of the majority party usually becomes the committee chair. (The majority party in each house controls committee leadership.) Other senior members of the majority party become subcommittee chairs, whereas their counterparts from the minority party gain influence as ranking minority members. The numerous subcommittees in the House and Senate offer multiple opportunities for power and status.

After the Republicans gained control of the House in 1994, Speaker of the House Newt Gingrich made a major break with the seniority system by rejecting three Republicans who were in line to become committee chairs. Gingrich passed over the three to choose committee members whom he thought would be more conservative and more aggressive in promoting the Republican program. Speakers have not appointed House committee chairs in this fashion since the first part of this century, when "Uncle Joe" Cannon ruled the chamber with an iron fist.[30] Gingrich also instituted term limits for committee and subcommittee chairs, restricting their tenure to six years.

The way in which committees and subcommittees are led and organized within Congress is significant because much public policy decision making takes place there. The first step in drafting legislation is to collect information on the issue. Committee staffers research the problem, and hearings may be held to take testimony from witnesses who have some special knowledge on the subject.

The meetings at which subcommittees and committees actually debate and amend legislation are called *markup sessions*. The process by which committees reach decisions varies. In many committees, there is a strong tradition of decision by consensus. The chair, the ranking minority member, and others in these committees work hard, in formal committee sessions and in informal negotiations, to find a middle ground on issues that divide committee members. In other committees, members exhibit strong ideological and partisan sentiments. However, committee and subcommittee leaders prefer to find ways to overcome inherent ideological and partisan divisions so that they can build compromise solutions that will appeal to the broader membership of their house. The skill of committee leaders in assembling coalitions that produce legislation that can pass on the floor of their house is critically important.

Oversight: Following Through on Legislation

It is often said in Washington that "knowledge is power." For Congress to retain its influence over the programs it creates, it must be aware of how the agencies responsible for them are administering them. To that end, legislators and their committees engage in **oversight**, the process of reviewing agency operations to determine whether the agency is carrying out policies as Congress intended.

Congress performs its oversight function in a number of different ways. The most visible is the hearing. Hearings may be part of a routine review or the by-product of information that reveals a major problem with a program or with an agency's administrative practices. Another way Congress keeps track of what departments and agencies are doing is by requesting reports on specific agency practices and operations. Also, a good deal of congressional oversight takes place informally. There is ongoing contact between committee and subcommittee leaders and agency administrators, and between committee staffers and top agency staffers.

Congressional oversight of the executive branch has sharply increased since the early 1970s.[31] A primary reason for this increase was that Congress gave itself the staff necessary to watch over the growing federal government.[32] In addition to significantly expanding the staffs of individual legislators and of House and Senate committees, Congress enhanced its analytical capabilities by creating the Congressional Budget Office and by strengthening the Government Accounting Office (GAO) and the Congressional Research Service of the Library of Congress.

Majoritarian and Pluralist Views of Committees

Government by committee vests a tremendous amount of power in the committees and subcommittees of Congress—and especially their leaders. This is particularly true of the House, which has more decentralized patterns of influence than the Senate and is more restrictive about letting members amend legislation on the floor. Committee members can bury a bill by not reporting it to the full House or Senate. The influence of committee members extends even further, to the floor debate. Many of them also make up the conference committees charged with developing compromise versions of bills.

In some ways, the committee system enhances the force of pluralism in American politics. Representatives and senators are elected by the voters in particular districts and states, and they tend to seek membership on the committees that make the decisions most important to their constituents. Members from farm areas, for example, want membership on the House and Senate Agriculture Committees. As a result, committees with members who represent constituencies with an unusually strong interest in their policy area are predisposed to write legislation favorable to those constituencies.

The committees have a majoritarian aspect as well. The membership of most committees tend to resemble the general ideological profiles of the two parties' congressional contingents. Even if a committee's views are not in line with those of the full membership, it is constrained in the legislation it writes because bills cannot become law unless they are passed by the parent chamber and by the other house. Consequently, in formulating legislation, committees anticipate what other representatives and senators will accept. The parties within each chamber also have means of rewarding members who are the most loyal to party priorities. Party committees and the party leadership within each chamber make committee assignments and respond to requests for transfers from less prestigious to more prestigious committees. Those whose voting is the most in line with the party get better assignments.[33]

In the Gingrich-led House of Representatives, committee-based pluralism has been reduced. First, by violating the seniority norm in selecting chairs, Gingrich served notice on all chairs that they served at his pleasure. Second, on occasion Gingrich would publicly side with other members of a committee when the chair pursued policy goals he opposed.

Leaders and Followers in Congress

Above the committee chairs is another layer of authority in the organization of the House and Senate. The Democratic and Republican leaders in each house work to maximize the influence of their own party while trying to keep their chamber functioning smoothly and efficiently. The operation of the two houses is also influenced by the rules and norms that each chamber has developed over the years.

The Leadership Task

Each of the two parties elect leaders in each of the two houses. In the House of Representatives, the majority party's leader is the **Speaker of the House**, who, gavel in hand, chairs sessions from the ornate rostrum at the front of the chamber. The Speaker's counterpart in the opposing party is the minority leader. The Speaker is a constitutional officer, but the Constitution does not list the Speaker's duties. The minority leader is not mentioned in the Constitution, but that post has evolved into an important party position in the House.

The Constitution makes the vice president of the United States the president of the Senate. But in practice the vice president rarely visits the Senate chamber unless there is a possibility of a tie vote, in which case he can break the tie. The *president pro tempore* (president "for the time"), elected by the majority party, is supposed to chair the Senate in the vice president's absence, but by custom this constitutional position is entirely honorary.

The real power in the Senate resides in the **majority leader**. As in the House, the top position in the opposing party is that of minority leader. Technically, the majority leader does not preside over Senate sessions (members rotate in the president pro tempore's chair); but he or she does schedule legislation in consultation with the minority leader. More broadly, party leaders play a critical role in getting bills through Congress. The most significant function that leaders play is steering the bargaining and negotiating over the content of legislation. When an issue divides their party, their house, the two houses, or their house and the White House, the leaders must take the initiative to work out a compromise.

Day in, day out, much of what leaders do is to meet with other members of their house to try to strike deals that will yield a majority on the floor. Beyond trying to engineer tradeoffs that will win votes, the party leaders must persuade others (often powerful committee chairs) that theirs is the best deal possible. After serving his first years as Senate majority leader, Bob Dole said he thought "majority pleader" was a more apt title.[34]

As recently as the 1950s, strong leaders dominated the legislative process. In the contemporary Congress, however, it has been difficult for leaders to control rank-and-file members because they have independent electoral bases in their districts and states and receive the vast bulk of their campaign funds from nonparty sources. Contemporary party leaders are coalition builders, not autocrats. Newt Gingrich, however, is a throwback to an earlier style of leadership. Gingrich won the fierce loyalty and support of rank-and-file Republicans by his hard work for the party and for his dynamic vision for the Republican platform in the 1994 congressional campaign, the Contract with America. However, while Gingrich was successful in getting almost all of the Contract's provisions through the House, gaining acclaim as the most effective Speaker in recent history, his leadership position was threatened when charges of ethical violations resulted in an unprecedented reprimand by the House and a $300,000 fine. By early 1997 it was reported that ambitious committee chairmen and others were moving to fill the void left by the weakened Speaker.[35]

Rules of Procedure

The operations of the House and Senate are structured by both formal rules and informal norms of behavior. Rules in each chamber are mostly matters of parliamentary procedure. For example, they govern the scheduling of legislation, outlining when and how certain types of legislation can be brought to the floor.

As noted earlier, an important difference between the two chambers is the House's use of its Rules Committee to govern floor debate. Lacking a similar committee to act as a "traffic cop" for legislation approaching the floor, the Senate relies on unanimous consent agreements to set the starting time and length of debate. If one senator objects to an agreement, it does not take effect. Senators do not routinely object to unanimous consent agreements, however, because they will need them when bills of their own await scheduling by the leadership.

A senator who wants to stop a bill badly enough may start a **filibuster** and try to talk the bill to death. By historical tradition, the Senate gives its members the right of unlimited debate. The record for holding the floor belongs to Republican Senator Strom Thurmond of South Carolina, for a twenty-four-hour, eighteen-minute marathon.[36] In the House, no member is allowed to speak for more than an hour without unanimous consent.

After a 1917 filibuster by a small group of senators killed President Wilson's bill to arm merchant ships—a bill favored by a majority of senators—the Senate finally adopted **cloture**, a means of limiting debate. A petition signed by sixteen senators initiates a cloture vote. It now takes the votes of sixty senators to invoke cloture. Although there is considerable criticism of the filibuster, there is no significant movement within the Senate to reform the rules of debate.

Norms of Behavior

Both houses have codes of behavior that help keep them running. These codes are largely unwritten norms, although some have been formally adopted as rules. Members of Congress recognize that they must eliminate personal conflict, lest Congress dissolve into bickering factions unable to work together. One of the most celebrated norms is that members show respect for their colleagues in public deliberations. During floor debate, bitter opponents still refer to one another in such terms as "my good friend, the senior senator from . . ." or "my distinguished colleague."

Probably the most important norm of behavior in Congress is that individual members should be willing to bargain with one another. Policymaking is a process of give and take; it demands compromise. However, it is important to point out that members of Congress are not expected to violate their consciences on policy issues simply to strike a deal. Rather, they are expected to listen to what others have to say and to make every effort to reach a reasonable compromise. Obviously, if they all stick rigidly to their own view, they will never agree on anything. Moreover, few policy matters are so clear-cut that compromise destroys one's position.

Some important norms have changed in recent years, most notably the notion that junior members of the House and Senate should serve apprenticeships and defer to their party and committee elders during their first couple of years in Congress. When seventy-three new Republicans entered the House after the GOP sweep in the 1994 elections, these freshmen served notice that they would use their size to change the way things were done in Congress.

These Republican freshmen did have an impact, most notably in pushing Speaker Gingrich to hold fast on principle in his negotiations with President Clinton. The freshmen thought that there is too much compromise in American politics and that political parties should stand firmly for what they believe in.[37]

The Legislative Environment

In this section, we examine the broader legislative environment that affects decision making in Congress. More specifically, we look at the influence on legislators of political parties, the president, constituents, and interest groups. The first two influences push Congress toward majoritarian democracy. The other two are pluralist influences on congressional policymaking.

Political Parties

The national political parties might appear to have limited resources at their disposal to influence lawmakers. They do not control the nominations of House and Senate candidates. Candidates receive the bulk of their funds from individual contributors and political action committees, not from the national parties. Nevertheless, the parties are strong forces in the legislative process. The party leaders and various party committees within each house can help or hinder the efforts of rank-and-file legislators to get on the right committees, get their bills and amendments considered, and climb onto the leadership ladder themselves. Moreover, party members on a committee

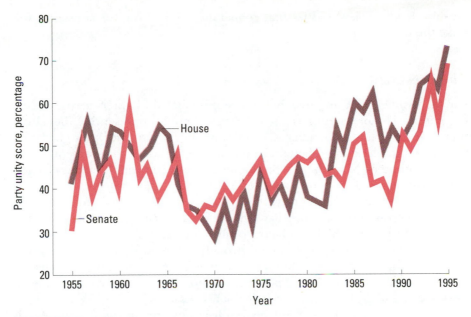

FIGURE 8.4   *Rising Partisanship*
The lines in this graph show the percentages of representatives and senators who voted with their party on party unity votes. (Party unity votes are those in which a majority of one party votes one way and a majority of the other party votes the opposite way.) The rising percentage of party unity votes indicates that congressional parties are more frequently at odds with each other. In a true majoritarian system, parties vote against each other on all key issues. (Sources: Norman J. Ornstein, Thomas E. Mann, and Michael J. Malbin (eds.), Vital Statistics on Congress, 1995–1996 *(Washington, D.C.: Congressional Quarterly Press, 1994), p. 208; and Dan Carney, "As Hostilities Rage on the Hill, Partisan-Vote Rate Soars,"* Congressional Quarterly Weekly Report, *27 January 1996, p. 199.)*

tend to act as agents of their party as they search for solutions to policy problems.[38]

The most significant reason that the parties are important in Congress is, of course, that Democrats and Republicans have different ideological views. Both parties have diversity, but as Figure 8.4 illustrates, Democrats increasingly tend to vote one way and Republicans the other. The primary reason why partisanship has been rising is that the parties are becoming more homogeneous.[39] The liberal wing of the Republican party has practically disappeared, and the party is unified around a conservative agenda for America. Likewise, the conservative wing of the Democratic party has declined. As the parties have sorted themselves out, their ideological wingspans have shrunk.

Some applaud this rising partisanship because it is a manifestation of majoritarianism. When congressional parties are more unified, it gives voters a stronger means of influencing public policy choices through their selection of representatives and senators. Others are skeptical of majoritarianism, believing that Congress is more productive and responsible when it relies on bipartisanship. In their view, parties that cooperate in searching for consensus will serve the nation better.

The President

Unlike members of Congress, the president is elected by voters across the entire nation. The president has a better claim, then, to representing the nation than does any single member of Congress. But it can also be argued that Congress as a whole has a better claim than the president to representing the majority of voters. Nevertheless, presidents capitalize on their popular election and usually act as though they are speaking for the majority.

During the twentieth century, the public's expectations of what the president can accomplish in office have grown enormously. We now expect the president to be our chief legislator: to introduce legislation on major issues and to use his influence to push bills through Congress.[40] This is much different from our early history, when presidents felt constrained by the constitutional doctrine of separation of powers and had to have members of Congress work confidentially for them during legislative sessions.[41]

Today the White House is openly involved not only in the writing of bills but also in their development as they wind their way through the legislative process. If the White House does not like a bill, it tries to work out a compromise with key legislators in order to have the legislation amended. On issues of the greatest importance, the president himself may meet with individual legislators to persuade them to vote a certain way. To monitor daily congressional activities and lobby for the administration's policies, there are hundreds of legislative liaison personnel who work for the executive branch.

Although members of Congress grant presidents a leadership role in proposing legislation, they jealously guard the power of Congress to debate, shape, and pass or defeat any legislation the president proposes. Congress often clashes sharply with the president when his proposals are seen as ill-advised.

Constituents

Constituents are the people who live and vote in a legislator's district or state. As much as members of Congress want to please their party's leadership or the president by going along with their preferences, they have to think about what the voters back home want. If they displease enough people by the way they vote, they might lose their seats in the next election.

Constituents' influence contributes to pluralism, because the diversity of America is mirrored in the geographical basis of representation in the House and Senate. A representative from Los Angeles, for instance, may need to be sensitive to issues of particular concern to constituents whose backgrounds are Korean, Vietnamese, Hispanic, African American, or Jewish. A representative from Montana will have few such constituents but must pay particular attention to issues involving minerals and mining. A senator from Nebraska will give higher priority to agricultural issues than to urban issues. Conversely, a

The State of the Union
The Constitution requires that the president "shall from time to time give to the Congress Information of the State of the Union, and recommend to their Consideration such Measures as he shall judge necessary." Here President Clinton fulfills that requirement in his first State of the Union Address.

senator from New York will be hypersensitive to issues involving the cities. All these constituencies, enthusiastically represented by legislators who want to do a good job for the people back home, push and pull Congress in many different directions.

Interest Groups

As we pointed out in Chapter 7, interest groups are one way constituents influence Congress. Because they represent a vast array of vocational, regional, and ideological groupings within our population, interest groups exemplify pluralist politics. Interest groups press members of Congress to take a particular course of action, believing sincerely that what they prefer is also best for the country. Legislators, in turn, are attentive to interest groups because these organizations represent citizens, some of whom live back home in the district or state. Lobbies are also sources of useful information and potentially of political support (and in some instances, campaign contributions) for members of Congress.

Because the four external sources of influence on Congress—parties, the president, constituents, and interest groups—push legislators in both majoritarian and pluralist directions, Congress exhibits aspects of both pluralism and majoritarianism in its operations. We will return to the conflict between pluralism and majoritarianism at the end of this chapter.

The Dilemma of Representation: Trustees or Delegates?

When candidates for the House and Senate campaign for office, they routinely promise to work hard for their district's or state's interests. When they get to Washington, though, they all face a troubling dilemma: What their constituents want may not be what the people across the nation want.

Members of Congress are often criticized for being out of touch with the people they are supposed to represent. This charge does not seem justified. A typical week in the life of a representative means working in Washington, then boarding a plane and flying back to the home district. There the representative spends time meeting with individual constituents and talking to civic groups, church gatherings, business associations, labor unions, and the like. A survey of House members during a nonelection year showed that each made an average of thirty-five trips back to his or her district, spending an average of 138 days there.[42] Legislators work extraordinarily hard at keeping in touch with voters, at finding out what is on their constituents' minds. The problem is how to act on that knowledge.

Are members of Congress bound to vote the way their constituents want them to vote, even if it means voting against their conscience? Some say no. They argue that legislators must be free to vote in line with what they think is best. This view has long been associated with the eighteenth-century English political philosopher Edmund Burke (1729–1797). Burke, who served in Parliament, told his constituents in Bristol that "you choose a member, indeed; but when you have chosen him, he is not a member of Bristol, but he is a member of *Parliament*."[43] Burke reasoned that representatives are sent by their constituents to vote as they think best. As **trustees**, representatives are obligated to consider the views of constituents, but they are not obligated to vote according to those views if they think they are misguided.

Others hold that legislators are duty-bound to represent the majority view of their constituents, that they are **delegates** with instructions from the people at home on how to vote on critical issues. And delegates, unlike trustees, must be prepared to vote against their own policy preferences.

Members of Congress are subject to two opposing forces, then. While the interests of their districts encourage them to act as delegates, their interpretation of the larger national interest calls on them to be trustees. Given these conflicting role definitions, it is not surprising that Congress is not clearly either a body of delegates or one of trustees. Research has shown, however, that members of Congress are more apt to take the delegate role on issues that are of great concern to their constituents.[44] But much of the time, what constituents really want is not clear. Many issues are not highly visible back home, they cut across the constituency to affect it in different ways, or constituents only partially understand them. For such issues, no delegate position is obvious.

Pluralism, Majoritarianism, and Democracy

The U.S. Congress is often criticized for being too pluralist and not majoritarian enough. The federal budget deficit, discussed at the beginning of this chapter, provides a case in point. Americans are deeply concerned about the large deficits that have plagued our national budgets in recent years. Indeed, that concern was apparent to both President Clinton and the Republican congressional leadership when, in May 1997, they finally agreed to a plan for balancing the budget by 2002. Both Democrats and Republicans in Congress have repeatedly called for reductions in the budget deficits. But when spending bills have come before Congress, legislators' concern has turned to what the bills will or will not do for their district or state. Appropriations bills usually include pork barrel projects that benefit specific districts or states and further add to the deficit.

Such projects get into the budget through bargaining among members; as we saw earlier in this chapter, congressional norms encourage it. Members of Congress try to win projects and programs that will benefit their constituents and thus help them at election time. To win approval of such projects, members must be willing to vote for other legislators' projects in turn. This type of system obviously promotes pluralism (and spending).

In recent years legislators have taken several steps to reduce the national deficit. The balanced budget agreement of 1997 was perhaps the most significant. However, critics contend that Congress will have to largely abandon pluralism if it is ever to balance the budget. Indeed, a primary motivation for the line-item veto was to give the president a tool to strip such projects from the budget. Yet those who favor pluralism are quick to point out that many different constituencies are well served by an appropriations process that allows for pluralism. Proponents of pluralism also argue that the makeup of Congress generally reflects that of the nation, that different members of Congress represent farm areas, oil and gas areas, low-income inner cities, industrial areas, and so on. They point out that America itself is pluralistic, with a rich diversity of economic, social, religious, and racial groups, and that even if our own representatives and senators do not represent our particular viewpoint, it is likely that someone in Congress does.[45]

The House Republicans' push to enact the Contract with America represented a concerted effort to move the national government toward a more majoritarian system. By presenting the voters in 1994 with a platform of policies they promised to pass, GOP House candidates were emulating candidates running for Parliament in a responsible party system (recall Chapter 6).

With the 104th Congress (1995–1996) now over, how might this bold experiment be evaluated? What was most impressive was the exceptional unity of House Republicans in voting for the bills that were part of the Contract with

TABLE 8.1   A Contract Fulfilled?

The Republicans' Contract with America "was born on a snowy weekend in February 1994. . . . At a conference of House Republicans in Salisbury, Maryland, a direction was set for making sure citizens could clearly understand what the Republican party stood for and meant to deliver if ever given a chance to control the federal legislative process."* House Republicans delivered on their promise, but many of the Contract's proposals never became law.

Policy Proposal	Outcome
Apply labor laws to Congress	Passed and signed into law
Prohibit unfunded mandates	Passed and signed into law
Balanced Budget Amendment	Passed House but failed by a single vote in the Senate
Line item veto	Passed and signed into law
Violent crime	
Truth in sentencing	Passed House, died in the Senate; also added to an appropriations bill that was vetoed
Relax exclusionary rule	Passed House but died in the Senate
Welfare reform	Passed and signed into law
Tax reform	
$500-a-child tax credit	Did not become law
Capital gains tax cut	Did not become law
Family Reinforcement Act	
Tax credits for adoption, senior care	Passed and signed into law
National defense	
Restrict U.S. troops under U.N. flag	Passed House but died in the Senate
Increase defense spending	Passed and signed into law
Reduce Soc. Sec. earnings limit	Passed and signed into law
Roll back regulations	Efforts to weaken Superfund and Clean Water Act failed to pass
Legal reform	
Securities litigation	Clinton veto overturned by Congress
Product liability	Passed by Congress but vetoed by Clinton
Term limits	Defeated in the House

* *Contract with America* (New York: Times Books, 1994), p. 4.

America. Almost all of the bills passed with relatively few defections in the Republican ranks. The Republican House candidates kept the promise they made in the 1994 campaign that they would pass the Contract if they won a majority. Yet a good portion of the Contract, including some of its most visible provisions—a balanced budget amendment, term limits for members of Congress, and a $500-per-child tax credit and capital gains tax cut—never became law (see Table 8.1). Although Republicans could blame Democrat Bill Clinton for vetoing some important parts of the Contract, one of the problems was the Republican majority in the Senate. A number of GOP voted against some of the bills when they reached the Senate. Although they gave the Republicans a landslide victory in 1994, voters were not of one mind on the Contract.

While they seemingly embraced majoritarianism with the Contract with America, the Republicans of the 104th Congress did not completely abandon pluralism. Interest groups played far too important a role in the 104th Congress for it to be judged an example of majoritarian democracy. Although increased party unity in legislators' voting and the Contract with America have both enhanced majoritarianism in Congress, the House and the Senate still remain more pluralistic than majoritarian in nature.

Summary

Congress writes the laws of the land and attempts to oversee their implementation. It helps to educate us about new issues as they appear on the political agenda. Most important, members of Congress represent us, working to see to it that interests from home and from around the country are heard throughout the policy-making process.

We count on Congress to do so much that criticism about how well it does some things is inevitable. However, certain strengths are clear. The committee system fosters expertise; representatives and senators who know the most about particular issues have the most influence over them. And the structure of our electoral system keeps legislators in close touch with their constituents.

Bargaining and compromise play important roles in the congressional policy-making process. Some find this disquieting. They want less deal making and more adherence to principle. This thinking is in line with the desire for a more majoritarian democracy. Others defend the current system, arguing that the United States is a large, complex nation and the policies that govern it should be developed through bargaining among various interests.

There is no clear-cut answer on whether a majoritarian or a pluralist legislative system provides better representation for voters. Our system is a mix of pluralism and majoritarianism. It serves minority interests that might otherwise be neglected or even harmed by an unthinking or uncaring majority. At the same time, congressional parties work to represent the broader interests of the American people.

Key Terms

reapportionment
impeachment
incumbent
gerrymandering
casework
descriptive representation
racial gerrymandering
veto
pocket veto
line item veto
standing committee
joint committee

select committee
conference committee
seniority
oversight
Speaker of the House
majority leader
filibuster
cloture
constituents
trustee
delegate

Selected Readings

Fenno, Richard F., Jr. *Home Style.* Boston: Little, Brown, 1978. A classic analysis of how House members interact with constituents during visits to their home districts.

Glaser, James. *Race, Campaign Politics, and the Realignment in the South.* New Haven, Conn.: Yale University Press, 1996. This examination of congressional races in the South looks at how Democratic candidates try to build biracial coalitions.

Herrnson, Paul S. *Congressional Elections.* Washington, D.C.: Congressional Quarterly Press, 1995. Herrnson's study is a comprehensive look at congressional candidates and the electorate.

Thomas, Sue. *How Women Legislate.* New York: Oxford University Press, 1994. Using surveys of state legislators, the author details how women are different from men in the way they do their jobs.

World Wide Web Resources

Project VoteSmart's Congressional Information Center. Keep track of your member of Congress. See how members voted on bills, get biographical information, access the Congressional Record, and follow links to other congressional information services. Also find the status of current legislation and see how members are evaluated by interest groups. Use the "zipper" to find your member of Congress by zip code and to send "netgrams."
<www.vote-smart.org/congress/congress.html>

Library of Congress. View current library exhibitions and retrieve current news and events. A highlight of this home page is the "American Memory," which contains historical collections (viewable on the Net) for the "National Digital Library."
<www.loc.gov>

House of Representatives. Retrieve information on current and recent legislation and information on members, committees, and other congressional organizations.
<www.house.gov>

Senate. Visitors can get information from and about Senate members, search the member directory, read about Senate history, and search a glossary of Senate terms.
<www.senate.gov>

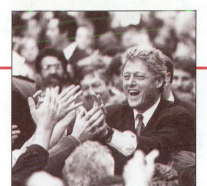

9

The Presidency

Bill Clinton promised to hit the ground running when he came to Washington. He had ambitious plans to reorient the country's priorities—"putting people first," as he had stressed in his campaign. His strategy for reviving the lagging economy was to create an investment program that would improve the nation's infrastructure, increase educational opportunities, and enhance training for those whose skills were not adequate for the demands of today's job market.

Clinton's first step was a modest $16.3 billion economic stimulus package, introduced less than a month after he took office. The legislation was intended to give a jump start to an economy that had performed poorly for the previous three years. It provided additional money for a variety of programs, including summer youth employment, AIDS care, child immunization, highway construction, Pell grants for college students, water projects, and Head Start. The biggest component of the package was simply a continuation of unemployment compensation.

The big Democratic majority in the House easily approved the bill in mid-March. In the Senate, Appropriations Committee chair Robert Byrd, a Democrat, was so eager to demonstrate his support to the president that he devised a complicated legislative strategy to get the bill through without any Republican amendments. Byrd's actions incensed the Republicans, who began a filibuster. The Democrats needed three Republican votes to break the filibuster, but the Republicans held firm in their unanimous opposition to the bill. Clinton resisted compromise at first, and by the time he reluctantly realized that the bill could not get through without concessions to the Republicans, Senate minority leader Bob Dole knew that his party had beaten the president. At the end of April, Clinton finally gave up on the economic stimulus package; Congress later enacted a narrowly focused bill extending unemployment benefits.

The new president had gone eyeball to eyeball with Bob Dole and suffered a humiliating defeat. Clinton himself bore much of the responsibility for the bill's failure. He never convinced the American people that the bill was vital. (The economy did, in fact, sharply improve in the months to come, despite the lack of a stimulus package.) The Republicans had made Clinton understand that without bipartisan support, he wouldn't be able to get much

Bridge for Sale
When he gave his acceptance speech at the 1996 Democratic convention, President Bill Clinton gave an optimistic assessment of the nation's health but was generally cautious in outlining plans for a second term. Using an evocative phrase, he said repeatedly that his goal was to "build a bridge to the twenty-first century." Clinton wanted to position the Democrats as the party of the future, while drawing a subtle contrast between himself and a seventy-three-year-old opponent whom he wanted to portray as the candidate of a generation whose time had passed.

through the Congress. Rather than hitting the ground running, Bill Clinton had simply hit the ground.[1]

As we analyze the various facets of the presidency, bear in mind one recurring question: Is the presidency primarily an instrument of pluralist democracy, serving small but vocal constituencies, or does the office promote majoritarian democracy by responding primarily to public opinion? In the case we have just discussed, President Clinton thought that both pluralist and majoritarian politics would work in his favor. In fact, neither did. That is, he thought the public would back him, but it was apathetic, and he thought that interest groups benefiting from the bill would help him get the legislation through, but these organizations had little influence with the Republicans. In addition to examining the majoritarian and pluralist sides of presidential politics, we focus in this chapter on a number of other important questions. What are the powers of the presidency? How is the president's advisory system organized? How does the separation of powers between the executive and legislative branches affect public policymaking? Finally, what are the particular issues and problems that presidents face in foreign affairs?

The Constitutional Basis of Presidential Power

When the presidency was created, the colonies had just fought a war of independence; their reaction to British domination had focused on the autocratic rule of King George III. Thus the delegates to the Constitutional Convention were extremely wary of unchecked power and were determined not to create an all-powerful, dictatorial presidency.

The delegates' fear of a powerful presidency was counterbalanced by their desire for strong leadership. The Articles of Confederation—which did not provide for a single head of state—had failed to bind the states together into a unified nation (see Chapter 2). The delegates knew they had to create some type of effective executive office. Their task was to provide national leadership without allowing any opportunity for tyranny.

Initial Conceptions of the Presidency

Debates over the nature of the office began. Should there be one president or a presidential council or committee? Should the president be chosen by Congress and remain largely subservient to that body?

The final structure of the presidency reflected the "checks and balances" philosophy that had shaped the entire Constitution. In the minds of the delegates, they had imposed important limits on the presidency through the powers specifically delegated to Congress and the courts. Those counterbalancing powers would act as checks, or controls, on presidents who might try to expand the office beyond its proper bounds.

The Powers of the President

The requirements for the presidency are set forth in Article II of the Constitution: the president must be a U.S.-born citizen, at least thirty-five years old, who has lived in the United States for a minimum of fourteen years. Article II also sets forth the responsibilities of presidents. In view of the importance of the office, the constitutional description of the president's duties is surprisingly brief and vague. This vagueness has led to repeated conflict about the limits of presidential power.

The major presidential duties and powers listed in the Constitution can be summarized as follows:

- *Serve as administrative head of the nation.* The Constitution gives little guidance on the president's administrative duties. It states merely that "the executive Power shall be vested in a President of the United States of America" and that "he shall take Care that the Laws be faithfully executed." These imprecise directives have been interpreted to mean that the president is to supervise and offer leadership to various departments, agencies, and programs created by Congress. In practice, a chief executive spends much more time making policy decisions for his cabinet departments and agencies than enforcing existing policies.

- *Act as commander in chief of the military.* In essence, the Constitution names the president as the highest ranking officer in the armed forces. But it gives Congress the power to declare war. The framers no doubt intended Congress to control the president's military power; nevertheless, presidents have initiated military action without the approval of Congress.[2] The entire Vietnam War was fought without a congressional declaration of war.

- *Convene Congress.* The president can call Congress into special session on "extraordinary Occasions," although this has rarely been done. He must also periodically inform Congress of "the State of the Union."

- *Veto legislation.* The president can **veto** (disapprove) any bill or resolution enacted by Congress, with the exception of joint resolutions that propose constitutional amendments. Congress can override a presidential veto with a two-thirds vote in each house.

- *Appoint various officials.* The president has the authority to appoint federal court judges, ambassadors, cabinet members, other key policymakers, and many lesser officials. Many appointments are subject to Senate confirmation.

- *Make treaties.* With the "Advice and Consent" of at least two-thirds of those senators voting at the time, the president can make treaties with foreign powers. The president is also to "receive Ambassadors," a phrase that presidents have interpreted to mean the right to formally recognize other nations.

- *Grant pardons.* The president can grant pardons to individuals who have committed "Offenses against the United States, except in Cases of Impeachment."

The Expansion of Presidential Power

The framers' limited conception of the president's role has given way to a considerably more powerful interpretation. In this section, we look beyond the presidential responsibilities explicitly listed in the Constitution and examine the additional sources of power that presidents have used to expand the authority of the office. First, we look at the claims that presidents make about "inherent" powers implicit in the Constitution. Second, we turn to congressional grants of power to the executive branch. Third, we discuss the influence that comes from a president's political skills. Finally, we analyze how a president's popular support affects his political power.

The Inherent Powers

Several presidents have expanded the power of the office by taking actions that exceeded commonly held notions of the president's proper authority.

These men justified what they had done by saying that their actions fell within the **inherent powers** of the presidency. From this broad perspective, presidential power derives not only from those duties clearly outlined in Article II but also from inferences that may be drawn from the Constitution.

When a president claims a power that has not been considered part of the chief executive's authority, he forces the Congress and the courts to either acquiesce to his claim or restrict it. In doing so, he runs the risk of suffering a politically damaging rebuff by either body. However, when presidents succeed in claiming a new power, they leave to their successors the legacy of a permanent expansion of presidential authority.

Claims of inherent powers often come at critical points in the nation's history. During the Civil War, for example, Abraham Lincoln issued a number of orders that exceeded the accepted limits of presidential authority and usurped powers constitutionally conferred on Congress . Lincoln said the urgent nature of the South's challenge to the Union forced him to act without waiting for congressional approval. His rationale was simple: "Was it possible to lose the nation and yet preserve the Constitution?"[3] In other words, Lincoln circumvented the Constitution in order to save the nation. Subsequently, Congress and the Supreme Court approved Lincoln's actions. That approval gave added legitimacy to the theory of inherent powers—a theory that over time has transformed the presidency.

Congressional Delegation of Power

Presidential power grows when presidents successfully challenge Congress, but in many instances Congress willingly delegates power to the executive branch. As the American public pressures the national government to solve various problems, Congress, through a process called **delegation of powers**, gives the executive branch more responsibility to administer programs that address those problems. One example of delegation of congressional power occurred in the 1930s, during the Great Depression, when Congress gave Franklin Roosevelt's administration wide latitude to do what it thought was necessary to solve the nation's economic ills.

When Congress concludes that the government needs flexibility in its approach to a problem, the president is often given great freedom in how or when to implement policies. Richard Nixon was given discretionary authority to impose a freeze on wages and prices in an effort to combat escalating inflation. If Congress had been forced to debate the timing of this freeze, merchants and manufacturers would surely have raised their prices in anticipation of the event. Instead, Nixon was able to act suddenly, and the freeze was imposed without warning. (We discuss congressional delegation of authority to the executive branch in more detail in Chapter 10.)

However, at other times Congress believes that too much power has accumulated in the executive branch, and it enacts legislation to reassert congressional authority. During the 1970s, many representatives and senators agreed that Congress's role in the American political system was declining, that presidents were exercising power that rightfully belonged to the legislative branch. The most notable reaction was the passage of the War Powers Resolution (1973), which was directed toward ending the president's ability to pursue armed conflict without explicit congressional approval.

The President's Power to Persuade

A president's influence in office comes not only from his assigned responsibilities but also from his political skills and from how effectively he uses the resources of his office. A classic analysis of the use of presidential resources is offered by Richard Neustadt in his book *Presidential Power*, which discusses how presidents gain, lose, or maintain their influence. Neustadt's initial premise is simple: "Presidential power is the power to persuade."[4] Presidents, for all their resources—a skilled staff, extensive media coverage of presidential actions, the great respect the country holds for the office—must depend on others' cooperation to get things done. Harry Truman echoed Neustadt's premise when he said, "I sit here all day trying to persuade people to do the things they ought to have sense enough to do without my persuading them. . . . That's all the powers of the President amount to."[5]

Ability in bargaining, dealing with adversaries, and choosing priorities, according to Neustadt, separate above-average presidents from mediocre ones. A president must make wise choices about which policies to push and which to put aside until he can find more support. He must decide when to accept compromises and when to stand on principles. He must know when to go public and when to work behind the scenes.

A president's political skills can be important in affecting outcomes in Congress. The chief executive cannot intervene in every legislative struggle. He must choose his battles carefully, then try to use the force of his personality and the prestige of his office to forge an agreement among differing factions. In terms of getting members to vote a certain way, presidential influence is best described as taking place "at the margins." That is, presidents don't have the power to consistently move large numbers of votes one way or the other. They can, however, affect some votes—possibly enough to affect the outcome of a closely fought piece of legislation.[6]

Neustadt stresses that a president's influence is related to his professional reputation and prestige. When a president pushes hard for a bill that Congress eventually defeats or emasculates, the president's reputation is hurt. The public perceives him as weak or as showing poor judgment, and Congress becomes even less likely to cooperate with him in the future. President Clinton was clearly damaged by his failure to gain passage of his ambitious plan to reform the nation's health care system.

The President and the Public

Neustadt's analysis suggests that a popular president is more persuasive than an unpopular one. A popular president has more power to persuade because he can use his public support as a resource in the bargaining process.[7] Members of Congress who know that the president is highly popular back home have more incentive to cooperate with the administration.

A familiar aspect of the modern presidency is the effort presidents devote to mobilizing public support for their programs. A president uses televised addresses (and the press coverage surrounding them), remarks to reporters, and public appearances to speak directly to the American people and convince them of the wisdom of his policies.

In recent years, presidents have increased their direct communication with the American people; as Figure 9.1 illustrates, the number of public presidential appearances has grown sharply since World War II. Obviously, modern technology has contributed to this growth. Nonetheless, the increase in public appearances and speeches represents something more than increased visibility for the president and his views. The power of the presidency has also changed fundamentally. The decline of party and congressional leadership hastened the rise of the public president; at the same time, the president's direct communication with the American people made it more difficult for political parties and Congress to reinvigorate themselves.[8]

Presidential popularity is typically at its highest during a president's first year in office. This "honeymoon period" affords the president a particularly good opportunity to use public support to get some of his programs through Congress.[9] When Ronald Reagan made a televised appeal for support for a legislative proposal during his first year in office, some members of Congress received calls and letters that ran ten to one in favor of the president. At the beginning of his second term, however, congressional offices typically received an equal number of negative and positive responses after a Reagan appeal.[10] Clearly, the public viewed Reagan with a more skeptical eye than it had four years earlier.

Several factors generally explain the rise and fall in presidential popularity. First, public approval of the job done by a president is affected by economic conditions, such as inflation and unemployment, as Figure 9.2 shows. Second, a president is affected by unanticipated events of all types that occur during his administration.[11] When American embassy personnel were taken hostage in Teheran by militantly anti-American Iranians, Carter's popularity soared. This "rally 'round the flag" support for the president eventually gave way to frustration with his inability to gain the hostages' release, and Carter's popularity plummeted. The third factor that affects presidential popularity is American involvement in a war. Lyndon Johnson, for example, suffered a loss of popularity during his escalation of the American effort in Vietnam.[12]

Presidents closely monitor their popularity, because it is widely regarded as a basic report card on how well they are performing their duties. A president's popularity can change dramatically during the course of a term. In the aftermath of the Gulf War, roughly nine in ten Americans approved of President Bush's performance in office. A month before the 1992 election, however, fewer than four in ten Americans approved of Bush.

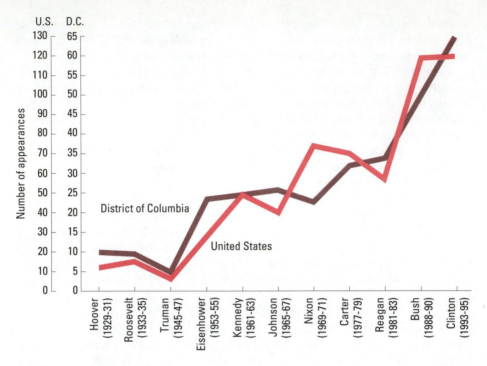

FIGURE 9.1 *Going Public*
This graph depicts the average number of public appearances made in a year by presidents from 1929 to 1990.* The increase in presidential public appearances is driven in large part by the efforts of presidents to rally public support for their proposals and policies.
*Only the first three years of their first terms were examined; the fourth year was not tabulated in order to exclude appearances arranged with an eye toward an upcoming election. Gerald Ford's term is also excluded for this reason. The Bush figures are for his first two years only. (Source: Samuel Kernell,
Going Public, *2nd ed. (Washington, D.C.: Congressional Quarterly Press, 1993), p. 102. Copyright © 1993 by Congressional Quarterly Press. Used with permission.)*

The strategy of leading by courting public opinion has considerable risks. It is not easy to move public opinion, and presidents who plan to use it as leverage in dealing with Congress are left highly vulnerable if public support for their position does not materialize. When Bill Clinton came into office, he was strongly predisposed toward governing by leading public opinion. His strategy worked poorly, though, as he was frequently unsuccessful in rallying the public to his side on issues crucial to his administration. Communicating with the public is crucial to a modern president's success, but so too is an ability to form bipartisan coalitions in Congress and broad interest group coalitions.

Presidents' obsessive concern with public opinion can be defended as a means of furthering majoritarian democracy: The president tries to gauge what the people want so that he can offer policies that reflect popular preferences.

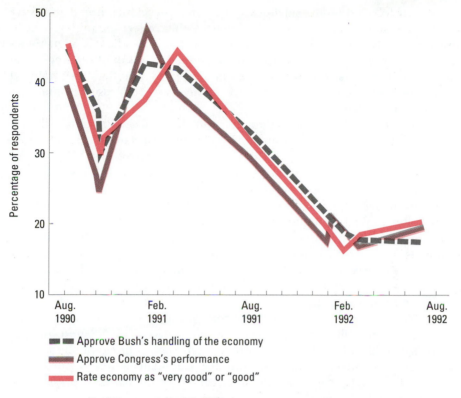

Percentage of respondents

Aug. 1990 — Feb. 1991 — Aug. 1991 — Feb. 1992 — Aug. 1992

- ■ ■ ■ Approve Bush's handling of the economy
- ▬▬▬ Approve Congress's performance
- ▬▬▬ Rate economy as "very good" or "good"

FIGURE 9.2   *Bad Economy, Bad Poll Ratings*

As the public's perception of economic conditions declined during the Bush years, people's confidence in the president's handling of the economy declined in tandem. Notice that confidence in Congress's performance took a similar tumble. Yet in the 1992 elections, most congressional incumbents were reelected, although President Bush was voted out of office. As we discussed in Chapter 8, people judge the Congress as a whole much differently than they judge their own members of the House and Senate. (Source: Gary C. Jacobson, "Congress: Unusual Year, Unusual Election," in The Elections of 1992, Michael Nelson, ed. (Washington, D.C.: Congressional Quarterly Press, 1993), p. 163. Copyright © 1993 by Congressional Quarterly Press. Used with permission.)

The Electoral Connection

In his farewell address to the nation, Jimmy Carter lashed out at the interest groups that had plagued his presidency. Interest groups, he said, "distort our purposes because the national interest is not always the sum of all our single or special interests." Carter noted the president's singular responsibility: "The president is the only elected official charged with representing all the people."[13] Like all other presidents, Carter quickly recognized the dilemma of majoritarianism versus pluralism after he took office. The president must try to please countless separate constituencies while trying to do what is best for the whole country.

It is easy to stand on the sidelines and say that presidents should always try to follow a majoritarian path, pursuing policies that reflect the preferences of most citizens. However, simply by running for office, candidates align themselves with particular segments of the population. As a result of their electoral strategy, their identification with activists in their party, and their own political views, candidates come into office with an interest in pleasing some constituencies more than others.

Each candidate attempts to put together an electoral coalition that will provide at least the minimum 270 (out of 538) electoral votes needed for election. As the campaign proceeds, each candidate tries to win votes from different groups of voters through his stand on various issues. Because issue stances can cut both ways—attracting some voters but driving others away—candidates may try to finesse an issue by being deliberately vague. However, a candidate who is noncommittal on too many issues appears wishy-washy. And future presidents do not build their political careers without working strongly for and becoming associated with important issues and constituencies. Moreover, after the election is over, the winning candidate wants to claim that he has been given a **mandate**, or endorsement, by the voters to carry out the policies he campaigned on. Newly chosen presidents make a majoritarian interpretation of the electoral process, claiming that their election-day victory is an expression of the direct will of the people. However, more dispassionate observers usually find it difficult to document concrete evidence of broad public support for the range of specific policies a winning candidate wants to pursue. As Feature 9.1 suggests, the "mandate" that came out of the 1996 presidential election is muddled at best.

A central reason why it is difficult to read the president's political tea leaves from election results is that the president is elected independently of Congress. Often this leads to **divided government**, with one party controlling the White House and the other party controlling at least one house of Congress. President Bush, for example, had to work with a Democratic-controlled House and Senate throughout all four years of his term. This may seem politically schizophrenic, with the electorate saying one thing by electing a president and another by electing a majority in Congress that opposes his policies. This does not appear to bother the American people, however: polls often show that the public feels it is desirable for control of the government to be divided between Republicans and Democrats.[14] As Table 9.1 shows, divided government has become more and more frequent.

Voters appear to use quite different criteria when choosing a president than they do when choosing congressional representatives. As one scholar has noted, "Presidential candidates are evaluated according to their views on national issues and their competence in dealing with national problems. Congressional candidates are evaluated on their personal character and experience and on their devotion to district services and local issues."[15] This congressional independence is another reason why contemporary presidents work so hard to gain public support for their policies.[16]

Scholars are divided as to the impact of divided government. One study showed that just as much significant legislation gets passed and signed into law

Back from the Dead

President Bill Clinton's easy victory over Bob Dole came as no surprise—the polls had been predicting it throughout the campaign. What was surprising, however, was that only a year earlier it had looked as though it would be the *Republican* candidate who would roll to an easy victory.

Although fortune appeared to turn quickly on the Republicans, viewing the election within a broader historical context suggests that 1996 strongly favored the Democratic candidate. The country was at peace and the nation's economy had been performing strongly since the beginning of the Clinton administration. In postwar America, the party controlling the White House has usually been successful in winning reelection when there was both peace and prosperity. What beat Bob Dole was not the mistakes he made in strategy or that he wasn't more telegenic. What beat him was four years of a steady, growing economy. Although the economy wasn't the only issue in the 1996 campaign, pocketbook issues were central to the public's decision to give four more years to Bill Clinton.

Still, if a Clinton victory seemed foreordained in 1996, why had Clinton looked so weak for the first three years of his term? The public certainly had doubts about Clinton and, indeed, his popularity ratings were unimpressive during his first three years. His first two years in office disappointed even his most ardent followers. His ill-fated economic stimulus package, a budget deficit reduction bill that included some tax increases on upper-income Americans, and the defeat of his health care reform bill, his most important legislative priority, all contributed to a widely held perception of presidential failure. Compounding Clinton's problems was the fact that he came across to the public as wavering and unsteady, as if he wasn't quite sure what he believed in.

The congressional election in 1994 was a disaster for Clinton. Not only had the Republicans won a huge and unexpected victory, taking over both houses of Congress, but by just about everyone's account the election was a referendum on Clinton's first two years in office. As Newt Gingrich led a blitzkrieg through the House with his Contract with America, the Democrats seemed stunned by the tidal wave that hit them.

Fortunately for Clinton, the Republicans overplayed their hand—they saw a mandate to sharply reduce the size and scope of government. Americans do want a small government, but they also want extensive government services. Although this is contradictory, public opinion is not subject to logic tests. When Clinton refused to go along with their extensive budget cuts, the Republicans refused to appropriate money to keep large segments of the government running. Clinton stood fast and parts of the government shut down. But the public sided with Clinton and it was Newt Gingrich who was on the defensive.

After the shattering repudiation of his administration in 1994, Clinton critically reassessed his performance and began talking with Dick Morris, a political consultant who had advised Clinton during his years in Arkansas. Morris pushed Clinton to move toward the moderate middle of the political

(continued)

spectrum, and he convinced the president that he needed to shed his image as a big-spending liberal. Especially noteworthy was Clinton's support for a welfare reform bill denounced by liberals in his own party. In the 1992 campaign Clinton had promised to "end welfare as we know it," and his signature on the legislation in 1996 sent a loud signal to the American people that he was a different kind of Democrat. At the same time, he remained steadfast in his support for education, the environment, and gun control—all issues popular with the American people and all issues on which the Republicans do poorly.

As Clinton skillfully and strategically positioned his party in line with public opinion on a wide range of issues, the public's perception of the economy grew more generous. There was clearly a lag as the public remained unconvinced for some time that the recession of the Bush years had fully ended and that the recovery was significant and enduring. When Bill Clinton faced the voters in the 1996 campaign, he could claim credit for an economy that had produced 10.5 million jobs during his term, had steadily expanded, and had low unemployment and low inflation. At the same time, the budget deficit had been reduced by more than half and the country was at peace. For Bill Clinton, it was the best of times.

TABLE 9.1   Unified and Divided Party Control of Government, 1901–1996
Divided government exists when one party controls the White House and the other party controls one or both houses of Congress. Earlier in this century, divided government was rare. In recent years, however, it has become common.

Year	President	Senate	House
1901–1903	R	R	R
1903–1905	R	R	R
1905–1907	R	R	R
1907–1909	R	R	R
1909–1911	R	R	R
1911–1913	R	R	D
1913–1915	D	D	D
1915–1917	D	D	D
1917–1919	D	D	D
1919–1921	D	R	R
1921–1923	R	R	R
1923–1925	R	R	R
1925–1927	R	R	R
1927–1929	R	R	R
1929–1931	R	R	R
1931–1933	R	R	D
1933–1935	D	D	D

(continued)

TABLE 9.1   **Unified and Divided Party Control of Government, 1901–1996 (cont.)**

Year	President	Senate	House
1935–1937	D	D	D
1937–1939	D	D	D
1939–1941	D	D	D
1941–1943	D	D	D
1943–1945	D	D	D
1945–1947	D	D	D
1947–1949	D	R	R
1949–1951	D	D	D
1951–1953	D	D	D
1953–1955	R	R	R
1955–1957	R	D	D
1957–1959	R	D	D
1959–1961	R	D	D
1961–1963	D	D	D
1963–1965	D	D	D
1965–1967	D	D	D
1967–1969	D	D	D
1969–1971	R	D	D
1971–1973	R	D	D
1973–1975	R	D	D
1975–1977	R	D	D
1977–1979	D	D	D
1979–1981	D	D	D
1981–1983	R	R	D
1983–1985	R	R	D
1985–1987	R	R	D
1987–1989	R	D	D
1989–1991	R	D	D
1991–1993	R	D	D
1993–1995	D	D	D
1995–1996	D	R	R

Source: James A. Thurber, "An Introduction to Presidential-Congressional Rivalry," in Rivals of
Power, *ed. James A. Thurber (Washington, D.C.: Congressional Quarterly Press, 1996), pp. 8–9.
Copyright © 1996 by Congressional Quarterly Press. Used with permission.*

when there is divided government as when one party controls both the White
House and Congress.[17] Using different approaches, other scholars have shown
that divided governments are in fact less productive than unified ones.[18]
Despite these differences in the scholarly literature, political scientists generally
do not believe that divided government produces **gridlock**, a situation where
government is incapable of acting on important policy issues.[19] There is a
strong tradition of bipartisan policymaking in Congress, which facilitates cooperation when the government is divided. The rising partisanship in Congress
(recall Figure 8.4) may, however, make divided government more of a problem.

The Executive Branch Establishment

As the president tries to maintain the support of his electoral coalition for the policies he pursues, he draws on the great resources of the executive branch of government. The president has a White House staff that helps him formulate policy. The vice president is another resource; his duties within the administration vary according to his relationship with the president. The president's cabinet secretaries—the heads of the major departments of the national government—play a number of roles, including the critical function of administering the programs that fall within their jurisdictions.

The Executive Office of the President

The president depends heavily on his key aides. They advise him on crucial political choices, devise the general strategies the administration will follow in pursuing congressional and public support, and control access to the president to ensure that he has enough time for his most important tasks. Consequently, he needs to trust and respect these top staffers; many in a president's inner circle of assistants are long-time associates. The president's personal staff constitutes the White House Office.

Presidents typically have a chief of staff, who may be a first among equals, or, in some administrations, the unquestioned leader of the staff. There is also a national security adviser to provide daily briefings on foreign and military affairs and longer-range analyses of issues confronting the administration. The Council of Economic Advisers is also located in the White House. Senior domestic policy advisers help determine the administration's basic approach to such areas as health, education, and social services.

Below these top aides are the large staffs that serve them and the president. These staffs are organized around certain specialties. Some staff members work on political matters, such as liaison with interest groups, relations with ethnic and religious minorities, and party affairs. One staff deals exclusively with the media, and a legislative liaison staff lobbies the Congress for the administration. The large Office of Management and Budget (OMB) analyzes budget requests, is involved in the policymaking process, and also examines agency management practices. This extended White House executive establishment, including the White House Office, is known as the **Executive Office of the President**. The Executive Office employs close to 1,600 individuals and has an annual budget of nearly $200 million.[20]

No one agrees about a "right way" for a president to organize his White House staff. However, one factor that influences how a president uses his senior staff is the degree to which he delegates authority to them. For example, Carter immersed himself in the policymaking process to ensure that he made all the significant decisions himself.

When Bill Clinton took over the White House, he instituted a loose staff structure that gave many top staffers direct access to him. Clinton's choice for his chief of staff was Mack McLarty, a friend since childhood and a successful Arkansas businessman who had no Washington experience. This appointment seemed to suggest that Clinton really wanted to be his own chief of staff, deeply involved in the nuts and bolts of White House policymaking. The president's undisciplined style and his tendency to take too much on led to considerable criticism of White House operations.[21] Clinton soon recognized that his staff structure was too inefficient and undisciplined. In June 1994, McLarty was moved aside to become a senior adviser to Clinton, and Leon Panetta, the president's budget director, became the new chief of staff. Panetta had served in Congress for many years, and he made clear improvements in White House operations before his departure at the end of Clinton's first term.

The Vice President

The vice president's primary function is to be ready and able to take over the presidency if anything happens to the president during his term in office. Traditionally, vice presidents have not been used in any important advisory capacity. Instead, presidents tend to give them political chores—campaigning, fund raising, and "stroking" the party faithful. This is often the case because vice presidential candidates are chosen for reasons that have more to do with the political campaign than with governing the nation. However, Vice President Al Gore's responsibilities extended far beyond such political chores. His high visibility along with his popularity among the party faithful made him an early favorite to capture the Democratic nomination for president in 2000.

The Cabinet

The president's **cabinet** is composed of the heads of the departments in the executive branch and a small number of other key officials, such as the head of the Office of Management and Budget and the ambassador to the United Nations. The cabinet has expanded greatly since George Washington formed his first cabinet, which included an attorney general and the secretaries of state, treasury, and war. Clearly, the growth of the cabinet to fourteen departments reflects the growth of government responsibility and intervention in areas such as energy, housing, and transportation.

In theory, the members of the cabinet constitute an advisory body that meets with the president to debate major policy decisions. In practice, however, cabinet meetings have been described as "vapid non-events in which there has been a deliberate non-exchange of information as part of a process of mutual non-consultation."[22] Why is this so? First, the cabinet has become rather large. Counting department heads, other officials of cabinet rank, and presidential aides, it is a body of at least twenty people—a size that many presidents find unwieldy for the give-and-take of political decision making. Second, most cabinet members have limited areas of expertise and simply cannot contribute much to deliberations in policy areas they know little about. The secretary of defense, for example, would probably be a poor choice to help decide important issues of agricultural policy. Third, although cabinet members have impressive backgrounds, they may not be personally close to the president or easy for him to work with. The president often chooses cabinet members because of their reputations, or he may be guided by a need to give his cabinet some racial, ethnic, geographic, sexual, or religious balance.

Finally, modern presidents do not rely on the cabinet to make policy because they have such large White House staffs, which offer most of the advisory support they need. And, in contrast to cabinet secretaries, who may be pulled in different directions by the wishes of the president and those of their clientele groups, staffers in the White House Office are likely to see themselves as being responsible to the president alone. Thus, despite periodic calls for the cabinet to be a collective decision-making body, cabinet meetings seem doomed to be little more than academic exercises. In practice, presidents prefer the flexibility of ad hoc groups, specialized White House staffs, and the advisers and cabinet secretaries with whom they feel most comfortable.

More broadly, presidents use their personal staffs and the large Executive Office of the President to centralize control over the entire executive branch. The vast size of the executive branch and the number and complexity of decisions that must be made each day pose a challenge for the White House. Each president must be careful to appoint people to top administrative positions who are passionate about the president's goals and skillful enough to lead others in the executive branch to fight for the president's program instead of for their own agendas.[23] To fulfill more of their political goals and policy preferences, modern presidents have given their various staffs more responsibility for overseeing decision making throughout the executive branch.[24]

The President as National Leader

With an election behind him and the resources of his office at hand, a president is ready to lead the nation. Each president enters office with a general vision of how government should approach policy issues. During his term, a president spends much of his time trying to get Congress to enact legislation that reflects his general philosophy and specific policy preferences.

From Political Values . . .

Presidents differ greatly in their views of the role of government. Lyndon Johnson had a strong liberal ideology concerning domestic affairs. He believed that government has a responsibility to help disadvantaged Americans. In describing his vision of justice in his inaugural address, Johnson used the words *justice* and *injustice* as code words for *equality* and *inequality*. They were used six times in his speech; *freedom* was used only twice. Johnson used his popularity, his skills, and the resources of his office to press for a "just" America—a "Great Society."[25]

To achieve his Great Society, Johnson sent Congress an unprecedented package of liberal legislation. He launched such projects as the Job Corps (which created centers and camps offering vocational training and work experience to youths aged sixteen to twenty-one), Medicare (which provided medical care for the elderly), and the National Teacher Corps (which paid teachers to work in impoverished neighborhoods). Supported by huge Democratic majorities in Congress during 1965 and 1966, he had tremendous success in getting his proposals through. Liberalism was in full swing.

In 1985, exactly twenty years after Johnson's inaugural speech, Ronald Reagan took his oath of office for the second time. Addressing the nation, Reagan reasserted his conservative philosophy. He emphasized *freedom*, using the term fourteen times, and failed to mention justice or equality once. He turned Johnson's philosophy on its head, declaring that "government is not the solution to our problem. Government is the problem." During his presidency, Reagan worked to undo many welfare and social service programs, and cut funding for such programs as the Job Corps and food stamps. By the end of his term there had been a fundamental shift in federal spending, with sharp increases in defense spending and "decreases in federal social programs [which] served to defund Democratic interests and constituencies."[26]

. . . To Policy Agenda

The roots of particular policy proposals, then, can be traced to the more general political ideology of the president. Presidential candidates outline that philosophy of government during their campaigns for the White House. But when the hot rhetoric of the presidential campaign meets the cold reality of what is possible in Washington, the newly elected president must make some hard choices about what to push for during the coming term. These choices are reflected in the bills the president submits to Congress, as well as in the degree to which he works for their passage. The president's bills, introduced by his allies in the House and Senate, always receive a good deal of initial attention. In the words of one Washington lobbyist, "When a president sends up a bill, it takes first place in the queue. All other bills take second place."[27]

The president's role in legislative leadership is largely a twentieth-century phenomenon. Not until the Budget and Accounting Act of 1921 did executive branch departments and agencies have to clear their proposed budget bills with the White House. Before this, the president did not even coordinate proposals for how much the executive branch would spend on all the programs it administered. Later, Franklin D. Roosevelt required that all major legislative proposals by an agency or department be cleared by the White House. No longer could a department submit a bill without White House support.[28]

Roosevelt's influence on the relationship between the president and Congress went far beyond this new administrative arrangement. With the nation in the midst of the Great Depression, Roosevelt began his first term in 1933 with an ambitious array of legislative proposals. During the first hundred days Congress was in session, it enacted fifteen significant laws, including the Agricultural Adjustment Act, the act creating the Civilian Conservation Corps, and the National Industrial Recovery Act. Never had a president demanded— and received—so much from Congress. Roosevelt's legacy was that the president would henceforth provide aggressive leadership for Congress through his own legislative program.

Chief Lobbyist

When Franklin D. Roosevelt and Harry Truman first became heavily involved in preparing legislative packages, political scientists typically described the process as one in which "the president proposes and Congress disposes." In other words, once the president sends his legislation to Capitol Hill, Congress decides on its own what to do with it. Over time, though, presidents have become increasingly active in all stages of the legislative process. The president is expected not only to propose legislation but also to make sure that it passes (see Figure 9.3).

The president's efforts to influence Congress are reinforced by the work of his legislative liaison staff. All departments and major agencies have legislative specialists as well. These department and agency people work with the White House liaison staff to coordinate the administration's lobbying on major issues.

The **legislative liaison staff** is the communications link between the White House and Congress. As a bill slowly makes its way through Congress, liaison staffers advise the president or a Cabinet secretary on the problems that emerge. They specify what parts of a bill are in trouble and may have to be modified or dropped. They tell their boss what amendments are likely to be offered, which members of Congress need lobbying, and what the chances are for the passage of the bill with or without certain provisions. Decisions on how the administration will respond to such developments must then be reached. For example, when the Reagan White House realized that it was still a few votes short of victory on a budget bill in the House, it reversed its opposition to a sugar price-support bill. This attracted the votes of representatives from Louisiana and Florida, two sugar-growing states, for the budget bill. The White House would not call what happened a deal but it noted that "adjustments and considerations" had been made.[29]

A certain amount of the president's job consists of stereotypical arm-twisting—pushing reluctant legislators to vote a certain way. Yet most day-in, day-out interactions between the White House and Congress tend to be more subtle, with the liaison staff trying to build consensus by working cooperatively with legislators. The White House also works directly with interest groups in its efforts to build support for legislation.[30] Interest groups can quickly reach the constituents who are most concerned about a bill, using their communications network to quickly mobilize members to write, call, or e-mail their members of Congress.

Although much of the liaison staff's work with Congress is done in a cooperative spirit, agreement cannot always be reached. When Congress passes a bill the president opposes, he may veto it and send it back to Congress; as we noted earlier, Congress can override a veto with a two-thirds majority of those voting in each house. Presidents use their veto power sparingly, but the threat that a president will veto an unacceptable bill increases his bargaining lever-

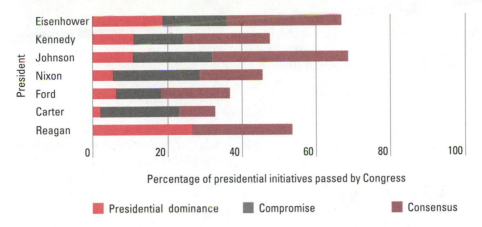

FIGURE 9.3   *Legislative Success*

Presidents vary considerably in their ability to convince Congress to enact the legislation that they send to Capitol Hill. Eisenhower and Johnson got about two-thirds of their proposals enacted, whereas Jimmy Carter was successful only one-third of the time. There is also substantial variation in the degree to which presidents have had to compromise to get their bills enacted. The category "presidential dominance" refers to presidential initiatives that were opposed in Congress but that opponents failed to defeat or alter. "Compromise" represents initiatives that Congress changed significantly before enacting. "Consensus" refers to initiatives for which there was no real opposition in Congress. All remaining legislation for each president failed to pass Congress. (Source: Adapted and reprinted by permission of the publishers from Mark A. Peterson, Legislating Together: The White House and Capitol Hill from Eisenhower to Reagan *(Cambridge, Mass.: Harvard University Press, 1990). Copyright © 1990 by the President and Fellows of Harvard College.)*

age with members of Congress. We have also seen that a president's leverage with Congress is enhanced when he is riding high in the public opinion polls and hindered when the public is critical of his performance.[31]

Party Leader

Part of the president's job is to lead his party. This is very much an informal duty, with no prescribed tasks. In fact, presidents can operate effectively without the help of a national party apparatus. Lyndon Johnson was contemptuous of the Democratic National Committee. He saw to it that the committee's budget was cut and refused some advisers' request that he replace its ineffectual head. Johnson thought a weak national committee would allow him to control party affairs from the White House. Like other modern presidents, Johnson believed he would be most effective communicating directly with the American people and did not see the need for national, state, or local party officials to be intermediaries in the process of coalition building.[32]

Work with the party may be more important for gaining the presidency than for actually governing. During the 1996 campaign, Vice President Al Gore campaigned tirelessly for Democratic candidates at all levels and did his best to raise money for the party. Regardless of whether the Clinton-Gore ticket won reelection, he wanted to position himself to make a likely run for the presidency in 2000. Working to shore up support among party activists was seen by Gore as a critical step toward gaining the nomination.[33]

The President as World Leader

The president's leadership responsibilities extend beyond the Congress and the nation into the international arena. Each administration tries to further what it sees as the country's best interests in its relations with allies, adversaries, and the developing countries of the world. In this role, the president must be ready to act as diplomat and crisis manager.

Foreign Relations

From the end of World War II to the beginning of the Bush administration, presidents were preoccupied with containing communist expansion around the globe. Now, with the collapse of communism in the Soviet Union and Eastern Europe, American presidents have entered a new era in international relations. The new presidential job description places much more emphasis on managing economic relations with the rest of the world. Trade relations are an especially difficult problem, because presidents must balance the conflicting interests of foreign countries (many of them our allies), the interests of particular American industries, the overall needs of the American economy, and the demands of the legislative branch.

The decline of communism has not enabled the president to ignore security issues. The world remains a dangerous place, and regional conflicts can still embroil the United States. When Iraq invaded and quickly conquered Kuwait in August 1990, President George Bush responded to protect our economic interests and to stand beside our Arab allies in the area. It was, said one journalist, a "dazzling performance. In roughly four days, Bush organized the world against Saddam Hussein."[34]

Crisis Management

Periodically the president faces a grave situation in which conflict is imminent or a small conflict threatens to explode into a larger war. Handling such episodes is a critical part of the president's job. Thus, voters may make the candidates' personal judgment and intelligence primary considerations in how they cast their ballots. A major reason for Barry Goldwater's crushing defeat in the 1964 election was his warlike image. His bellicose rhetoric scared many Americans. Fearing that Goldwater would be too quick to resort to nuclear weapons, they voted for Lyndon Johnson instead.

A president must be able to exercise good judgment and remain cool in crisis situations. John Kennedy's behavior during the Cuban missile crisis of

1962 has become a model of effective crisis management. When the United States learned that the Soviet Union had placed missiles containing nuclear warheads in Cuba, Kennedy sought the advice of a group of senior aides. An armed invasion of Cuba and air strikes against the missiles were two options considered. In the end, Kennedy decided on a less dangerous response: a naval blockade of Cuba. The Soviet Union thought better of prolonging its challenge to the United States and soon agreed to remove its missiles. For a short time, though, the world held its breath over the very real possibility of a nuclear war.

Are there guidelines for what a president should do in times of crisis or at other important decision-making junctures? Drawing on a range of advisers and opinions is certainly one.[35] Not acting in unnecessary haste is another. A third is having a well-designed, formal review process that promotes thorough analysis and open debate.[36] A fourth guideline is rigorously examining the chain of reasoning that has led to the option chosen, to ensure that presumptions have not been subconsciously equated with what is actually known to be true. Still, these are rather general rules and provide no assurance that mistakes will not be made. Each crisis is a unique event.

Presidential Character

How does the public assess which presidential candidate has the best judgment and a character suitable to the office? Americans must make a broad evaluation of the candidates' personalities and leadership styles. The character issue emerged in 1992 when the Bush campaign harshly attacked Bill Clinton for evasiveness about how he avoided the Vietnam draft. Also, many people had interpreted Clinton's earlier acknowledgment on *60 Minutes* that he was responsible for "causing pain in my marriage" as an indirect admission of marital infidelity.[37]

The character issue continued to dog Clinton in the White House. Questions were raised about an investment that he and Hillary Rodham Clinton had made in the Whitewater land development project. Allegations of sexual misconduct also reemerged in 1997 when the Supreme Court unanimously rejected Clinton's claim that, as president, he had temporary immunity to civil suits arising from incidents that allegedly occurred before he took office. The ruling cleared the way for Paula Jones, a former Arkansas state employee, to proceed with her sexual harassment suit against Clinton.[38]

A president's character is clearly relevant to his performance in office. His actions in office reflect something more than ideology and politics; they also reflect the moral, ethical, and psychological forces that comprise his character. However, candidates don't come neatly labeled as having healthy or unhealthy presidential characters. Although voters make their own estimations of how presidents will behave in office, there is no guarantee that those evaluations will turn out to be accurate. And a candidate's character must still be weighed along with other factors, including ideology, party affiliation, and stances on specific issues.

A Difference in Character
The personalities of Calvin Coolidge and John F. Kennedy led to considerably different styles of presidential leadership. Coolidge's motto, "Let well enough alone," says much about his approach to the presidency. "Vigorous" was the term commonly used to describe Kennedy, and it's an apt description of his presidency as well. Historian Arthur Schlesinger, Jr., said of Kennedy, "His presidential life was instinct with action."

Summary

When the delegates to the Constitutional Convention met to design the government of this new nation, they had trouble shaping the office of the president. They struggled to find a balance between an office that was powerful enough to provide unified leadership but not so strong that presidents could use their powers to become tyrants or dictators. The initial conceptions of the presidency have slowly been transformed over time, as presidents have adapted the office to meet the nation's changing needs. The trend has been to expand presidential power. Some of this expansion has come from presidential actions taken under claims of inherent powers. Congress has also delegated a great deal of power to the executive branch, further expanding the role of the president.

Because the president is elected by the entire nation, he can claim to represent all citizens when proposing policy; this broad electoral base equips the presidency to be an institution of majoritarian democracy. Whether the presidency actually operates in a majoritarian manner depends on several factors—the individual president's perception of public opinion on specific issues, the relationship between public opinion and the president's political ideology, and the extent to which the president is committed to pursuing his values through his office.

The executive branch establishment has grown rapidly, and the White House has become a sizable bureaucracy. New responsibilities of the twentieth-century presidency are particularly noticeable in the area of legislative leadership. Now a president is expected to be a policy initiator for Congress, as well as a lobbyist who guides his bills through the legislative process.

The presidential "job description" for foreign policy has also changed considerably. Post-World War II presidents had been preoccupied with containing the spread of communism, but with the collapse of communism in the Soviet Union and Eastern Europe, international economic relations now loom largest as a priority for presidents. However, national security issues remain because regional conflicts can directly involve the interests of the United States.

Key Terms

veto
inherent powers
delegation of powers
mandate
divided government

gridlock
Executive Office of the President
cabinet
legislative liaison staff

Selected Readings

Campbell, Colin, and Bert A. Rockman, eds. *The Clinton Presidency*. Chatham, N.J.: Chatham House, 1996. A first effort by political scientists to evaluate Bill Clinton's presidency.

Jones, Charles O. *The Presidency in a Separated System*. Washington, D.C.: Brookings Institution, 1994. Jones argues that ours is not a presidency-centered system and that policy initiation in Congress is more independent of the executive branch than most scholars realize.

Neustadt, Richard E. *Presidential Power*. Rev. ed. New York: Wiley, 1980. Neustadt's classic work examines the president's power to persuade.

Skowronek, Stephen. *The Politics Presidents Make*. Cambridge, Mass.: Harvard University Press, 1993. A sweeping, magisterial analysis of the cycles of presidential history.

Thurber, James A. *Rivals for Power*. Washington, D.C.: Congressional Quarterly Press, 1996. An excellent collection of essays reviewing the major issues in executive-legislative relations.

World Wide Web Resources

The White House. The highlight of this White House home page is the "interactive citizen handbook," an Internet guide to how to be a good citizen. Also available are White House tours and entry into White House "briefing rooms." Enter the briefing rooms to get current information on White House speeches, statements, and press releases as well as current government statistics.
<www.whitehouse.gov.>

Presidential Address. This page is sponsored by the University of Oklahoma Law Center. It allows the visitor to retrieve all state of the union and inaugural addresses dating back to George Washington. Other historically significant presidential speeches are also available.
<www.law.uoknor.edu/ushist.html>

10

The Bureaucracy

On May 11, 1996, ValuJet flight 592 took off from the Miami airport and headed north. A few minutes later smoke began to fill the cabin, and the pilot turned the plane around to return to Miami. Before it could reach the airport, however, the plane lost power and nose-dived into an alligator-infested swamp in the Everglades. None of the 109 on board survived.

Plane crashes are shocking, not just because of the carnage but because commercial airline crashes are so rare. Even more shocking than the crash was the revelation that the Federal Aviation Administration (FAA), the regulatory agency charged with setting, monitoring, and enforcing airline safety standards, had previously documented a poor maintenance record by ValuJet. Yet the agency had done little to force ValuJet to improve its repair and record-keeping practices.

The cause of the crash appears to have been some used oxygen canisters, which were loaded by mistake. Why weren't correct procedures followed? Beyond the individual errors in judgment are the financial pressures brought on the airlines by deregulation. Until the late 1970s, airline pricing was oligopolistic, with common fares approved by the government. Today, airlines compete vigorously, and many cut-rate start-ups like ValuJet have taken market share away from major carriers like United, American, and Delta.

Many of the new low-cost carriers save money by farming out maintenance work to subcontractors who can do the work more cheaply. Indeed, it was a subcontractor who loaded the fatal canisters onto flight 592. This has made the FAA's work more difficult, as its work force has not expanded to match the increasing number of companies running or servicing commercial airlines.[1]

But why is this so? Why doesn't the FAA just add inspectors and write more regulations to improve its monitoring of carriers and subcontractors? Americans surely want commercial airliners to be as safe as possible. Yet, at the same time that Americans want government to reduce the risks of everyday life, there is also great pressure to cut the budget, reduce the deficit, and shrink the size of government. As we'll explore in this chapter, Americans don't want big government, but they want the services big government provides. The controversy over the bureaucracy's role is not just a function of majoritarian opinion that is contradictory; it is also due to the fact that majoritarianism is often

Flight to Oblivion
After ValuJet flight 592 crashed into the Everglades, the FAA was roundly criticized for failing to do a better job of monitoring airline maintenance and safety standards. After reviewing its own performance, the FAA announced that it was taking steps to improve its supervision of maintenance subcontractors, such as Sabretech, the company that worked for ValuJet at the time of the crash. In September of 1996 ValuJet began flying again on a limited basis.

pitted against pluralism. One reason the FAA did not take more concerted action against ValuJet prior to the crash is that any government rebuke of the carrier would have jeopardized the company's future. (After the crash, the FAA did force the company to suspend its service.) More broadly, one of the FAA's responsibilities is to promote the airline industry, and it is thus lobbied heavily on both business and safety issues by large and small carriers alike. Beyond our focus on pluralist and majoritarian dynamics in bureaucratic politics, we will also look closely at why it is that Americans dislike government so much. Finally, we will discuss reforms that might make government work better.

Organization Matters

A nation's laws and policies are administered, or put into effect, by a variety of departments, agencies, bureaus, offices, and other government units, which together are known as its *bureaucracy.* **Bureaucracy** actually means any large, complex organization in which employees have very specific job responsibilities and work within a hierarchy of authority. The employees of these government units have become known somewhat derisively as **bureaucrats**.

We study bureaucracies because they play a central role in the governments of modern societies. In fact, organizations are a crucial part of any society, no matter how elementary. For example, the organization of a preindustrial tribe is not merely a quaint aspect of its evolution but is critical to the survival of its members.

The organization of modern governmental bureaucracies also reflects their need to survive. The environment of modern bureaucracies, filled with conflicting political demands and the ever-present threat of budget cuts, can be no less hostile than that of preindustrial tribes. The way a given government bureaucracy is organized also reflects the needs of its clients. The bottom line, however, is that the manner in which any bureaucracy is organized affects how well it is able to accomplish its tasks.

Unfortunately, "if organization matters, it is also the case that there is no one best way of organizing."[2] Although greater autonomy may improve the performance of public schools, it may not be a good solution for improving a state social welfare agency, where a primary goal is to treat its clients equally, and provide the same benefits to people with the same needs and circumstances. The study of bureaucracy, then, centers around finding solutions to the many different kinds of problems faced by large government organizations.

The Development of the Bureaucratic State

A common complaint voiced by Americans is that the national bureaucracy is too big and tries to accomplish too much. To the average citizen, the federal government may seem like an octopus—its long arms reach just about everywhere.

The Growth of the Bureaucratic State

American government seems to have grown unchecked during this century. As one observer noted wryly, "The assistant administrator for water and hazardous materials of the Environmental Protection Agency presided over a staff larger than Washington's entire first administration."[3] Yet even during George Washington's time, bureaucracies were necessary. No one argued then about the need for a postal service to deliver mail or a treasury department to maintain a system of currency. However, government at all levels (national, state, and local) has grown enormously in the twentieth century.[4] There are a number of major reasons.

A principal cause of government expansion is the increasing complexity of society. George Washington did not have an assistant administrator for water and hazardous materials because there was no need for one. A National Aeronautics and Space Administration (NASA) was not necessary until rockets were invented.

Another reason government has grown is that the public's attitude toward business has changed. Throughout most of the nineteenth century, business was generally autonomous, and any government intervention in the economy that might limit that autonomy was considered inappropriate. This attitude began to change toward the end of the nineteenth century, as more Americans became aware that the end product of a laissez-faire approach was not always highly competitive markets that benefited consumers.

Gradually, government intervention came to be accepted as necessary to protect the integrity of markets. And if government was to police unfair business practices effectively, it needed administrative agencies. During the twentieth century, new bureaucracies were organized to regulate specific industries. Among them are the Securities and Exchange Commission (SEC), which oversees securities trading, and the Food and Drug Administration (FDA), which tries to protect consumers from unsafe food, drugs, and cosmetics.

Through bureaucracies such as these, government has become a referee in the marketplace, developing standards of fair trade, setting rates, and licensing individual businesses for operation. As new problem areas have emerged, government has added new agencies, further expanding the scope of its activities.

General attitudes about government's responsibilities in the area of social welfare have changed too. An enduring part of American culture is the belief in self-reliance. People are expected to overcome adversity on their own, to succeed on the basis of their own skills and efforts. Yet, certain segments of our population are believed to deserve government support, because we so value their contribution to society or have come to believe that they cannot realistically be expected to overcome adversity on their own.[5]

This belief goes as far back as the nineteenth century. The government provided pensions to Civil War veterans. Later, programs to help mothers and children were developed.[6] In the wake of the Great Depression, the Social Security Act became law, creating a fund that workers pay into and then collect income from during old age. In the 1960s, the government created programs designed to help minorities. As the government made these new commitments, it also made new bureaucracies or expanded existing ones.

Finally, government has grown because ambitious, entrepreneurial agency officials have expanded their organizations and staffs to take on added responsibilities. Each new program that is developed leads to new authority. Larger budgets and staffs, in turn, are necessary to support that authority.

Can We Reduce the Size of Government?

When candidates for Congress and the presidency campaign, they typically "run against the government"—even if they are incumbents. Government is unpopular: Americans have little confidence in its capabilities and feel that it wastes money and is out of touch with the people (see Figure 10.1). Americans want a smaller government that costs less and performs better.

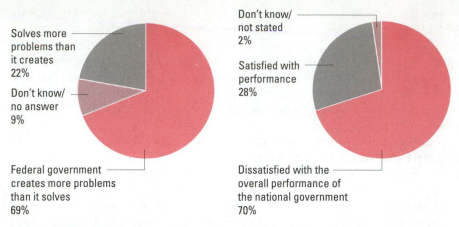

FIGURE 10.1 *We Hate Government (in General)*
Americans demonstrate little confidence in government when asked about its general capabilities. Poll results show that citizens believe government creates more problems than it solves and are dissatisfied with its performance. (Source: American Enterprise, *March-April 1993, p. 89.)*

If government is to become smaller, bureaucracies will have to be eliminated or reduced in size. Serious budget cuts also require serious reductions in programs. Not surprisingly, presidents and members of Congress face a tough job when they try to cut specific programs. Each government bureaucracy performs a service of value to some sector of society. For example, farmers want the price supports of the U.S. Department of Agriculture. Builders profit from programs offered by the U.S. Department of Housing and Urban Development. And labor unions want a vigorous Occupational Safety and Health Administration. Interest groups that have a stake in an agency almost always resist efforts to cut back its scope.

As for the public, people's attitudes toward government in general tell only part of the story.[7] When asked about specific programs or functions of government, citizens tend to be highly supportive. As Figure 10.2 shows, public support for expensive government endeavors (including guaranteeing a job for all who want one, which would be a significant expansion of government's reach into the economy) is considerable.

Given interest group and public support, it is rare for the government to abolish a department or agency. But agencies are not immune to change. Major reorganizations, in which programs are consolidated and the size and scope of activities are reduced, are not uncommon.

The tendency for big government to endure reflects the tension between majoritarianism and pluralism. Even when the public as a whole wants a smaller national government, that sentiment can be undermined by the strong desire of different segments of society for government to continue performing

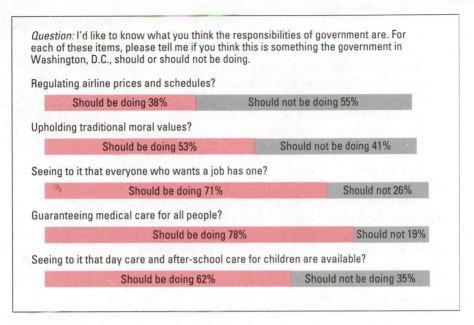

Question: I'd like to know what you think the responsibilities of government are. For each of these items, please tell me if you think this is something the government in Washington, D.C., should or should not be doing.

Regulating airline prices and schedules?

Should be doing 38% | Should not be doing 55%

Upholding traditional moral values?

Should be doing 53% | Should not be doing 41%

Seeing to it that everyone who wants a job has one?

Should be doing 71% | Should not 26%

Guaranteeing medical care for all people?

Should be doing 78% | Should not 19%

Seeing to it that day care and after-school care for children are available?

Should be doing 62% | Should not be doing 35%

FIGURE 10.2   We Like Government (in Particular)
Americans are critical of government, believing that it tries to do too much, has become too powerful, and wastes a lot of money. When asked about specific programs, however, they tend to be much more supportive of what the government is doing. (Source: Adapted from a November 1987 New York Times/CBS News *poll. Berman, Larry, ed.* Looking Back on the Reagan Presidency. *Baltimore, Md.: Johns Hopkins University Press, 1990, p. 307. Reprinted with permission.)*

some valuable function for them. Lobbies that represent these segments work strenuously to convince Congress and the administration that certain agencies' funding is vital and that any cuts ought to come out of other agencies' budgets.

Bureaus and Bureaucrats

We often think of the bureaucracy as a monolith. In reality, the bureaucracy in Washington is a disjointed collection of departments, agencies, bureaus, offices, and commissions—each a bureaucracy in its own right.

The Organization of Government

By examining the basic types of government organizations, we can better understand how the executive branch operates. In our discussion, we pay particular attention to the relative degree of independence of these organizations and to their relationship with the White House.

Departments   **Departments** are the biggest units of the executive branch, covering broad areas of government responsibility. As noted in Chapter 9, the secretaries (heads) of the departments, along with a few other key officials, form the president's cabinet. The current cabinet departments are State, Treasury, Defense, Interior, Agriculture, Justice, Commerce, Labor, Health and Human Services, Housing and Urban Development, Transportation, Energy, Education, and Veterans Affairs. Each of these massive organizations is broken down into subsidiary agencies, bureaus, offices, and services.

Independent Agencies   Within the executive branch, there are also many **independent agencies** that are not a part of any cabinet department. Instead, they stand alone and are controlled to varying degrees by the president. Some, among them the CIA, are directly under the president's control. Others, such as the Federal Communications Commission, are structured as **regulatory commissions**. Each commission is run by a small number of commissioners appointed to fixed terms by the president. Some commissions were formed to guard against unfair business practices. Others were formed to protect the public from unsafe products. Although presidents don't have direct control over these regulatory commissions, they can strongly influence their direction through their appointments of new commissioners.

Government Corporations   Finally, Congress has also created a small number of **government corporations**. The services these executive branch agencies perform theoretically could be provided by the private sector, but Congress has decided that the public is better served by these organizations having some link with the government. For example, the national government maintains the postal service as a government corporation because it feels that Americans need low-cost, door-to-door service for all kinds of mail, not just for profitable routes or special services. In some instances, the private sector does not have enough financial incentive to provide an essential service. This is the case with the financially troubled Amtrak train line.[8]

The Civil Service

The national bureaucracy is staffed by about three million civilian employees, who account for about 2.4 percent of the U.S. work force.[9] Most of those government workers are hired under the requirements of the **civil service**. The civil service was created by the Pendleton Act (1883). The objective of the act was to reduce patronage—the practice of filling government positions with the president's political allies or cronies. The civil service fills jobs on the basis of merit and sees to it that workers are not fired for political reasons.

The vast majority of the national government's workers are employed outside Washington. One reason for this decentralization is to make government offices accessible to the people they serve. Decentralization is also a way to distribute jobs and income across the country. Members of Congress, of course, are only too happy to place some of the "pork" back home, so that their constituents will credit them with the jobs and money that government installations create.

Like most large organizations, the federal government has taken steps to try to make its work force mirror the larger population in terms of race and gender (on gender, see Politics in a Changing America 10.1). Minorities have substantial representation within the federal government's work force, but at the highest level of the civil service, minorities are underrepresented.[10]

Presidential Control over the Bureaucracy

Civil service and other reforms have effectively insulated the vast majority of government workers from party politics. An incoming president can appoint fewer than 1 percent of all executive branch employees.[11] Still, presidential appointees fill the top policymaking positions in government. Appointing loyal people and developing mechanisms for White House control of agencies are means by which presidents try to get the individual parts of the executive branch to be responsive to their goals.

Each new president establishes an extensive personnel review process to find appointees who are both politically compatible and qualified in their field. Although the president selects some people from his campaign staff, cabinet secretaries, assistant secretaries, agency heads, and the like tend to be drawn directly from business, universities, and government itself.

Because so few of their own appointees are in each department and agency, presidents often believe that they do not have enough control over the bureaucracy. Presidents find that the bureaucracy is not always as responsive as they might like, for a number of reasons. Principally, pluralism can pull agencies in a direction other than that favored by the president. The Department of Transportation may want to move toward more support for mass transit, but politically it cannot afford to ignore the preferences of highway builders. An agency administrator must often try to broker a compromise between conflicting groups rather than pursue a position that holds fast and true to the president's ideology. Bureaucracies must also follow—at least in general terms—the laws governing the programs they are entrusted with, even if the president doesn't agree with some of those statutes. However, although government bureaucracies may sometimes frustrate the president, by and large their policies move in the direction set by the White House.

Administrative Policymaking: The Formal Processes

Many Americans wonder why agencies sometimes actually make policy rather than merely carry it out. Administrative agencies are, in fact, authoritative policymaking bodies, and their decisions on substantive issues are legally binding on the citizens of this country.

Politics in a Changing America 10.1

Does Gender Make a Difference?

When the U.S. Forest Service was sued for discriminating against women employees, it signed a consent decree pledging to hire enough women at each level of the organization so that its employment mix would be similar to the gender composition of the rest of the American work force. It moved quickly to hire more women in all types of jobs.

It is easy to applaud the Forest Service for tackling discrimination within its ranks in order to create more opportunities for women. Clearly, it makes a difference for women, who can now compete more fairly for better jobs with increased responsibility and better pay. But does it make a difference in how the Forest Service operates? Does employing more women have an impact on the Forest Service's policy decisions? After all, the primary job of the Forest Service is to manage publicly owned forests—is there a distinctly "feminine" approach to managing trees?

Recent research demonstrates that men and women in the Forest Service are different in important ways. A survey of those working for the agency shows that women are decidedly more concerned about environmental protection. Women in the Forest Service are more likely to believe that there are limits to the number of people the earth can support, that the balance of nature is easily upset, that economic growth should be "steady-state," and that humans are abusing the environment.

The Forest Service must balance the needs of consumers for wood products with the desire of Americans to have our forests preserved for generations to come. But if a larger percentage of employees entering the Forest Service believes we need to do more to protect the environment, then the existing balance between development and preservation is likely to be challenged.

The influx of women into the agency is too recent to measure whether these attitudes have carried over into new policies. Furthermore, basic policy is set by Congress and by the president's appointees who run the agency. Inevitably, though, the different mix of men and women within the Forest Service is going to affect policy, just as adding a lot more liberals or con-

(continued)

Administrative Discretion

What are executive agencies set up to do? To begin with, cabinet departments, independent agencies, and government corporations are creatures of Congress. Congress creates a new department or agency by enacting a law that describes the organization's mandate, or mission. As part of that mandate, Congress grants to the agency the authority to make certain policy decisions. Congress long ago recognized that it has neither the time nor the technical expertise to make all policy decisions. Ideally, it sets general guidelines for policy and expects agencies to act within those guidelines. The latitude that

Politics in a Changing America 10.1 (continued)

servatives to an agency would change it. The National Forest Products Association, a trade group of businesses that develop or use public-forest resources, has warned its members that "the sharp changes in the demographic characteristics of Forest Service employees will lead to further deemphasis on commodity production and to increasing emphasis accorded to non-timber resource values." In other words, more women in the agency means a different outlook on how to manage the nation's forests.

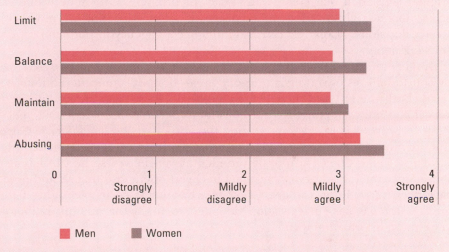

Source: Greg Brown and Charles C. Harris, "The Implications of Work Force Diversification in the U.S. Forest Service," *Administration and Society* 25 (May 1993), pp. 85–113.

Average response based on placement of respondents on a four-point scale.
Limit = We are approaching the limit of the number of people the earth can support.
Balance = The balance of nature is very delicate and easily upset.
Maintain = To maintain a healthy economy we will have to develop a "steady-state" economy, where industrial growth is controlled.
Abusing = Humankind is severely abusing the environment.

Congress gives agencies to make policy in the spirit of their legislative mandate is called **administrative discretion**.

Congress often is vague about its intent when setting up a new agency or program. At times a problem is clear-cut, but the solution is not; yet Congress is under pressure to act. So it creates an agency or program to show that it is concerned and responsive, but it leaves it to administrators to develop specific solutions. For example, the 1934 enabling legislation that established the FCC recognized a need for regulation in the burgeoning radio industry. But Congress avoided tackling several sticky issues by giving the FCC the ambiguous directive that broadcasters should "serve the public interest, convenience, and necessity."[12] In other cases, a number of obvious solutions to a problem may be available, but lawmakers cannot agree on which one is best. Compromise wording is thus often ambiguous, papering over differences and ensuring conflict over administrative regulations as agencies try to settle lingering policy disputes.

The wide latitude Congress gives administrative agencies often leads to charges that government is out of control, a power unto itself. But such claims are frequently exaggerated. If Congress is unhappy with an agency's actions, it can pass laws invalidating specific policies. This method of control may seem cumbersome, but Congress does have periodic opportunities to amend the original legislation that created an agency or program. Over time, Congress makes increasingly detailed policy decisions, often affirming or modifying agency decisions.[13] Congress can also influence an agency through appropriations legislation.

In general, then, the bureaucracy is not out of control. But Congress has chosen to limit its own oversight in one area—domestic and international security. Both the FBI and the CIA have enjoyed a great deal of freedom from formal and informal congressional constraints because of the legitimate need for secrecy in their operations. During the years that the legendary J. Edgar Hoover ran the FBI (1924–1972), it was something of a rogue elephant, independent of both Congress and the president. Over the years, the CIA has also abused its need for privacy by engaging in covert operations that should never have been carried out. Congress, however, has increased its oversight of the agency and has passed legislation designed to force the administration to share more information with it.

Rule Making

Agencies exercise their policymaking through formal administrative procedures, usually rule making. **Rule making** is the administrative process that results in regulations. **Regulations** are rules that govern the operation of government programs. When an agency issues regulations, it is using the discretionary authority granted to it by Congress to implement a program or policy enacted into law.

Because they are authorized by congressional statutes, regulations have the effect of law. Regulations are first published as proposals to give all interested parties an opportunity to comment on them and to try to persuade the agency to adopt, alter, or withdraw them. When the FDA issued proposed regulations requiring manufacturers of vitamins and dietary supplements to substantiate the health claims made for their products on the label, the industry fought the regulations vigorously. The manufacturers also asked Congress for relief. Although it was responsible for the legislation authorizing the regulations, Congress passed a one-year moratorium on the proposed rules. Congress seemed to want to have it both ways, ensuring the integrity of food and drugs while protecting the business interests of industry constituents.

The regulatory process is controversial because regulations often require individuals and corporations to act against their own self-interest. In this case, the producers of vitamins and dietary supplements resented the implication

Weighing the Evidence
As it oversees the safety of food, drugs, cosmetics, and medical devices, the Food and Drug Administration must weigh the benefits of each against any possible health risk. Here, author Karen Berger, who wrote a book about women deciding to use breast implants, testifies at an FDA hearing considering the banning of silicone gel implants due to health fears.

that they were making false claims and reminded policymakers that they employ many people to make products that consumers want. The FDA must, however, balance its desire not to put people out of work through overregulation with its concern that people not be misled or harmed by false labeling.

Administrative Policymaking: Informal Politics

When an agency is considering a new regulation, and all the evidence and arguments have been presented, how does an administrator reach a decision? Because policy decisions typically address complex problems that lack a single satisfactory solution, they rarely exhibit mathematical precision and efficiency.

The Science of Muddling Through

In his classic analysis of policymaking, "The Science of Muddling Through," Charles Lindblom compared the way policy might be made in the ideal world with the way it is formulated in the real world.[14] The ideal rational decision-making process, according to Lindblom, begins with an administrator tackling a problem by ranking values and objectives. After the objectives are clarified, the administrator thoroughly considers all possible solutions to the problem. The administrator comprehensively analyzes alternative solutions, taking all relevant factors into account. Finally, the administrator chooses the alternative that is seen as the most effective means of achieving the desired goal and solving the problem.

Lindblom claims that this "rational-comprehensive" model is unrealistic. To begin with, policymakers have great difficulty defining precise values and goals. Administrators at the U.S. Department of Energy, for example, want to be sure that supplies of home heating oil are sufficient each winter. At the same time, they want to reduce dependence on foreign oil. Obviously, the two goals are not fully compatible. How do administrators decide which is more important? And how do they relate them to the other goals of the nation's energy policy?

Real-world decision making parts company with the ideal in another way: The policy selected cannot always be the most effective means to the desired end. Even if a tax at the pump is the most effective way to reduce gasoline consumption during a shortage, motorists' anger would make this theoretically "right" decision politically difficult. So the "best" policy is often the one on which most people can agree. However, political compromise may mean that the government is able to solve only part of a problem.

Finally, critics of the rational-comprehensive model point out that policymaking can never be based on truly comprehensive analysis. Time is of the essence, and problems are often too pressing to wait for a complete study.

In short, policymaking tends to be characterized by **incrementalism**, with policies and programs changing bit by bit, step by step.[15] Decision makers are constrained by competing policy objectives, opposing political forces, incomplete information, and the pressures of time. They choose from a limited number of feasible options that are almost always modifications of existing policies rather than wholesale departures from them. However, over time, such incremental changes can significantly alter a program.[16]

The Culture of Bureaucracy

How an agency makes decisions and performs its tasks is greatly affected by the people who work there—the bureaucrats. Americans often find their interactions with bureaucrats frustrating because bureaucrats are inflexible (they go by the book) or lack the authority to get things done. Top administrators, too, can also become frustrated with the bureaucrats who work for them.

Why do people act bureaucratically? Individuals who work for large organizations cannot help but be affected by the culture of bureaucracy. Modern bureaucracies develop explicit rules and standards in order to make operations more efficient and to guarantee fair treatment of their clients. But within each organization, **norms** (informal, unwritten rules of behavior) also develop and influence the way people act on the job.

Bureaucracies are often influenced in their selection of policy options by the prevailing customs, attitudes, and expectations of the people working within them. Departments and agencies commonly develop a sense of mission where a particular objective or a means for achieving it is emphasized. The Army Corps of Engineers, for example, is dominated by engineers who define the agency's objective as protecting citizens from floods by means of building dams. There could be other objectives, and there are other methods of achieving this one, but the engineers promote the solutions that fit their conception of what the agency should be doing.

Despite budget cutbacks, adverse public opinion, and other constraints that make their job difficult, most bureaucrats work hard and try to serve the public as best they can. Those agencies with a clear sense of mission are likely to have a strong esprit de corps that adds to the bureaucrats' motivation. Bureaucrats' caution and close adherence to agency rules offer a measure of consistency. It would be unsettling if government employees interpreted rules as they pleased. Simply put, bureaucrats "go by the book" because "the book" consists of the laws and regulations of this country, as well as the internal rules and norms of a particular agency. Americans expect to be treated equally before the law, and bureaucrats work with that expectation in mind.

Problems in Implementing Policy

The development of policy in Washington is the end of one phase of the policymaking cycle and the beginning of another. After policies have been developed, they must be implemented. **Implementation** is the process of putting specific policies into operation. It is important to study implementation because policies do not always do what they were designed to do.

Implementation may be difficult because the policy to be carried out is not always clearly stated. Policy directives to bureaucrats sometimes lack clarity and leave them with too much discretion. When John Frohnmayer headed the National Endowment for the Arts (NEA), he fought legislation intended to prohibit federal funding for "obscene" art. He believed such legislation infringed upon artistic freedom. After a bitter fight in Congress, a compromise required that NEA grants be restricted to works that fall within "general standards of decency." But what exactly is a "general standard of decency"? It was left to the NEA—with an administrator hostile to the very idea of a decency standard—to figure it out.[17]

Implementation can also be problematic because of the sheer complexity of some government endeavors. Toxic cleanups, for example, pose complex engineering, political, and financial problems. Inevitably, regional EPA offices and key actors on the local level engage in considerable negotiations at each stage of the process.[18] The more organizations and levels of government involved, the more difficult it is to coordinate implementation.

Policymakers can create implementation difficulties by ignoring the administrative capabilities of an agency they have chosen to carry out a program. This happened in 1981 when the Reagan administration and Congress instructed the Social Security Administration to expand its review of those citizens receiving disability insurance benefits. The state agencies that carried out the reviews, had been doing between 20,000 to 30,000 cases a quarter. The same agencies were ordered to review 100,000 to 150,000 cases a quarter. As the number of people terminated increased, so did the legal appeals to reverse the terminations, and the backlog of unresolved cases grew sharply. With the administrative system inundated with more cases than it could handle, the problems with the program reached crisis proportions.

Obstacles to effective implementation can create the impression that nothing the government does succeeds, but programs can and do work. Problems in implementation demonstrate why patience and continual analysis are necessary ingredients of successful policymaking. To return to a term we used earlier, implementation is by its nature an *incremental* process, in which trial and error eventually lead to policies that work.

Reforming the Bureaucracy: More Control or Less?

As we saw at the beginning of this chapter, organization matters. How bureaucracies are designed directly affects how effective they are in accomplishing their tasks.[19] Administrative reforms have taken many different approaches in recent years as the criticism of government has mounted.[20] A central question that overrides much of the debate over bureaucratic reform is whether we need to establish more control over the bureaucracy or less.

Deregulation

Many people believe that government is too involved in **regulation**, intervention in the natural workings of business markets to promote some social goal. For example, government might regulate a market to ensure that products pose no danger to consumers. Through **deregulation**, the government reduces its role and lets the natural market forces of supply and demand take over. Considerable deregulation took place in the 1970s and 1980s, notably in the airline, trucking, financial services, and telecommunications industries.

In telecommunications, for example, consumers had no choice in choosing a long-distance vendor—one could call on the Bell system or not call at all. After an out-of-court settlement broke up the Bell system in 1982, AT&T was awarded the right to sell the long-distance services that had previously been provided by that system, but it now had to face competition from other long-distance carriers, like MCI and Sprint. Consumers have benefited from the competition, and more recently, competition has opened up for local phone service as well.

Deciding on an appropriate level of deregulation is particularly difficult for health and safety issues. Companies within a particular industry may legitimately claim that health and safety regulations are burdensome, making it difficult for them to earn sufficient profits or compete effectively with foreign manufacturers. But, the drug-licensing procedures used by the FDA illustrate

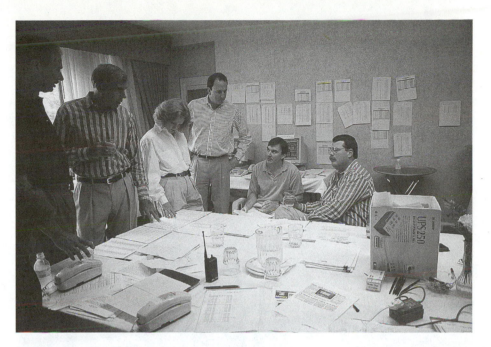

Bureaucrats, Planners, Auctioneers
The Federal Communications Commission plays a central role in overseeing the nation's telecommunications industry. These FCC bureaucrats did the planning that led to the 1994 sale of airwave licenses for paging and data transmission services. The successful auction yielded $617 million for the federal government.

the potential danger of deregulating such policy areas. The thorough and lengthy process the FDA uses to evaluate drugs has as its ultimate validation the thalidomide case in the 1960s. Dr. Frances Kelsey, who was assigned to evaluate the sedative, demanded that all FDA drug-testing requirements be met, despite the fact that the drug was already in use in other countries. Before the tests were completed, news came pouring in from Europe that some women who had taken thalidomide during pregnancy were giving birth to babies without arms, legs, or ears. Strict adherence to government regulation protected Americans from the same tragic consequences.

Nevertheless, the pharmaceutical industry has been highly critical of the FDA, claiming that the licensing procedures are so complex that drugs of great benefit are kept from the marketplace for years with people suffering from diseases denied access to new treatments. They have encouraged the FDA to adopt faster procedures.

Although the FDA has been resistant to doing anything that would compromise what it sees as necessary precautions, in recent years, the AIDS epidemic has brought about some concessions. The FDA has issued new rules expediting the availability of experimental drugs, and more generally, the FDA has adopted a somewhat speedier timetable for clinical tests of new drugs.[21]

Fly the Unfriendly Skies
With the deregulation of the airline industry, increased traffic on many routes has tested the
capacity of the Federal Aviation Administration to ensure safety in the air. Air traffic con-
trollers form the front line of the FAA's safety efforts. The responsibility of their job and the
acute concentration it requires make the controllers' work extremely stressful.

The conflict over how far to take deregulation reflects the traditional dilemma of choosing between freedom and order. A strong case can be made for deregulated business markets, in which free and unfettered competition benefits consumers and promotes productivity. The strength of capitalist economies comes from the ability of individuals and firms to compete freely in the marketplace, and the regulatory state places restrictions on this freedom. But without regulation, nothing ensures that marketplace participants will act responsibly.

Monitoring, Accountability, and Responsiveness

Bureaucracies must also strive to be responsive to the public, to provide services in an efficient and accessible manner. In the past few years, a management reform program known as **total quality management (TQM)** has increasingly gotten attention. Although initially directed at improving the quality of manufacturing, it is now being adapted to organizations (such as government bureaucracies) that provide services as their "product." The principles of TQM include listening to the customer, relying on teamwork, focusing on continually improving quality, breaking down barriers between parts of organizations, and engaging in participatory management.[22]

Most Americans believe that government has a long way to go toward treating its clients like "customers." Yet in an era when people are highly antagonistic toward government and budgets are tight, government bureaucrats know they need to do better.

The compelling philosophy behind TQM led the Clinton administration to launch its "reinventing government" initiative, aimed at improving the management of the national government. It has had some short-term successes, but there is no shortage of problems with TQM.[23] The single most important rule of TQM is to listen to your customers in an effort to serve them better. But for a government agency, who is the customer? Are the Department of Agriculture's customers the farmers who want the agency to spend a lot of money providing them with services and subsidies, or are they the taxpayers who want the agency to minimize the amount of money spent by government? TQM does not solve this basic conflict between pluralism and majoritarianism.

Summary

As the scope of government activity has grown during the twentieth century, so too has the bureaucracy. The executive branch has evolved into a complex set of departments, independent agencies, and government corporations. The way in which these various bureaucracies are organized matters a great deal because the way they are structured affects their ability to carry out their tasks.

Through the administrative discretion granted them by Congress, these bodies make policy decisions through rule making and adjudication that have the force of law. In making policy choices, agency decision makers are influenced by their external environment, especially the White House, Congress, and interest groups. Internal norms and the need to work cooperatively with others both inside and outside their agencies also influence decision makers.

The most serious charge facing the bureaucracy is that it is unresponsive to the will of the people. In fact, the White House, Congress, interest groups, and public opinion act as substantial controls on the bureaucracy. Still, to many Americans, the bureaucracy seems too big, too costly, and too intrusive. Reducing the size and scope of bureaucratic activity is difficult, because pluralism characterizes our political system. The entire executive branch may appear too large, and each of us can point to agencies that we believe should be reduced or eliminated. Yet each bureaucracy has its supporters. Bureaucracies survive because they provide important services to groups of people, and those people—no matter how strong their commitment to shrinking the government—are not willing to sacrifice their own benefits.

Plans for reforming the bureaucracy to make it work better are not in short supply. Proponents of deregulation believe our economy would be more productive if we freed the marketplace from the heavy hand of government supervision. Opponents believe that deregulation involves considerable risk and that we ought to be very careful in determining which markets and business practices can be subjected to less government supervision. To prevent disasters such as the thalidomide episode and the savings and loan scandal, government bureaucracies must be able to monitor the behavior of people inside and outside of government, and supervise business practices in a wide range of industries. However, most people continue to believe that the overall management of bureaucracies is poor and that government needs to be more customer-driven.

Key Terms

bureaucracy
bureaucrat
department
independent agency
regulatory commission
government corporation
civil service
administrative discretion

rule making
regulations
incrementalism
norms
implementation
regulation
deregulation
total quality management (TQM)

Selected Readings

Eisner, Marc Allen. *Regulatory Politics in Transition.* Baltimore: Johns Hopkins University Press, 1993. Eisner offers an overview of regulation in different periods of American history.

Harris, Richard A., and Sidney M. Milkis. *The Politics of Regulatory Change,* 2d ed. New York: Oxford University Press, 1996. A study of how the regulatory regime of the Reagan years affected policymaking at the Federal Trade Commission and the Environmental Protection Agency.

Howard, Philip K. *The Death of Common Sense.* New York: Warner Books, 1994. A sharp attack on government bureaucracies for being too inflexible and for not giving agency officials more discretion in solving problems.

Kerwin, Cornelius M. *Rulemaking: How Government Agencies Write Law and Make Policy.* Washington, D.C.: Congressional Quarterly Press, 1994. An inside look at how agencies write regulations to carry out the laws they must administer.

World Wide Web Resources

Fedworld. This site is operated by the National Technical Information Service (of the Department of Commerce). A "central access point" for U.S. government information on-line, it allows you to "locate, order, and have government information delivered to you." It also contains information on federal employment opportunities, abstracts of recent government reports (from all agencies), links to departments for which Fedworld provides home pages (Federal Energy

Regulatory Commission, IRS, Treasury), and the World-News Connection (access to non-U.S. media sources).

Federal Communications Commission. This home page provides access to the FCC's Daily Digest, policy agenda, agendas of open meetings, consumer information, a link to the text of the 1996 Telecommunications Act (which includes Internet policy) and the FCC's implementation schedule, and speeches made by commissioners.

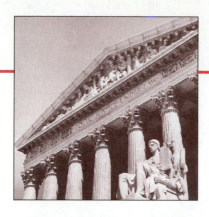

11

The Courts

"We're going to kill him politically—this little creep. Where did he come from?" asked feminist activist Florence Kennedy.[1] Her target was Judge Clarence Thomas, who had just been nominated by President George Bush for a seat on the nation's highest court, the Supreme Court of the United States. Thomas was a staunch conservative. His 1991 appointment, to replace the retiring liberal Justice Thurgood Marshall, would put many liberal decisions at risk.

Thomas endured a determined effort by a range of liberal organizations, including the American Civil Liberties Union and the National Organization for Women, to scuttle his confirmation by the U.S. Senate (a constitutional requirement). He weathered days of questioning from the Senate Judiciary Committee, declining to express his opinions about policies and approaches to constitutional interpretation and thus stymieing his opponents. Thomas's nomination seemed assured until a last-minute witness, Professor Anita Hill, came forward with charges that Thomas had made unwanted advances when she had worked for him ten years earlier. Thomas categorically denied the charges and characterized the process as "a high-tech lynching."[2]

Suddenly, the hearing galvanized the press and the public. A transfixed nation watched the riveting testimony of Hill, Thomas, and a parade of corroborating witnesses. Thomas's critics heaved charges of sexism; his champions leveled charges of racism. The committee failed to unearth convincing proof of Hill's allegations. (National polls at the time showed Americans believed Thomas over Hill by a margin of two to one.) In the end, the Senate voted by a slim margin—fifty-two to forty-eight—to confirm Thomas's nomination.

Upon taking the oath of office, Thomas withdrew into his work, secure in the knowledge that the Constitution now placed him above his detractors. For her part, Anita Hill became a much-sought-after celebrity for liberal and feminist causes. For his part, Thomas has the consolation of serving on the nation's highest court for the rest of his life. "They can say what they want about me," Thomas later remarked to a friend, "but I'm going to be making law for a long time."[3]

The Supreme Court is like a cloister: Outsiders find it very difficult to know what transpires inside. This is especially true of the events that take place in the conference room where the justices gather twice weekly to cast tentative decisions on cases that have recently been argued.

"She Said. He Said."
President George Bush nominated forty-three-year-old Clarence Thomas to the nation's high-est court in 1991. As Thomas was on the verge of confirmation, Anita Hill, a former Thomas assistant, stepped forward to assert that Thomas had made unwanted advances years earlier. Her charges nearly scuttled Thomas's nomination.

After hearing arguments in two important 1995 cases related to issues of race, Thomas spoke fervently in the conference room of his own struggles with racial segregation and bigotry. (The justices reported these events to their assistants, who spoke without attribution to a reporter.) As Thomas saw it, race-based solutions (such as forcing whites and blacks to attend the same schools or giving African Americans special advantages in securing contracts or employment) are misdirected and harmful because they rest on the patronizing belief that blacks are inherently inferior. The solution, Thomas averred, is to ensure equality of opportunity and to remove government from the business of racial classifications. The Constitution, Thomas declared, should be color-blind.[4] He cast his votes accordingly.

A single vote can make a difference. In both 1995 cases, the justices split five to four, with Thomas in the majority. As a result, the Court curtailed the government's power to fashion remedies to racial discrimination in the name of equality and allowed more room for freedom to flourish.[5] These cases and others have signaled a conservative shift in the Court's ideological center—a shift that is largely unaffected by representative institutions or majority rule.

Judges confront conflicting values in the cases brought before them, and in crafting their decisions, judges—especially Supreme Court justices—make policy. Their decisions become the precedents other judges use to rule in similar cases. Judges make public policy to the extent that they influence decisions in other courts.

The power of the courts to shape policy creates a difficult problem for democratic theory. According to that theory, the power to make law resides only in the people or their elected representatives. When judges undo the work of elected majorities, they risk depriving the people of the right to make the laws to govern themselves.

Court rulings—especially Supreme Court rulings—extend far beyond any particular case. Judges are students of the law, but they remain human beings. They have their own opinions about the values of freedom, order, and equality. And although all judges are constrained by statutes and precedents from expressing their personal beliefs in their decisions, some judges are more prone than others to interpret laws in light of those beliefs.

America's courts are deeply involved in the life of the country and its people. Some courts, such as the Supreme Court, make fundamental policy decisions vital to the preservation of freedom, order, and equality. Through checks and balances, the elected branches link the courts to democracy, and the courts link the elected branches to the Constitution. But does it work? Can the courts exercise political power within the pluralist model? Or are judges simply sovereigns in black robes, making decisions independent of popular control? This chapter tries to answer these questions by exploring the role of the judiciary in American political life.

National Judicial Supremacy

Section 1 of Article III of the Constitution creates "one supreme Court." The founders were divided on the need for other national courts, so they deferred to Congress the decision to create a national court system. Those who opposed the creation of national courts believed that such a system would usurp the authority of the state courts.[6] Congress considered the issue in its first session and, in the Judiciary Act of 1789, gave life to a system of federal (that is national) courts that would coexist with the courts in each state but be independent of them. Federal judges would also be independent of popular influences because the Constitution provided for their virtual lifetime appointment.

In the early years of the Republic, the federal judiciary was not considered a particularly powerful branch of government. It was especially difficult to recruit and keep Supreme Court justices. They spent much of their time as individual traveling judges ("riding circuit"); disease and transportation were everyday hazards. The justices met as the Supreme Court only for a few weeks in February and August.[7] John Jay, the first chief justice, refused to resume his duties in 1801 because he concluded that the Court could not muster the "energy, weight, and dignity" to contribute to national affairs.[8] But a period of profound change began in 1801 when President John Adams appointed his secretary of state, John Marshall, to the position of chief justice.

Judicial Review of the Other Branches

Shortly after Marshall's appointment, the Supreme Court confronted a question of fundamental importance to the future of the new republic: If a law enacted by Congress conflicts with the Constitution, which should prevail? The question arose in the case of *Marbury v. Madison* (1803), which involved a controversial series of last-minute political appointments.

The High Court held, in Marshall's forceful argument, that the Constitution was "the fundamental and paramount law of the nation" and that "an act of the legislature repugnant to the constitution is void." In other words, when an act of the legislature conflicts with the Constitution—the nation's highest law—that act is invalid. Marshall's argument vested in the judiciary the power to weigh the validity of congressional acts:

> It is emphatically the province and duty of the judicial department to say what the law is. Those who apply the rule to particular cases, must of necessity expound and interpret that rule. . . . If a law be in opposition to the constitution, if both the law and the constitution apply to a particular case, so that the court must either decide that case conformably to the law, disregarding the constitution; or conformably to the constitution, disregarding the law; the court must determine which of these conflicting rules governs the case. This is the very essence of judicial duty.[9]

The decision in *Marbury v. Madison* established the Supreme Court's power of **judicial review**—the power to declare congressional acts invalid if they violate the Constitution.* Subsequent cases extended the power to cover presidential acts as well.[10]

Marshall expanded the potential power of the Supreme Court to equal or exceed the power of the other branches of government. Should a congressional act (or, by implication, a presidential act) conflict with the Constitution, the Supreme Court claimed the power to declare the act void. The judiciary would be a check on the legislative and executive branches, consistent with the principle of checks and balances embedded in the Constitution. Judicial review gave the Supreme Court the final word on the meaning of the Constitution.

The exercise of judicial review—an appointed branch's checking of an elected branch in the name of the Constitution—appears to run counter to democratic theory. But, in nearly two hundred years of practice, the Supreme Court has invalidated fewer than 150 provisions of national law. Only a small number have had great significance for the political system.[11] The Court did produce a bumper crop of four invalidations in 1995, but only one—involving handgun possession near a school—merited broad media and scholarly attention. Moreover, there are mechanisms to override judicial review (constitutional amendment) and to control the excesses of the justices (impeachment). In addition, the Court can respond to the continuing struggle among competing interests (a struggle that is consistent with the pluralist model) by reversing itself.

Judicial Review of State Government

The establishment of judicial review of national laws made the Supreme Court the umpire of the national government. When acts of the national govern-

---

*The Supreme Court had earlier upheld an act of Congress in *Hylton v. United States,* 3 Dallas 171 (1796). *Marbury v. Madison* was the first exercise of the power of a court to invalidate an act of Congress.

ment conflict with the Constitution, the Supreme Court can declare those acts invalid. But suppose state laws conflict with the Constitution, national laws, or federal treaties? Can the U.S. Supreme Court invalidate them as well?

The Court answered in the affirmative in 1796. The case involved a British creditor who was trying to collect a debt from the state of Virginia.[12] Virginia law canceled debts owed British subjects, yet the Treaty of Paris (1783), in which Britain formally acknowledged the independence of the colonies, guaranteed that creditors could collect such debts. The Court ruled that the Constitution's supremacy clause (Article VI), which embraces national laws and treaties, nullified the state law.

The states continued to resist the yoke of national supremacy. Advocates of strong states' rights conceded that the supremacy clause obligates state judges to follow the Constitution when state law conflicts with it; however, they maintained that the states were bound only by their own interpretation of the Constitution. The Supreme Court said no, ruling that it had the authority to review state court decisions that called for the interpretation of national law.[13] National supremacy required the Supreme Court to impose uniformity on federal law; otherwise, the Constitution's meaning would vary from state to state. The people, not the states, had ordained the Constitution; and the people had subordinated state power to it in order to establish a viable national government. In time, the Supreme Court would use its judicial review power in nearly 1,200 instances to invalidate state and local laws on issues as diverse as abortion, the death penalty, the rights of the accused, and reapportionment.[14]

The Exercise of Judicial Review

These early cases, coupled with other historic decisions, established the components of judicial review:

- The power of the courts to declare national, state, and local laws invalid if they violate the Constitution
- The supremacy of national laws or treaties when they conflict with state and local laws
- The role of the Supreme Court as the final authority on the meaning of the Constitution

This political might—the power to undo decisions of the representative branches of the national and state governments—lay in the hands of appointed judges, people who were not accountable to the electorate. Did judicial review square with democratic government?

Alexander Hamilton had foreseen and tackled the problem in *Federalist* No. 78. Writing during the ratification debates surrounding the adoption of the Constitution (see Chapter 2), Hamilton maintained that despite the power of judicial review, the judiciary would be the weakest of the three branches of government because it lacked "the strength of the sword or the purse." The judiciary, wrote Hamilton, had "neither FORCE nor WILL, but only judgment."

Although Hamilton was defending legislative supremacy, he argued that judicial review was an essential barrier to legislative oppression.[15] He recognized that the power to declare government acts void implied the superiority of the courts over the other branches. But this power, he contended, simply reflects the will of the people declared in the Constitution as opposed to the will of the legislature expressed in its statutes. Judicial independence, guaranteed by lifetime tenure and protected salaries, frees judges from executive and legislative control, minimizing the risk of their deviating from the law established in the Constitution. If judges make a mistake, the people or their elected representatives have the means to correct the error, through constitutional amendments and impeachment.

Their lifetime tenure does free judges from the direct influence of the president and Congress. And although mechanisms to check judicial power are in place, these mechanisms require extraordinary majorities and are rarely used. When they exercise the power of judicial review, then, judges can and occasionally do operate counter to majoritarian rule by invalidating the actions of the people's elected representatives (see Compared with What? 11.1 for a discussion of the nature of judicial review in other governments, democratic and nondemocratic).

The Organization of Courts

The American court system is complex, partly as a result of our federal system of government. Each state runs its own court system and no two states' courts are identical. In addition, we have a system of courts for the national government. The national, or federal, courts coexist with the state courts (see Figure 11.1). Individuals fall under the jurisdiction of both court systems. They can sue or be sued in either system, depending mostly on what their case is about. Litigants file nearly all cases (99 percent) in the state courts.[16]

Some Court Fundamentals

Criminal and Civil Cases   A crime is a violation of a law that forbids or commands an activity. Criminal laws are defined in each state's penal code, as are punishments for violations. Because crime is a violation of public order, the government prosecutes **criminal cases**. Maintaining public order through the criminal law is largely a state and local function. Criminal cases brought by the national government represent only a small fraction of all criminal cases prosecuted in the United States.

Courts decide both criminal and civil cases. **Civil cases** stem from disputed claims to something of value. Disputes arise from accidents, contractual obligations, and divorce, for example. Often the parties disagree over tangible issues (possession of property, custody of children), but civil cases can involve more abstract issues too (the right to equal accommodations, damages for pain and suffering). The government can be a party to civil disputes, called on to defend its actions or to allege wrongdoing.

Procedures and Policymaking   Most civil and criminal cases never go to trial. In a criminal case, a defendant's lawyer and the prosecutor might plea bargain,

Compared with What? 11.1

Judicial Review

The U.S. Constitution does not explicitly give the Supreme Court the power of judicial review. In a controversial interpretation, the Court inferred this power from the text and structure of the Constitution. Other countries, trying to avoid political controversy over the power of their courts to review legislation, explicitly define that power in their constitutions. For example, Japan's constitution, inspired by the American model, went beyond it in providing that "the Supreme Court is the court of last resort with power to determine the constitutionality of any law, order, regulation, or official act."

The basic objection to the American form of judicial review is an unwillingness to place federal judges, who are usually appointed for life, above representatives elected by the people. Some constitutions explicitly deny judicial review. For example, Article 84 of the recently revised Belgian constitution (1994) firmly asserts that "the authoritative interpretation of laws is solely the prerogative of the Legislative authority."

The logical basis of judicial review—that government is responsible to a higher authority—can take interesting forms in other countries. In some, judges can invoke an authority higher than the constitution—God, an ideology, or a code of ethics. For example, both Iran and Pakistan provide for an Islamic review of all legislation. (Pakistan also has the American form of judicial review.)

By 1992, about seventy countries—most in Western Europe, Latin America, Africa, and the Far East—had adopted some form of judicial review. Australia, Brazil, Canada, India, Japan, and Pakistan give their courts a full measure of judicial review power. Australia and Canada come closest to the American model of judicial review, but the fit is never exact. And wherever courts exercise judicial review, undoing it requires extraordinary effort. For example, in Australia the federal parliament has no recourse after a law is declared unconstitutional by the high court but to redraft the offending act in a manner prescribed by the court. In the United States, overruling judicial review by the Supreme Court would require a constitutional amendment.

Governments with a tradition of judicial review share some common characteristics: stability, competitive political parties, distribution of power (akin to separation of powers), a tradition of judicial independence, and a high degree of political freedom. Is judicial review the cause or the consequence of these characteristics? More likely than not, judicial review contributes to stability, judicial independence, and political freedom. And separation of powers, judicial independence, and political freedom contribute to the effectiveness of judicial review.

Some constitutional courts possess extraordinary power compared with the American model. The German constitutional court, for example, has the power to rectify the failure of the nation's lawmakers to act. In 1975, for example, the German constitutional court nullified the legalization of abortion and declared that the government had a duty to protect unborn human life

(continued)

Compared with What? 11.1 (continued)

against all threats. The court concluded that the German constitution required the legislature to enact legislation protecting the fetus.

Some judges take their power at face value. South Africa created a constitutional court in 1995 and gave it powers on a par with the legislative and executive branches. In its first major decision, the court's eleven appointed justices abolished the death penalty, a decades-old practice that placed South Africa among the nations with the highest rate of capital punishment. "Everyone, including the most abominable of human beings, has a right to life, and capital punishment is therefore unconstitutional," declared the court's president.

The Supreme Court of India offers an extreme example of judicial review. In 1967, the court held that the Indian parliament could not change the fundamental rights sections of the country's constitution, even by constitutional amendment. The parliament then amended the constitution to secure its power to amend the constitution. The Supreme Court upheld the amendment but declared that any amendments that attacked the "basic structure" of the constitution would be invalid. In India, the Supreme Court is truly supreme.

Switzerland's Supreme Federal Tribunal is limited by the country's constitution to ruling on the constitutionality of cantonal laws (the Swiss equivalent of our state laws). It lacks the power to nullify laws passed by the national assembly. Through a constitutional initiative or a popular referendum, the Swiss people may exercise the sovereign right to determine the constitutionality of federal law. In Switzerland, the people are truly supreme.

Sources: Henry J. Abraham, *The Judicial Process,* 6th ed. (New York: Oxford University Press, 1993), pp. 270–310; Chester J. Antineau, *Adjudicating Constitutional Issues* (London: Oceana, 1985), pp. 1–6; Jerold L. Waltman and Kenneth M. Holland, *The Political Role of Law Courts in Modern Democracies* (New York: St. Martin's Press, 1988), pp. 46, 99–100; Robert L. Hardgrave, Jr., and Stanley A. Kochanek, *India: Government and Politics in a Developing Nation,* 4th ed. (New York: Harcourt Brace Jovanovich, 1986), p. 93; Howard W. French, "South Africa's Supreme Court Abolishes Death Penalty," *New York Times,* 7 June 1995, p. A3.

which means they negotiate the severity and number of charges; the defendant pleads guilty in return for a reduction in the more serious charges or a promise to seek less severe punishment. In a civil case, one side may be using a lawsuit as a threat to exact a concession from the other. Often, the parties settle their dispute. Less frequently, cases end with *adjudication,* a court judgment resolving the parties' claims and ultimately enforced by the government. When trial judges adjudicate cases, they may offer written reasons to support their decisions. When the issues or circumstances of cases are novel, judges may publish *opinions,* explanations justifying their rulings.

Judges make policy in two different ways. Occasionally, in the absence of legislation, they use rules from prior decisions. We call this body of rules the

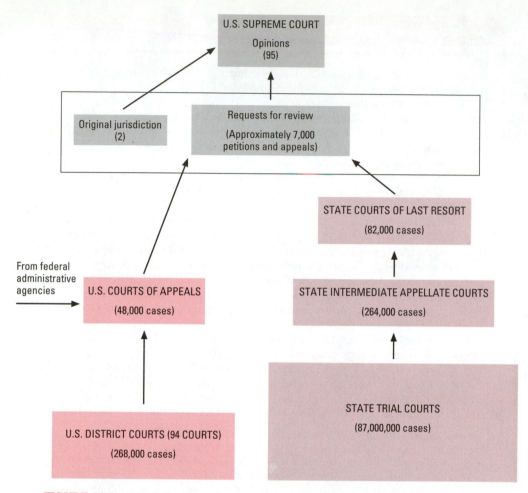

FIGURE 11.1 **The Federal and State Court Systems, 1995**
The federal courts have three tiers: district courts, courts of appeals, and the Supreme Court. The Supreme Court was created by the Constitution; all other federal courts were created by Congress. Most litigation occurs in state courts. The structure of state courts varies from state to state; usually, there are minor trial courts for less serious cases, major trial courts for more serious cases, intermediate appellate courts, and supreme courts. State courts were created by state constitutions. (Sources: National Center for State Courts, "State Court Caseload Statistics," Annual Report, 1994 (Williamsburg, Va.: National Center for State Courts, 1996); Administrative Office of the United States Courts, Statistics Division, Analysis and Reports Branch; Clerk's Office, Supreme Court of the United States; "Foreword," 109 Harvard Law Review 344 (1995).)

common, or **judge-made, law**. The roots of the common law lie in the English legal system. Contracts, property, and torts (an injury or wrong to the person or property of another) are common-law domains. The second area of judicial lawmaking involves the application of statutes enacted by legislatures. The judicial interpretation of legislative acts is called *statutory construction*. To determine how a statute should be applied, judges look for the legislature's intent, reading reports of committee hearings and debates. If these sources do not clarify the statute's meaning, the court does so. With or without legislation to guide them, judges look to the relevant opinions of higher courts for authority to decide the issues before them.

The federal courts are organized in three tiers, as a pyramid. At the bottom of the pyramid are the **U.S. district courts**, where litigation begins. In the middle are the **U.S. courts of appeals**. At the top is the Supreme Court of the United States. To *appeal* means to take a case to a higher court. The courts of appeals and the Supreme Court are appellate courts; with few exceptions, they only review cases that have already been decided in lower courts.

The U.S. District Courts

There are ninety-four federal district courts in the United States. Each state has at least one district court, and no district straddles more than one state.[17] In 1995, there were 649 full-time federal district court judges, and they received almost 268,000 new criminal and civil cases.[18]

The district courts are the entry point for the federal court system. When trials occur in the federal system, they take place in the federal district courts. Here is where witnesses testify, lawyers conduct cross-examinations, and judges and juries decide the fate of litigants. More than one judge may sit in each district court, but each case is tried by a single judge, sitting alone. Federal magistrates assist district judges, but they lack independent judicial authority. In 1996, there were 416 full-time magistrates.

Sources of Litigation   Today, the authority of U.S. district courts extends to

- federal criminal cases as defined by national law (for example, robbery of a federally insured bank or interstate transportation of stolen securities);
- civil cases brought by individuals, groups, or government alleging violation of national law (for example, failure of a municipality to implement pollution-control regulations required by a national agency);
- civil cases brought against the national government (for example, a vehicle manufacturer sues the motor pool of a government agency for its failure to take delivery of a fleet of new cars); and
- civil cases between citizens of different states when the amount in controversy exceeds $50,000 (for example, when a citizen of New York sues a citizen of Alabama in a U.S. district court in Alabama for damages stemming from an auto accident that occurred in Alabama).

The U.S. Courts of Appeals

All cases resolved in a U.S. district court and all decisions of federal administrative agencies can be appealed to one of the thirteen U.S. courts of appeals.

These courts, with a corps of 167 full-time judges, receive around forty-eight thousand new cases in 1995.[19] Each appeals court hears cases from a geographic area known as a *circuit*. The United States is divided into twelve circuits.*

Appellate Court Proceedings   Appellate court proceedings are public, but they usually lack courtroom drama. There are no jurors, witnesses, or cross-examinations; these are features of the trial courts. Appeals are based strictly on the rulings made and procedures followed in the trial courts. Suppose, for example, that in the course of a criminal trial, a U.S. district judge allows the introduction of evidence that convicts a defendant but was obtained under questionable circumstances. The defendant can appeal on the ground that the evidence was obtained in the absence of a valid search warrant and so was inadmissible. The issue on appeal is the admissibility of the evidence, not the defendant's guilt or innocence. If the appellate court agrees with the trial judge's decision to admit the evidence, the conviction stands. If the appellate court disagrees with the trial judge and rules that the evidence is inadmissible, the defendant must be retried without the incriminating evidence or be released.

It is common for litigants to try to settle their dispute while it is on appeal. Occasionally, litigants abandon their appeals for want of resources or resolve. Most of the time, however, appellate courts adjudicate the cases.

The courts of appeals are regional courts. They usually convene in panels of three judges to render judgments. The judges receive written arguments known as briefs (which are also sometimes submitted in trial courts). Often the judges hear oral arguments and question the lawyers to probe their arguments.

Precedents and Making Decisions

Following review of the briefs and, in many appeals, oral argument, the three-judge panel will meet to reach a judgment. When an appellate opinion is published, its influence can reach well beyond the immediate case. For example, a lawsuit turning on the meaning of the Constitution produces a ruling which then serves as a **precedent** for subsequent cases; that is, the decision becomes a basis for deciding similar cases in the same way. At the appellate level, precedent requires that opinions be written.

Making decisions according to precedent is central to the operation of our legal system, providing continuity and predictability. The bias in favor of existing decisions is captured by the Latin expression *stare decisis*, which means "let the decision stand." But the use of precedent and the principle of *stare decisis* do not make lower-court judges cogs in a judicial machine. "If precedent clearly governed," remarked one federal judge, "a case would never get as far as the Court of Appeals: the parties would settle."[20]

---

*The thirteenth court, the U.S. Court of Appeals for the Federal Circuit, is not a regional court; it specializes in appeals involving patents, contract claims against the federal government, and federal employment cases.

Judges on the courts of appeals direct their energies to correcting errors in district court proceedings and interpreting the law (in the course of writing opinions). When judges interpret the law, they often modify existing laws. In effect, they are making policy. Judges are politicians in the sense that they exercise political power, but the black robes that distinguish judges from other politicians signal constraints on their exercise of power.

Uniformity of Law   Decisions by the courts of appeals ensure a measure of uniformity in the application of national law. The courts of appeals harmonize the decisions of district judges within their region so that laws are applied uniformly.

The regional character of the courts of appeals undermines uniformity somewhat because the courts are not bound by the decisions of other circuits. The percolation of cases up through the federal system of courts virtually guarantees that at some point two or more courts of appeals, working with similar sets of facts, are going to interpret the same law differently. However, the problem of conflicting decisions in the intermediate federal courts can be corrected by review in the Supreme Court, where policymaking, not error correction, is the paramount goal.

The Supreme Court

Above the west portico of the Supreme Court Building are inscribed the words EQUAL JUSTICE UNDER LAW. At the opposite end of the building, above the east portico, are the words JUSTICE THE GUARDIAN OF LIBERTY. These mottoes reflect the Court's difficult task: achieving a just balance among the values of freedom, order, and equality. Consider how the values came into conflict in two controversial issues the Court has faced in recent years.

Flag burning as a form of political protest pits the value of order, or the government's interest in maintaining a peaceful society, against the value of freedom, including the individual's right to vigorous and unbounded political expression. In two flag-burning cases, the Supreme Court affirmed constitutional protection for unbridled political expression, including the emotionally charged act of desecrating a national symbol.[21]

School desegregation pits the value of equality (in this case, equal educational opportunities for minorities) against the value of freedom (the rights of parents to send their children to neighborhood schools). In *Brown v. Board of Education*, the Supreme Court carried the banner of racial equality by striking down state-mandated segregation in public schools. The justices recognized the disorder their decision would create in a society accustomed to racial bias, but in this case equality clearly outweighed freedom. Twenty-four years later, the Court was still embroiled in controversy over equality when it ruled that race could be a factor in university admissions (to diversify the student body), in the *Bakke* case.[22] Having secured equality for blacks, the Court then had to confront the charge that it was denying whites the freedom to compete for admission. The controversy continued in 1995 as a new majority of conservative justices limited race-based preferences in government policies.[23]

The Supreme Court makes national policy. Because its decisions have far-reaching effects on all of us, it is vital that we understand how it reaches those decisions. With this understanding, we can better evaluate how the Court fits within our model of democracy.

Access to the Court

There are rules of access that must be followed to bring a case to the Supreme Court. Also important is a sensitivity to the justices' policy and ideological preferences. The notion that anyone can take a case all the way to the Supreme Court is true only in theory, not fact.

The Supreme Court's cases come from two sources. A few arrive under the Court's **original jurisdiction**, conferred by Article III, Section 2, of the Constitution, which gives the Court the power to hear and decide "all Cases affecting Ambassadors, other public Ministers and Consuls, and those in which a State shall be a Party." Cases falling under the Court's original jurisdiction are tried and decided in the Court itself; the cases begin and end there. For example, the Court is the first and only forum in which legal disputes between states are resolved.

Most cases enter the Supreme Court from the U.S. courts of appeals or the state courts of last resort. This is the Court's **appellate jurisdiction**. These cases have been tried, decided, and reexamined as far as the law permits in other federal or state courts. The Court exercises judicial power under its appellate jurisdiction only because Congress gives it the authority to do so. Congress may change (and, perhaps, eliminate) the Court's appellate jurisdiction. This is a powerful but rarely used weapon in the congressional arsenal of checks and balances.

Litigants in state cases who invoke the Court's appellate jurisdiction must satisfy two conditions: first, the case must reach the end of the line in the state court system. Litigants cannot jump at will from state to federal arenas of justice. Second, the case must raise a **federal question**, an issue covered under the Constitution, federal laws, or national treaties. However, even most cases that meet these conditions do not reach the High Court.

Since 1925, the Court has exercised substantial (today, nearly complete) control over its **docket**, or agenda. The Court selects a handful of cases (less than one hundred) for consideration from the seven thousand or more requests filed each year. These requests take the form of petitions for *certiorari*, in which a litigant seeking review asks the Court "to become informed" of the lower-court proceedings. For the vast majority of cases, the Court denies the petition for *certiorari*, leaving the decision of the lower court undisturbed. No explanations accompany cases that are denied review, so they have little or no value as court rulings.

The Court grants a review only when four or more justices agree that a case warrants full consideration. This unwritten rule is known as the **rule of four**. With advance preparation by their law clerks, who screen petitions and pre-

The Supreme Court, 1996 Term: The Starting Lineup
The justices of the Supreme Court of the United States, pictured from left to right: Clarence Thomas, Antonin Scalia, Sandra Day O'Connor, Anthony Kennedy, David Souter, Stephen Breyer, John Paul Stevens, Chief Justice William Rehnquist, Ruth Bader Ginsburg.

pare summaries, all nine justices make these judgments at conferences held twice a week.[24]

The Solicitor General

Why does the Court decide to hear certain cases but not others? The best evidence scholars have adduced suggests that agenda-setting depends on the individual justices, who vary in their decision-making criteria and on the issues raised by the cases. Occasionally, justices will weigh the ultimate outcome of a case when granting or denying review. At other times, justices will grant or deny review based on disagreement among the lower courts or because delay in resolving the issues would impose alarming economic or social costs.[25] The solicitor general plays a vital role in the Court's agenda setting.

The **solicitor general** represents the national government before the Supreme Court. Appointed by the president, the solicitor general is the third-ranking official in the U.S. Department of Justice (after the attorney general and the deputy attorney general). The solicitor general's duties include determining whether the government should appeal lower-court decisions; reviewing and modifying, when necessary, the briefs filed in government appeals; and deciding whether the government should file an ***amicus curiae* brief*** in any appellate court.[26] The objective is to create a cohesive program for the executive branch in the federal courts. Solicitors general are a "formidable

---

* *Amicus curiae* is Latin for "friend of the court." Amicus briefs can be filed with permission of the Court. They allow groups and individuals who are not parties to the litigation but have an interest in it to influence the Court's thinking and, perhaps, its decision.

force" in the process of setting the Supreme Court's agenda.[27] Their influence in bringing cases to the Court and arguing them there has earned the Solicitor General the informal title of the "tenth justice."

Decision Making

Once the Court grants review, attorneys submit written arguments (briefs). Oral arguments, limited to thirty minutes for each side, usually follow. From October through April, the justices spend four hours a day, five or six days a month hearing arguments. They reach no collective decision at oral argument. A tentative decision is reached only after they have met in conference.

Our knowledge of the dynamics of decision making on the Supreme Court is all secondhand. However, Justice Antonin Scalia, who joined the Court in 1986, remarked that "not much conferencing goes on." By *conferencing*, Scalia meant efforts to persuade others to change their views by debating points of disagreement. "To call our discussion of a case a conference," he said, "is really something of a misnomer. It's much more a statement of the views of each of the nine Justices, after which the totals are added and the case is assigned" for an opinion.[28] Votes remain tentative until the opinion announcing the Court's judgment is issued.

Judicial Restraint and Judicial Activism　How do the justices decide how to vote on a case? According to some scholars, legal doctrines and past decisions explain their votes. This explanation, which is consistent with the majoritarian model, anchors the justices closely to the law and minimizes the contribution of their personal values. This view is embodied in the concept of **judicial restraint**, which maintains that legislators, not judges, should make the laws. Judges are said to exercise judicial restraint when they hew closely to statutes and previous cases in reaching their decisions. Other scholars contend that the value preferences and resulting ideologies of the justices provide a more powerful interpretation of their voting.[29] This view is embodied in the concept of **judicial activism**, which maintains that judges should interpret laws loosely, using their power to promote their preferred social and political goals. Judges are said to exercise judicial activism when they are apt to interpret existing laws and rulings with little regard to precedent and to interject their own values into court decisions. Judicial activism, which is consistent with the pluralist model, sees the justices as actively promoting their value preferences.

Judgment and Argument　The voting outcome is the **judgment**, the decision on who wins and who loses. The justices often disagree, not only on winners and losers but also on the reasons for their judgments.

After voting, the justices in the majority must draft an opinion setting out the reasons for their decision. The **argument** is the kernel of the opinion—its logical content, as distinct from facts, rhetoric, and procedure. If all justices agree with the judgment and the reasons supporting it, the opinion is unanimous. Agreement with a judgment, but for different reasons than those set forth in the majority opinion is called a **concurrence**. Or a justice can **dissent** if

Choosing Sides
*Justices Ruth Bader Ginsburg (left) and Sandra Day O'Connor (right) are occasional allies
on issues of abortion and gender equality. But O'Connor parts company with Ginsburg and
tends to side with Chief Justice William Rehnquist (center) on matters dealing with racial
equality and federalism. The justices are pictured here in the conference room of the Supreme
Court building.*

she or he disagrees with a judgment. Both concurring and dissenting opinions
may be drafted in addition to the majority opinion.

The Opinion   After the conference, the chief justice writes the majority opinion or assigns that responsibility to another justice in the majority. If the chief
justice is not in the majority, the writing or assigning responsibility rests with
the most senior associate justice in the majority. An opinion may have to be
rewritten several times to accommodate colleagues who remain unpersuaded
by the draft. Justices can change their votes, and perhaps alter the judgment,
up until the decision is officially announced.

Justices in the majority frequently try to muffle or stifle dissent in order
to encourage institutional cohesion. Since the mid-1940s, however, unity has
been more difficult to obtain.[30] Gaining agreement from the justices today is
akin to negotiating with nine separate law firms. Nevertheless, the justices
must be keenly aware of the slender foundation of their authority, which
rests largely on public respect. That respect is tested whenever the Court
ventures into areas of controversy. Freedom of speech and religion, racial
equality, and the right to privacy have led the Court into controversy in this
century.

Strategies on the Court

If we start with the assumption that the justices attempt to stamp their own policy views on the cases they review, we should expect typical political behavior from them. Because the justices are grappling with conflict on a daily basis, they probably have well-defined ideologies that reflect their values. Scholars and journalists have attempted to pierce the veil of secrecy that shrouds the Court from public view and analyze the justices' ideologies.[31]

The beliefs of most justices can be located on the two-dimensional model of political values discussed in Chapter 1 (see Figure 1.2). Liberal justices, such as John Paul Stevens and Ruth Bader Ginsburg, choose freedom over order, and equality over freedom. Conservative justices—Antonin Scalia and Clarence Thomas, for example—choose order over freedom, and freedom over equality. These choices translate into policy preferences as the justices struggle to win votes or retain coalitions.

As in any group of people, the justices also vary in intellectual ability, advocacy skills, social graces, temperament, and the like. They argue for the support of their colleagues, offering information in the form of drafts and memoranda to explain the advantages and disadvantages of voting for or against an issue. And the justices make occasional, if not regular, use of friendship, ridicule, and appeals to patriotism to mold their colleagues' views.

The Chief Justice

The chief justice is only one of nine justices, but he has several important functions based on his authority. Apart from his role in forming the docket and directing the Court's conferences, the chief justice can also be a social leader, generating solidarity within the group. Sometimes, a chief justice can embody intellectual leadership. Finally, the chief justice can provide policy leadership, directing the Court toward a general policy position.

When presiding at the conference, the chief justice can control the discussion of issues, although independent-minded justices are not likely to acquiesce to his views. Moreover, justices today rarely engage in a debate of the issues in the conference. Rather, they use their law clerks as ambassadors between justices' chambers and, in effect, "run the Court without talking to one another."[32]

Judicial Recruitment

Neither the Constitution nor national law imposes formal requirements for appointment to the federal courts. Once appointed, district court and appeals judges must reside in the district or circuit to which they are appointed. The president appoints judges to the federal courts, and all nominees must be confirmed by the Senate. Congress sets, but cannot lower, a judge's compensation.

State courts operate somewhat similarly. Governors appoint judges in more than half the states, often in consultation with judicial nominating commissions. In many of these states, voters decide whether judges should be retained in office. In some states, nominees must be confirmed by the state legislature. Contested elections for judgeships are unusual.

The Appointment of Federal Judges

The Constitution states that federal judges shall hold their commission "during good Behaviour," which in practice means for life.* A president's judicial appointments, then, are likely to survive his administration, providing a kind of political legacy. The appointment power assumes that the president is free to identify candidates and appoint judges who favor his policies.

Judicial vacancies occur when sitting judges resign, retire, or die. Vacancies also arise when Congress creates new judgeships to handle increasing caseloads. In both cases, the president nominates a candidate, who must be confirmed by the Senate. The president has the help of the Justice Department, which screens candidates before the formal nomination, subjecting serious contenders to FBI investigation. The department and the Senate vie for control in the appointment of district and appeals judges.

The "Advice and Consent" of the Senate   For district and appeals vacancies, the practice called **senatorial courtesy** forces presidents to share the nomination power with members of the Senate. The Senate will not confirm a nominee who is opposed by the senior senator from the nominee's state, if that senator is a member of the president's party. The Justice Department searches for acceptable candidates and polls the appropriate senator for her or his reaction to them.

The Senate Judiciary Committee conducts a hearing for each judicial nominee. The chairman exercises a measure of control in the appointment process that goes beyond senatorial courtesy. If a nominee is objectionable to the chairman, he or she can delay a hearing or hold up other appointments until the president and the Justice Department find an alternative. However, committee chairs are usually loathe to place obstacles in a president's path, especially when they may want presidential support for their own policies and constituencies.

The American Bar Association   The American Bar Association (ABA), the biggest organization of lawyers in the United States, has been involved in screening candidates for the federal bench since 1946.[33] Its role is defined by custom, not law. At the president's behest, the ABA's Standing Committee on the Federal Judiciary routinely rates prospective appointees, using a three-value scale: "well qualified," "qualified" and "not qualified." Presidents do not always agree with the committee's judgment, but the overwhelming majority of appointees to the federal bench since 1946 have had the ABA's blessing.

---

*Only twelve federal judges have been impeached. Of these, seven were convicted in the Senate and removed from office. Three judges were impeached by the Senate in the 1980s. In 1992, Alcee Hastings became the first such judge to serve in Congress.

Recent Presidents and the Federal Judiciary

President Jimmy Carter wanted to base judicial appointments on merit and make the judiciary more representative of the general population. He appointed substantially more blacks, women, and Hispanics to the federal bench than did any of his predecessors or his immediate successors. (Nearly all Carter judges were Democrats.)

Clearly, President Reagan did not share Carter's second objective. Only 2 percent of Reagan's appointments were blacks and only 8 percent were women; in contrast, 14 percent of Carter's appointments were blacks and 16 percent were women (see Figure 11.2). Four percent of Reagan judges were Hispanics, compared to 6 percent of Carter judges. Bush's record on women and minority appointments was better than Reagan's. President Clinton's appointments stand in stark contrast to his conservative predecessors. For the first time in history, more than half of a president's judicial appointments have been women or minorities.

It seems clear that political ideology, not demographics, lies at the heart of judicial appointments. Reagan and Bush sought nominees with particular policy preferences in order to leave their stamp on the judiciary well into the twenty-first century. Clinton is animated by the same goal. The Reagan-Bush legacy is considerable: They appointed nearly two-thirds of all judges sitting today.[34]

Appointment to the Supreme Court

The president is not shackled by senatorial courtesy when it comes to nominating a Supreme Court justice. However, appointment to the Court attracts more intense public scrutiny than do lower-level appointments, effectively narrowing the president's options and focusing attention on the Senate's advice and consent.

Of the 146 men and 2 women nominated to the Court, 28—or about 1 in 5—have failed to receive Senate confirmation. The most important factor in the rejection of a nominee is partisan politics. The most recent nominee to be rejected, on partisan and ideological grounds, was Judge Robert H. Bork.

Sixteen of the twenty-two Supreme Court nominees since 1950 have had prior judicial experience in federal or state courts. This tendency toward "promotion" from within the judiciary may be based on the idea that judges' previous opinions are good predictors of their future opinions on the High Court. After all, a president is handing out a powerful lifetime appointment; it makes sense to want an individual who is sympathetic to his views.

The resignation of Chief Justice Warren Burger in 1986 gave Reagan the chance to elevate Associate Justice William H. Rehnquist to the position of chief justice. Rehnquist faced stern questioning from critics during his Senate confirmation hearings. (Testimony from Supreme Court nominees is a relatively recent phenomenon; it began in 1925.) Reagan then nominated Antonin Scalia, a judge in a federal court of appeals, as Rehnquist's replacement. Rehnquist and Scalia did not try to defend their judicial records; they argued that judicial independence meant that they could not be called to ac-

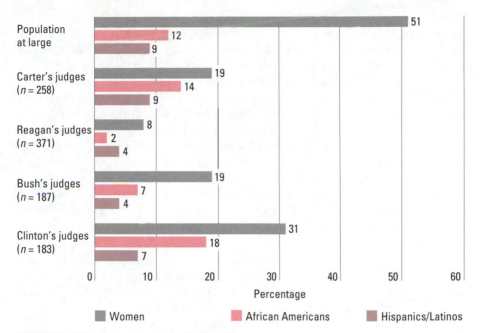

FIGURE 11.2 *Diversity on the Federal Courts*

To what extent should the courts reflect the diverse character of the population? President Jimmy Carter sought to make the federal courts more representative of the population by appointing more blacks, Hispanics, and women. Ronald Reagan's appointments reflected neither the lawyer population nor the population at large. Bush's appointments were somewhat more representative than Reagan's on race and gender criteria. Clinton's nominees represent a dramatic departure in appointments, especially in terms of race and gender. (Sources: Sheldon Goldman, "Judicial Selection Under Clinton: A Midterm Examination," Judicature 78, pp. 276–291 (1995), with additional data kindly provided by Professor Goldman; U.S. Bureau of the Census, Statistical Abstract of the United States, 1993 (Washington, D.C.: U.S. Government Printing Office, 1993), Table No. 644.)

count for their decisions before the Senate. Both judges also ducked discussing issues that might come to the Court for fear of compromising their impartiality. Both were confirmed by the Republican-controlled Senate.[35]

In 1987, when Justice Lewis F. Powell, Jr., resigned, Reagan had an opportunity to shift the ideological balance on the Court toward a more conservative consensus. He nominated Bork, a conservative, to fill the vacancy. Although Bork advocated judicial restraint, some of his critics maintained that he was really a judicial activist draped in the robes of judicial restraint. Bork's critics charged that his true purpose, spelled out in his prodigious writings, was to advance his conservative ideology from the High Court.

The hearings concluded after several days of televised testimony from Judge Bork and a parade of witnesses. Liberals formed a temporary anti-Bork coalition of feminist, labor, environmental, senior citizen, abortion rights, and civil rights groups. They put aside their disagreements and mounted a massive campaign to defeat the nomination, overwhelming conservative efforts to buttress Bork. By the time the hearings ended, public opinion had shifted against him. Although his defeat was a certainty, Bork insisted that the Senate vote on his nomination, hoping for a sober discussion of his record. But the rancor never abated. Bork was defeated by a vote of 42 to 58, the biggest vote margin by which the Senate has ever rejected a Supreme Court nominee.

The rules of the game for appointment to the High Court appeared to have changed in 1990 when President Bush plucked David H. Souter from relative obscurity to replace liberal justice William J. Brennan, Jr. Souter fit the model of other nominees: He had extensive judicial experience as a justice on the New Hampshire Supreme Court and had recently been appointed to the federal court of appeals. But his views on provocative topics were undetectable because he had written little and spoken less on privacy, abortion, religious liberty, and equal protection. Furthermore, during Senate confirmation hearings, he successfully avoided or deflected the most controversial topics. Souter was confirmed by the Senate, 90–9.

Recall from the beginning of this chapter that George Bush left an additional stamp on the Supreme Court when he nominated a conservative black judge, Clarence Thomas, to replace ailing Thurgood Marshall.[36] Thomas has proved a strong ally for other conservatives on the Court.

President Clinton made his mark on the Court in 1993 when Associate Justice Byron R. White announced his retirement. Clinton chose Ruth Bader Ginsburg for the vacancy; she has been an active civil rights litigator, a law professor, and a federal judge. Some Court watchers described her as the Thurgood Marshall of women's rights because of her tireless efforts to alter the legal status of women. Ginsburg's Senate confirmation hearing revealed little of her constitutional philosophy beyond her public record. Ginsburg declined to reveal her constitutional value preferences. She cruised through to a 96–3 confirmation vote in the Senate.

Justice Harry Blackmun's resignation in 1994 gave Clinton a second opportunity to leave his imprint on the Court. After six weeks of deliberation, Clinton chose federal appeals judge Stephen G. Breyer for the coveted appointment. Breyer's moderate pragmatic views made him a consensus candidate. He sailed through tame confirmation hearings to take his place as the 108th justice.

The Consequences of Judicial Decisions

Of all the lawsuits begun in the United States, the overwhelming majority end without a court judgment. Many civil cases are settled, or the parties give up, or the courts dismiss the suits because they are beyond the legitimate bounds of judicial resolution. Most criminal cases end with a **plea bargain,** the defendant's admission of guilt in exchange for a less severe punishment. Only about 10 percent of criminal cases in the federal district courts are tried; an equally small percentage of civil cases are adjudicated.

Furthermore, the fact that a judge sentences a criminal defendant to ten years in prison or a court holds a company liable for $11 billion in damages does not guarantee that the defendant will lose his freedom or the company will give up any assets. In the case of the criminal defendant, the road of seeking an appeal following trial and conviction is well traveled and, if nothing else, serves to delay the day when no alternative to prison remains. In civil cases, the immediate consequence of a judgment may also be an appeal, which delays the day of reckoning.

Supreme Court Rulings: Implementation and Impact

When the Supreme Court makes a decision, it relies on others to implement it, to translate policy into action. How a judgment is implemented rests in good measure on how it was crafted. Remember that the justices, in preparing their opinions, must work to hold their majorities together, to gain greater, if not unanimous support for their arguments. This forces them to compromise in their opinions, to moderate their arguments, and introduces ambiguity into many of the policies they articulate. Ambiguous opinions affect the implementation of policy. For example, when the Supreme Court issued its order in 1955 to desegregate public school facilities "with all deliberate speed,"[37] judges who opposed the Court's policy dragged their feet in implementing it.

Because the Supreme Court confronts issues freighted with deeply felt social values or fundamental political beliefs, its decisions have impact beyond the immediate parties in a dispute. The Court's decision in *Roe v. Wade* legalizing abortion generated heated public reaction. Groups opposing abortion vowed to overturn the decision; groups favoring the freedom to obtain an abortion moved to protect the right they had won. Within eight months of the decision, more than two dozen constitutional amendments had been introduced in Congress, although none managed to carry the extraordinary majority required for passage.

Public Opinion and the Supreme Court

Democratic theorists have a difficult time reconciling a commitment to representative democracy with a judiciary that is not accountable to the electorate yet has the power to undo legislative and executive acts. This difficulty may simply be a problem for theorists, however. The policies coming from the Supreme Court, although lagging years behind public opinion, rarely seem out of line with the public's ideological choices.[38] Surveys in several controversial areas reveal that the Court seldom departs from majority sentiment or trends.[39] The evidence squarely supports the view that the Supreme Court reflects public opinion at least as often as other elected institutions.[40]

There are at least three explanations for the Court's reflecting majority sentiment. First, the modern Court has shown deference to national laws and policies, which typically echo national public opinion. Second, the Court moves closer to public opinion during periods of crisis. And, third, rulings that reflect the public view are subject to fewer changes than rulings that depart from public opinion.

Finally, the evidence also supports the view that the Court seldom influences public opinion. The Court enjoys only moderate popularity, and its decisions are not much noticed by the public. With few exceptions, there is no evidence of shifting public opinion before and after a Supreme Court ruling.[41]

The Courts and Models of Democracy

How far should judges stray from existing statutes and precedents? Supporters of the majoritarian model would argue that judges must refrain from injecting their own values into their decisions. If the law places too much (or not enough) emphasis on equality or order, the elected legislature, not the courts, can change the law. In contrast, those who support the pluralist model maintain that the courts are a policymaking branch of government. It is thus legitimate for the individual values and interests of judges to mirror group interests and preferences and for judges to consciously attempt to advance group interests as they see fit.

The argument that our judicial system fits the pluralist model gains support from a legal procedure called a **class action**. A class action is a device for assembling the claims or defenses of similarly situated individuals so that they can be tried in a single lawsuit. A class action makes it possible for people with small individual claims and limited financial resources to aggregate their claims and resources in order to make a lawsuit viable. Since the 1940s, class action suits have been the vehicles through which groups have asserted claims involving civil rights, legislative apportionment, and environmental problems. For example, schoolchildren have sued (through their parents) under the banner of class action to rectify claimed racial discrimination on the part of school authorities, as in *Brown v. Board of Education*.

Abetting the class action is the resurgence of state supreme courts' fashioning policies consistent with group preferences. State courts may serve as the staging areas for legal campaigns to change the law in the nation's highest court. They also exercise substantial influence over policies that affect citizens daily, including the rights and liberties enshrined in their state constitutions, statutes, and common law.[42]

Furthermore, a state court can avoid review by the U.S. Supreme Court by basing its decision solely on state law or by plainly stating that its decision rests on both state and federal law. If the U.S. Supreme Court is likely to render a restrictive view of a constitutional right, and the judges of a state court are inclined toward a more expansive view, the state judges can use the state ground to avoid Supreme Court review. In a period when the nation's highest court is moving in a decidedly conservative direction, some state courts have become safe havens for liberal values.

When judges reach decisions, they pay attention to the views of other courts, and not just those above them in the judicial hierarchy. State and federal court opinions are the legal storehouse from which judges regularly draw their ideas. Often the issues that affect individual lives—property, family, contracts—are grist for state courts, not federal courts.

State courts have become renewed arenas for political conflict with litigants—individually or in groups—vying for their preferred policies. The multiplicity of the nation's court system, with overlapping state and federal responsibilities, provides alternative points of access for individuals and groups to present and argue their claims. This description of the courts fits the pluralist model of government.

Summary

The power of judicial review, claimed by the Supreme Court in 1803, placed the judiciary on an equal footing with Congress and the president. The principle of checks and balances can restrain judicial power through several means, such as constitutional amendments and impeachment. But restrictions on that power have been infrequent, leaving the federal courts to exercise considerable influence through judicial review and statutory construction.

The federal court system has three tiers. At the bottom are the district courts, where litigation begins and most disputes end. In the middle are the courts of appeals. At the top is the Supreme Court. The ability of judges to make policy increases as they move up the pyramid from trial courts to appellate courts to the Supreme Court.

The Supreme Court, free to draft its agenda through the discretionary control of its docket, harmonizes conflicting interpretations of national law and articulates constitutional rights. It is helped at this crucial stage by the solicitor general, who represents the executive branch of government before the High Court. The solicitor general's influence with the justices affects their choice of cases to review.

Political allegiance and complementary values are necessary conditions for appointment by the president to the coveted position of judge. The president and senators from the same party share the power of appointment of federal district and appellate judges. The president has more leeway in the nomination of Supreme Court justices, although all nominees must be confirmed by the Senate.

Courts inevitably fashion policy for each of the states and for the nation. They provide multiple points of access for individuals to pursue their preferences and so fit the pluralist model of democracy. Furthermore, the class action enables people with small individual claims and limited financial resources to pursue their goals in court, reenforcing the pluralist model.

Judges confront both the original and the modern dilemmas of government. The impact of their decisions can extend well beyond a single case. Some democratic theorists are troubled by the expansion of judicial power. But today's courts fit within the pluralist model and usually are in step with what the public wants.

As the U.S. Supreme Court heads in a more moderate direction, some state supreme courts have become safe havens for more liberal policies on civil rights and civil liberties. The state court systems have overlapping state and national responsibilities, offering groups and individuals many access points to present and argue their claims.

Key Terms

judicial review

criminal case

civil case

common (judge-made) law

U.S. district courts

U.S. courts of appeals

precedent
stare decisis
original jurisdiction
appellate jurisdiction
federal question
docket
rule of four
solicitor general
amicus curiae brief

judicial restraint
judicial activism
judgment
argument
concurrence
dissent
senatorial courtesy
plea bargain
class action

Selected Readings

Baum, Lawrence. *American Courts: Process and Policy.* 3d ed. Boston: Houghton Mifflin, 1994. A comprehensive review of trial and appellate courts in the United States that addresses their activities, describes their procedures, and explores the processes that affect them.

Coffin, Frank M. *On Appeal: Court, Lawyering, and Judging.* New York: Norton, 1994. A close look at the workings of a federal appellate court and the ways in which its chief judge reaches decisions.

O'Brien, David M. *Storm Center: The Supreme Court in American Politics.* 4th ed. New York: Norton, 1996. A primer on the Supreme Court, its procedures, personalities, and political influence.

Salokar, Rebecca Mae. *The Solicitor General: The Politics of Law.* Philadelphia: Temple University Press, 1992. A timely and well-researched empirical assessment of one of the least known but most important offices in the national government.

World Wide Web Resources

OYEZ. The U.S. Supreme Court has recorded its public proceedings from 1955 to the present. "Oyez. Oyez. Oyez."—a Web site developed at Northwestern University—contains an archive of the most important arguments and decisions. Download and install the free player from RealAudio <www.realaudio.com>, navigate to the OYEZ site, and the audio files will stream in real time to your desktop.
<oyez.at.nwu.edu/oyez.html> and <//court.it-services.nwu.edu/oyez/>

The Legal Information Institute, Cornell University. The institute maintains a megasite of law-related materials including a searchable database of Supreme Court opinions since 1990.

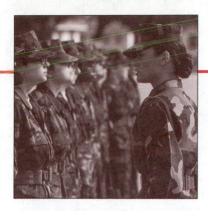

12

Civil Liberties and Civil Rights

University of Michigan student Jake Baker posted shockingly explicit sex stories to an electronic bulletin board, one of the thousands of news groups that form the worldwide collection of networked information called Usenet. Baker wrote fictional fantasies that frequently included rape and violence to women and girls. In one story in which Baker graphically described the torture, rape, and murder of a woman, he gave the victim the name of a classmate at the University of Michigan.[1] Baker's stories could be read by millions of people every day. Some read them and moved on. Others were appalled and complained.

Eventually, university officials acted. Baker admitted writing the stories, waived his right to an attorney, and provided his e-mail password so officials could read his electronic mail. Shortly thereafter, the university president suspended Baker without a hearing. He was told to pack his bags and leave the university immediately.[2]

Had Baker committed a crime? If so, what was it? Writing fiction is not a crime, even when it describes harmful acts. However, after reading his private e-mail, prosecutors decided to charge Baker with making threats to kill or kidnap in electronic messages transmitted via the Internet to a correspondent in Canada. U.S. commerce law prohibits the interstate or international transmission of threats to injure or kidnap a victim. The law carries a penalty of up to five years of imprisonment.

Colorado contractor Randy Pech believed that free competition usually means the lowest bidder gets the job when his company, Adarand Constructors, bid for work installing highway guardrails in Colorado. However, of the five companies that construct and maintain the state's guardrails, Adarand Constructors is the only one owned by a white man. Each of the other four companies has been designated a "Disadvantaged Business Enterprise," or DBE.

The government's objective in designating some businesses as DBEs is to promote affirmative action. **Affirmative action** is a commitment by a business, employer, school, or other public or private institution to expand opportunities for women, blacks, Hispanic Americans, and members of other minority groups. Affirmative action embraces a wide range of policies, from special recruitment efforts to numerical goals and quotas.

In 1987, Congress passed a law requiring the U.S. Department of Transportation to set aside at least 10 percent of its highway construction funds for businesses owned by women or members of designated racial minorities. The set-aside policy restricts free competition in order to give DBEs business. This meant that in Colorado, a DBE did not have to submit the lowest bid to win the guardrail contract, provided Pech's company was the lowest bidder. In 1989, Pech submitted the lowest bid for a guardrail job, but the general contractor awarded the work to Gonzales Construction, a DBE. Pech challenged the law, claiming that it unconstitutionally discriminated on the basis of race.[3]

Pech believed that the government's actions violated his constitutional right to equal protection. The Fourteenth Amendment declares that no *state* shall deny any person equal protection. While there is no equivalent constitutional provision compelling the national government to treat persons equally, the Supreme Court has held that the Fifth Amendment's due process guarantee embraces the equal protection principle. Was the national government's affirmative action policy consistent with the Supreme Court's conception of equal protection? (We will explore the Court's answer later in this chapter.)

In the case of Jake Baker, the government acted to maintain order—that is, to ensure the peace and safety of the community. The government viewed Baker's private correspondence as evidence of a threat of imminent harm. Baker's attorney, joined by the American Civil Liberties Union, urged dismissal of the government's case. They maintained that the free speech clause of the First Amendment protected Baker from government action. A federal judge, Avern Cohn, sat at the center of the controversy, holding in the balance Baker's freedom and the community's demand for order. He held that, in the absence of a threat to act, Baker's communications were protected by the First Amendment.[4]

In the case of Randy Pech, the government acted to promote equality. In this case, the government's policy to advance minority- and women-owned businesses disrupted the free competition of the marketplace and thereby imposed an unequal burden on Randy Pech. As we shall see later in this chapter, the conflict intensifies when we recognize that Americans advocate competing conceptions of equality.

How well do the courts respond to clashes that pit freedom against order in some cases and freedom against equality in others? Are freedom, order, or equality ever unconditional? In this chapter, we explore some value conflicts that the judiciary has resolved. You will be able to judge from the decisions in these cases whether American government has met the challenge of democracy by finding the appropriate balance between freedom and order and between freedom and equality.

The value conflicts described in this chapter revolve around claims or entitlements that rest on law. Although we concentrate here on conflicts over constitutional issues, the Constitution is not the only source of people's rights. Government at all levels can—and does—create rights through laws written by legislatures and regulations issued by bureaucracies.

We begin this chapter with the Bill of Rights and the freedoms it protects. Then we take a closer look at the role of the First Amendment in the original conflict between freedom and order. Next we turn to the Fourteenth Amendment and the limits it places on the states. Then we examine the Ninth Amendment and its relationship to issues of personal autonomy. We then examine the threat to the democratic process when judges transform policy issues into constitutional issues. We end with an examination of the Fourteenth Amendment's promise of equal protection, which sets the stage for the modern dilemma of government: the struggle between freedom and equality.

The Bill of Rights

You may remember from Chapter 2 that the omission of a bill of rights was the most important obstacle to the adoption of the Constitution by the states. Eventually, the First Congress approved twelve amendments and sent them to the states for ratification. In 1791, ten were ratified, and the nation had a bill of rights.

The Bill of Rights imposed limits on the national government but not on the state governments.* During the next seventy-seven years, litigants pressed the Supreme Court to extend the amendments' restraints to the states, but the Court refused until well after the adoption of the Fourteenth Amendment in 1868. Before then, protection from repressive state government had to come from state bills of rights.

The U.S. Constitution guarantees Americans numerous liberties and rights. In this chapter we explore a number of them. We will define and distinguish civil liberties and civil rights. (On some occasions, we will use the terms interchangeably.) **Civil liberties** are freedoms that are guaranteed to the individual. The guarantees take the form of restraints on government. For example, the First Amendment declares that "Congress shall make no law . . . abridging the freedom of speech." Civil liberties declare what the government cannot do. In contrast, civil rights declare what the government must do or provide.

Civil rights are powers or privileges that are guaranteed to the individual and protected against arbitrary removal at the hands of the government or other individuals. The right to vote and the right to a jury trial in criminal cases are civil rights embedded in the Constitution. Today, civil rights also embrace laws that further certain values. The Civil Rights Act of 1964, for example, furthered the value of equality by establishing the right to nondiscrimination in places of public accommodations and the right to equal employment opportunity.

The Bill of Rights lists both civil liberties and civil rights. When we refer to the rights and liberties of the Constitution, we mean the protections enshrined in the Bill of Rights and in the first section of the Fourteenth Amendment.[5] The list includes freedom of religion, freedom of speech and of the press, the right to assemble peaceably and to petition the government, the

---

* Congress considered more than one hundred amendments in its first session. One that was not approved would have limited the power of the states to infringe on the rights of conscience, speech, press, and jury trial in criminal cases. James Madison thought this amendment was the "most valuable" of the list, but it failed to muster a two-thirds vote in the Senate.

right to bear arms, the rights of the criminally accused, the requirement of due process, and the equal protection of the laws.

Freedom of Religion

> Congress shall make no law respecting an establishment of religion, or prohibiting the free exercise thereof.

Religious freedom was very important to the colonies, and later to the states. That importance is reflected in its position in the Bill of Rights: first, in the very first amendment. The First Amendment guarantees freedom of religion in two clauses: the **establishment clause** prohibits laws establishing religion; the **free-exercise clause** prevents the government from interfering with the exercise of religion. Together they ensure that the government can neither promote nor inhibit religious beliefs or practices.

At the time of the Constitutional Convention, many Americans, especially in New England, maintained that government could and should foster religion, specifically Protestantism. However, many more Americans agreed that this was an issue for state governments, that the national government had no authority to meddle in religious affairs. The religion clauses were drafted in this spirit.[6]

The Supreme Court has refused to interpret the religion clauses definitively. The result is an amalgam of rulings, the cumulative effect of which is that freedom to believe is unlimited, but freedom to practice a belief can be limited. Religion cannot benefit directly from government actions (for example, government cannot make contributions to churches or synagogues), but it can benefit indirectly from those actions (for example, government can supply books on secular subjects for use in all schools—public, private, and parochial).

The Establishment Clause

The provision that "Congress shall make no law respecting an establishment of religion" bars government sponsorship or support of religious activity. The Supreme Court has consistently held that the establishment clause requires government to maintain a position of neutrality toward religions and to maintain that position in cases that involve choices between religion and nonreligion. However, the Court never has interpreted the clause as barring all assistance that incidentally aids religious institutions.

Government Support of Religion   In 1879, the Supreme Court contended, quoting Thomas Jefferson, that the establishment clause erected "a wall of separation between church and state."[7] That wall was breached somewhat in 1947, when the justices upheld a local government program that provided free transportation to parochial school students.[8] The breach seemed to widen in 1968, when the Court held constitutional a government program in which parochial school students borrowed state-purchased textbooks.[9] The objective of the program, reasoned the majority, was to further educational opportunity. The students, not the schools, borrowed the books, and the parents, not the church, realized the benefits.

But in 1971, in *Lemon v. Kurtzman*, the Court struck down a state program that would have helped pay the salaries of teachers hired by parochial schools to give instruction in secular subjects.[10] The justices proposed a three-pronged test for determining the constitutionality of government programs and laws under the establishment clause:

- They must have a secular purpose (such as lending books to parochial school students).

- Their primary effect must not be to advance or inhibit religion.

- They must not entangle the government excessively with religion.

A program or law missing any prong would be unconstitutional.

The program at issue in *Lemon* failed on the last ground: To be sure that they did not include religious instruction in their lessons, the government would have to constantly monitor the secular teachers. Such supervision would entangle the government in religious activity. However, in a 1997 test of the establishment clause, the Court held that "A federally funded program providing supplemental, remedial instruction to disadvantaged children on a neutral basis is not invalid under the Establishment Clause when such instruction is given on the premises of sectarian schools by government employees pursuant to a program containing safeguards" such as that of a New York program which, in the eyes of the Court, did not "run afoul of the three primary criteria" cited in *Lemon*.[11]

School Prayer   The Supreme Court has consistently equated prayer in public schools with government support of religion. In 1962, it struck down the daily reading of this twenty-two-word nondenominational prayer in New York's public schools: "Almighty God, we acknowledge our dependence upon Thee, and we beg Thy blessings upon us, our parents, our teachers, and our country."[12]

In the years since that decision, new challenges on the issue of school prayer continue to find their way to the Supreme Court. In 1985, the Court struck down a series of Alabama statutes requiring a moment of silence for meditation or voluntary prayer in elementary schools.[13] In 1992, the Court ruled, 5 to 4, that public schools may not include nondenominational prayers in graduation ceremonies.[14]

The establishment clause creates a problem for government. Support for all religions at the expense of nonreligion seems to pose the least risk to social order. Tolerance of the dominant religion at the expense of other religions risks minority discontent, but support for no religion (neutrality between religion and nonreligion) risks majority discontent.

The Free-Exercise Clause

The free-exercise clause of the First Amendment states that "Congress shall make no law . . . prohibiting the free exercise [of religion]." The Supreme

Court has struggled to avoid absolute interpretations of this restriction so as not to violate its complement, the establishment clause. An example: Suppose Congress grants exemptions from military service to individuals who have religious scruples against war. These exemptions could be construed as a violation of the establishment clause because they favor some religious groups over others. But if Congress forces conscientious objectors to fight—to violate their religious beliefs—the government would run afoul of the free-exercise clause. In fact, Congress has granted military draftees such exemptions. But, the Supreme Court has avoided a conflict between the establishment and free-exercise clauses by equating religious objection to war with any deeply held humanistic opposition to it.[15]

In the free-exercise cases, the justices have distinguished religious beliefs from actions based on those beliefs. Beliefs are inviolate, beyond the reach of government control. But the First Amendment does not protect antisocial actions. Consider conflicting values about saluting the flag, working on the Sabbath, and using drugs as religious sacraments.

Saluting the Flag   The values of order and religious freedom clashed in 1940, when the Court considered the first of two cases involving compulsory flag saluting in the public schools. In *Minorsville School District v. Gobitis*, a group of Jehovah's Witnesses challenged the law on the ground that the action forced them to worship graven images, which their faith forbids.[16] Order won, in an 8–1 decision. "The mere possession of religious convictions," wrote Justice Felix Frankfurter, "which contradict the relevant concerns of a political society does not relieve the citizen from the discharge of political responsibilities."

Three years later, however, the Court reversed itself in **West Virginia State Board of Education v. Barnette**. *Gobitis* was decided on the narrow issue of religious belief versus saluting the flag. In *Barnette*, the justices chose to focus instead on the broader issue of freedom of expression. In stirring language, Justice Robert H. Jackson argued in the majority opinion that no one could be compelled by the government to declare any belief:

> If there is any fixed star in our constitutional constellation, it is that no official, high or petty, can prescribe what shall be orthodox in politics, nationalism, religion, or other matters of opinion or force citizens to confess by word or act their faith therein. If there are any circumstances which permit an exception, they do not now occur to us.[17]

Working on the Sabbath   The modern era of free-exercise thinking begins with **Sherbert v. Verner** (1963). Adeil Sherbert was a Seventh-Day Adventist who was disqualified from receiving unemployment benefits after declining a job that required working on Saturday, which was her Sabbath. In a 7–2 decision, the Supreme Court ruled that the disqualification imposed an impermissible burden on Sherbert's free exercise of religion. The First Amendment, declared the majority, protected observance as well as belief. A neutral law that burdens the free exercise of religion is subject to **strict scrutiny**. This means the law may be upheld only if the government can demonstrate that the law is justified by a "compelling governmental interest" and is the least restrictive means for achieving that interest.[18]

Using Drugs as Sacrament   Partaking of illegal substances as part of a religious sacrament forces believers to violate the law. For example, the Rastafarians and members of the Ethiopian Zion Coptic Church smoke marijuana in the belief that it is the body and blood of Christ. Obviously, taking to an extreme the freedom to practice religion can result in a license to engage in illegal conduct. And even when such conduct stems from deeply held convictions, government resistance to it is understandable. The inevitable result is a clash between religious freedom and social order.

The courts used the compelling-government-interest test for many years and on that basis invalidated most laws restricting free exercise. But in 1990, the Supreme Court abruptly and unexpectedly rejected its longstanding rule, tipping the balance in favor of social order. In *Employment Division v. Smith*, two members of the Native American Church sought an exemption from an Oregon law that made the possession or use of peyote a crime.[19] (Peyote is a cactus that contains the hallucinogen mescaline. Native Americans have used it for centuries in their religious ceremonies.) Oregon rejected the two church members' applications for unemployment benefits after they were dismissed from their drug-counseling jobs for using peyote. Oregon believed it had a compelling interest in proscribing the use of certain drugs according to its own drug laws.

Justice Antonin Scalia, writing for the 6–3 majority, examined the conflict between freedom and order through the lens of majoritarian democratic thought. He observed that the Court has never held that an individual's religious beliefs excuse him or her from compliance with an otherwise valid law prohibiting conduct that government is free to regulate. Allowing exceptions to every state law or regulation affecting religion "would open the prospect of constitutionally required exemptions from civic obligations of almost every conceivable kind." Scalia cited as examples compulsory military service, payment of taxes, vaccination requirements, and child-neglect laws. Laws that indirectly restrict religious practices are acceptable; only laws aimed at religious groups are constitutionally prohibited.

The political response to *Employment Division v. Smith* was an example of pluralism in action. An unusual coalition of religious and nonreligious groups (including the National Association of Evangelicals, the American Civil Liberties Union, the National Islamic Prison Foundation, and B'nai B'rith) organized to restore the more restrictive strict scrutiny test. The alliance established in Congress what it had lost in the Supreme Court. In 1993, President Bill Clinton signed into law the Religious Freedom Restoration Act (RFRA). The law once again required government to satisfy the strict scrutiny standard before it could institute measures that interfere with religious practices. However, the Supreme Court seemed to have the last word when, in 1997, it held that Congress had exceeded its power and that the RFRA was unconstitutional because it "contradicts vital principles necessary to maintain separation of powers and the federal balance."[20]

Freedom of Expression

> Congress shall make no law . . . abridging the freedom of speech, or of the press; or the right of the people peaceably to assemble, and to petition the government for a redress of grievances.

James Madison introduced the initial versions of the speech clause and the press clause of the First Amendment in the House of Representatives in June 1789. One was merged with the religion and peaceable assembly clauses to yield the First Amendment.

The sparse language of the First Amendment seems perfectly clear: "Congress shall make no law . . . abridging the freedom of speech, or of the press." Yet a majority of the Supreme Court has never agreed that this "most majestic guarantee" is absolutely inviolable.[21] Historians have long debated the framers' intentions regarding these **free-expression clauses**. The dominant view is that the clauses confer the right to unrestricted discussion of public affairs.[22] Other scholars, examining much the same evidence, conclude that few, if any, of the framers clearly understood the clause; moreover, they insist that the First Amendment does not rule out prosecution for seditious statements (statements inciting insurrection).[23]

Careful analysis of the records of the period supports the view that the press clause prohibited only the imposition of **prior restraint**—censorship before publication. Publishers could not claim protection from punishment if works that had already been published were later deemed improper, mischievous, or illegal. Today, however, the clauses are deemed to bar not only most forms of prior restraint but also after-the-fact prosecution for political and other discourse.

The Supreme Court has evolved two approaches to the resolution of claims based on the free-expression clauses. First, government can regulate or punish the advocacy of ideas, but only if it can prove an intent to promote lawless action and demonstrate that a high probability exists that such action will occur. Second, government may impose reasonable restrictions on the means for communicating ideas, which can incidentally discourage free expression.

Suppose, for example, that a political party advocates nonpayment of personal income taxes. Government cannot regulate or punish that party for advocating nonpayment, because the standards of proof—that the act be directed to inciting or producing imminent lawless action and that the act be judged likely to produce such action—do not apply. But government can impose restrictions on the way the party's candidates communicate what they are advocating. Government can bar them from blaring messages from loudspeakers in residential neighborhoods at 3:00 A.M.

Freedom of Speech

The starting point for any modern analysis of free speech is the **clear and present danger test** formulated by Justice Oliver Wendell Holmes in the Supreme Court's unanimous decision in *Schenck v. United States* (1919). Charles T. Schenck and his fellow defendants were convicted under a federal criminal statute for attempting to disrupt World War I military recruitment by distributing leaflets claiming that conscription was unconstitutional. The government believed this behavior threatened the public order. At the core of the Court's opinion, as Holmes wrote, was the view that

> the character of every act depends upon the circumstances in which it is done....The most stringent protection of free speech would not protect a man in falsely shouting fire in a theatre and causing a panic....The question in every case is whether the words used are used in such circumstances and are of such a nature as to create a *clear and present danger* that they will bring about the substantive evils that Congress has a right to prevent. It is a question of proximity and degree. When a nation is at war many things that might be said in time of peace are such a hindrance to its effort that their utterance will not be endured so long as men fight and that no Court could regard them as protected by any constitutional right. [Emphasis added.][24]

Because the actions of the defendants in *Schenck* were deemed to create a clear and present danger to the United States at that time, the Supreme Court upheld the defendants' convictions. The clear and present danger test helps to distinguish the advocacy of ideas, which is protected, from incitement, which is not.

In 1925 the Court issued a landmark decision in *Gitlow v. New York*.[25] Benjamin Gitlow was arrested for distributing copies of a "left-wing manifesto" that called for the establishment of socialism through strikes and class action of any form. Gitlow was convicted under a state criminal anarchy law; Schenck had been convicted under a federal law. For the first time, the Court assumed that the First Amendment speech and press provisions applied to the states through the due process clause of the Fourteenth Amendment. Still, a majority of the justices affirmed Gitlow's conviction.

The protection of advocacy faced yet another challenge in 1948 when eleven members of the Communist Party were charged with violating the Smith Act—a federal law making the advocacy of force or violence against the United States a criminal offense. The leaders were convicted, although the government introduced no evidence that they actually urged people to commit specific violent acts. The Supreme Court mustered a majority for its decision to uphold the convictions under the act, but it could not get a majority to agree on the reasons in support of that decision. The biggest bloc of four justices announced the plurality opinion in 1951, arguing that the government's interest was substantial enough to warrant criminal penalties.[26] The justices interpreted the threat to government to be the gravity of the advocated action "discounted by its improbability." In other words, a single soap-box orator advocating revolution stands a low chance of success. But a well-organized, highly disciplined political movement advocating revolution in the tinderbox of unstable political conditions stands a greater chance of success. In broadening the meaning of clear and present danger, the Court held that the government was justified in acting preventively rather than waiting until revolution is about to occur.

By 1969, the pendulum had swung back in the other direction: That year, in ***Brandenburg v. Ohio***, a unanimous decision extended the freedom of speech to new limits.[27] Clarence Brandenburg, the leader of the Ohio Ku Klux Klan, had been convicted under a state law for advocating racial strife at a Klan rally. His comments, which had been filmed by a television crew, included threats against government officials.

The Court reversed Brandenburg's conviction because the government had failed to prove that the danger was real. The Court went even further and declared that threatening speech is protected by the First Amendment unless the government can prove that such advocacy is "directed to inciting or producing imminent lawless action and is likely to produce such action."

Symbolic Expression   Symbolic expression, or nonverbal communication, generally receives less protection than pure speech. But the courts have upheld certain types of symbolic expression. ***Tinker v. Des Moines Independent County School District*** (1969) involved three public school students who wore black arm bands to school to protest the Vietnam War. Principals in their school district had prohibited the wearing of arm bands on the ground that such conduct would provoke a disturbance; the district suspended the students. The Supreme Court overturned the suspensions. Justice Abe Fortas declared for the majority that the principals had failed to show that the forbidden conduct would substantially interfere with appropriate school discipline:

> Undifferentiated fear or apprehension is not enough to overcome the right to freedom of expression. Any departure from absolute regimentation may cause trouble. Any variation from the majority's opinion may inspire fear. Any word spoken, in class, in the lunchroom, or on the campus, that deviates from the views of another person may start an argument or cause a disturbance. But our Constitution says we must take this risk.[28]

The flag is an object of deep veneration in our society, yet its desecration is also a form of symbolic expression protected by the First Amendment. In 1989, a divided Supreme Court struck down a Texas law that barred the desecration of venerated objects. Congress then enacted the Flag Protection Act of 1989 in an attempt to overcome the constitutional flaws of the Texas decision.

The Supreme Court nullified the federal flag-burning statute in *United States v. Eichman* (1990). By a vote of 5 to 4, the justices reaffirmed First Amendment protection for all expression of political ideas. The vote was identical to the Texas case, with conservative justices Scalia and Kennedy joining with the liberal wing to forge an unusual majority. The majority placed the same emphasis on freedom that it had in the Texas case, including a quotation from its earlier opinion: "'If there is a bedrock principle underlying the First Amendment, it is that the Government may not prohibit the expression of an idea simply because society finds the idea itself offensive or disagreeable.' Punishing desecration of the flag dilutes the very freedom that makes this emblem so revered, and worth revering."[29]

In this opinion, the Court majority relied on the substantive conception of democratic theory, which embodies the principle of freedom of speech. Yet a May 1990 poll revealed that most people wanted to outlaw flag burning as a means of expressing political opinions and that a clear majority favored a constitutional amendment to that end.[30] The procedural conception of democratic theory states that government should do what the people want. In the case of flag burning, then, the people are willing to abandon the freedom-of-speech principle embodied in the substantive view of democracy.

Free Speech Versus Order: Obscenity   The Supreme Court has always viewed ob-scene material—words, music, books, magazines, films—as outside the bounds of constitutional protection, which means that states may regulate or even ban obscenity. However, difficulties arise in determining what is obscene and what is not.

In ***Miller v. California*** (1973), its most recent major attempt to clarify con-stitutional standards governing obscenity, the Court declared that a work—play, film, or book—is obscene and may be regulated by government if (1) the work taken as a whole appeals to prurient interest ("prurient" means having a tendency to excite lustful thoughts); (2) the work portrays sexual conduct in a patently offensive way; and (3) the work taken as a whole lacks serious literary, artistic, political, or scientific value.[31] Local community standards govern ap-plication of the first and second prongs of the *Miller* test.

Feminism, Free Expression, and Equality   Traditionally, civil liberties conflict with demands for social order. However, civil liberties may also be viewed in conflict with demands for equality. In the 1980s, city officials in Indianapolis, Indiana, influenced by feminist theorists, invoked equality principles to justify legislation restricting freedom of expression. Specifically, they argued that pornography is sex discrimination.[32]

The ordinance banned pornographic material according to the following argument: Government interest in equality outweighs any First Amendment interest in communication. Pornography affects thoughts; it conditions society to subordinate women impermissibly. An ordinance regulating expression will regulate and control the underlying unacceptable conduct.

United States District Court judge Sarah Evans Barker confronted the tradeoff between equality and freedom in a pluralist democracy. Judge Barker declared the ordinance unconstitutional, stating that it went beyond the cate-gories of unprotected expression (such as child pornography) to suppress oth-erwise protected expression.

Interest groups that use the democratic process to carve exceptions to the First Amendment benefit at the expense of everyone's rights. Although efforts to restrict behavior that leads to humiliation and degradation of women may be necessary and desirable, "free speech, rather than being the enemy," wrote Judge Barker, "is a long-tested and worthy ally. To deny free speech in order to engineer social change in the name of accomplishing a greater good for one sector of our society erodes the freedom of all."[33]

In this recasting of a freedom-versus-order issue into a freedom-versus-equality framework Judge Barker's tradeoff protected freedom. Her judgment was affirmed by the U.S. Court of Appeals in 1985 and affirmed without argu-ment by the Supreme Court in 1986. However, in the next confrontation—and, in a pluralist democracy there will surely be others—equality may prove the victor.

Freedom of the Press

The First Amendment guarantees that government "shall make no law . . . abridging the freedom . . . of the press." Although it originally was adopted as a restriction on the national government, since 1931 the Supreme Court has held the free-press guarantee to apply to state and local governments as well.

The ability to collect and report information without government interference was (and still is) thought to be essential to a free society. The print media continue to use and defend the freedom conferred on them by the framers. However, the electronic media have had to accept some government regulation stemming from the scarcity of broadcast frequencies (see Chapter 4).

Defamation of Character   Libel is the written defamation of character.* A person who believes his or her name and character have been harmed by false statements in a publication can institute a lawsuit against the publication and seek monetary compensation for the damage. Such a lawsuit can impose limits on freedom of expression; at the same time, false statements impinge on the rights of individuals. In a landmark decision in **New York Times v. Sullivan** (1964), the Supreme Court declared that freedom of the press takes precedence—at least when the defamed individual is a public official.[34] The Court unanimously agreed that the First Amendment protects the publication of all statements— even false ones—about the conduct of public officials except when statements are made with actual malice (with knowledge that they are false or in reckless disregard of their truth or falsity). Citing John Stuart Mill's 1859 treatise *On Liberty*, the Court declared that "even a false statement may be deemed to make a valuable contribution to public debate, since it brings about the clearer perception and livelier impression of truth, produced by its collision with error."

Three years later, the Court extended this protection to apply to suits brought by any public figures, whether a government official or not. **Public figures** are people who assume roles of prominence in the affairs of society or who thrust themselves to the forefront of public controversy—including officials, actors, writers, television personalities, and others. These people must show actual malice on the part of the publisher that prints false statements about them. Because the burden of proof is so great, few plaintiffs prevail.

Prior Restraint and the Press   In the United States, freedom of the press has primarily meant protection from prior restraint, or censorship. The Supreme Court's first encounter with a law imposing prior restraint on a newspaper was in *Near v. Minnesota* (1931).[35] In Minneapolis Jay Near published a scandal sheet in which he attacked local officials, charging that they were in league with gangsters.[36] Minnesota officials obtained an injunction to prevent Near

---

*Slander is the oral defamation of character. The durability of the written word usually means that libel is a more serious accusation than slander.

from publishing his newspaper under a state law that allowed such action against periodicals deemed "malicious, scandalous, and defamatory."

The Supreme Court struck down the law, declaring that prior restraint is a special burden on a free press. Chief Justice Charles Evans Hughes forcefully articulated the need for a vigilant, unrestrained press: "The fact that the liberty of the press may be abused by miscreant purveyors of scandal does not make any the less necessary the immunity of the press from previous restraint in dealing with official misconduct." Although the Court acknowledged that prior restraint may be permissible in exceptional circumstances, it did not specify those circumstances, nor has it yet done so.

Consider another case, which occurred during a war, a time when the tension between government-imposed order and individual freedom is often at a peak. In 1971, Daniel Ellsberg, a special assistant in the Pentagon, delivered portions of a classified U.S. Department of Defense study to the *New York Times* and the *Washington Post*. By making the documents public, he hoped to discredit the Vietnam War and thereby end it. The U.S. Department of Justice sought to restrain the *Times* and the *Post* from publishing the documents, contending that publication would prolong the war and embarrass the government. The case was quickly brought before the Supreme Court.

Three days later, in a 6–3 decision in **New York Times v. United States** (1971), the Court concluded that the government had not met the heavy burden of proving that immediate, inevitable, and irreparable harm would follow publication.[37] The majority expressed its view in a brief unsigned opinion; individual and collective concurring and dissenting views added nine opinions to the decision. Two justices maintained that the First Amendment offers absolute protection against government censorship, no matter what the situation. But the other justices left the door ajar for the imposition of prior restraint in the most extreme and compelling of circumstances.

Freedom of Expression Versus Maintaining Order The courts have consistently held that freedom of the press does not override the requirements of law enforcement. A grand jury called a Louisville, Kentucky, reporter, who had researched and written an article about drug-related activities, to identify people he had seen in possession of marijuana or in the act of processing it. The reporter refused to testify, maintaining that freedom of the press shielded him from inquiry. In a closely divided decision, the Supreme Court in 1972 rejected this position.[38] The Court declared that no exception exists to the rule that all citizens have a duty to give their government whatever testimony they are capable of giving.

The Supreme Court again confronted the conflict between free expression and order in 1988.[39] The principal of a St. Louis high school had deleted articles on divorce and teenage pregnancy from the school's newspaper on the ground that the articles invaded the privacy of the individuals who were the focus of the stories. Three student editors claimed that the principal's censorship interfered with the newspaper's function as a public forum, a role protected by the First Amendment. The principal maintained that the newspaper was just an extension of classroom instruction and was thus not protected by the First Amendment.

In a 5–3 decision, the Court upheld the principal's actions in sweeping terms. Educators may limit speech within the confines of the school curriculum and speech that might seem to bear the approval of the school provided their actions serve any "valid educational purpose."

The Rights to Assemble Peaceably and to Petition the Government

The final clause of the First Amendment states that "Congress shall make no law . . . abridging . . . the right of the people peaceably to assemble, and to petition the Government for a redress of grievances." The framers meant that the people have the right to assemble peaceably *in order to* petition the government. Today, however, the right to assemble peaceably is equated with the right of free speech and a free press, independent of whether or not the government is petitioned. Precedent has merged these rights and made them equally indivisible.[40] Government cannot prohibit peaceful political meetings and cannot brand as criminals those who organize, lead, and attend such meetings.[41]

The clash of interests in cases involving these rights illustrates a continuing effort to define and apply fundamental principles. The need for order and stability has tempered the concept of freedom. And when freedom and order conflict, the justices of the Supreme Court, who are responsible only to their consciences, strike the balance.

The Right to Bear Arms

The Second Amendment declares

> A well-regulated militia being necessary to the security of a free State, the right of the people to keep and bear arms shall not be infringed.

Gun-control advocates assert that the amendment protects the right of the states to maintain *collective* militias. Gun-use advocates assert that the amendment protects the right of *individuals* to own and use guns. There are good arguments on both sides.

Federal firearms regulations did not come into being until Prohibition, so the Supreme Court had little to say on the matter. In 1939, however, a unanimous Court upheld a 1934 federal law requiring the taxation and registration of machine guns and sawed-off shotguns. The Court held that the Second Amendment protects a citizen's right to own ordinary militia weapons; sawed-off shotguns did not qualify for protection.[42] Restrictions on gun ownership (for example, registration and licensing) have passed constitutional muster. However, outright prohibitions on gun ownership (for example, a ban on handguns) might run afoul of the amendment.

Applying the Bill of Rights to the States

The major purpose of the Constitution was to structure the division of power between the national government and the state governments. Even before it was amended, the Constitution set some limits on both the nation and the states with regard to citizens' rights. It barred both governments from passing **bills of attainder**, laws that make an individual guilty of a crime without a trial. They were also prohibited from enacting **ex post facto laws**, laws that declare an action a crime after it has been performed. And it barred both nation and states from impairing the **obligation of contracts**, the obligation of the parties in a contract to carry out its terms.

Although initially the Bill of Rights seemed to apply only to the national government, various litigants have pressed the claim that its guarantees also apply to the states. In response to one such claim, Chief Justice John Marshall affirmed that the provisions of the Bill of Rights served only to limit national authority. "Had the framers of these amendments intended them to be limitations on the powers of the state governments," wrote Marshall, "they would have . . . expressed that intention."[43]

Change came with the Fourteenth Amendment, which was adopted in 1868. The due process clause of that amendment is the linchpin that holds the states to the provisions of the Bill of Rights.

The Fourteenth Amendment: Due Process of Law

Section 1 . . . . No State shall make or enforce any law which shall abridge the privileges or immunities of citizens of the United States; nor shall any State deprive any person of life, liberty, or property, without due process of law. . . .

Most freedoms protected in the Bill of Rights today apply as limitations on the states. And many of the standards that limit the national government serve equally to limit state governments. These changes have been achieved through the Supreme Court's interpretation of the due process clause of the Fourteenth Amendment: "nor shall any State deprive any person of life, liberty, or property, without due process of law." The clause has two central meanings. First, it requires the government to adhere to appropriate procedures. Second, it forbids unreasonable government action. The Supreme Court has used the first meaning of the due process clause as a sponge, absorbing or incorporating the procedural specifics of the Bill of Rights and spreading or applying them to the states.

The Fundamental Freedoms

In 1897, the Supreme Court declared that the states are limited by the Fifth Amendment's prohibition on taking of private property without providing just compensation.[44] The Court accomplished its goal by absorbing that prohibition into the due process clause of the Fourteenth Amendment, which applies to the states. Thus, one Bill of Rights protection—but only that one—applied to both the states and the national government, as illustrated in Figure 12.1. In 1925, the Court assumed that the due process clause protected the First Amendment speech and press liberties from impairment by the states.[45]

The inclusion of other Bill of Rights guarantees within the due process clause faced a critical test in **Palko v. Connecticut** (1937).[46] Frank Palko had been charged with homicide in the first degree. He was convicted of second degree murder, however, and sentenced to life imprisonment. The state of Connecticut appealed and won a new trial; this time Palko was found guilty of first-degree murder and sentenced to death. Palko appealed the second conviction on the ground that it violated the protection against double jeopardy guaranteed to him by the Fifth Amendment. This protection applied to the states, he contended, because of the Fourteenth Amendment's due process clause.

The Supreme Court upheld Palko's second conviction. In his opinion for the majority, Justice Benjamin N. Cardozo formulated principles that were to direct the Court's actions for the next three decades. He noted that some Bill of Rights guarantees—such as freedom of thought and speech—are fundamental, and that these fundamental rights are absorbed by the Fourteenth Amendment's due process clause and are therefore applicable to the states. These rights are essential, argued Cardozo, because "neither liberty nor justice would exist if they were sacrificed." Trial by jury and other rights, although valuable and important, are not essential to liberty and justice, and therefore are not absorbed by the due process clause. "Few would be so narrow or provincial," Cardozo claimed, "as to maintain that a fair and enlightened system of justice would be impossible" without these other rights. In other words, only some provisions of the Bill of Rights—the "fundamental" provisions—were absorbed into the due process clause and made applicable to the states. Because protection against double jeopardy was not one of them, Palko died in Connecticut's gas chamber in April 1938.

The next thirty years saw slow but perceptible change in the standard for determining whether a Bill of Rights guarantee was fundamental. The reference point changed from the idealized "fair and enlightened system of justice" in *Palko* to the more realistic "American scheme of justice" thirty years later.[47] Case after case tested various guarantees that the Court found to be fundamental. By 1969, when *Palko* was finally overturned, the Court had found most of the Bill of Rights applicable to the states.

Criminal Procedure: The Meaning of Constitutional Guarantees

"The history of liberty," remarked Justice Frankfurter, "has largely been the history of observance of procedural safeguards."[48] The safeguards embodied in the Fourth through Eighth Amendments to the Constitution specify how government must behave in criminal proceedings. Their application to the states has reshaped American criminal justice in the last four decades

The Supreme Court

Due process clause of the Fourteenth Amendment

Amendments I, IV, portions of V, VI, VIII, IX

Bill of Rights

State and local governments

FIGURE 12.1   *The Incorporation of the Bill of Rights*
The Supreme Court has used the due process clause of the Fourteenth Amendment as a sponge, absorbing most—but not all—of the provisions in the Bill of Rights and applying them to state and local governments. All provisions in the Bill of Rights apply to the national government.

in two steps. The first step is the judgment that a guarantee asserted in the Bill of Rights also applies to the states. The second step requires that the judiciary give specific meaning to the guarantee. If the rights are fundamental, their meaning cannot vary from state to state. But life is not quite so simple under the U.S. Constitution. The concept of federalism is sewn into the constitutional fabric, and the Supreme Court recognizes that there may be more than one way to prosecute the accused while heeding fundamental rights.

Consider, for example, the right to a jury trial in criminal cases, which is guaranteed by the Sixth Amendment. This right was made obligatory on the states in *Duncan v. Louisiana* (1968). The Supreme Court later held that the right applied to all nonpetty criminal cases—those in which the penalty for conviction was more than six months' imprisonment.[49] But the Court did not require that state juries have twelve members, the number required for federal criminal proceedings. The Court permits jury size to vary from state to state, although it set the minimum number at six. Furthermore, it has not imposed on the states the federal requirement of a unanimous jury verdict.

In contrast, the Court left no room for variation in its definition of the fundamental right to an attorney, also guaranteed by the Sixth Amendment. Clarence Earl Gideon was a penniless vagrant accused of breaking into and robbing a pool hall. Because Gideon could not afford a lawyer, he asked the state to provide him with legal counsel for his trial. The state refused, and

Gideon was subsequently convicted and sentenced to five years in the Florida State Penitentiary. From his cell, Gideon appealed to the U.S. Supreme Court, claiming that his conviction should be struck down because the state had denied him his Sixth Amendment right to counsel. (Gideon was also without counsel in this appeal; he filed a hand-lettered "pauper's petition" with the Court, after studying law texts in the prison library. When the Court agreed to consider his case, he was assigned a prominent Washington attorney, Abe Fortas, who later became a Supreme Court justice.)[50]

In its landmark decision in *Gideon v. Wainwright* (1963), the Court set aside Gideon's conviction and extended to the states the Sixth Amendment right to counsel.[51] The state retried Gideon, who this time had the assistance of a lawyer, and the court found him not guilty. In subsequent rulings that stretched over more than a decade, the Court specified at what points in the course of criminal proceedings a defendant is entitled to a lawyer (from arrest to trial, appeal, and beyond). These pronouncements are binding on all states.

During this period the Court also came to grips with another procedural issue: informing suspects of their constitutional rights. Ernesto Miranda was arrested in Arizona in connection with the kidnapping and rape of an eighteen-year-old woman. After the police questioned him for two hours and the woman identified him, Miranda confessed to the crime. An Arizona court convicted him on the basis of that confession—although he was never told he had the right to counsel and the right not to incriminate himself. Miranda appealed his conviction, which was overturned by the Supreme Court in 1966.[52]

The Court based its decision in *Miranda v. Arizona* on the Fifth Amendment privilege against self-incrimination. According to the Court, warnings are necessary to dispel the coercion that is inherent in custodial interrogation without counsel. The Court does not require warnings if a person is only in custody without questioning or subject to questioning without arrest. But in *Miranda* the Court found the combination of custody and interrogation sufficiently intimidating to require warnings before questioning. These statements are known today as the *Miranda* **warnings**. Among them:

- You have the right to remain silent.
- Anything you say can be used against you in court.
- You have the right to talk to a lawyer of your own choice before questioning.
- If you cannot afford to hire a lawyer, a lawyer will be provided without charge.

The Fourth Amendment guarantees that "the right of the people to be secure in their persons, houses, papers, and effects, against unreasonable searches and seizures, shall not be violated." The Court made this right applicable to the states in *Wolf v. Colorado* (1949).[53] But, although the Court found that protection from illegal searches by state and local government was a fundamental right, it refused to apply to the states the **exclusionary rule** that evidence obtained from an illegal search and seizure cannot be used in a trial.

The justices considered the exclusionary rule again in *Mapp v. Ohio* (1961).[54] An Ohio court had found Dolree Mapp guilty of possessing obscene materials after an admittedly illegal search of her home for a fugitive. The Ohio Supreme Court affirmed her conviction, and she appealed to the U.S. Supreme Court. In a 6–3 decision, the Court declared that "all evidence obtained by searches and seizures in violation of the Constitution is, by [the Fourth Amendment], inadmissible in a state court." The decision was historic. It placed the exclusionary rule within the confines of the Fourth Amendment and required all levels of government to operate according to the provisions of that amendment.

The struggle over the exclusionary rule took a new turn in 1984, when the Court reviewed *United States v. Leon*.[55] In this case, a judge had issued a search warrant without "probable cause" having been firmly established. The police, relying on the warrant, found large quantities of illegal drugs. The Court, by a vote of 6 to 3, established the **good faith exception** to the exclusionary rule. The justices held that the state could introduce at trial evidence seized on the basis of a mistakenly issued search warrant. The exclusionary rule, argued the majority, is not a right but a remedy justified by its ability to deter illegal police conduct. Such a deterrent effect was not a factor in *Leon:* The police acted in good faith. Hence, the Court decided, there is a need for an exception to the rule.

The exclusionary rule continues to divide the Supreme Court. In 1990, the justices again reaffirmed the rule, but only by a bare 5–4 majority.[56] The current Supreme Court line-up has a more conservative bent, which suggests that the battle over the exclusionary rule has not ended.

The Ninth Amendment and Personal Autonomy

> The enumeration in the Constitution, of certain rights, shall not be construed to deny or disparage others retained by the people.

The wording and history of the Ninth Amendment remain an enigma; the evidence supports two different views. The amendment may protect rights that are not enumerated, or it may simply protect state governments against the assumption of power by the national government.[57] The meaning of the amendment was not an issue until 1965, when the Supreme Court used it to protect privacy, a right that is not enumerated in the Constitution.

Controversy: From Privacy to Abortion

In *Griswold v. Connecticut* (1965), the Court struck down, by a vote of 7 to 2, a seldom-used Connecticut statute that made the use of birth control devices a crime.[58] Justice Douglas, writing for the majority, asserted that the "specific guarantees in the Bill of Rights have penumbras [partially illuminated regions surrounding fully lit areas]" that give "life and substance" to broad, unspecified protections in the Bill of Rights. Several specific guarantees in the First, Third, Fourth, and Fifth Amendments create a zone of privacy, Douglas argued, and this zone is protected by the Ninth Amendment and is applicable to the states by the due process clause of the Fourteenth Amendment.

Griswold established a zone of personal autonomy, protected by the Constitution, which was the basis of a 1973 case that sought to invalidate state antiabortion laws. In ***Roe v. Wade*** (1973), the Court in a 7–2 decision declared unconstitutional a Texas law making it a crime to obtain an abortion except for the purpose of saving the woman's life.[59]

Justice Harry A. Blackmun, who authored the majority opinion, based the decision on the right to privacy protected by the due process clause of the Fourteenth Amendment. The Court declared that in the first three months of pregnancy, the abortion decision must be left to the woman and her physician. In the interest of protecting the woman's health, states may restrict but not prohibit abortions in the second three months of pregnancy. Finally, in the last three months of pregnancy, states may regulate or even prohibit abortions to protect the life of the fetus except when medical judgment determines that an abortion is necessary to save the woman's life. In all, the Court's ruling affected the laws of forty-six states.

The dissenters—Justices White and Rehnquist—were quick to assert what critics have frequently repeated since the decision: The Court's judgment was directed by its own dislikes, not by any constitutional compass. In the absence of guiding principles, they asserted, the majority justices simply substituted their views for the views of the state legislatures whose abortion regulations they invalidated.[60]

The composition of the Court shifted under President Ronald Reagan. His elevation of William Rehnquist to chief justice in 1986 and his appointments of Antonin Scalia in 1986 and Anthony Kennedy in 1988 raised new hope among abortion foes and old fears among advocates of choice.

A perceptible shift away from abortion rights materialized in *Webster v. Reproductive Health Services* (1989). In *Webster,* the Court upheld the constitutionality of a Missouri law that denied the use of public employees or publicly funded facilities in the performance of an abortion unless the woman's life was in danger.[61] Furthermore, the law required doctors to perform tests to determine whether fetuses twenty weeks and over could survive outside the womb. This was the first time that the Court upheld significant government restrictions on abortion.

The Court has since moved cautiously down the road toward greater government control of abortion. In 1990, the justices split on two state parental notification laws. Then, a new coalition—forged by Reagan and Bush appointees O'Connor, Souter, and Kennedy—reaffirmed *Roe* yet tolerates additional restrictions on abortion. In *Planned Parenthood v. Casey* (1992), the Court opted for O'Connor's test that restrictions must not place "an undue burden" on a woman's ability to choose an abortion. The Court remains deeply and bitterly divided on abortion.[62]

The abortion issue pits freedom against order. The decision to bear or beget children should be free from government control. Yet government has a legitimate interest in protecting and preserving life, including fetal life, as part

of its responsibility to maintain an orderly society. Rather than choose between freedom and order, the majority on the Court has loosened constitutional protection on abortion rights and cast the politically divisive issue into
the state legislative process, where elected representatives can thrash out the
conflict.

Personal Autonomy and Sexual Orientation

The right-to-privacy cases may have opened a Pandora's box of divisive social
issues. Does the right to privacy embrace private homosexual acts between
consenting adults? Consider the case of Michael Hardwick, who was arrested
in 1982 in his Atlanta bedroom while having sex with another man. In a standard approach to prosecuting homosexuals, Georgia charged him under a
state criminal statute with the crime of sodomy, which means oral or anal in-
tercourse. Hardwick sued to challenge the law's constitutionality. He won in
the lower courts. However, in a bitterly divided ruling in 1986, the Supreme
Court held in *Bowers v. Hardwick* that the Constitution does not protect homosexual relations between consenting adults, even in the privacy of their
own homes.[63]

The appointments of conservatives to replace liberals on the Court casts
freedom-preferring policies such as gay rights in continued jeopardy.
However, Clinton's appointments of Ginsburg and Breyer signal movement
toward a liberal view. That the Court will soon reverse course on matters of
personal autonomy is unlikely. It will take several more liberal Court appointments and the right cases to create the conditions for a change in direction.

Issues around sexual orientation have shifted toward the states, where various groups continue to assert their political power. Thus, the pluralist
model provides one solution for groups dissatisfied with rulings from the nation's highest court. State courts and state legislatures have demonstrated
their receptivity to positions that are probably untenable in the federal
courts.

Two Conceptions of Equality

Most Americans support **equality of opportunity**, the idea that people
should have an equal chance to develop their talents and that effort and ability should be rewarded equitably. This form of equality glorifies personal
achievement and free competition, and allows everyone to play on a level field
where the same rules apply to all. Special recruitment efforts aimed at identifying qualified minority or female job applicants, for example, ensure that
everyone has the same chance starting out. Low-bid contracting illustrates
equality of opportunity, because every bidder has the same chance to compete
for work.

Americans are far less committed to **equality of outcome**, which means
greater uniformity in social, economic, and political power among different

social groups. Equality of outcome can occur only if we restrict the free competition that is the basis of equality of opportunity. For example, schools and businesses aim at equality of outcome when they allocate admissions or jobs on the basis of race, gender, or disability, which are unrelated to ability. (Some observers refer to these allocations as quotas, while others call them goals. The difference is subtle. A quota *requires* that a specified, proportional share of some benefit go to a favored group. A goal *aims* for proportional allocation of benefits, without requiring it.) The government seeks equality of outcome when it adjusts the rules to handicap some bidders and favor others. The vast majority of Americans, however, consistently favor low-bid contracting and merit-based admissions and employment over preferential treatment.[64] Quota- or goal-based policies muster only modest support (see Figure 12.2).

Quota policies generate the most opposition because they confine competition. Quotas limit advancement for some individuals and ensure advancement for others by taking into account factors unrelated to ability. Quotas seem to be at odds with individual initiative. In other words, equality clashes with freedom. To understand the ways government resolves this conflict, we have to understand the development of civil rights in this country.

The struggle of blacks has been a beacon lighting the way for Native Americans, Hispanic Americans, women, and the disabled. Each of these groups has confronted **invidious discrimination.** Discrimination is simply the act of making or recognizing distinctions. When making distinctions among people, discrimination may be benign (that is, harmless) or invidious (harmful).

The Civil War Amendments

The Civil War amendments were adopted to provide freedom and equality to black Americans. The Thirteenth Amendment, ratified in 1865, provided that

> neither slavery nor involuntary servitude . . . shall exist within the United States, or any place subject to their jurisdiction.

The Fourteenth Amendment was adopted three years later. It provides first that freed slaves are citizens:

> All persons born or naturalized in the United States, and subject to the jurisdiction thereof, are citizens of the United States and of the State wherein they reside.

As we saw earlier in this chapter, it also prohibits the states from abridging the "privileges or immunities of citizens of the United States" or depriving "any person of life, liberty, or property, without due process of law." The amendment then goes on to protect equality under the law, declaring that no state shall

> deny to any person within its jurisdiction the equal protection of the laws.

FIGURE 12.2 *Public Attitudes Toward Preferential Treatment*
Polls since the 1970s have revealed low levels of support for preferential policies aiding minorities and women in employment and college admissions. More than 80 percent of Americans consistently favor using ability as the only criterion for hiring and college entrance decisions. Depending on how poll questions are worded, the level of support for race- and gender-based preferences appears to now be somewhat higher than it was in the seventies, though it has declined again somewhat in the last few years. QUESTION 1: Some people say that to make up for past discrimination, women and members of minority groups should be given preferential treatment in getting jobs and places in college. Others say that ability, as determined by test scores, should be the main consideration. Which point of view comes closer to how you feel on the subject? (Gallup) QUESTION 2: Do you believe that where there has been job discrimination against blacks (women) in the past, preference in hiring and promotion should be given to blacks (women) today? (CBS/NYT) QUESTION 3: Some people say that because of past discrimination, blacks should be given preference in hiring and promotion. Others say that such a preference in hiring and promotion of blacks is wrong because it gives blacks advantages they haven't earned. What about your opinion—are you for or against preferential hiring and promotion of blacks? (NES) (Source: Charlotte Steeh and Maria Krysan, "Affirmative Action and the Public, 1970–1995," Public Opinion Quarterly 60, 1996, 128–158.)

The Fifteenth Amendment, adopted in 1870, added a measure of political equality:

> The right of citizens of the United States to vote shall not be denied or abridged by the United States or by any State on account of race, color, or previous condition of servitude.

American blacks were thus free and politically equal—at least according to the Constitution. But for many years the courts sometimes thwarted the efforts of other branches to protect these constitutional rights.

Congress and the Supreme Court: Lawmaking Versus Law Interpreting

In the years after the Civil War, Congress went to work to protect the rights of black citizens. In 1866, lawmakers passed a civil rights act that granted all citizens—white and black—the right to make and enforce contracts, sue or be sued, give evidence, and inherit, purchase, lease, sell, hold, or convey property. Later, in the Civil Rights Act of 1875, Congress attempted to guarantee blacks equal access to public accommodations (streetcars, inns, parks, theaters, and the like).

While Congress was enacting laws to protect the civil rights of black citizens, the Supreme Court weakened some of those rights. In 1873, the Court ruled that the Civil War amendments had not changed the relationship between the state and national governments.[65] State citizenship and national citizenship remained separate and distinct. According to the Court, the Fourteenth Amendment did not obligate the states to honor the rights guaranteed by U.S. citizenship. In effect, the Court stripped the amendment of its power to secure for black citizens the freedoms guaranteed by the Bill of Rights.

In 1883, the Court struck down the public accommodations section of the Civil Rights Act of 1875.[66] The justices declared that the national government could prohibit only government action that discriminated against blacks; private acts of discrimination or acts of omission by a state were beyond the reach of the national government.

In case after case, the Court refused to see racial discrimination as an act that the national government could prohibit. By tolerating racial discrimination, the justices abetted **racism**, the belief that there are inherent differences among the races that determine people's achievement and that one's own race is superior to, and thus has a right to dominate, others.

The Court's decisions gave the states ample room to maneuver around civil rights laws. In the matter of voting rights, for example, states that wanted to bar black men from the polls simply used nonracial means to do so. One popular tool was the **poll tax**, first imposed by Georgia in 1877. This was a tax of $1 or $2 on every citizen who wanted to vote. The tax was not a burden for most whites. But many blacks were tenant farmers, who did not have any extra money for voting. Other bars to black suffrage included literacy tests, minimum education requirements, and a grandfather clause that restricted suffrage to men who could establish that their grandfathers were eligible to vote before 1867 (three years before the Fifteenth Amendment declared that race could not be used to deny individuals the right to vote).[67] Intimidation and violence were also used to keep blacks from the polls.

The Roots of Racial Segregation

Well before the Civil War, **racial segregation** was a way of life in the South: Blacks lived and worked separately from whites. After the war, southern states began to enact Jim Crow laws that enforced segregation. (*Jim Crow* was a derogatory term for a black person.) Once the Supreme Court took the teeth out of the Civil Rights Act of 1875, such laws proliferated. They required blacks to live in separate (generally inferior) areas and restricted them to separate sections of hospitals, separate cemeteries, separate schools, and separate sections of streetcars, trains, jails, and parks. Each day, in countless ways, they were reminded of the inferior status accorded them by white society.

In 1892, Homer Adolph Plessy—who was seven-eighths Caucasian—took a seat in a "whites only" car of a Louisiana train. He refused to move to the car reserved for blacks and was arrested. Plessy argued that Louisiana's law mandating racial segregation on its trains was an unconstitutional infringement on both the privileges and immunities guaranteed by the Fourteenth Amendment and its equal protection clause. The Supreme Court disagreed. The majority in *Plessy v. Ferguson* (1896) upheld state-imposed racial segregation.[68] They based their decision on the **separate-but-equal doctrine**, which held that separate facilities for blacks and whites satisfied the Fourteenth Amendment so long as they were equal. The lone dissenter, John Marshall Harlan, who envisioned a "color-blind Constitution," wrote this in his dissenting opinion:

> We boast of the freedom enjoyed by our people above all other peoples. But it is difficult to reconcile that boast with a state of the law which, practically, puts the brand of servitude and degradation upon a large class of our fellow citizens—our equals before the law. The thin disguise of "equal" accommodations for passengers in railroad coaches will not mislead any one, nor atone for the wrong this day done.[69]

Three years later, the Supreme Court extended the separate-but-equal doctrine to the schools.[70] The justices ignored the fact that black educational facilities (and most other "colored only" facilities) were far from equal to those reserved for whites.

By the end of the nineteenth century, racial segregation was firmly and legally entrenched in the American South. Although constitutional amendments and national laws to protect equality under the law were in place, the Supreme Court's interpretation of those amendments and laws rendered them ineffective. Several decades would pass before any change was discernible.

The Dismantling of School Segregation

By the middle of the twentieth century, public attitudes toward race relations were slowly changing. Black troops had fought with honor—albeit in segregated military units—in World War II. Blacks and whites were working together in unions and in service and religious organizations. Social change and court decisions suggested that government-imposed segregation was vulnerable.

President Harry S Truman risked his political future with his strong support of blacks' civil rights. In 1947, he established the President's Committee on Civil Rights. The committee's report, issued later that year, became the agenda for the civil rights movement over the next two decades. It called for national laws prohibiting racially motivated poll taxes, segregation, and brutality against minorities, and for guarantees of voting rights and equal employment opportunity. In 1948, Truman ordered the **desegregation** (the dismantling of authorized racial segregation) of the armed forces.

In 1947, the U.S. Department of Justice had begun to submit briefs to the courts in support of civil rights. Perhaps the department's most important intervention came in *Brown v. Board of Education.*[71] This case was the culmination of twenty years of planning and litigation on the part of the National Association for the Advancement of Colored People (NAACP) to invalidate racial segregation in public schools.

Linda Brown was a black child whose father tried to enroll her in a white public school in Topeka, Kansas. Brown's request was refused because of Linda's race. A federal district court found that the black public school was, in all major respects, equal in quality to the white school; therefore, according to the *Plessy* doctrine, Linda was required to go to the black public school. Brown appealed the decision.

Brown v. Board of Education reached the Supreme Court in late 1951. The justices delayed argument on the sensitive race issue, placing it beyond the 1952 national election. *Brown* was merged with four similar cases into a class action (see Chapter 11). The class action was supported by the NAACP and coordinated by Thurgood Marshall, who would later become the first black justice to sit on the Supreme Court. The five cases squarely challenged the separate-but-equal doctrine. By all tangible measures (standards for teacher licensing, teacher-pupil ratios, library facilities), the two school systems in each case—one white, the other black—were equal. The issue was legal separation of the races.

On May 17, 1954, Chief Justice Earl Warren, who had recently joined the Court, delivered a single opinion covering four of the cases. Warren spoke for a unanimous Court when he declared that "in the field of public education the doctrine of 'separate but equal' has no place. Separate educational facilities are inherently unequal,"[72] depriving the plaintiffs of the equal protection of the laws. Segregated facilities generate in black children "a feeling of inferiority . . . that may affect their hearts and minds in a way unlikely ever to be undone."[73] In short, the nation's highest court found that state-imposed public school segregation was found to violate the equal protection clause of the Fourteenth Amendment.

The Court deferred implementation of the school desegregation decisions until 1955. Then, in *Brown v. Board of Education II*, it ruled that school systems must desegregate "with all deliberate speed" and assigned the process of supervising desegregation to the lower federal courts.[74]

Some states quietly complied with the *Brown* decree. Others did little to desegregate their schools. And many communities in the South defied the Court, sometimes violently. This resistance, along with the Supreme Court's "all deliberate speed" order, placed a heavy burden on federal judges to dismantle what was the fundamental social order in many communities.[75] Gradual desegregation under *Brown* was in some cases no desegregation at all. By 1969, a unanimous Supreme Court ordered that the operation of segregated school systems must stop "at once."[76]

Two years later, the Court approved several remedies to achieve integration, including busing, racial quotas, and the pairing or grouping of noncontiguous school zones. But these remedies applied only to *de jure* **segregation**, government-imposed segregation (for example, government assignment of whites to one school and blacks to another within the same community). Court-imposed remedies did not apply to *de facto* **segregation**, segregation that is not the result of government influence (for example, racial segregation resulting from residential patterns).

Public opinion strongly opposed the busing approach, and Congress sought limits on busing as a remedy. In 1974, a closely divided Court ruled that lower courts could not order busing across school district boundaries unless each district had practiced racial discrimination or unless school district lines had been deliberately drawn to achieve racial segregation.[77]

The Civil Rights Movement

Although the NAACP concentrated on school desegregation, it also made headway in other areas. The Supreme Court responded to NAACP efforts in the late 1940s by outlawing the whites-only primary elections in the South, declaring them to be in violation of the Fifteenth Amendment. The Court also declared segregation on interstate bus routes to be unconstitutional and desegregated restaurants and hotels in the District of Columbia. Despite these and other decisions that chipped away at existing barriers to equality, the realization of equality would require the political mobilization of the people—black and white—into what is now known as the **civil rights movement**.

Civil Disobedience

Rosa Parks, a black woman living in Montgomery, Alabama, sounded the first call to action. That city's Jim Crow ordinances required blacks to sit in the back of the bus and empowered drivers to order blacks to vacate an entire row to make room for one white or to order blacks to stand even when some seats were vacant. In December 1955, Parks boarded a city bus on her way home from work and took an available seat in the front of the bus; she refused to give up her seat when the driver asked her to do so and was arrested and fined $10 for violating the city ordinance.

Under the leadership of a charismatic twenty-six-year-old Baptist minister named Martin Luther King, Jr., Montgomery's black community responded to Parks's arrest with a boycott of the city's bus system. A **boycott** is a refusal to do business with a company or individual, as an expression of disapproval or a means of coercion. A year after the boycott began, the federal courts ruled that segregated transportation systems violated the equal protection clause of the Constitution.

In 1957, King helped organize the Southern Christian Leadership Council (SCLC) to coordinate civil rights activities. King was totally com-

A Modern-Day Moses
Martin Luther King, Jr., was a Baptist minister who believed in the principles of nonviolent protest practiced by India's Mohandas ("Mahatma") Gandhi. This photograph, taken in 1963 in Baltimore, captures the crowd's affection for King, the man many thought would lead them to a new Canaan of racial equality. King, who won the Nobel Peace Prize in 1964, was assassinated in 1968 in Memphis, Tennessee.

mitted to nonviolent action to bring racial issues into the light. To that end, he advocated **civil disobedience**, the willful but nonviolent breach of unjust laws.

Martin Luther King, Jr., had risen to worldwide prominence by August, 1963, when he organized and led "A March for Jobs and Freedom," in Washington, D.C. More than 250,000 people, black and white, gathered peaceably at the Lincoln Memorial to hear King speak. "I have a dream," he told them, "that my little children will one day live in a nation where they will not be judged by the color of their skin but by the content of their character"[78]

The Civil Rights Act of 1964

President Lyndon B. Johnson considered civil rights his top legislative priority. Within months after he assumed office, Congress passed the Civil Rights Act of 1964, the most comprehensive legislative attempt ever to erase racial discrimination in the United States. Among its many provisions, the act

- Entitled all persons to "the full and equal enjoyment" of goods, services, and privileges in places of public accommodation without discrimination on the grounds of race, color, religion, or national origin
- Established the right to equality in employment opportunities
- Strengthened voting rights legislation
- Created the Equal Employment Opportunity Commission (EEOC), and charged it with hearing and investigating complaints of job discrimination*
- Provided that funds could be withheld from federally assisted programs that were administered in a discriminatory manner

President Johnson's goal was a "great society." Soon a constitutional amendment and a series of civil rights laws were in place to help him meet his goal.

- The Twenty-fourth Amendment, ratified in 1964, banned poll taxes in primary and general elections for national office.
- The Economic Opportunity Act of 1964 focused on education and training to combat poverty.
- The Voting Rights Act of 1965 empowered the attorney general to send voter registration supervisors to areas in which fewer than half the eligible minority voters had been registered. This act has been credited with doubling black voter registration in the South in only five years.[79]
- The Fair Housing Act of 1968 banned discrimination in the rental or sale of most housing.

The Continuing Struggle over Civil Rights

However, civil rights on the books do not ensure civil rights in action. While Congress has tried to restore and expand civil rights enforcement, in recent years the Supreme Court has weakened it. The Court restricted minority contractor set-asides of state public works funds, an arrangement it had approved in 1980. (Recall that a set-aside is a purchasing or contracting provision that reserves a certain percentage of funds for minority-owned contractors.) The five-person majority held that past societal discrimination alone cannot serve as the basis for rigid quotas.[80]

Buttressed by Republican appointees, the Supreme Court continued to narrow the scope of national civil rights protections in a string of decisions that suggested the ascendancy of a new conservative majority more concerned with freedom than equality.[81] To counter the Court's changing interpretations of civil rights laws, liberals turned to Congress to restore and enlarge earlier Court decisions by writing them into law. The result was a comprehensive new

---

*Since 1972, the EEOC has had the power to institute legal proceedings on behalf of employees who allege that they have been victims of illegal discrimination.

civil rights bill. The Civil Rights Act of 1991 reversed or altered twelve Court decisions that had narrowed civil rights protections. The new law clarified and expanded earlier legislation and increased the costs to employers for intentional, illegal discrimination. Continued resentment generated by equal outcomes policies would move the battle back to the courts, however.

Civil Rights for Other Minorities

Recent civil rights laws and court decisions protect members of all minority groups. The Supreme Court underscored the breadth of this protection in an important decision in 1987.[82] The justices ruled unanimously that the Civil Rights Act of 1866 (known today as Section 1981) offered broad protection against discrimination to all minorities. Previously, members of white ethnic groups could not invoke the law in bias suits. Under the 1987 decision, members of *any* ethnic group—Italian, Iranian, Norwegian, or Chinese, for example—can recover money damages if they prove they have been denied a job, excluded from rental housing, or subjected to another form of discrimination prohibited by the law. The 1964 Civil Rights Act offers similar protections but specifies strict procedures for filing suits that tend to discourage litigation.

Clearly the civil rights movement has had an effect on all minorities. Here we examine the civil rights struggles of three groups—Native Americans, Hispanic Americans, and the disabled.

Native Americans

In 1924, Indians received U.S. citizenship. Until that time, they were considered members of tribal nations whose relations with the U.S. government were determined by treaties. The agencies responsible for administering Indian reservations kept Native Americans poor and dependent on the national government. And Indian lands continued to shrink through the 1950s and into the 1960s—despite signed treaties and the religious significance of portions of the lands they lost.

Anger bred of poverty, unemployment, and frustration with an uncaring government exploded into militant action in November 1969, when several American Indians seized Alcatraz Island, an abandoned island in San Francisco Bay. The group cited an 1868 Sioux treaty that entitled them to unused federal lands; they remained on the island for a year and a half. In 1973, armed members of the American Indian Movement seized eleven hostages at Wounded Knee, South Dakota—the site of an 1890 massacre of two hundred Sioux (Lakota) by U.S. cavalry troops. They remained there, occasionally exchanging gunfire with federal marshals, for seventy-one days until the government agreed to examine the treaty rights of the Oglala Sioux.[83]

In 1946, Congress enacted legislation establishing an Indian claims commission to compensate Native Americans for land that had been taken from them. In the 1970s, the Native American Rights Fund and other groups used that legislation to win important victories in the courts. The tribes won the return of lands in the Midwest and in the states of Oklahoma, New Mexico, and Washington. In 1980, the Supreme Court ordered the national government to

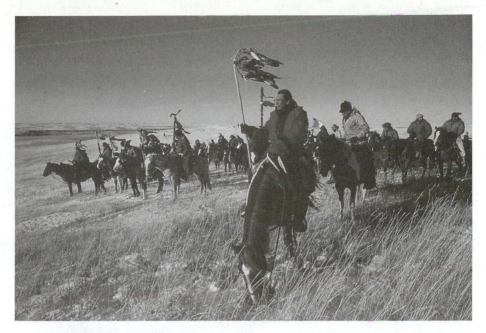

Bury My Heart
Native American mourners gathered at Wounded Knee, South Dakota, on December 29, 1990, to remember a tragedy. On that site a hundred years earlier, Seventh Cavalry soldiers massacred two hundred Sioux—including women and children. Descendants of the survivors traveled by foot and horseback to mark the anniversary and to honor their heritage.

pay the Sioux $117 million plus interest for the Black Hills of South Dakota, which had been stolen from them a century before. Other cases, involving land from coast to coast, are still pending.

The special status accorded Indian tribes in the Constitution has proved attractive to a new breed of Indian leaders. Some of the 557 recognized tribes have successfully instituted casino gambling on their reservations, even in the face of state opposition to their plans. Congress has allowed these developments provided that the tribes spend their profits on Indian assistance programs. The wealth created by casino gambling and other ventures funded with gambling profits may prove to be Native Americans' most effective weapon for retaining and regaining their heritage.

Hispanic Americans

Many Hispanic Americans have a rich and deep-rooted heritage in America, but until the 1920s, that heritage was largely confined to the southwestern states and particularly California. Then, unprecedented numbers of Mexican and Puerto Rican immigrants came to the United States in search of employment and a better life. Like blacks who had migrated to northern cities, most of them found poverty and discrimination.

A Long Climb
In 1990 the Americans with Disabilities Act brought people with physical or mental
disabilities under the protections embodied in the Civil Rights Act of 1964. Mandated
changes such as access to public places for those using wheelchairs now permit individuals
such as these to live fuller and more productive lives.

World War II gave rise to another influx of Mexicans, this time primarily courted to work farms in California. But by the late 1950s, most farm workers—blacks, whites, and Hispanics—were living in poverty. Those Hispanic Americans who lived in cities fared little better. Yet millions of Mexicans continued to cross the border into the United States, both legally and illegally. The effect was to depress the value of farm labor in California and the Southwest.

The Hispanic American population continues to grow. The 20 million Hispanics living in the United States in the 1970s were still mainly Puerto Rican and Mexican American, but they were joined by immigrants from the Dominican Republic, Colombia, Cuba, Ecuador, and elsewhere. Although civil rights legislation helped them to an extent, they are among the poorest and least-educated groups in the United States.

Voter registration and voter turnout among Hispanics are lower than among other groups. Also, voter turnout depends on effective political advertising, and Hispanics are not targeted as often as other groups with political messages that they can understand. But despite these stumbling blocks, Latinos have started to exercise a measure of political power.

Hispanics occupy positions of power in national and local arenas. The 104th Congress (1995–1997) convened with a diverse group of eighteen Hispanic House members. They form the Congressional Hispanic Caucus, an informal bipartisan group dedicated to voicing and advancing issues affecting Hispanic Americans. The National Hispanic Caucus of State Legislators, which has 250 members, has a similar mission. Latinos have won the mayoralties of San Antonio, San Diego, Denver, and Miami. President Clinton appointed two Hispanics to his first cabinet.

Disabled Americans

Forty-three million disabled Americans gained recognition in 1990 as a protected minority with the enactment of the Americans with Disabilities Act (ADA). The law extends the protections embodied in the Civil Rights Act of 1964 to people with physical or mental disabilities, including people with AIDS and recovering alcoholics, and drug abusers. It guarantees them access to employment, transportation, public accommodations, and communication services.

Advocates for the disabled found a ready model in the existing civil rights laws. Opponents argued that the changes mandated by the 1990 law (such as access for those confined to wheelchairs) could cost billions of dollars, but supporters replied that the costs would be offset by an equal or greater reduction in federal aid to disabled people, who would rather be working.

A change in the law, no matter how welcome, does not ensure a change in attitudes. Laws that end racial discrimination do not extinguish racism, and laws that ban biased treatment of the disabled cannot mandate their acceptance. But, civil rights advocates predict that bias against the disabled, like similar attitudes toward other minorities, will wither as they become full participants in society.

Gender and Equal Rights: The Women's Movement

Together with such unconventional political activities as protests and sit-ins, conventional political tools such as the ballot box and the lawsuit have brought minorities in America a measure of equality. The Supreme Court has expanded the array of legal weapons available to all minorities to help them achieve social equality. Women, too, have benefited from this change.

Protectionism

Until the early 1970s, laws that affected the civil rights of women were based on traditional views of the relationship between men and women. At the heart of these laws was **protectionism**—the notion that women must be sheltered from life's harsh realities. And protected they were, through laws that discriminated against them in employment and other areas. With few exceptions, women were also "protected" from voting until early in the twentieth century.

Protectionism reached a peak in 1908, when the Court upheld an Oregon law limiting the number of hours women could work.[84] The decision was rife with assumptions about the nature and role of women, and it gave wide latitude to laws that "protected" the "weaker sex." However, in 1991, the Supreme Court clearly moved away from protectionism by striking down an employer's policy excluding women capable of bearing children from jobs that involve exposure to toxic substances that could harm a developing fetus. Relying on amendments to the 1964 Civil Rights Act, the court declared that "women as capable of doing their jobs as their male counterparts may not be forced to choose between having a child and having a job."[85]

Political Equality for Women

In 1878, Susan B. Anthony, a women's rights activist, persuaded a U.S. senator from California to introduce a constitutional amendment requiring that "the right of citizens of the United States to vote shall not be denied or abridged by the United States or by any State on account of sex." The amendment was introduced and voted down a number of times over the next twenty years. Meanwhile, a number of states—primarily in the Midwest and West—did grant limited suffrage to women.

By the early 1900s the movement for women's suffrage had became a political battle to amend the Constitution. The battle was won in 1920, when the **Nineteenth Amendment** gave women the right to vote in the wording first suggested by Anthony.

Prohibiting Sex-Based Discrimination

The movement to provide equal rights to women advanced a step with the passage of the Equal Pay Act of 1963. That act requires equal pay for men and women doing similar work. However, to remove the restrictions of protectionism, women needed equal opportunity for employment. They got it in the Civil Rights Act of 1964 and later legislation. The EEOC, which had been created by that law, was empowered to act on behalf of victims of invidious sex discrimination, or **sexism**.

Stereotypes Under Scrutiny

After nearly a century of protectionism, the Supreme Court began to take a closer look at gender-based distinctions. In 1971, it struck down a state law that gave men preference over women in administering the estate of a person who died without naming an administrator.[86] Two years later, the justices declared that paternalism operated to "put women not on a pedestal, but in a cage."[87] They then proceeded to strike down several gender-based laws that either prevented or discouraged departures from "proper" sex roles. In 1976, the Court finally developed a workable standard for reviewing these kinds of laws: Gender-based distinctions are justified only if they serve some important government purpose.[88]

The courts have not been reluctant to extend to women the *constitutional* guarantees won by blacks. In 1994, the Supreme Court extended the Constitution's equal protection guarantee by forbidding the exclusion of potential jurors on the basis of their sex.[89] The 1994 decision completed a constitutional revolution in jury selection that began in 1986 with a bar against juror exclusions based on race.

In 1996, the Court spoke with uncommon clarity when it declared that the men-only admissions policy of the Virginia Military Institute (VMI), a state-supported military college, violated the equal protection clause of the Fourteenth Amendment. In an effort to meet women's demands to enter VMI—and to stave off continued legal challenges—Virginia had established a separate-but-equal institution called the Virginia Women's Institute for Leadership (VWIL). Writing for a six-member majority in **United States v. Virginia,** Justice Ruth Bader Ginsburg applied a demanding test she labeled "skeptical scrutiny" to official acts that deny individuals rights or responsibilities based on their sex. "Parties who seek to defend gender-based government action," she wrote, "must demonstrate an 'exceedingly persuasive justification' for that action." Ginsburg declared that "women seeking and fit for a VMI-quality education cannot be offered anything less, under the State's obligation to afford them genuinely equal protection."[90] The upshot is that distinctions based on sex are almost as suspect as distinctions based on race.

The Equal Rights Amendment

Policies protecting women, based largely on sexual stereotypes, have been woven into the legal fabric of American life. This protectionism has limited the freedom of women to compete with men socially and economically on an equal footing. However, the Supreme Court has been hesitant to extend the principles of the Fourteenth Amendment beyond issues of race. If constitutional interpretation imposes such a limit, then only a constitutional amendment can overcome it.

The National Women's party, one of the few women's groups that did not disband after the Nineteenth Amendment was enacted, first introduced the **Equal Rights Amendment (ERA)** in 1923. The ERA declared that "equality of rights under the law shall not be denied or abridged by the United States or any State on account of sex."

A national coalition of women's rights advocates generated enough support to get the ERA through Congress in 1972. However, the ERA died on July 1, 1982, still three states short of adoption.

Despite its failure, some scholars argue that for practical purposes, the Supreme Court has implemented the ERA through its decisions. It has struck down distinctions based on sex and held that stereotyped generalizations of sexual differences must fall.[91] In recent rulings, the Court has held that states may require employers to guarantee job reinstatement to women returning from maternity leave and that sexual harassment in the workplace is illegal, and that a hostile work environment will be judged by a reasonable perception of abuse rather than a demonstration of psychological injury.[92]

Affirmative Action: Equal Opportunity or Equal Outcome?

In his vision of the Great Society, President Johnson linked economic rights with civil rights, and equality of outcome with equality of opportunity. "Equal opportunity is essential, but not enough," he declared. "We seek not just legal equity but human ability, not just equality as a right and a theory but equality as a fact and equality as a result."[93] This commitment led to affirmative action programs to expand opportunities for women, minorities, and the disabled.

Affirmative action embraces a range of public and private programs, policies, and procedures, including special recruitment, preferential treatment, and quotas in job training and professional education, employment, and the awarding of government contracts. The point of these programs is to move beyond equality of opportunity to equality of outcome.

Arguments for affirmative action programs (from increased recruitment efforts to quotas) tend to use the following reasoning: Certain groups have historically suffered invidious discrimination, denying them educational and economic opportunities. To eliminate the lasting effects of such discrimination, the public and private sectors must take steps to provide access to good education and jobs. If the majority once used discrimination to hold groups back, discriminating to benefit those groups is fair. Therefore, quotas are a legitimate means to provide a place on the ladder of success.[94]

Affirmative action opponents maintain that quotas for designated groups necessarily create invidious discrimination (in the form of reverse discrimination) against individuals who are themselves blameless. Moreover, they say, quotas lead to admission, hiring, or promotion of the less qualified at the expense of the well qualified. In the name of equality, such policies thwart individuals' freedom to succeed. Do preferential poli-

Right Remedied
Cheryl Hopwood and others challenged preferential admissions policies at the University of Texas Law School. Hopwood's victory cast doubt on the viability of other government-sponsored preference policies.

cies in other nations offer lessons for us? See Compared with What 12.1 to learn the answer.

Reverse Discrimination

The Supreme Court confronted an affirmative action quota program for the first time in *Regents of the University of California v. Bakke*.[95] Allan Bakke, a thirty-five-year-old white man, had twice applied for admission to the University of California Medical School at Davis. He was rejected both times. The school had reserved sixteen places in each entering class of one hundred for qualified minority applicants, as part of the university's affirmative action program. Bakke's qualifications (college grade point average and test scores) exceeded those of

Compared with What? 12.1

How Other Nations Struggle with Affirmative Action

Americans are not alone in their disagreements over affirmative action. Controversies, and even bloodshed, have been the order of the day in countries where certain groups receive government-sanctioned preferences over others.

India, Sri Lanka, Malaysia, Nigeria, Australia, and Canada are among the nations with affirmative action policies of their own. The phraseology of these policies may differ somewhat from the American model. Although Australia and Canada use the American label *affirmative action,* India refers to its policy as *positive discrimination.* Nigeria's preferential policy is designed to "reflect the federal character of the country." In Malaysia, the constitution recognizes the "special position" of the Malays (the dominant group) and reserves a share of public benefits (including government jobs, educational scholarships, and land) for them.

The particular problems created by the affirmative action policy in India recently claimed international attention. The untouchables, a pariah group, have long been the chief beneficiary of the nation's preferential policies. In 1990, the government of India decided to strengthen its policy of positive discrimination by reserving more than half of all government jobs for members of the lower castes.

Although the job quotas proved popular among the lower castes, who make up well over half of India's population, they generated deep resentment among the higher castes. Students from the higher castes have traditionally viewed government jobs as a way to secure their middle-class expectations. The new ruling made government jobs much more difficult for them to obtain. Regardless of their academic success, many high-caste students will be passed over for government jobs. In a singularly gruesome form of protest, scores of young upper-caste men and women have set themselves ablaze. And when the Indian courts issued a temporary injunction that halted the government's affirmative action plan, terrorists who supported the plan protested by bombing a train, killing dozens of people. Tension is likely to remain high in Indian society, given the country's ancient caste hierarchy and an economy that is not expanding rapidly enough to satisfy every interest.

One recent study of preferential policies has aimed to generalize from the experiences of many nations. The cultures, politics, and economies of nations with preferential policies vary enormously. The groups benefiting from these policies also vary; they may be locally or nationally dominant, or they may be poor and relatively powerless politically.

Despite these variables, nations with affirmative action policies seem to share some common patterns. First, although often defined as temporary, preferential policies tend to persist and even expand to embrace more individuals and groups. Second, benefits tend to flow disproportionately to members of recipient groups who are already more fortunate. Third, antagonism among groups tends to increase in the wake of the implementation of

(continued)

Compared with What? 12.1 (continued)

preferential policies. The reactions of groups that do not benefit from such policies range from a change in voting behavior to violence, even civil war. And fourth, false claims of membership in designated beneficiary groups increase.

These observations have implications for majoritarian and pluralist models of democracy. All governments broker conflict in varying degrees. Under a majoritarian model, group demands could lead quickly to conflict and instability, because majority rule leaves little room for compromise. A pluralist model allows different groups to get a piece of the pie. By parceling out benefits, pluralism mitigates disorder in the short term. But in the long term, repeated demands for increased benefits can spark instability. A vigorous pluralist system should provide acceptable mechanisms (legislative, executive, bureaucratic, judicial) to vent such frustrations and yield a new allocation of benefits.

Sources: Donald L. Horowitz, *Ethnic Groups in Conflict* (Berkeley: University of California Press, 1985); *Facts on File,* 19 October 1990, pp. 784–785; Edward W. Desmond, "Fatal Fires of Protest," *Time,* 15 October 1990, p. 63; and Thomas Sowell, *Race and Culture: A World View* (New York: Basic Books, 1994).

any of the minority students admitted in the two years his applications were rejected. Bakke contended, first in the California courts, then in the Supreme Court, that he was excluded from admission solely on the basis of race. He argued that the equal protection clause of the Fourteenth Amendment and the Civil Rights Act of 1964 prohibited this reverse discrimination.

The Court's decision in *Bakke* contained six opinions and spanned 154 pages. But even after careful analysis of the decision, discerning what the Court had decided was difficult: No opinion had a majority. One bloc of four justices opposed the medical school's plan; a second bloc of four justices supported the plan. Justice Lewis F. Powell, Jr., agreed with parts of both arguments. With the first bloc, he argued that the school's rigid use of racial quotas violated the equal protection clause of the Fourteenth Amendment. With the second bloc, he contended that the use of race was permissible as one of several admissions criteria. Powell cast the deciding vote ordering the medical school to admit Bakke. Despite the confusing multiple opinions, the Court signaled its approval of affirmative action programs in education that use race as a *plus* factor (one of many such factors) but not as *the* factor (one that alone determines the outcome).

Other cases followed. In 1979, the Court upheld a voluntary affirmative action plan that gave preferences to blacks in an employee training program.[96] Five years later, however, the Court held that affirmative action did not exempt minorities (typically the most recently hired employees) from traditional work rules, which generally specify that the last hired are the first fired. Layoffs must proceed by seniority, declared the Court, unless minority employees can demonstrate that they are actual victims of their employer's discrimination.[97]

In 1995, the Supreme Court struck a sharp blow to the legal foundations of government policies that award benefits on the basis of race, signaling an end to equal outcomes policies. Recall Randy Pech's lawsuit challenging a government set-aside program for minority contractors. Writing for a 5–4 majority in *Adarand Constructors v. Peña,* Justice Sandra Day O'Connor declared that such programs must be subject to the most searching judicial inquiry (what the Court calls "strict scrutiny") and must be "narrowly tailored" to achieve a "compelling government interest."[98] Few, if any, programs can satisfy the Court's stringent requirements for constitutionality. (The Court sent the case back to the trial court so that it could evaluate the facts in light of the "strict scrutiny" approach.)

Quota policies are now under serious threat from several quarters. In 1996, a federal appeals court, relying on the *Adarand* case, rejected the use of race or ethnicity as the determining factor in law school admissions. Meanwhile, the governing board of the University of California has voted to scrap its race-based admissions policy. And legislative movements in more than a dozen states aim to curtail or eliminate racial preferences in educational admissions and financial aid. Colorado, for example, has begun to offer college scholarships on the basis of need rather than race.[99] The biggest showdown to date regarding the future of affirmative action occurred during the 1996 elections. California voters were asked to approve or reject a ballot initiative to amend the state constitution as follows:

> Neither the State of California, nor any of its political subdivisions or agents, shall use race, sex, color, ethnicity or national origin as a criterion for either discriminating against, or granting preferential treatment to, any individual or group in the operation of the State's system of public employment, public education or public contracting.

The initiative passed with 54 percent of the vote.

The Politics of Affirmative Action

A comprehensive review of nationwide surveys conducted over the past twenty years reveals an unsurprising truth: that blacks favor affirmative action programs and whites do not. Women and men do not differ on this issue. The gulf between the races was wider in the 1970s than it is today, but the moderation results from shifts among blacks, not whites. Perhaps the most important finding is that "whites' views have remained essentially unchanged over 20 years."[100]

How do we account for the persistence of equal outcomes policies? A majority of Americans have consistently rejected explicit race or gender preferences for the awarding of contracts, employment decisions, and college admissions, regardless of the groups such preferences benefit. Nevertheless, preference policies have survived and thrived under both Democrats and Republicans. The list of protected groups has expanded beyond African Americans to include Hispanic Americans, Native Americans, Asian Pacific Americans, Subcontinental Asian Americans, and women. Politicians have a powerful motive—votes—to expand the number of protected groups and the benefits such policies provide.

The conflict between freedom and equality will continue as other individuals and groups press their demands through litigation and legislation. The choice the country makes will depend on whether and to what extent Americans are prepared to change their minds on these thorny issues.

Summary

When they established the new government of the United States, the states and the people compelled the framers, through the Bill of Rights, to protect their freedoms. In their interpretation of these ten amendments, the courts, especially the Supreme Court, have taken on the task of balancing freedom and order.

The First Amendment protects several freedoms: freedom of religion, freedom of speech and of the press, and the freedom to assemble peaceably and petition the government. The establishment clause demands government neutrality toward religions and between the religious and the nonreligious. According to judicial interpretations of the free-exercise clause, religious beliefs are inviolable, but the Constitution does not protect antisocial actions in the name of religion. Extreme interpretations of the religion clauses could bring the clauses into conflict with each other.

Freedom of expression encompasses freedom of speech, freedom of the press, and the right to assemble peaceably and petition the government. Freedom of speech and freedom of the press have never been held to be absolute, but the courts have ruled that the Bill of Rights gives them far greater protection than other freedoms. Exceptions to free-speech protections include some forms of symbolic expression, and obscenity. Press freedom has had broad constitutional protection because a free society depends on the ability to collect and report information without government interference. The rights to assemble peaceably and to petition the government stem from the guarantees of freedom of speech and of the press. Each freedom is equally fundamental, but the right to exercise them is not absolute.

The adoption of the Fourteenth Amendment in 1868 extended the guarantees of the Bill of Rights to the states. The due process clause became the vehicle for applying specific provisions of the Bill of Rights—one at a time, case after case—to the states. The designation of a right as fundamental also called for a definition of that right. The Supreme Court has tolerated some variation from state to state in the meaning of certain constitutional rights. The Court has also imposed a duty on governments to inform citizens of their rights so that they are equipped to exercise them.

As it fashioned new fundamental rights from the Constitution, the Supreme Court has become embroiled in controversy. The right to privacy served as the basis for the right of women to terminate a pregnancy, which in turn suggested a right to personal autonomy. The abortion controversy is still raging, and the justices have called a halt to the extension of personal privacy in the name of the Constitution.

Americans want equality, but they disagree on the extent to which government should guarantee it. At the heart of this conflict is the distinction between equal opportunities and equal outcomes.

Congress enacted the Civil War amendments—the Thirteenth, Fourteenth, and Fifteenth Amendments—to provide full civil rights to black Americans. In the late nineteenth century, the Supreme Court interpreted the amendments very narrowly, declaring that they did not restrain individuals from denying civil rights to blacks and that they did not apply to powers that were reserved for the states. The Court's rulings had the effect of denying the vote to most blacks and of institutionalizing racism, making racial segregation a fact of daily life.

Through a series of court cases spanning two decades, the Court slowly dismantled segregation in the schools. The battle for desegregation culminated in the *Brown* cases in 1954 and 1955, in which a now-supportive Supreme Court declared segregated schools to be inherently unequal and therefore unconstitutional. The Court also ordered the desegregation of all schools and upheld the use of busing to do so.

Gains in other civil rights areas came more slowly. The motivating force was the civil rights movement, led by Martin Luther King, Jr., until his assassination in 1968. King believed strongly in civil disobedience and nonviolence, strategies that helped secure for blacks equality in voting rights, public accommodations, higher education, housing, and employment opportunity.

Civil rights activism and the civil rights movement worked to the benefit of all minority groups; in fact, they benefited all Americans. Native Americans obtained some redress for past injustices. Hispanic Americans came to recognize the importance of group action to achieve economic and political equality. Disabled Americans won civil rights protections enjoyed by African Americans and others. And civil rights legislation removed the protectionism that was, in effect, legalized discrimination against women in education and employment.

Despite legislative advances in the area of women's rights, the states did not ratify the Equal Rights Amendment. Still, the struggle for ratification produced several positive results, heightening awareness of women's roles in society and mobilizing their political power. And legislation and judicial rulings implemented much of the amendment's provisions in practice. The Supreme Court now judges sex-based classification with "skeptical scrutiny," meaning that distinctions based on sex are almost as suspect as distinctions based on race.

Government and business instituted affirmative action programs to counteract the results of past discrimination. These provide preferential treatment for women, minorities, and the disabled in a number of areas that affect individuals' economic opportunity and well-being. In effect, such programs discriminate to remedy earlier discrimination. When programs make race the determining factor in awarding contracts, offering employment, or granting admission to educational institutions, the courts will be skeptical of their validity. Notwithstanding congressional efforts to reverse some Supreme Court decisions, a conservative majority on the Court has emerged to roll back the equality-preferring policies of the more liberal bench that held sway through the 1980s.

Many of the civil liberties and civil rights that Americans enjoy today were defined by the courts. This raises a basic issue. By offering constitutional protection to certain public policies, the courts may be threatening the democratic process, the process that gives the people a say in government through their elected representatives. One thing is certain, however: The challenge of democracy requires the constant balancing of freedom, order and equality.

Key Terms

affirmative action	establishment clause
civil liberties	free-exercise clause
civil rights	strict scrutiny

free-expression clauses
prior restraint
clear and present danger test
public figures
bill of attainder
ex post facto law
obligation of contracts
Miranda warnings
exclusionary rule
good faith exception
equality of opportunity
equality of outcome
invidious discrimination
racism

poll tax
racial segregation
separate-but-equal doctrine
desegregation
de jure segregation
de facto segregation
civil rights movement
boycott
civil disobedience
protectionism
Nineteenth Amendment
sexism
Equal Rights Amendment (ERA)

Key Cases

Lemon v. Kurtzman
West Virginia State Board of Education v. Barnette
Sherbert v. Verner
Brandenburg v. Ohio
Tinker v. Des Moines Independent County School District
Miller v. California
New York Times v. Sullivan
New York Times v. United States
Palko v. Connecticut
Gideon v. Wainwright
Griswold v. Connecticut
Roe v. Wade
Bowers v. Hardwick
Plessy v. Ferguson
Brown v. Board of Education
Brown v. Board of Education II
United States v. Virginia
Regents of the University of California v. Bakke
Adarand Constructors v. Peña

Selected Readings

Berger, Raoul. *Government by Judiciary: The Transformation of the Fourteenth Amendment.* Cambridge, Mass.: Harvard University Press, 1977. This provocative work argues that the framers of the Fourteenth Amendment had narrow aims and that the Supreme Court, especially since 1954, has disregarded this historical legacy in its promotion of freedom and equality.

Branch, Taylor. *Parting the Waters: America in the King Years, 1954–1963.* New York: Simon & Schuster, 1988. A riveting, Pulitzer Prize-winning narrative history and biography of the King years.

Browning, Rufus P., Dale Rogers Marshall, and David H. Tabb. *Racial Politics in American Cities.* New York: Longman, 1990. This collection of essays documents the continuing struggle for minority access to political power in cities across the United States.

Carter, Stephen L. *The Culture of Disbelief: How American Law and Politics Trivialize Religious Devotion.* New York: Basic Books, 1993. In this wide-ranging, thoughtful work, Carter argues that Americans can simultaneously preserve separation of church and state, embrace American spirituality, and avoid treating believers with disdain.

Garrow, David. *Liberty and Sexuality: The Right to Privacy and the Making of* Roe *v.* Wade. New York: Macmillan, 1994. This is a comprehensive, historical narrative of the fundamental right to sexual privacy.

Levy, Leonard W. *The Establishment Clause: Religion and the First Amendment.* New York: Macmillan, 1986. This searching study of the establishment clause claims that the view that government can assist all religions is historically groundless. Levy argues that it is unconstitutional for government to provide aid to any religion.

Lewis, Anthony. *Make No Law: The Sullivan Case and the First Amendment.* New York: Random House, 1991. This is an enlightening study of a great constitutional decision. Lewis illuminates the history and evolution of the First Amendment guarantees of free expression and free press.

Smolla, Rodney A. *Free Speech in an Open Society.* New York: Alfred A. Knopf, 1993. A lucid examination covering a wide range of contemporary problems in free speech, such as flag burning.

Sniderman, Paul M., and Thomas Piazza. *The Scar of Race.* Cambridge, Mass.: Belknap Press of Harvard University Press, 1993. The authors of this insightful study argue that the problems of race cannot be reduced to racism. On many racial issues, white Americans are open to argument and persuasion, even though they disagree on racial policies.

Verba, Sidney, and Gary R. Orren. *Equality in America: The View From the Top.* Cambridge, Mass.: Harvard University Press, 1985. Two political scientists isolate different meanings of equality, then analyze the opinions of American leaders on the application of equality of opportunity across a range of policy areas.

World Wide Web Resources

The American Civil Liberties Union Freedom Network. Check out this site to get up-to-the-minute reports on the state of civil liberties around the nation.
<www.aclu.org>

The Freedom Forum First Amendment Center. The Freedom Forum First Amendment Center at Vanderbilt University was founded December 15, 1991, the two-hundredth anniversary of the ratification of the Bill of Rights to the U.S. Constitution. The Center serves as a forum for dialogue, discussion, and debate on free-expression and freedom-of-information issues. The Center was created by the Freedom Forum, a financially independent, nonpartisan, international organization dedicated to a free press, free speech, and a free spirit.
<www.fac.org>

Justice on Campus. The Justice on Campus Project's mission is to preserve free expression and due process rights at universities. You will find a Jake Baker link here as well as other university-inspired restrictions on free expression.
<Joc.mit.edu>

Native American Resources. A wealth of links to issues related to native peoples.
<www.cowboy.net/native/>

Latinoweb. A fine source for content links addressing the concerns of Spanish-speaking people.

<www.latinoweb.com/favision/resource.htm>

Asian American Resources. A good source for links to other relevant sites.

<www.mit.edu:8001/afs/athena.mit.edu/user/i/r/irie/www/aar.html>

Universal Black Pages. This site is a comprehensive source of information related to the black experience.

The National Organization for Women (NOW) Home Page. A very useful home page that provides access to NOW policy statements, press releases, and research, as well as links to women's resources on the Internet.

13

Public Policy

Kimber Reynolds returned home to Fresno, California, from her fashion design college to take part in a friend's wedding. She was walking out of a trendy restaurant when two men on motorcycles stopped her on the way to her car. One man grabbed her purse; Reynolds grabbed it back. The man put a .357 Magnum in her ear and shot her to death.

The Fresno police quickly identified two suspects. The gunman, Joe Davis, died in a shoot-out when the police tried to apprehend him. The other, Doug Walker, was captured and pleaded guilty as an accessory to the crime. He was sentenced to nine years in prison. Both Davis and Walker had recently been paroled from prison. When Reynolds' father, Mike, found out that with "good behavior" Walker could again be paroled after serving less than half of his sentence, he knew he had to do something.

After meeting with some judges and attorneys he knew, Mike Reynolds launched a campaign to put a "three strikes and you're out" initiative on the state ballot. The measure required that anyone convicted of a third serious crime be sentenced to a minimum of twenty-five years in prison. Fed up with violent crime, Californians responded enthusiastically to Reynolds' crusade.

Caught off guard by an issue that seemed to have sprung from nowhere, state legislators rushed to introduce legislation that would accomplish much the same goals as Reynolds' initiative. In March 1994, a three-strikes bill passed the California legislature and was signed into law in California. That November, 72 percent of California voters cast ballots in favor of the referendum, giving the state its second three-strikes law.

Three strikes won overwhelming support despite the fact that many judges, district attorneys, and criminologists thought such a law would overwhelm prison capacity and reduce repeat offenders' incentive to plea bargain, thus increasing the need for time-consuming and expensive trials. Today, the California court system is buckling under the weight of these additional trials and the state budgets more for its prisons than for its colleges and universities.[1]

Mike Reynolds and millions of other Californians were willing to endure these additional costs and problems because they were sick of revolving-door justice, in which violent criminals are paroled after they have served only part

A Death, Then Outrage

After Kimber Reynolds (top left) was brutally murdered, her father was grief-stricken. Reminiscing about her childhood, Mike Reynolds described her as his "little buddy." His grief turned to political advocacy, however, and "three strikes and you're out" is now law in California. Ironically, three strikes would not necessarily have kept Kimber's murderer, Joe Davis (above), off the streets prior to his assault on her. Davis had only two prior felonies before he shot her to death. Doug Walker (left) was convicted as an accessory and sentenced to nine years in prison.

of their sentences. A year after three strikes, crime was down in California, though the reasons are surely more complex than just the mandatory sentencing under the new law.

Mike Reynolds and the volunteers he attracted to this cause put the issue of repeat offenders and revolving-door justice on California's political agenda. In turn, California's size and visibility worked to put three strikes on the national agenda. Other states took up the issue, and President Clinton endorsed three strikes as part of a national crime package enacted in 1994. (However, most violent crimes are prosecuted under state, not federal, law.)

In this case, an issue arose because a political activist effectively capitalized on the anger of other citizens. But how do issues usually reach the political agenda? And what happens to them once they are there? Previous chapters have focused on individual institutions of government. Here we focus on government more broadly and ask how policymaking takes place across institutions. We first identify different types of public policies and then analyze the stages in the policymaking process. We then examine how policy is made when many competing interest groups are trying to influence the outcome and how the relationships between those groups, and between such groups and different parts of government, structure the policymaking process. Finally, we take a closer look at specific public policies. We begin with an examination of policies relating to the economy. Then, we discuss policies that provide for "the general welfare": social insurance and public assistance.

Government Purposes and Public Policies

In Chapter 1, we noted that virtually all citizens are willing to accept limitations on their personal freedom in return for various benefits of government. We defined the major purposes of government as maintaining order, providing public benefits, and promoting equality. Different governments place different values on each broad purpose, and those differences are reflected in their public policies. A **public policy** is a general plan of action adopted by a government to solve a social problem, counter a threat, or pursue an objective.

Whatever their form and effectiveness, all policies have this in common: They are the means by which government pursues certain goals in specific situations. People disagree about public policies because they disagree about one or more of the following elements: the goals that government should have, the means it should use to meet them, and how the situation at hand should be perceived.

How do policymakers attempt to achieve their goals? As a starting point, we will divide all government approaches to solving problems into four broad types: We can analyze public policies according to whether they prohibit, protect, promote, or provide.

Some policies are intended to prohibit behaviors that endanger society. All governments outlaw murder, robbery, and rape. Governments that emphasize order tend to favor policies of prohibition, which instruct people in what they must not do (drink liquor, have abortions, use illegal drugs).

Government policies can also protect certain activities, business markets, or special groups of citizens. For example, taxes were once levied on colored margarine (a butter substitute) to reduce its sales and protect the dairy industry from competition. Regulations concerning the testing of new drugs are intended to protect citizens from harmful side effects. Although governments argue that these kinds of regulations serve the public good, some people believe that most protective legislation is unwarranted government interference.

Policies can also promote social activities that are important to the government. For instance, our government has used advertising to urge people to buy bonds or to join the army. To promote railroad construction in the 1860s, Congress granted railroad companies huge tracts of public land as rights-of-way through western states.

The government also promotes activities through favorable treatment within the tax structure. Because it amounts to a loss of government revenue, the technical term for this form of government promotion is *tax expenditure.* For example, the government encourages people to buy their own homes by allowing them to deduct the interest they pay on their mortgage from their taxable income.

Finally, public policies can provide benefits directly to citizens, either collectively or selectively. Collective benefits are facilities or services that all residents share (mail service, roads, schools, street lighting, libraries, parks). Selective benefits go to certain groups of citizens (poor people, farmers, veterans, college students). Collective benefits can be more difficult to deliver because they require either the construction of facilities (roads, dams, sewer systems) or the creation of organizations (transportation agencies, power companies, sanitation departments) to provide them. Many selective benefits are simply payments to individuals in the form of food stamps, subsidies, pensions, and loans. The payments are made because the recipients are particularly needy or powerful, or both.

The Policymaking Process

We distinguish government policies according to their approach, not simply to create an inventory of problem-solving methods but also to emphasize the relationship between policy and process. By *process* we mean the configuration of participants involved, the procedures used for decision making, and the degree of cooperation or conflict usually present. The premise is simple: Different kinds of policies affect the political process in different ways.

The Effect of Policy

One basic reason for the various policymaking processes is that different approaches to public policy affect people in different ways. If a policy proposal affects a well-organized constituency adversely, that constituency will fight it aggressively. When the Clinton administration proposed legislation to raise fees on the use of federal land for grazing, western ranchers who wanted to maintain the relatively low rates they were paying resisted bitterly.

Other policies pit well-organized groups against each other. Action for Children's Television and other organizations promoting children's educational programming have long pressured the Federal Communications Commission (FCC) to require broadcasters to air more high-quality shows for young viewers. The National Association for Broadcasters, representing 1,400 local TV stations, fought against such rules.

A Policymaking Model

We can separate the policymaking process into four stages: agenda setting, policy formulation, implementation, and policy evaluation.[2] Figure 13.1 shows the four stages in sequence. As you will see, policymaking is a circular process; the end of one phase is really the beginning of another.

Agenda Setting **Agenda setting** is the part of the process during which problems are defined as political issues. Many problems confront Americans in their daily lives, but government is not actively working to solve them all. For example, the problem of poverty among the elderly did not suddenly arise during the 1930s, but that is when inadequate income for the elderly was defined as a political problem. When the government begins to consider acting on an issue it has previously ignored, we say that the issue has become part of the political agenda.

Why does an existing social problem become redefined as a political problem? There is no single reason; many different factors can stimulate new thinking about a problem. Sometimes, highly visible events or developments push issues onto the agenda. Issues may also be placed on the agenda through the efforts of scholars and activists, to get more people to pay attention to a condition of which the public is generally unaware. The probability that a certain problem will move onto the agenda is also affected by who controls the government and broad ideological shifts. Agenda building may also involve redefining old issues so that people look at them in different ways.[3]

Policy Formulation **Policy formulation** is that stage of the policymaking process in which formal policy proposals are developed and officials decide whether to adopt them. The most obvious kind of policy formulation is the proposal of a measure by the president or the development of legislation by Congress. Administrative agencies also formulate policy through the regulatory process. Courts formulate policy, too, when their decisions establish new interpretations of the law.

Implementation Policies are not self-executing; **implementation** is the process by which they are carried out. When regulations are issued by agencies in Washington, some government bodies must then put those policies into effect. In the case of the 1990 Americans with Disabilities Act, for example, the owners of office buildings would probably not have repositioned their water fountains simply because Washington published new regulations. Administrative bodies at the regional, state, or local level had to inform them of the rule, give them a timetable for compliance, communicate the penalties for noncompliance, answer questions, and report to Washington on how well the regulations are working.

As pointed out in Chapter 10, one of the biggest problems at the implementation stage of policymaking is coordination. After officials in Washington enact a law and write the subsequent regulations, people outside Washington typically are designated to implement the policy. The agents may be local officials, state administrators, or federal bureaucrats headquartered in regional

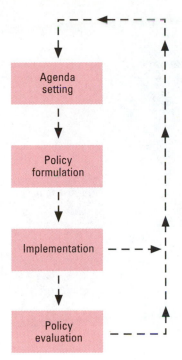

FIGURE 13.1   The Policymaking Process
This model, one of many possible ways to depict the policymaking process, shows four policymaking stages. Feedback on program operations and performance from the last two stages stimulates new cycles of the process.

offices around the country. Although it may sound highly technical, implementation is very much a political process. It involves a great deal of bargaining and negotiation among different groups of people in and out of government.

Policy Evaluation   **Policy evaluation** is the analysis of public policy. Although there is no one method of determining how well a policy is working, evaluation tends to draw heavily on approaches used by academics, including cost-effectiveness analysis and various statistical methods designed to provide concrete measurements of program outcomes. Although technical, the studies can be quite influential in decisions on whether to continue, expand, alter, reduce, or eliminate programs.

One interesting example of policy evaluation involves weaponry used in the Persian Gulf War. For the first time, the United States made extensive use of "smart bombs"—bombs that are electronically guided to their targets. During the war the Pentagon touted the effectiveness of these weapons, showing the American public dramatic videotapes of smart bombs hitting targets in Iraq. Later, a thorough and dispassionate study by Congress's General Accounting Office comparing the very expensive smart bombs and far cheaper "dumb bombs" showed no difference in their accuracy. This is the kind of policy evaluation that is most useful: directly comparing different ways of achieving the same goal, and determining the relative effectiveness and efficiency of each approach.

A Winning Team
The Supreme Court's power to formulate policy has never been illustrated more dramatically than when it declared in 1954 that segregation in public schools is unconstitutional. The team of litigators that won this momentous case was (left to right) George E. C. Hayes, Thurgood Marshall, and James Nabrit, Jr.

Evaluation is part of the policymaking process, because it helps to identify problems and issues that arise from current policy. In other words, evaluation studies provide **feedback** to policymakers on program performance. (The dotted line in Figure 13.1 represents a feedback loop. Problems that emerge during the implementation stage also provide feedback to policymakers.) By drawing attention to emerging problems, policy evaluation influences the political agenda. Thus, we have come full circle. The end of the process—evaluating whether the policy is being implemented as it was envisioned when it was formulated—is the beginning of a new cycle of public policymaking.

Issue Networks

Within any issue area, a number—often a very large number—of interest groups try to influence policy decisions. Representatives from these organizations interact with each other and with government officials on a recurring basis. The ongoing interaction produces both conflict and cooperation.

Government by Policy Area

The various individuals and organizations that work in a particular policy area form a loosely knit community. More specifically, those "who share expertise in a policy domain and who frequently interact constitute an issue network."[4] The boundaries and membership of an **issue network** are hardly precise, but in general terms networks include members of Congress, committee staffers, agency officials, lawyers, lobbyists, consultants, scholars, and public relations specialists.

Political scientists have long analyzed policymaking by issue area. However, the issue network framework is a relatively new tool. In the 1950s, policy communities were typically much smaller, with a few key committee or subcommittee chairs, a top agency official, and a couple of lobbyists from the principal trade groups negotiating behind the scenes to settle important policy questions. Political scientists used to call such small, tightly knit policy communities *iron triangles.* Iron triangles were thought to be relatively autonomous and to operate by consensus. The explosion in the number of interest groups and the growth of government and overlapping jurisdictions put an end to iron triangles. Today, policy communities are much more open and much more conflictual.

The Case of Telecommunications

The telecommunications industry provides a useful illustration of the changing nature of politics in Washington. Once a harmonious iron triangle, telecommunications is today a large issue network filled with conflict.

Until fairly recently, the telecommunications industry was dominated by American Telephone & Telegraph (AT&T), which, with its affiliated Bell System telephone companies around the country, constituted a monopoly.[5] Customers had no choice but to use the phone lines and phone equipment of "Ma Bell." Within the telecommunications iron triangle—a policymaking community made up of some key members of Congress, the Federal Communications Commission, and AT&T—policymaking was usually consensual and uncontroversial.

In 1974, the U.S. Department of Justice brought a lawsuit against the corporation, charging it with illegal monopolistic behavior in the telecommunications industry. The eventual outcome of the suit was an out-of-court settlement that required AT&T to give up control over local operating service. The Bell System was broken up into seven independent regional telephone companies (the "Baby Bells"). AT&T was allowed to retain its long-distance service, but it would have to compete against other long-distance carriers. The giant telephone company had fallen victim to a growing belief among academics and policymakers that government regulation was hampering the economy by restricting competition and lessening the incentives for innovation, as well as limiting the price and product choices available to consumers. Thus, telecommunications was deregulated.[6]

Today, policymaking in telecommunications bears no resemblance to an iron triangle. After the AT&T divestiture, competition among businesses selling various communications services and equipment became even more intense. Many new companies emerged to join the highly fractious issue network. Much of the political conflict that ensued involved fights between the Baby Bells and long-distance carriers, each side wanting to expand into new markets while protecting their current markets from encroachment by would-be competitors.

Three important developments in telecommunications have forced the government to abandon this regulatory framework. First were various technological innovations, such as cellular phones and other forms of wireless communication, which were either not anticipated by the consent decree or excluded from it. Second was the pivotal convergence of various technologies. One of the more significant examples is that telephone lines became critically important to computer users as the electronic transmission of data and digital communications became more feasible.

Third was the fact that entrepreneurs began to see the future as one in which the strongest companies—or at least those that survived the tumultuous changes in the marketplace—would be those that were alliances of many different businesses with expertise in individual products. Such alliances could offer an array of services to customers through integrated technology. These developments forced the government to move toward a truly deregulated market with legislation passed in 1996. Telecommunications firms can now enter virtually any business and package these services together. Local phone companies can offer long-distance services, and vice versa.[7]

As Figure 13.2 shows, the changes in the industry have led to an issue network characterized not so much by political alliances as by business alliances. Mergers, acquisitions, joint ventures, and cross-ownership arrangements have created many firms with far-reaching interests.[8] (The figure depicts the industry in the spring of 1994, and the changes have accelerated since then.) Generally though, issue network politics is characterized by rapidly changing coalitions as partners on one issue become opponents on the next. Conflict within the telecommunications issue network is chronic. No one controls telecommunications policymaking, but many organizations and individuals have a say in it. With hundreds of lobbies active in many important policy areas, issue network politics has come to characterize contemporary policymaking in Washington.

Issue Networks and Democracy

For many years, political scientists have described American democracy as a system in which different constituencies work energetically to influence policies of concern to them. Policymaking is seen as a response to these groups rather than to majority will. This is a considerably different conception of democracy from the more traditional perspective, that policies reflect what most people want. It is a pluralist, not a majoritarian, view of American government.

In a number of ways, issue networks promote pluralist democracy. They are open systems, populated by a wide range of interest groups. Decision making is not centralized in the hands of a few key players; policies are formulated in a participatory fashion. But there is still no guarantee that all relevant interests are represented, and those with greater financial resources have an advantage. Nevertheless, issue networks provide access to government for a diverse set of competing interests and thus further the pluralist ideal.[9]

FIGURE 13.2   The Telecommunications Issue Network

There is no one way to draw an issue network. This graphic illustrates the different types of relationships among the different private sector groups involved in the telecommunications industry. Recent trends in the industry are toward more and more mergers and acquisitions as companies try to expand into integrated, large-scale entities that can provide a range of services that will be popular in the future. The congressional committees and units of the executive branch specified in this figure are those with primary responsibility for telecommunications policymaking. (Source: Jeffrey M. Berry, "The Dynamic Qualities of Issue Networks," paper delivered at the annual meeting of the American Political Science Association, New York City, September 1994. Used with permission.)

For those who prefer majoritarian democracy, however, issue networks are an obstacle to achieving their vision of how government should operate. The technical complexity of contemporary issues makes it especially difficult for the public at large to exert control over policy outcomes. However, although issue networks promote pluralism, keep in mind that majoritarian influences on policymaking are still significant. The broad contours of public opinion can be a dominant force on highly visible issues. Elections, too, send messages to policymakers about the most widely discussed campaign issues. What issue networks have done, however, is facilitate pluralist politics in policy areas in which majoritarian influences are weak.

Public Policies

In this segment we look at specific public policies. We concentrate on policies based on the authority of the national government to tax and spend for the general welfare. But it is important to recognize that state and local governments play a vital role in shaping and directing the policies that emanate from Washington. For example, in 1996 the national government largely abandoned setting standards for the allocation of welfare benefits. Now states may impose their own standards for recipients.[10]

Economic Policy

Keynesian theory, developed by John Maynard Keynes, a British economist, holds that government can stabilize the economy through a combination of fiscal and monetary policies. **Fiscal policies**, which are enacted by the president and Congress, involve changes in government spending and taxing. When demand for goods and services is too low, according to Keynes, government should either spend more itself—hiring people and thus giving them money—or cut taxes, giving people more of their own money to spend. When demand is too great, the government should either spend less or raise taxes, giving people less money to spend. **Monetary policies**, which are largely determined by the Federal Reserve Board, involve changes in the money supply and operate less directly on the economy. Increasing the amount of money in circulation increases demand and thus increases price inflation. Decreasing the money supply decreases aggregate demand and inflationary pressures.

Despite some problems with the assumptions of Keynesian theory, capitalist countries have widely adopted it in some form.[11] At one time or another, virtually all have used the Keynesian technique of **deficit financing**—spending in excess of tax revenues—to combat an economic slump. The objective of deficit financing is to inject extra money into the economy to stimulate aggregate demand.

In 1946, the year Keynes died, Congress passed an employment act establishing "the continuing responsibility of the national government to... promote maximum employment, production and purchasing power." It also created the **Council of Economic Advisors (CEA)** within the Executive Office of the President to advise the president on maintaining a stable economy.

Although most economists accept Keynesian theory in its broad outlines, they depreciate its political utility. Some argue that government spending programs take too long to enact in Congress and to implement through the bureaucracy. As a result, jobs are created not when they are needed but years later, when the crisis may have passed and government spending needs to be reduced. Also, government spending is easier to start than to stop, because the groups that benefit from spending programs tend to defend them even when they are no longer needed. A similar criticism applies to tax policies. Politically, it is much easier to cut taxes than to raise them.

Recognizing these limitations of fiscal policies, **monetarists** argue that government can control the economy's performance effectively only by controlling the nation's money supply. Monetarists favor a long-range policy of small but steady growth in the amount of money in circulation rather than frequent manipulation of monetary policies.

Monetary policies in the United States are under the control of the **Federal Reserve System**, which acts as the country's central bank. At the top of the system is the board of governors, seven members appointed by the president for staggered terms of fourteen years. The president designates one member of the board to be its chairperson, serving a four-year term that extends beyond the president's term of office.

When Ronald Reagan came to office in 1981, he embraced a school of thought called **supply-side economics** to deal with the double-digit inflation that the nation was experiencing. Keynesian theory argues that inflation results when consumers, businesses, and governments have more money to spend than there are goods and services to buy. The standard Keynesian solution is to reduce demand (for example, by increasing taxes). Supply-siders argue that inflation can be lowered more effectively by increasing the supply of goods. (That is, they stress the supply side of the economic equation.) Specifically, they favor tax cuts to stimulate investment (which, in turn, leads to the production of more goods) and less government regulation of business (again, to increase productivity—which they hold will yield more, not less, government revenue). Supply-siders believe that government interferes too much with the efforts of individuals to work, save, and invest.

Tax Policies   Tax policy is designed to provide a continuous flow of income. A major text on government finance says that tax policy is sometimes changed to accomplish one or more of several objectives:

- To adjust overall revenue to meet budget outlays
- To make the tax burden more equitable for taxpayers
- To help control the economy by raising taxes (thus decreasing demand) or by lowering taxes (thus increasing demand)[12]

In 1986 Congress passed one of the most sweeping tax reform laws in history. The new policy reclaimed a great deal of revenue by eliminating many deductions for corporations and wealthy citizens. By eliminating many tax brackets, the new tax policy approached the idea of a flat tax—one that requires everyone to pay at the same rate. A flat tax has the appeal of simplicity, but it violates the principle of **progressive taxation**, under which the rich pay proportionately higher taxes than the poor. Governments can rely on progressive taxation to redistribute wealth and thus promote economic equality.

After the 1986 tax reform there were only two tax rates—15 and 28 percent. In 1990 Bush was forced to violate his pledge of "no new taxes" by creating a third tax rate, 31 percent. Clinton created a fourth level, 40 percent in 1993, moving toward a more progressive tax structure.

Spending Policies The national government spends hundreds of billions of dollars every year. Where does the money go? To understand current expenditures, it is a good idea to examine national expenditures over time, as in Figure 13.3. The effect of World War II is clear: Spending for national defense rose sharply after 1940, peaked at about 90 percent of the budget in 1945, and fell to about 30 percent in peacetime. The percentage allocated to defense rose again in the early 1950s, reflecting rearmament during the Cold War with the Soviet Union. Thereafter, the share of the budget devoted to defense decreased steadily (except for the bump during the Vietnam War in the late 1960s), until the trend was reversed by the Carter administration in the 1970s and shot upwards during the Reagan presidency. Defense spending significantly decreased under Bush and continued to go down under Clinton.

Government payments to individuals (social security checks) consistently consumed less of the budget than national defense until 1971. Since then, payments to individuals have accounted for the largest portion of the national budget, and they have been increasing. Net interest payments have also increased substantially in recent years, reflecting the rapidly growing national debt. Pressure from payments for national defense, individuals, and interest on the national debt has squeezed all other government outlays.

National spending has increased from about 15 percent of gross domestic product (GDP) soon after World War II to over 20 percent, most recently at the price of a growing national deficit. There are two major explanations for this steady increase in government spending. One is bureaucratic, the other political.

The bureaucratic explanation for spending increases involves **incremental budgeting**: Bureaucrats, in compiling their funding requests for the coming year, traditionally ask for the amount they got the current year plus some increment to fund new projects. Because Congress has already approved the agency's budget for the current year, it pays little attention to the agency's current size (the largest part of its budget), and focuses instead on the extra money (the increment) requested for the next year. As a result, few agencies are ever cut back, and spending continually goes up.

Recent reactions to the budget deficit have substantially checked the practice of incremental budgeting. When the Republicans took over control of Congress in 1995, they largely disregarded Clinton's FY 1996 budget and proceeded to slash government programs. Only after Clinton vetoed five appropriations bills and the government experienced two historic shutdowns did the president and Congress compromise on spending.[13] Nevertheless, the final

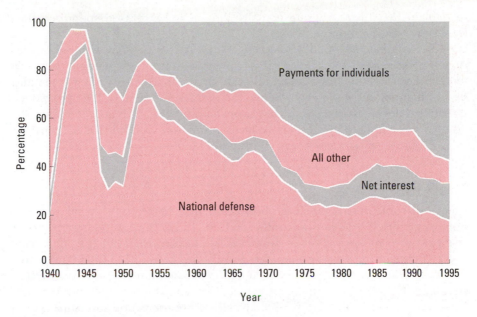

FIGURE 13.3   *National Government Outlays over Time*
This chart plots the percentage of the annual budget devoted to four major expense categories over time. It shows that significant changes have occurred in national spending since 1940. During World War II, defense spending consumed more than 80 percent of the national budget. Defense again accounted for most national expenditures during the Cold War of the 1950s. Since then, the military's share of expenditures has declined, while payments to individuals (mostly in the form of social security benefits) have increased dramatically. Also, as the graph shows, the proportion of the budget paid in interest on the national debt has increased substantially since the 1970s. (Source: Executive Office of the President, Budget of the United States Government, Fiscal Year 1997: Historical Tables *(Washington, D.C.: U.S. Government Printing Office, 1996), pp. 23–24.)*

spending bill for FY 1996 was judged by an outside expert to be "one of the most significant reversals in the course of government since World War II."[14]

Certain government programs are effectively immune to budget reductions, because they have been enacted into law and enshrined in politics. For example, social security legislation guarantees certain benefits to program participants when they retire. Medicare and veterans' benefits also entitle citizens to certain payments. Because these payments have to be made under existing law, they represent **uncontrollable outlays**. In Clinton's FY 1997 budget, nearly two-thirds of all budget outlays were uncontrollable or relatively uncontrollable—mainly payments to individuals under social security, Medicare, and public assistance; interest on the national debt; and farm price supports.

To be sure, Congress could change the laws to abolish such entitlement payments (benefits to which individuals are legally entitled). But politics argues against large-scale reductions. The Republicans in Congress drew public criticism for "reducing" spending on health care, even though they took pains to explain that their program actually allowed for increased spending; they were only "cutting the rate of increase."[15]

What spending cuts would be acceptable to or even popular with the public? At the most general level, voters favor cutting government spending, but they tend to favor maintaining "government programs that help needy people and deal with important national problems."[16] A perplexed Congress, trying to reduce the budget deficit, faces a public that favors funding programs at even higher levels than those favored by most lawmakers.[17] Moreover, spending for the most expensive of these programs—social security and Medicare—is uncontrollable.

Social Insurance

The most controversial purpose of government is to promote social and economic equality. To do so may conflict with the freedom of some citizens, for it requires government action to redistribute income from rich to poor. This choice between freedom and equality constitutes the modern dilemma of government. Today, almost every modern nation may be characterized as a **welfare state**, serving as the provider and protector of individual well-being through economic and social programs. **Social welfare programs** are government programs designed to provide the minimum living conditions necessary for all citizens. Income for the elderly, health care, subsidized housing, and nutrition are among the concerns addressed by government social welfare programs.

Since the late nineteenth century, there has been a growing tendency for governments to offer **social insurance**, which is government-backed protection against loss by individuals, regardless of need. The most common forms of social insurance offer health protection and guard against losses from worker sickness, injury, and disability; old age; and unemployment. The first example of social insurance in the United States was workers' compensation. Beginning early in this century, most states created systems of insurance that compensated workers who lost income because they were injured in the workplace.

Social insurance benefits are distributed to recipients without regard to their economic status. Such programs are examples of **entitlements**—benefits to which every eligible person has a legal right and that government cannot deny. National entitlement programs consume about half of every dollar of government spending; the largest entitlement program is social security.

Social Security   **Social security** is social insurance that provides economic assistance to people faced with unemployment, disability, or old age; it is financed by taxes on employers and employees. Initially, social security benefits were distributed only to the aged, the unemployed, and surviving spouses—most of whom were widows—with dependent children. Today, social security also provides medical care for the elderly and income support for the disabled.

The social security taxes collected today pay the benefits of today's retirees. Thus, social security (and social insurance in general) is not a form of savings; it is a pay-as-you-go tax system. Today's workers support today's elderly. For that reason the solvency of the social security program will soon be tested. As the baby boomer generation retires, beginning about 2010, politicians will face an inevitable dilemma: lower benefits and generate the ire of retirees or raise taxes and generate the ire of taxpayers.

Today, few argue against the need for social security. But debate surrounds the extent of coverage and the level of benefits. "The [Social Security] Act is the most successful program of the modern state," declared Nobel Prize laureate Paul Samuelson. Yet Milton Friedman, another Nobel laureate and social security opponent, labeled the act "a sacred cow that no politician can criticize." How can two renowned economists maintain such dramatically different views? Samuelson is a liberal in the Keynesian tradition; he favors equality over freedom. According to his view, social security lifted the elderly from destitution by redistributing income from workers (who have growing incomes) to the elderly (who have little or no income). Friedman is a libertarian and a monetarist; he favors freedom over equality. Because social security limits freedom in order to provide economic equality, Friedman would no doubt prefer that the program be scaled back or even eliminated. However, the political risks associated with social security cutbacks are too great for most politicians to bear. As a group, older Americans exercise enormous political power. People at or near retirement age now make up almost 30 percent of the potential electorate, and voter turnout among older Americans is reported to be about twice that of younger people.[18]

Medicare On July 30, 1965, President Johnson signed a bill that provided a number of health benefits to the elderly and the poor. The **Social Security Act** was amended to provide **Medicare**, health care for all people aged sixty-five or older. Fearful of the power of the American Medical Association (AMA), which then opposed any form of government-provided medical care, the Democrats confined their efforts to a compulsory hospitalization-insurance plan for the elderly. (This is known today as Part A of Medicare.) In addition, the bill contained a version of an alternative Republican plan, which called for voluntary government-subsidized insurance to cover physician's fees. (This is known today as Part B of Medicare.) A third program, added a year later, is called *Medicaid*; it provides medical aid to the poor through federally assisted state health programs. Medicaid is a need-based comprehensive medical and hospitalization program: if you are poor, you qualify.

Today part A of Medicare is compulsory insurance that covers certain hospital services for people aged sixty-five and older. Workers pay a tax; retirees pay premiums deducted from their social security payments. Payments for necessary services are made by the national government directly to participating hospitals and other qualifying facilities. Part B of Medicare is a voluntary program of medical insurance for people aged sixty-five and older who pay the premiums.

Health Care for Everyone Medicare provides health care for the elderly. Medicaid provides health care for the poor. Yet the United States is the only major industrialized nation without a universal health-care system. Nearly everyone maintains that the U.S. health-care system needs fixing. However, the American public remains divided on the remedy. The Clinton administration's effort to reform health care has held firm to its objective of universal coverage, but none of the proposed approaches to that end has gained the support of a majority of Americans.

Politics in a Changing America 13.1

The Feminization of Poverty

When we examine the composition of poor families, especially over the past twenty-five years, we observe a dramatic and disturbing trend. One in every two poor Americans resides in a family in which a woman is the sole householder, or head of the household (see graph). Thirty years ago, only one in every four poor people lived in such a family. What accounts for this dramatic upward shift in the proportion of female-headed poor families?

This century bears witness to extraordinary changes for women. Women won the right to vote and to own property. Women also gained a measure of legal and social equality (see Chapter 12). But increases in the rates of divorce, marital separation, and adolescent pregnancy have cast more and more women in the head-of-household role. Caring for children competes with women's ability to work. Affordable child care is out of reach for many single parents. In the absence of a national child care policy, single women with young children face limited employment opportunities and lower wages in comparison to full-time workers. These factors and others contribute to the **feminization of poverty,** the fact that a growing percentage of all poor Americans are women or the dependents of women.

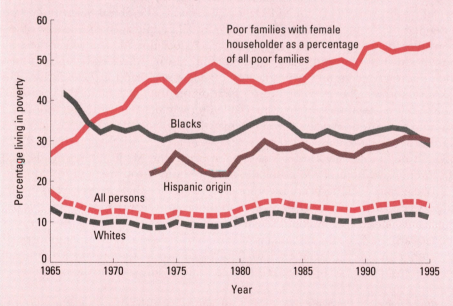

Sources: Barbara Ehrenreich and Frances Fox Piven, "The Feminization of Poverty," *Dissent* (Spring 1984), 162–170; Harrell R. Rodgers, Jr., *Poor Women, Poor Families: The Economic Plight of America's Female-Headed Households,* 2d ed. (Armonk, N.Y.: M. E. Sharpe, 1990).

Source for data: U.S. Bureau of the Census, U.S. Department of Commerce, *Poverty in the United States, 1992,* Current Population Reports, Series P-60, No. 185 (Washington, D.C.: U.S. Government Printing Office, 1993).

The health-care issue goes to the heart of the modern dilemma of government: We must weigh greater equality in terms of universal coverage and cost controls against a loss of freedom in markets for health care and in choosing a doctor.

Public Assistance

Public assistance is what most people mean when they use the terms *welfare* or *welfare payments*; it is government aid to individuals who can demonstrate a need for that aid. Although much public assistance is directed toward those who lack the ability or the resources to provide for themselves or their families, the poor are not the only recipients of welfare. Corporations, farmers, and college students are among the many recipients of government aid in the form of tax breaks, subsidized loans, and other benefits.

Public assistance programs instituted under the Social Security Act include (1) old-age assistance for the needy elderly not covered by old-age pension benefits, (2) aid to the needy blind, (3) aid to needy families with dependent children, and (4) aid to the totally and permanently disabled. Adopted initially as stopgap measures during the Depression, these programs have become entitlements. They are administered by the states, but the bulk of the funding comes from the national government's general tax revenues. Because the states also contribute to the funding of their public assistance programs, the benefits vary widely from state to state.

Until 1996, the national government imposed national standards on state welfare programs. It distributed funds to each state based on the proportion of its population living in poverty. That proportion is determined on the basis of a federally defined **poverty level**, or poverty threshold, which is the minimum cash income that will provide for a family's basic needs.

The national government's **food stamp program** aims to improve the diets of low-income households by supplementing their food-purchasing power. The nationally funded program is administered through local agencies, which distribute the stamps to needy individuals and families. The stamps are actually coupons that can be used to purchase food. Food stamp benefits are set nationally and do not vary from state to state.

Poverty was once a condition of old age. Social security changed that. Today, poverty is still related to age, but in the opposite direction: It is largely a predicament of the young. Twenty-two percent of persons younger than eighteen live in poverty.[19]

It is relatively easy to draw a portrait of the poor; it is much more difficult to craft policies that move them out of destitution. Although candidate Bill Clinton had promised to "end welfare as we know it," he was hard-pressed in 1996 to accept the welfare reform proposals served up by the Republican-led Congress. Eventually, President Clinton signed a compromise welfare reform bill into law. The bill he signed on August 22, 1996, eliminated a federal guarantee of cash assistance. The new measure impacted nearly all of the 12.8 million people on welfare and the 27 million receiving food stamps. It abolished the biggest public assistance program, **Aid to Families with Dependent Children (AFDC)**, affecting more than one-fifth of the families in America with children—some nine million children and four million parents.[20] In addition, most immigrants who arrived after the bill was signed would not be eligible for the majority of federal benefits and services.

Under the plan, individual adult recipients of welfare payments will have to become employed within two years. The law places the burden of job creation on the states. Families can receive no more than a total of five years' of benefits in a lifetime, and states can set a minimum limit much lower than that. However, even before signing the bill, Clinton already was granting waivers permitting states to offer extensions beyond the five-year limit, as long as recipients continue to look for work.

Under the old entitlement system, benefits varied dramatically from state to state. Nonetheless, for the 328 House members and 74 senators who voted for the bill (Republicans heavily in favor, Democrats split), devolving power to the states proved a prime force in the reform effort.

In effect, these reforms move away from promoting equal outcomes. For many impoverished people, the decline of national entitlement policies and the beginning of state experimentation will determine the course of their lives, and their children's lives, for years to come.

Summary

Government tries to solve problems through a variety of approaches. Some public policies prohibit; some protect; some promote; and some provide. The approach chosen can significantly affect the policymaking process.

Although there is much variation in the policymaking process, we can conceive of it as consisting of four stages. The first stage is agenda setting, the process by which problems become defined as political issues worthy of government attention. Once people in government feel that they should be doing something about a problem, an attempt at policy formulation will follow. All three branches of the national government formulate policy. Once policies have been formulated and ratified, administrative units of government must implement them. Finally, once policies are being carried out, they need to be evaluated. Implementation and program evaluation influence agenda building, because program shortcomings become evident during these stages. Thus, the process is really circular, with the end often marking the beginning of a new round of policymaking.

Policymaking in many areas can be viewed as an ongoing process of interaction within issue networks composed of actors inside and outside government. Each network is a way to communicate and exchange information and ideas about a particular policy area. In a network, lobbying coalitions form easily and dissolve rapidly as new issues arise. Issue networks place a high premium on expertise as public policy problems grow ever more complex.

Keynesian theory holds that the government should take an active role in dealing with inflation and unemployment, using fiscal and monetary policies to control aggregate demand. Monetarists believe fiscal policies are unreliable; they opt instead to use the money supply to affect aggregate demand. Supply-side economists focus on controlling the supply of goods and services rather than the demand for them.

In 1986, Congress enacted a sweeping tax reform law, which eliminated tax loopholes and drastically reduced the number of tax brackets. In a 1993 effort to reduce the deficit, President Clinton formulated a budget that moved toward a more progressive tax structure. When the Republicans gained control of Congress in 1995, they abandoned the informal policy of incremental budgeting and drastically cut spending on some programs.

Often, disagreements about public policy are disagreements about values. Some of the oldest and most costly domestic policies, such as social security and Medicare, pose choices between freedom and equality.

Today, the government plays an active role in providing benefits to the poor, the elderly, and the disabled. The object of these domestic policies is to alleviate conditions that individuals are powerless to prevent. This is the social welfare function of the modern state.

Government confers benefits on individuals through social insurance and public assistance. Social insurance is not based on need; public assistance (welfare) hinges on proof of need. In one form of social insurance—old-age benefits—a tax on current workers pays retired workers' benefits. Aid for the poor, by contrast, comes from the government's general tax revenues.

Programs to aid the elderly and the poor have been gradually transformed into entitlements. These government programs have reduced poverty among some groups, especially the elderly. However, poverty retains a grip on certain segments of the population.

Bill Clinton and the Republican-led Congress have reformed the welfare system. The biggest entitlement program (AFDC) is gone, and individual state programs will substitute for a single national policy. Food stamps remain a federal entitlement. Work requirements and time limits on welfare may break the cycle of dependency, but the reforms run the risk of endangering the neediest among us. Time and experience will likely tell whether this grand experiment will produce better outcomes.

Key Terms

public policy
agenda setting
policy formulation
implementation
policy evaluation
feedback
issue network
Keynesian theory
fiscal policies
monetary policies
deficit financing
Council of Economic Advisers (CEA)
monetarists
Federal Reserve System
supply-side economics

progressive taxation
incremental budgeting
uncontrollable outlays
welfare state
social welfare programs
social insurance
entitlements
social security
Social Security Act
Medicare
public assistance
poverty level
food stamp program
Aid to Families with Dependent
    Children (AFDC)

Selected Readings

Anderson, James E. *Public Policymaking*, 2d ed. Boston: Houghton Mifflin, 1994. A brief overview of the policymaking system.

Axelrod, Donald. *Budgeting for Modern Government*, 2d ed. New York: St. Martin's Press, 1995. A thorough explanation of the process of public budgeting, from agency requests to the finished budget. Excellent in evaluating criticisms and proposing reforms.

Baumgartner, Frank R., and Bryan D. Jones. *Agendas and Instability in American Politics*. Chicago: University of Chicago Press, 1993. A systematic analysis of how issues arise and how they fall off the national agenda.

Ellwood, David T. *Poor Support: Poverty in the American Family*. New York: Basic Books, 1988. Ellwood agrees with Murray's analysis (see below) but argues for incentives to break the grip of poverty. Ellwood's ideas have been part of the Clinton administration's effort to "end welfare as we know it."

Goldberg, Gertrude Schaffner, and Eleanor Kremen, eds. *The Feminization of Poverty: Only in America?* New York: Greenwood, 1990. This comparative study of poverty among females in seven capitalist and socialist countries argues that the feminization of poverty is not unique to the United States.

Katz, Michael B. *The Undeserving Poor: From the War on Poverty to the War on Welfare*. New York: Pantheon, 1989. A historical overview of the ideas and assumptions that shaped policies toward the poor from the 1960s through the 1980s.

Mackenzie, G. Calvin, ed. *The In-and-Outers*. Baltimore: Johns Hopkins University Press, 1987. A collection of essays examining the problems associated with the movement of people between the private sector and the executive branch.

Murray, Charles. *Losing Ground*. New York: Basic Books, 1985. An assessment of American social policy from 1950 to 1980. Murray argues that by attempting to remove the barriers to the good life for the poor, policymakers have created a poverty trap. Controversial in its day, Murray's analysis is taken as received wisdom today.

Penny, Timothy J., and Steven E. Schier. *Payment Due: A Nation in Debt, A Generation in Trouble*. Boulder, Colo: Westview Press, 1996. A former member of Congress (Penny) and a scholar collaborate in analyzing the problems in reducing the deficit and the consequences for America if we do not.

Pierson, Paul. *Dismantling the Welfare State*. New York: Cambridge University Press, 1994. The decline of support for welfare in the United States and Britain during the 1980s is viewed through a comparative lens.

Stein, Herbert. *On the Other Hand . . . Reflections on Economics, Economists, and Politics*. Washington, D.C.: American Enterprise Institute, 1995. The chairman of President Nixon's Council of Economic Advisers, Herbert Stein, examines controversies over economic growth, employment, taxes, and deficits, and the ideas of economists whose theories have influenced economic practice.

Wilson, William Julius. *The Truly Disadvantaged: The Inner City, the Underclass, and Public Policy*. Chicago: University of Chicago Press, 1987. Wilson argues that the decay of the inner city cannot be explained by racism alone and targets the class structure of ghetto neighborhoods as the most important factor in a complex web of reasons.

World Wide Web Resources

The Heritage Foundation. This is the home page for this conservative public policy think tank. In addition to "this week's top ten facts," visitors interested in public policy jobs can access the foundation's job bank. This page also provides its "Candidate Education Guide," the latest news on current issues (such as tax reform) and various foundation publications, including current and back issues of the foundation's magazine, *Policy Review: Journal of American Citizenship.*

Progressive Policy Institute. This is the home page of the Progressive Policy Institute of the Democratic Leadership Council. In addition to accessing information on the organization's history and ideology, visitors can access the institute's library, read current news articles about the DLC, and read current and back issues of the institute's "flagship magazine," *The New Democrat.*

Federal Reserve Board. In addition to explaining the structure and functions of the Federal Reserve Board, this site contains the famous "Beige Book" that reports on economic conditions in the nation eight times a year. It is an easy-to-read executive summary of business, manufacturing, and commercial activities in each of the system's twelve regional Federal Reserve banks.

Office of Management and Budget. The place to go to get recent versions of the federal budget. The site provides data as well as graphs and text.
<www.whitehouse.gov/WH/EOP/omb>

The Social Security Administration Home Page. Everything you always wanted to know about social security but were afraid to ask.
<www.ssa.gov>

The Urban Institute's Welfare Reform Overview. A detailed analysis of welfare reform issues, prepared by the Urban Institute, an independent Washington think tank.
<www.urban.org/welfare/overview.htm>

Appendices

The unanimous declaration of the thirteen
United States of America

When, in the course of human events, it becomes necessary for one people to dissolve the political bands which have connected them with another, and to assume, among the powers of the earth, the separate and equal station to which the laws of nature and of nature's God entitle them, a decent respect to the opinions of mankind requires that they should declare the causes which impel them to the separation.

We hold these truths to be self-evident: That all men are created equal; that they are endowed by their Creator with certain unalienable rights; that among these are life, liberty, and the pursuit of happiness; that, to secure these rights, governments are instituted among men, deriving their just powers from the consent of the governed; that whenever any form of government becomes destructive of these ends, it is the right of the people to alter or to abolish it, and to institute new government, laying its foundation on such principles, and organizing its power in such form, as to them shall seem most likely to effect their safety and happiness. Prudence, indeed, will dictate that governments long established should not be changed for light and transient causes; and accordingly all experience hath shown that mankind are more disposed to suffer, while evils are sufferable, than to right themselves by abolishing the forms to which they are accustomed. But when a long train of abuses and usurpations, pursuing invariably the same object, evinces a design to reduce them under absolute despotism, it is their right, it is their duty, to throw off such government, and to provide new guards for their future security. Such has been the patient sufferance of these colonies; and such is now the necessity which constrains them to alter their former systems of government. The history of the present King of Great Britain is a history of repeated injuries and usurpations, all having in direct object the establishment of an absolute tyranny over these states. To prove this, let facts be submitted to a candid world.

He has refused his assent to laws, the most wholesome and necessary for the public good.

He has forbidden his governors to pass laws of immediate and pressing importance, unless suspended in their operation till his assent should be obtained; and, when so suspended, he has utterly neglected to attend to them.

He has refused to pass other laws for the accommodation of large districts of people, unless those people would relinquish the right of representation in the legislature, a right inestimable to them, and formidable to tyrants only.

He has called together legislative bodies at places unusual, uncomfortable, and distant from the depository of their public records, for the sole purpose of fatiguing them into compliance with his measures.

He has dissolved representative houses repeatedly, for opposing, with manly firmness, his invasions on the rights of the people.

He has refused for a long time, after such dissolutions, to cause others to be elected; whereby the legislative powers, incapable of annihilation, have returned to the people at large for their exercise; the state remaining, in the mean time, exposed to all the dangers of invasions from without and convulsions within.

He has endeavored to prevent the population of these states; for that purpose obstructing the laws for naturalization of foreigners; refusing to pass others to encourage their migration hither, and raising the conditions of new appropriations of lands.

He has obstructed the administration of justice, by refusing his assent to laws for establishing judiciary powers.

He has made judges dependent on his will alone, for the tenure of their offices, and the amount and payment of their salaries.

He has erected a multitude of new offices, and sent hither swarms of officers to harass our people, and eat out their substance.

He has kept among us, in times of peace, standing armies, without the consent of our legislatures.

He has affected to render the military independent of, and superior to, the civil power.

He has combined with others to subject us to a jurisdiction foreign to our constitution, and unacknowledged by our laws, giving his assent to their acts of pretended legislation:

For quartering large bodies of armed troops among us;

For protecting them, by a mock trial, from punishment for any murders which they should commit on the inhabitants of these states;

For cutting off our trade with all parts of the world;

For imposing taxes on us without our consent;

For depriving us, in many cases, of the benefits of trial by jury;

For transporting us beyond seas, to be tried for pretended offenses;

For abolishing the free system of English laws in a neighboring province, establishing therein an arbitrary government, and enlarging its boundaries, so as to render it at once an example and fit instrument for introducing the same absolute rule into these colonies;

For taking away our charters, abolishing our most valuable laws, and altering fundamentally the forms of our governments;

For suspending our own legislatures, and declaring themselves invested with power to legislate for us in all cases whatsoever.

He has abdicated government here, by declaring us out of his protection and waging war against us.

He has plundered our seas, ravaged our coasts, burned our towns, and destroyed the lives of our people.

He is at this time transporting large armies of foreign mercenaries to complete the works of death, desolation, and tyranny already begun with circumstances of cruelty and perfidy scarcely paralleled in the most barbarous ages, and totally unworthy the head of a civilized nation.

He has constrained our fellow-citizens, taken captive on the high seas, to bear arms against their country, to become the executioners of their friends and brethren, or to fall themselves by their hands.

He has excited domestic insurrection among us, and has endeavored to bring on the inhabitants of our frontiers the merciless Indian savages, whose known rule of warfare is an undistinguished destruction of all ages, sexes, and conditions.

In every stage of these oppressions we have petitioned for redress in the most humble terms; our repeated petitions have been answered only by repeated injury. A prince, whose character is thus marked by every act which may define a tyrant, is unfit to be the ruler of a free people.

Nor have we been wanting in our attentions to our British brethren. We have warned them, from time to time, of attempts by their legislature to extend an unwarrantable jurisdiction over us. We have reminded them of the circumstances of our emigration and settlement here. We have appealed to their native justice and magnanimity; and we have conjured them, by the ties of our common kindred, to disavow these usurpations, which would inevitably interrupt our connections and correspondence. They, too, have been deaf to the voice of justice and of consanguinity. We must, therefore, acquiesce in the necessity which denounces our separation, and hold them, as we hold the rest of mankind, enemies in war, in peace friends.

We, therefore, the representatives of the United States of America, in General Congress assembled, appealing to the Supreme Judge of the world for the rectitude of our intentions, do, in the name, and by the authority of the good people of these colonies, solemnly publish and declare, that these United Colonies are, and of right ought to be, FREE AND INDEPENDENT STATES; that they are absolved from all allegiance to the British crown, and that all political connection between them and the state of Great Britain is, and ought to be, totally dissolved; and that, as free and independent states, they have full power to levy war, conclude peace, contract alliances, establish commerce, and do all other acts and things which independent states may of right do. And for the support of this declaration, with a firm reliance on the protection of Divine Providence, we mutually pledge to each other our lives, our fortunes, and our sacred honor.

JOHN HANCOCK
and fifty-five others

THE CONSTITUTION OF THE UNITED STATES OF AMERICA*

Preamble

We the people of the United States, in Order to form a more perfect Union, establish Justice, insure domestic Tranquility, provide for the common defense, promote the general Welfare, and secure the Blessings of Liberty to ourselves and our Posterity, do ordain and establish this Constitution for the United States of America.

Article I

Section 1 All legislative Powers herein granted shall be vested in a Congress of the United States, which shall consist of a Senate and a House of Representatives.

Section 2 The House of Representatives shall be composed of Members chosen every second Year by the people of the several States, and the Electors in each State shall have the Qualifications requisite for Electors of the most numerous Branch of the State Legislature.

No Person shall be a Representative who shall not have attained to the Age of twenty-five years, and been seven Years a Citizen of the United States, and who shall not, when elected, be an Inhabitant of that State in which he shall be chosen.

Representatives and direct Taxes shall be apportioned among the several States which may be included within this Union, according to their respective Numbers, *which shall be determined by adding to the whole Number of free persons, including those bound to Service for a Term of Years and excluding Indians not taxed, three-fifths of all other Persons.* The actual Enumeration shall be made within three Years after the first Meeting of the Congress of the United States, and within every subsequent Term of ten Years, in such Manner as they shall by Law direct. The Number of Representatives shall not exceed one for every thirty Thousand, but each State shall have at Least one Representative; *and until such enumeration shall be made, the State of New Hampshire shall be entitled to choose three, Massachusetts eight, Rhode-Island and Providence Plantations one, Connecticut five, New-York six, New Jersey four, Pennsylvania eight, Delaware one, Maryland six, Virginia ten, North Carolina five, South Carolina five, and Georgia three.*

When vacancies happen in the Representation from any State, the Executive Authority thereof shall issue Writs of Election to fill such Vacancies.

The House of Representatives shall choose their Speaker and other Officers; and shall have the sole Power of Impeachment.

Section 3 The Senate of the United States shall be composed of two Senators from each State, *chosen by the Legislature thereof,* for six Years; and each Senator shall have one Vote.

Immediately after they shall be assembled in Consequence of the first Election, they shall be divided as equally as may be into three Classes. The Seats of the Senators of the first Class

---

* Passages no longer in effect are printed in italic type.

shall be vacated at the Expiration of the second Year, of the second Class at the Expiration of the fourth Year, and of the third Class at the Expiration of the sixth Year, so that one-third may be chosen every second year; *and if Vacancies happen by Resignation or otherwise, during the Recess of the Legislature of any State, the Executive thereof may make temporary Appointments until the next meeting of the Legislature, which shall then fill such Vacancies.*

No Person shall be a Senator who shall not have attained to the Age of thirty Years, and been nine Years a Citizen of the United States, and who shall not, when elected, be an Inhabitant of that State for which he shall be chosen.

The Vice-President of the United States shall be President of the Senate, but shall have no Vote, unless they be equally divided.

The Senate shall choose their other Officers, and also a President *pro tempore,* in the absence of the Vice-President, or when he shall exercise the Office of President of the United States.

The Senate shall have the sole Power to try all Impeachments. When sitting for that purpose, they shall be on Oath or Affirmation. When the President of the United States is tried, the Chief Justice shall preside: And no person shall be convicted without the Concurrence of two-thirds of the Members present.

Judgment in Cases of Impeachment shall not extend further than to removal from Office, and disqualification to hold and enjoy any Office of honor, Trust, or profit under the United States: but the Party convicted shall nevertheless be liable and subject to Indictment, Trial, Judgment and punishment, according to Law.

Section 4   The Times, Places and Manner of holding Elections for Senators and Representatives, shall be prescribed in each state by the Legislature thereof; but the Congress may at any time by Law make or alter such Regulations, except as to the Places of choosing Senators.

The Congress shall assemble at least once in every Year, and such Meeting *shall be on the first Monday in December, unless they shall by Law appoint a different Day.*

Section 5   Each House shall be the Judge of the Elections, Returns and Qualifications of its own Members, and a Majority of each shall constitute a Quorum to do Business; but a smaller number may adjourn from day to day, and may be authorized to compel the Attendance of absent Members, in such Manner, and under such Penalties, as each House may provide.

Each House may determine the Rules of its Proceedings, punish its Members for disorderly Behaviour, and with the Concurrence of two-thirds, expel a Member.

Each House shall keep a Journal of its Proceedings, and from time to time publish the same, excepting such Parts as may in their Judgment require Secrecy; and the Yeas and Nays of the Members of either House on any question shall, at the Desire of one-fifth of those present, be entered on the journal.

Neither House, during the Session of Congress, shall, without the Consent of the other, adjourn for more than three days, nor to any other Place than that in which the two Houses shall be sitting.

Section 6   The Senators and Representatives shall receive a Compensation for their Services, to be ascertained by Law and paid out of the Treasury of the United States. They shall in all Cases except Treason, Felony and Breach of the Peace, be privileged from Arrest during their Attendance at the Session of their respective houses, and in going to and returning from the same; and for any Speech or Debate in either House, they shall not be questioned in any other place.

No Senator or Representative shall, during the Time for which he was elected, be appointed to any civil Office under the Authority of the United States, which shall have been created, or the Emoluments whereof shall have been increased, during such time; and no person holding any Office under the United States shall be a Member of either House during his continuance in Office.

Section 7 All Bills for raising Revenue shall originate in the House of Representatives; but the Senate may propose or concur with Amendments as on other bills.

Every Bill which shall have passed the House of Representatives and the Senate, shall, before it become a Law, be presented to the President of the United States; if he approve he shall sign it, but if not he shall return it with his Objections, to that House in which it originated, who shall enter the Objections at large on their Journal, and proceed to reconsider it. If after such reconsideration two-thirds of that House shall agree to pass the bill, it shall be sent, together with the objections, to the other House, by which it shall likewise be reconsidered, and, if approved by two-thirds of that House, it shall become a law. But in all such Cases the Votes of both Houses shall be determined by Yeas and Nays, and the Names of the Persons voting for and against the Bill shall be entered on the Journal of each House respectively. If any Bill shall not be returned by the President within ten Days (Sundays excepted) after it shall have been presented to him, the Same shall be a Law, in like Manner as if he had signed it, unless the Congress by their Adjournment prevent its Return, in which Case it shall not be a Law.

Every Order, Resolution, or Vote to which the Concurrence of the Senate and House of Representatives may be necessary (except on a question of Adjournment) shall be presented to the President of the United States; and before the Same shall take Effect, shall be approved by him, or being disapproved by him, shall be repassed by two-thirds of the Senate and House of Representatives, according to the Rules and Limitations prescribed in the Case of a Bill.

Section 8 The Congress shall have Power

To lay and collect Taxes, Duties, Imposts, and Excises, to pay the Debts and provide for the common Defence and general Welfare of the United States; but all Duties, Imposts and Excises shall be uniform throughout the United States;

To borrow money on the credit of the United States;

To regulate Commerce with foreign Nations, and among the several States, and with the Indian Tribes;

To establish an uniform Rule of Naturalization, and uniform Laws on the subject of Bankruptcies throughout the United States;

To coin Money, regulate the Value thereof, and of foreign Coin, and fix the Standard of Weights and Measures;

To provide for the Punishment of counterfeiting the Securities and current Coin of the United States;

To establish Post Offices and Post Roads;

To promote the Progress of Science and useful Arts by securing for limited times to Authors and Inventors the exclusive Right to their respective Writings and Discoveries;

To constitute Tribunals inferior to the Supreme Court;

To define and punish Piracies and Felonies committed on the high Seas and Offenses against the Law of Nations;

To declare War, grant Letters of Marque and Reprisal, and make rules concerning captures on land and water;

To raise and support Armies, but no Appropriation of Money to that Use shall be for a longer Term than two Years;

To provide and maintain a Navy;

To make rules for the Government and Regulation of the land and naval forces;

To provide for calling forth the Militia to execute the Laws of the Union, suppress Insurrections, and repel Invasions;

To provide for organizing, arming, and disciplining the Militia, and for governing such part of them as may be employed in the Service of the United States, reserving to the States respectively the Appointment of the Officers, and the Authority of training the Militia according to the discipline prescribed by Congress;

To exercise exclusive Legislation in all Cases whatsoever, over such District (not exceeding ten Miles square) as may, by Cession of particular States, and the acceptance of Congress, become the Seat of the Government of the United States, and to exercise like Authority over all places purchased by the Consent of the Legislature of the State, in which the same shall be, for Erection of Forts, Magazines, Arsenals, dock-Yards, and other needful Buildings;—And

To make all Laws which shall be necessary and proper for carrying into Execution the foregoing Powers, and all other powers vested by this Constitution in the Government of the United States, or in any Department or Officer thereof.

Section 9   *The Migration or Importation of such Persons as any of the States now existing shall think proper to admit shall not be prohibited by the Congress prior to the Year 1808; but a tax or duty may be imposed on such Importation, not exceeding ten dollars for each person.*

The privilege of the Writ of Habeas Corpus shall not be suspended, unless when in Cases of Rebellion or Invasion the public Safety may require it.

No Bill of Attainder or ex post facto Law shall be passed.

No capitation, or other direct, Tax shall be laid, unless in proportion to the Census or Enumeration herein before directed to be taken.

No Tax or Duty shall be laid on Articles exported from any State.

No Preference shall be given by any Regulation of Revenue to the ports of one State over those of another; nor shall Vessels bound to, or from, one State, be obliged to enter, clear, or pay Duties in another.

No Money shall be drawn from the Treasury, but in Consequence of Appropriations made by Law; and a regular Statement and Account of the Receipts and Expenditures of all public Money shall be published from time to time.

No Title of Nobility shall be granted by the United States: And no Person holding any Office or profit or Trust under them, shall, without the Consent of the Congress, accept of any present, Emolument, Office, or Title, of any kind whatever, from any King, Prince, or foreign state.

Section 10   No State shall enter into any Treaty, Alliance, or Confederation; grant Letters of Marque and Reprisal; coin Money; emit Bills of Credit; make any thing but gold and silver Coin a Tender in payment of Debts; pass any Bill of Attainder, ex post facto Law, or Law impairing the Obligation of Contracts, or grant any Title of Nobility.

No State shall, without the consent of Congress, lay any imposts or duties on imports or exports, except what may be absolutely necessary for executing its inspection laws: and the net produce of all duties and imposts, laid by any State on imports or exports, shall be for the use of the treasury of the United States; and all such laws shall be subject to the revision and control of the Congress.

No State shall, without the Consent of Congress, lay any duty of Tonnage, keep Troops or Ships of War in time of peace, enter into any Agreement or Compact with another State, or with a foreign power, or engage in War, unless actually invaded, or in such imminent Danger as will not admit of delay.

Article II

Section 1   The executive Power shall be vested in a President of the United States of America. He shall hold his Office during the Term of four years, and, together with the Vice-President, chosen for the same Term, be elected as follows:

Each State shall appoint, in such Manner as the Legislature thereof may direct, a Number of Electors, equal to the whole Number of Senators and Representatives to which the State may be entitled in the Congress; but no Senator or Representative, or person holding an Office of Trust or profit under the United States, shall be appointed an Elector.

The Electors shall meet in their respective States, and vote by Ballot for two persons, of whom one at least shall not be an Inhabitant of the same State with themselves. And they shall make a List of all the Persons voted for, and of the Number of Votes for each; which List they shall sign and certify, and transmit sealed to the Seat of Government of the United States, directed to the President of the Senate. The President of the Senate shall, in the presence of the Senate and House of Representatives, open all the Certificates, and the Votes shall then be counted. The person having the greatest Number of Votes shall be the President, if such Number be a Majority of the whole Number of Electors appointed; and if there be more than one who have such Majority, and have an equal number of Votes, then the House of Representatives shall immediately choose by Ballot one of them for President; and if no person have a Majority, then from the five highest on the List said House shall in like Manner choose the President. But in choosing the President the Votes shall be taken by States, the Representation from each State having one Vote; a quorum for this purpose shall consist of a Member or Members from two-thirds of the States, and a Majority of all the States shall be necessary to a Choice. In every Case, after the Choice of the President, the Person having the greatest Number of Votes of the Electors shall be the Vice-President. But if there should remain two or more who have equal votes, the Senate shall choose from them by Ballot the Vice-President.

The Congress may determine the Time of choosing the Electors and the Day on which they shall give their Votes; which Day shall be the same throughout the United States.

No person except a natural-born Citizen, *or a Citizen of the United States at the time of the Adoption of this Constitution,* shall be eligible to the Office of President; neither shall any Person be eligible to that Office who shall not have attained to the Age of thirty-five years, and been fourteen Years a Resident within the United States.

In Case of the Removal of the President from Office or of his Death, Resignation, or Inability to discharge the powers and Duties of the said Office, the same shall devolve on the Vice-President, and the Congress may by Law provide for the Case of Removal, Death, Resignation, or Inability, both of the President and Vice-President, declaring what Officer shall then act as President, and such

Officer shall act accordingly, until the disability be removed, or a President shall be elected.

The President shall, at stated Times, receive for his Services a Compensation, which shall neither be increased nor diminished during the period for which he shall have been elected, and he shall not receive within that Period any other Emolument from the United States, or any of them.

Before he enter on the execution of his Office, he shall take the following Oath or Affirmation:—"I do solemnly swear (or affirm) that I will faithfully execute the Office of the President of the United States, and will to the best of my Ability preserve, protect and defend the Constitution of the United States."

Section 2   The President shall be Commander in Chief of the Army and Navy of the United States, and of the Militia of the several States, when called into the actual Service of the United States; he may require the Opinion, in writing, of the principal Officer in each of the executive Departments, upon any subject relating to the Duties of their respective Offices, and he shall have Power to Grant Reprieves and Pardons for Offenses against the United States, except in Cases of Impeachment.

He shall have Power, by and with the Advice and Consent of the Senate, to make Treaties, provided two-thirds of the Senators present concur; and he shall nominate, and by and with the Advice and Consent of the Senate, shall appoint Ambassadors, other public Ministers and Consuls, Judges of the Supreme Court, and all other Officers of the United States, whose Appointments are not herein otherwise provided for, and which shall be established by Law: but Congress may by Law vest the Appointment of such inferior Officers, as they think proper, in the President alone, in the Courts of Law, or in the Heads of Departments.

The President shall have Power to fill up all Vacancies that may happen during the Recess of the Senate, by granting Commissions which shall expire at the End of their next Session.

Section 3   He shall from time to time give to the Congress Information of the State of the Union, and recommend to their Consideration such Measures as he shall judge necessary and expedient; he may, on extraordinary occasions, convene both Houses, or either of them, and in Case of Disagreement between them, with respect to the Time of Adjournment, he may adjourn them to such Time as he shall think proper; he shall receive Ambassadors and other public Ministers; he shall take Care that the Laws be faithfully executed, and shall Commission all the Officers of the United States.

Section 4   The President, Vice-President and all civil Officers of the United States shall be removed from Office on Impeachment for, and on Conviction of, Treason, Bribery, or other high Crimes and Misdemeanors.

Article III

Section 1   The judicial power of the United States shall be vested in one supreme Court, and in such inferior Courts as the Congress may from time to time ordain and establish. The Judges, both of the supreme and inferior Courts, shall hold their offices during good Behaviour, and shall, at stated Times, receive for their

Services a compensation which shall not be diminished during their Continuance in Office.

Section 2 The judicial Power shall extend to all Cases, in Law and Equity, arising under this Constitution, the Laws of the United States, and treaties made, or which shall be made, under their Authority;—to all cases affecting ambassadors, other public ministers and consuls;—to all cases of admiralty and maritime Jurisdiction;—to controversies to which the United States shall be a party;—to Controversies between two or more States;—*between a State and Citizens of another State*;—between Citizens of different States;—between Citizens of the same State claiming Lands under Grants of different States, and between a State, or the Citizens thereof, and foreign States, Citizens or Subjects.

In all Cases affecting Ambassadors, other public Ministers and Consuls, and those in which a State shall be Party, the supreme Court shall have original Jurisdiction. In all the other Cases before mentioned, the supreme Court shall have appellate Jurisdiction, both as to Law and Fact, with such Exceptions, and under such Regulations, as the Congress shall make.

The trial of all Crimes, except in Cases of Impeachment, shall be by Jury; and such Trial shall be held in the State where said Crimes shall have been committed; but when not committed within any State, the Trial shall be at such Place or Places as the Congress may by Law have directed.

Section 3 Treason against the United States shall consist only in levying War against them, or in adhering to their Enemies, giving them Aid and Comfort. No person shall be convicted of Treason unless on the Testimony of two Witnesses to the same overt Act, or on confession in open Court.

The Congress shall have power to declare the Punishment of Treason, but no Attainder of Treason shall work Corruption of Blood, or Forfeiture except during the Life of the Person attained.

Article IV

Section 1 Full Faith and Credit shall be given in each State to the public Acts, Records, and judicial Proceedings of every other State. And the Congress may by general Laws prescribe the Manner in which such Acts, Records, and Proceedings shall be proved, and the Effect thereof.

Section 2 The Citizens of each State shall be entitled to all Privileges and Immunities of Citizens in the several States.

A Person charged in any State with Treason, Felony, or other Crime, who shall flee from Justice, and be found in another State, shall on demand of the executive Authority of the State from which he fled, be delivered up, to be removed to the State having Jurisdiction of the crime.

No person held to Service or Labor in one State, under the Laws thereof, escaping into another, shall, in Consequence of any Law or Regulation therein, be discharged from such Service or Labor, but shall be delivered up on Claim of the party to whom such Service or Labor may be due.

Section 3 New States may be admitted by the Congress into this Union; but no new State shall be formed or erected within the Jurisdiction of any other State; nor any State be formed by the Junction of two or more States, or parts of States, without the Consent of the Legislatures of the States concerned as well as of the Congress.

The Congress shall have power to dispose of and make all needful Rules and regulations respecting the Territory or other property belonging to the United States; and nothing in this Constitution shall be so construed as to prejudice any Claims of the United States, or of any particular State.

Section 4 The United States shall guarantee to every State in this Union a Republican Form of Government, and shall protect each of them against Invasion; and on Application of the Legislature, or of the Executive (when the Legislature cannot be convened), against domestic Violence.

Article V

The Congress, whenever two-thirds of both Houses shall deem it necessary, shall propose Amendments to this Constitution, or, on the Application of the Legislatures of two-thirds of the several States, shall call a Convention for proposing Amendments, which, in either Case, shall be valid to all Intents and Purposes, as part of this Constitution, when ratified by the Legislatures of three-fourths of the several States, or by Conventions in three-fourths thereof, as the one or the other Mode of Ratification may be proposed by the Congress; provided *that no Amendment which may be made prior to the Year One thousand eight hundred and eight shall in any Manner affect the first and fourth Clauses in the Ninth Section of the first Article;* and that no State, without its Consent, shall be deprived of its equal suffrage in the Senate.

Article VI

All Debts contracted and Engagements entered into, before the Adoption of this Constitution, shall be as valid against the United States under this Constitution, as under the Confederation.

This Constitution, and the Laws of the United States which shall be made in Pursuance thereof; and all Treaties made, or which shall be made, under the Authority of the United States, shall be the supreme Law of the Land; and the Judges in every State shall be bound thereby, any thing in the Constitution or Laws of any State to the Contrary notwithstanding.

The Senators and Representatives before mentioned, and the Members of the several State Legislatures, and all executive and judicial Officers, both of the United States and of the several States, shall be bound by Oath or Affirmation to support this Constitution; but no religious Test shall ever be required as a qualification to any Office or public Trust under the United States.

Article VII

The Ratification of the Conventions of nine States shall be sufficient for the Establishment of this Constitution between the States so ratifying the same.

Done in Convention by the unanimous consent of the States present the Seventeenth day of September in the Year of our Lord one thousand seven hundred and Eighty-seven and of the Independence of the United States of America the Twelfth. In Witness whereof We have hereunto subscribed our Names.

GEORGE WASHINGTON
and thirty-seven others

*Amendments to the Constitution**

Amendment I

Congress shall make no law respecting an establishment of religion, or prohibiting the free exercise thereof; or abridging the freedom of speech, or of the press; or the right of the people peaceably to assemble, and to petition the government for a redress of grievances.

Amendment II

A well-regulated militia being necessary to the security of a free State, the right of the people to keep and bear arms shall not be infringed.

Amendment III

No soldier shall, in time of peace, be quartered in any house without the consent of the owner, nor in time of war, but in a manner to be prescribed by law.

Amendment IV

The right of the people to be secure in their persons, houses, papers, and effects, against unreasonable searches and seizures, shall not be violated, and no warrants shall issue but upon probable cause, supported by oath or affirmation, and particularly describing the place to be searched, and the persons or things to be seized.

Amendment V

No person shall be held to answer for a capital, or otherwise infamous crime, unless on a presentment or indictment of a grand jury, except in cases arising in the land or naval forces, or in the militia, when in actual service in time of war or public danger; nor shall any person be subject for the same offense to be twice put in jeopardy of life or limb; nor shall be compelled in any criminal case to be a witness against himself, nor be deprived of life, liberty, or property, without due process of law; nor shall private property be taken for public use without just compensation.

---

*The first ten amendments (the Bill of Rights) were adopted in 1791.

Amendment VI

In all criminal prosecutions, the accused shall enjoy the right to a speedy and public trial, by an impartial jury of the State and district wherein the crime shall have
been committed, which district shall have been previously ascertained by law, and
to be informed of the nature and cause of the accusation; to be confronted with
the witnesses against him; to have compulsory process for obtaining witnesses in
his favor, and to have the assistance of counsel for his defense.

Amendment VII

In suits at common law, where the value in controversy shall exceed twenty dollars,
the right of trial by jury shall be preserved, and no fact tried by a jury shall be otherwise reexamined in any court of the United States, than according to the rules of
the common law.

Amendment VIII

Excessive bail shall not be required, nor excessive fines imposed, nor cruel and unusual punishments inflicted.

Amendment IX

The enumeration in the Constitution, of certain rights, shall not be construed to
deny or disparage others retained by the people.

Amendment X

The powers not delegated to the United States by the Constitution, nor prohibited
by it to the States, are reserved to the states respectively, or to the people.

Amendment XI [Adopted 1798]

The judicial power of the United States shall not be construed to extend to any
suit in law or equity, commenced or prosecuted against one of the United States
by citizens of another state, or by citizens or subjects of any foreign state.

Amendment XII [Adopted 1804]

The electors shall meet in their respective States, and vote by ballot for President
and Vice-President, one of whom, at least, shall not be an inhabitant of the same
State with themselves; they shall name in their ballots the person voted for as
President, and in distinct ballots the person voted for as Vice-President, and they
shall make distinct lists of all persons voted for as President, and of all persons
voted for as Vice-President, and of the number of votes for each, which lists they
shall sign and certify, and transmit sealed to the seat of government of the
United States, directed to the President of the Senate;—the President of the
Senate shall, in the presence of the Senate and House of representatives, open

all the certificates and the votes shall then be counted;—the person having the greatest number of votes for President shall be the President, if such number be a majority of the whole number of electors appointed; and if no person have such majority, then from the persons having the highest numbers not exceeding three on the list of those voted for as President, the House of Representatives shall choose immediately, by ballot, the President. But in choosing the President, the votes shall be taken by States, the representation from each State having one vote; a quorum for this purpose shall consist of a member or members from two-thirds of the States, and a majority of all the States shall be necessary to a choice. And if the House of Representatives shall not choose a President whenever the right of choice shall devolve upon them, before *the fourth day of March* next following, then the Vice-President shall act as President, as in the case of the death or other constitutional disability of the President.

The person having the greatest number of votes as Vice-President shall be the Vice-President, if such number be a majority of the whole number of electors appointed; and if no person have a majority, then from the two highest numbers on the list the Senate shall choose the Vice-President; a quorum for the purpose shall consist of two-thirds of the whole number of Senators, and a majority of the whole number shall be necessary to a choice. But no person constitutionally ineligible to the office of President shall be eligible to that of Vice-President of the United States.

Amendment XIII [Adopted 1865]

Section 1   Neither slavery nor involuntary servitude, except as a punishment for crime whereof the party shall have been duly convicted, shall exist within the United States, or any place subject to their jurisdiction.

Section 2   Congress shall have power to enforce this article by appropriate legislation.

Amendment XIV [Adopted 1868]

Section 1   All persons born or naturalized in the United States, and subject to the jurisdiction thereof, are citizens of the United States and of the State wherein they reside. No State shall make or enforce any law which shall abridge the privileges or immunities of citizens of the United States; nor shall any State deprive any person of life, liberty, or property, without due process of law; nor deny to any person within its jurisdiction the equal protection of the laws.

Section 2   Representatives shall be apportioned among the several States according to their respective numbers, counting the whole number of persons in each State, excluding Indians not taxed. But when the right to vote at any election for the choice of Electors for President and Vice-President of the United States, Representatives in Congress, the executive and judicial officers of a State, or the members of the legislature thereof, is denied to any of the male inhabitants of such State, being twenty-one years of age and citizens of the United States, or in any way abridged, except for participation in rebellion, or other crime, the basis of representation therein shall be reduced in the proportion which the number of such male citizens shall bear to the whole number of male citizens twenty-one years of age in such State.

Section 3   No person shall be a Senator or Representative in Congress, or Elector of President and Vice-President, or hold any office, civil or military, under the United States, or under any State, who, having previously taken an oath, as a member of Congress, or as an officer of the United States, or as a member of any State legislature, or as an executive or judicial officer of any State, to support the Constitution of the United States, shall have engaged in insurrection or rebellion against the same, or given aid or comfort to the enemies thereof. Congress may, by a vote of two-thirds of each house, remove such disability.

Section 4   The validity of the public debt of the United States, authorized by law, including debts incurred for payment of pensions and bounties for services in suppressing insurrection or rebellion, shall not be questioned. But neither the United States nor any State shall assume or pay any debt or obligation incurred in aid of insurrection or rebellion against the United States, or any claim for the loss of emancipation of any slave; but all such debts, obligations, and claims shall be held illegal and void.

Section 5   The Congress shall have power to enforce, by appropriate legislation, the provisions of this article.

Amendment XV [Adopted 1870]

Section 1   The right of citizens of the United States to vote shall not be denied or abridged by the United States or by any State on account of race, color, or previous condition of servitude.

Section 2   The Congress shall have power to enforce this article by appropriate legislation.

Amendment XVI [Adopted 1913]

The Congress shall have power to lay and collect taxes on incomes, from whatever source derived, without apportionment among the several States, and without regard to any census or enumeration.

Amendment XVII [Adopted 1913]

Section 1   The Senate of the United States shall be composed of two Senators from each State, elected by the people thereof, for six years; and each Senator shall have one vote. The electors in each State shall have the qualifications requisite for electors of [voters for] the most numerous branch of the State legislatures.

Section 2   When vacancies happen in the representation of any State in the Senate, the executive authority of such State shall issue writs of election to fill such vacancies: *Provided,* that the Legislature of any State may empower the executive thereof to make temporary appointments until the people fill the vacancies by election as the Legislature may direct.

Section 3 This amendment shall not be so construed as to affect the election or term of any Senator chosen before it becomes valid as part of the Constitution.

Amendment XVIII [Adopted 1919, repealed 1933]

Section 1 After one year from the ratification of this article the manufacture, sale or transportation of intoxicating liquors within, the importation thereof into, or the exportation thereof from the United States and all territory subject to the jurisdiction thereof, for beverage purposes, is hereby prohibited.

Section 2 The Congress and the several States shall have concurrent power to enforce this article by appropriate legislation.

Section 3 This article shall be inoperative unless it shall have been ratified as an amendment to the Constitution by the legislatures of the several States, as provided by the Constitution, within seven years from the date of the submission thereof to the States by the Congress.

Amendment XIX [Adopted 1920]

Section 1 The right of citizens of the United States to vote shall not be denied or abridged by the United States or by any State on account of sex.

Section 2 The Congress shall have power to enforce this article by appropriate legislation.

Amendment XX [Adopted 1933]

Section 1 The terms of the President and Vice-President shall end at noon on the 20th day of January, and the terms of Senators and Representatives at noon on the 3d day of January, of the years in which such terms would have ended if this article had not been ratified; and the terms of their successors shall then begin.

Section 2 The Congress shall assemble at least once in every year, and such meetings shall begin at noon on the 3d day of January, unless they shall by law appoint a different day.

Section 3 If, at the time fixed for the beginning of the term of the President, the President-elect shall have died, the Vice-President-elect shall become President. If a President shall not have been chosen before the time fixed for the beginning of his term, or if the President-elect shall have failed to qualify, then the Vice-President-elect shall act as President until a President shall have qualified; and the Congress may by law provide for the case wherein neither a President-elect nor a

Vice-President-elect shall have qualified, declaring who shall then act as President, or the manner in which one who is to act shall be selected, and such persons shall act accordingly until a President or Vice-President shall have qualified.

Section 4   The Congress may by law provide for the case of the death of any of the persons from whom the House of Representatives may choose a President whenever the right of choice shall have devolved upon them, and for the case of the death of any of the persons from whom the Senate may choose a Vice-President whenever the right of choice shall have devolved upon them.

Section 5   Sections 1 and 2 shall take effect on the 15th day of October following the ratification of this article.

Section 6   This article shall be inoperative unless it shall have been ratified as an amendment to the Constitution by the Legislatures of three-fourths of the several States within seven years from the date of its submission.

Amendment XXI [Adopted 1933]

Section 1   The eighteenth article of amendment to the Constitution of the United States is hereby repealed.

Section 2   The transportation or importation into any State, Territory, or Possession of the United States for delivery or use therein of intoxicating liquors, in violation of the laws thereof, is hereby prohibited.

Section 3   This article shall be inoperative unless it shall have been ratified as an amendment to the Constitution by conventions in the several States, as provided in the Constitution, within seven years from the date of submission thereof to the States by the Congress.

Amendment XXII [Adopted 1951]

Section 1   No person shall be elected to the office of President more than twice, and no person who has held the office of President, or acted as President, for more than two years of a term to which some other person was elected President shall be elected to the office of President more than once. But this article shall not apply to any person holding the office of President when this article was proposed by the Congress, and shall not prevent any person who may be holding the office of President, or acting as President, during the term within which this article becomes operative from holding the office of President or acting as President during the remainder of such term.

Section 2   This article shall be inoperative unless it shall have been ratified as an amendment to the Constitution by the legislatures of three-fourths of the several States within seven years from the date of its submission to the States by the Congress.

Amendment XXIII [Adopted 1961]

Section 1 The District constituting the seat of Government of the United States shall appoint in such manner as the Congress may direct:

A number of electors of President and Vice-President equal to the whole number of Senators and Representatives in Congress to which the District would be entitled if it were a State, but in no event more than the least populous State; they shall be in addition to those appointed by the States, but they shall be considered for the purposes of the election of President and Vice-President, to be electors appointed by a State; and they shall meet in the District and perform such duties as provided by the twelfth article of amendment.

Section 2 The Congress shall have the power to enforce this article by appropriate legislation.

Amendment XXIV [Adopted 1964]

Section 1 The right of citizens of the United States to vote in any primary or other election for President or Vice-President, for electors for President or Vice-President, or for Senator or Representative in Congress, shall not be denied or abridged by the United States or any State by reason of failure to pay any poll tax or other tax.

Section 2 The Congress shall have the power to enforce this article by appropriate legislation.

Amendment XXV [Adopted 1967]

Section 1 In case of the removal of the President from office or of his death or resignation, the Vice-President shall become President.

Section 2 Whenever there is a vacancy in the office of the Vice-President, the President shall nominate a Vice-President who shall take office upon confirmation by a majority vote of both Houses of Congress.

Section 3 Whenever the President transmits to the President pro tempore of the Senate and the speaker of the House of Representatives his written declaration that he is unable to discharge the powers and duties of his office, and until he transmits to them a written declaration to the contrary, such powers and duties shall be discharged by the Vice-President as Acting President.

Section 4 Whenever the Vice-President and a majority of either the principal officers of the executive departments or of such other body as Congress may by law provide, transmit to the President pro tempore of the Senate and the Speaker of the House of Representatives their written declaration that the President is unable to discharge the powers and duties of his office, the Vice-President shall immediately assume the powers and duties of the office as Acting President.

Thereafter, when the President transmits to the President pro tempore of the Senate and the Speaker of the House of Representatives his written declaration that no inability exists, he shall resume the powers and duties of his office unless the Vice-President and a majority of either the principal officers of the executive department(s) or of such other body as Congress may by law provide, transmit within four days to the President pro tempore of the Senate and the Speaker of the House of Representatives their written declaration that the President is unable to discharge the powers and duties of his office. Thereupon Congress shall decide the issue, assembling within forty-eight hours for that purpose if not in session. If the Congress, within twenty-one days after receipt of the latter written declaration, or, if Congress is not in session, within twenty-one days after Congress is required to assemble, determines by two-thirds vote of both Houses that the President is unable to discharge the powers and duties of his office, the Vice-President shall continue to discharge the same as Acting President; otherwise, the President shall resume the powers and duties of his office.

Amendment XXVI [Adopted 1971]

Section 1   The right of citizens of the United States, who are eighteen years of age or older, to vote shall not be denied or abridged by the United States or by any State on account of age.

Section 2   The Congress shall have power to enforce this article by appropriate legislation.

Amendment XXVII [Adopted 1992]

No law, varying the compensation for the services of the senators and representatives shall take effect, until an election of representatives shall have intervened.

References

Chapter 1 / Dilemmas of Democracy
pp. 1–27

1. "Kevorkian Attends Another Michigan Death," *New York Times,* 30 January 1996, p. A8.

2. Jack Lessenberry, "In Tactical Change, Kevorkian Promises to Halt Suicide Aid," *New York Times,* 26 December 1993, p. 1.

3. Center for Political Studies of the Institute for Social Research, *Election Study 1992* (Ann Arbor: University of Michigan).

4. 1977 Constitution of the Union of Soviet Socialist Republics, Article 11, in *Constitutions of Countries of the World,* ed. A. P. Blaustein and G. H. Flanz (Dobbs Ferry, N.Y.: Oceana, 1971).

5. Karl Marx and Friedrich Engels, *Critique of the Gotha Programme* (New York: International Publishers, 1938), p. 10. Originally written in 1875 but published in 1891.

6. See the argument in Amy Gutman, *Liberal Equality* (Cambridge:Cambridge University Press, 1980), pp. 9–10.

7. See John H. Schaar, "Equality of Opportunity and Beyond," in *Equality,* NOMOS IX, ed. J. Roland Pennock and John W. Chapman (New York: Atherton Press, 1967), pp. 228–249.

8. Sam Vincent Meddis, "Crime's No Worse, But USA's Fear Grows," *USA Today* (International Edition), 28 October 1993, p. 1. See also Wesley G. Skogan, *Disorder and Decline: Crime and the Spiral of Decay in American Neighborhoods* (New York: Free Press, 1990), Chap. 2.

9. See generally Milton Friedman, *Capitalism and Freedom* (Chicago: University of Chicago Press, 1962).

10. The communitarian movement was founded by a group of ethicists and social scientists who met in Washington, D.C., in 1990 at the invitation of sociologist Amitai Etzioni and political theorist William Galston to discuss the declining state of morality and values in the United States. Etzioni became the leading spokesperson for the movement. See his *Rights and the Common Good: The Communitarian Perspective* (New York: St. Martin's Press, 1995), pp. iii–iv. The communitarian political movement should be distinguished from communitarian thought in political philosophy, which is associated with theorists such as Alasdair MacIntyre, Michael Sandel, and Charles Taylor, who wrote in the late 1970s and early 1980s. In essence, communitarian theorists criticized liberalism, which stressed freedom and individualism, as excessively individualistic. Their fundamental critique was that liberalism slights the values of community life. See Allen E. Buchanan, "Assessing the Communitarian Critique of Liberalism," *Ethics,* 99 (July 1989), pp. 852–882, and Patrick Neal and David Paris, "Liberalism and the Communitarian Critique: A Guide for the Perplexed," *Canadian Journal of Political Science,* 23 (September 1990), pp. 419–439. Communitarian philosophers attacked liberalism over the inviolability of civil liberties. In our framework, such issues involve the tradeoff between freedom and order. Communitarian and liberal theorists differ less concerning the tradeoff between freedom and equality. See William R. Lund, "Communitarian Politics and the Problem of Equality," *Political Research Quarterly,* 46 (September 1993), pp. 577–600. But

see also Susan Hekman, "The Embodiment of the Subject: Feminism and the Communitarian Critique of Liberalism," *Journal of Politics,* 54 (November 1992), pp. 1098–1119.

11. Etzioni, *Rights and the Common Good,* p. iv, and Etzioni, "Communitarian Solutions/What Communitarians Think," *The Journal of State Government,* 65 (January-March), pp. 9–11. For a critical review of the communitarian program, see Jeremiah Creedon, "Communitarian Manifesto," *Utne Reader* (July-August 1992), pp. 38–40.

12. Etzioni, "Communitarian Solutions/What Communitarians Think," p. 10. See also Lester Thurow, "Communitarian vs. Individualistic Capitalism," in Etzioni, *Rights and the Common Good,* pp. 277–282. Note, however, that government's role in dealing with issues of social and economic inequality is far less developed in communitarian writings than is its role in dealing with issues of order. In the same volume, an article by David Osborne, "Beyond Left and Right: A New Political Paradigm" (pp. 283–290), downplays the role of government in guaranteeing entitlements.

13. Etzioni, *Rights and the Common Good,* p. 17.

14. See James A. Stimson, Michael B. MacKuen, and Robert S. Erikson, "Dynamic Representation," *American Political Science Review,* 89 (September 1995), pp. 543–565.

15. See C. B. Macpherson, *The Real World of Democracy* (New York: Oxford University Press, 1975), pp. 58–59.

16. Thomas E. Cronin, *Direct Democracy* (Cambridge, Mass.: Harvard University Press, 1989), p. 47.

17. Jack Citrin, "Who's the Boss? Direct Democracy and Popular Control of Government," in *Broken Contract?,* ed. Stephen C. Craig (Boulder, Colo.: Westview, 1996), p. 271.

18. Lawrence K. Grossman, *The Electronic Republic* (New York: Viking, 1995).

19. M. Margaret Conway, *Political Participation in the United States,* 2nd ed. (Washington, D.C.: Congressional Quarterly, 1991), p. 44.

20. Benjamin I. Page and Robert Y. Shapiro, *The Rational Public* (Chicago: University of Chicago Press, 1992), p. 387.

21. See Robert A. Dahl, *Dilemmas of Pluralist Democracy* (New Haven, Conn.: Yale University Press, 1982), p. 5.

22. The classic statement on elite theory is C. Wright Mills, *The Power Elite* (New York: Oxford University Press, 1956).

23. See Robert A. Dahl, *Who Governs?* (New Haven, Conn.: Yale University Press, 1961). See also Clarence N. Stone, *Regime Politics* (Lawrence: University of Kansas Press, 1989); and John P. Heinz, Edward O. Laumann, Robert L. Nelson, and Robert H. Salisbury, *The Hollow Core* (Cambridge, Mass.: Harvard University Press, 1993).

24. Peter Bachrach and Morton S. Baratz, "Two Faces of Power," *American Political Science Review,* 56 (December 1962), pp. 947–952; and John Gaventa, *Power and Powerlessness* (Urbana: University of Illinois Press, 1980).

25. See, for example, Dan Clawson, Alan Neustadtl, and Denise Scott, *Money Talks* (New York: Basic Books, 1992).

26. Kay Lehman Schlozman and John T. Tierney, *Organized Interests and American Politics* (New York: Harper & Row, 1986).

27. E. E. Schattschneider, *The Semi-Sovereign People* (New York: Holt, Rinehart, & Winston, 1960), p. 35.

Chapter 2 / The Constitution pp. 28–55

1. Samuel Eliot Morison, *Oxford History of the American People* (New York: Oxford University Press, 1965), p. 172.

2. John Plamentz (rev. ed. by M. E. Plamentz and Robert Wokler), *Man and Society,* Vol. 1: *From the Middle Ages to Locke* (New York: Longman, 1992), pp. 216–218.

3. Extrapolated from U.S. Department of Defense, *Selected Manpower Statistics, FY 1982* (Washington, D.C.: U.S. Government Printing Office, 1983), Table 2-30, p. 130; and U.S. Bureau of the Census, *1985 Statistical Abstract of*

the United States (Washington, D.C.: U.S. Government Printing Office, 1985), Tables 1 and 2, p. 6.

4. Joseph T. Keenan, *The Constitution of the United States* (Homewood, Ill.: Dow-Jones-Irwin, 1975).

5. David P. Szatmary, *Shays' Rebellion: The Making of an Agrarian Insurrection* (Amherst: University of Massachusetts Press, 1980), pp. 82–102.

6. Robert H. Jackson, *The Struggle for Judicial Supremacy* (New York: Alfred A. Knopf, 1941), p. 8.

7. Forrest McDonald, *Novus Ordo Seclorum: The Intellectual Origins of the Constitution* (Lawrence: University Press of Kansas, 1985), pp. 205–209.

8. Donald S. Lutz, "The Preamble to the Constitution of the United States," *This Constitution,* 1 (September 1983), pp. 23–30.

9. Richard E. Neustadt, *Presidential Power: The Politics of Leadership* (New York: Wiley, 1960), p. 33.

10. Robert A. Goldwin, Letter to the Editor, *Wall Street Journal,* 30 August 1993, p. A11.

11. Herbert J. Storing, ed., *The Complete Anti-Federalist,* 7 vols. (Chicago: University of Chicago Press, 1981).

12. Alexis de Tocqueville, *Democracy in America,* 1835–1839, Reprint, ed. J. P. Mayer and Max Lerner (New York: Harper & Row, 1966), p. 102.

13. Jerold L. Waltman, *Political Origins of the U.S. Income Tax* (Jackson: University Press of Mississippi, 1985), p. 10.

Chapter 3 / Federalism   pp. 56–79

1. Rick Bragg, "Louisiana Stands Alone on Drinking at 18," *New York Times,* 23 March 1996, p. 1; "Louisiana Court Upholds Drinking Age of 21," *New York Times,* 3 July 1996, p. A17.

2. Ronald Reagan, "National Minimum Drinking Age: Remarks on Signing HR4616 into Law (17 July 1984)," *Weekly Compilation of Presidential Documents,* 23 July 1984, p. 1036.

3. *South Dakota v. Dole,* 483 U.S. 203 (1987).

4. Daniel J. Elazar, "Opening the Third Century of American Federalism: Issues and Prospects," *Annals of the American Academy of Political and Social Sciences,* 509 (May 1990), p. 14.

5. William H. Stewart, *Concepts of Federalism* (Lanham, Md.: University Press of America, 1984).

6. Edward Corwin, "The Passing of Dual Federalism," 36 *University of Virginia Law Review* 4 (1950).

7. See Daniel J. Elazar, *The American Partnership* (Chicago: University of Chicago Press, 1962); and Morton Grodzins, *The American System* (Chicago: Rand McNally, 1966).

8. Martha Derthick, "The Enduring Features of American Federalism," *The Brookings Review,* Summer 1989, p. 35.

9. *Baker v. Carr,* 369 U.S. 186 (1962); *Wesberry v. Sanders,* 376 U.S. 1 (1964); and *Reynolds v. Sims,* 377 U.S. 533 (1964).

10. *Seminole Tribe of Florida v. Florida,* 116 S. Ct. 1114 (1996).

11. *Idaho v. Coeur d'Alene Tribe,* — U.S. — (1997).

12. *Boerne v. Flores,* — U.S. — (1997).

13. *Printz v. United States,* — U.S. — (1997).

14. *McCulloch v. Maryland,* 4 Wheat. 316 (1819).

15. James T. Patterson, *The New Deal and the States: Federalism in Transition* (Princeton, N.J.: Princeton University Press, 1969).

16. *Brown v. Board of Education of Topeka,* 347 U.S. 483 (1954).

17. Advisory Commission on Intergovernmental Relations, *The Federal Role in the Federal System: The Dynamics of Growth* (A-86) (Washington, D.C.: U.S. Government Printing Office, 1981), p. 101.

18. Ronald Reagan, "Statement on Signing Executive Order Establishing the Presidential Advisory Committee on Federalism," 1981 Pub. Papers 341, 8 April 1981.

19. *Budget of the United States Government, FY 1997 Historical Tables* (Washington, D.C.: U.S. Government Printing Office, 1996), p. 257.

20. Joseph F. Zimmerman, *Contemporary American Federalism: The Growth of National Power* (New York: Praeger, 1992), Chap. 4.

21. Council of State Governments, *The Book of the States, 1994–95,* Vol. 30 (Lexington, Ky: Council of State Governments, 1994), pp. 580–581.

22. "Unfunded Federal Mandates," *Congressional Digest,* March 1995, p. 68.

23. U.S. Bureau of the Census, *Statistical Abstract of the United States: 1993* (Washington, D.C.: U.S. Government Printing Office, 1993), Table 466, p. 291.

24. Alice Rivlin, *Reviving the American Dream: The Economy, the States, and the Federal Government* (Washington, D.C.: Brookings Institution, 1992).

25. Michael A. Pagano and Ann O'M. Bowman, "The State of American Federalism, 1992–93" *Publius* 23 (Summer 1993), pp. 1–22.

Chapter 4 / Public Opinion, Political Socialization, and the Media
pp. 80–111

1. Gallup Organization, *Gallup Poll Monthly,* June 1995, p. 23.

2. Warren Weaver, Jr., "Death Penalty a Three Hundred–Year Issue in America," *New York Times,* 3 July 1976.

3. *Furman v. Georgia,* 408 U.S. 238 (1972).

4. *Gregg v. Georgia,* 248 U.S. 153 (1976).

5. "Fifty-six Executions This Year Were the Most Since 1957," *New York Times,* 30 December 1995, p. 10.

6. See Roberta S. Sigel, ed., *Political Learning in Adulthood: A Sourcebook of Theory and Research* (Chicago: University of Chicago Press, 1989).

7. Times Mirror Center for the People and the Press, *The New Political Landscape* (Washington, D.C.: 1994), p. 144; The Pew Center for the People and the Press, News Release, 29 February 1996, p. 28.

8. The wording of this question is criticized by R. Michael Alvarez and John Brehm in "When Core Beliefs Collide: Conflict, Complexity, or Just Plain Confusion?," a paper prepared for delivery at the annual meeting of the American Political Science Association, Washington, D.C., September 1993, p. 9. They argue that using the phrase "personal choice" (which they call a core value) triggers the psychological effect of reactance, or the feeling that a freedom has been removed. But this core value is precisely our focus in this analysis. Alvarez and Brehm favor using instead the battery of six questions on abortion that have been used in the General Social Survey. Those six questions are also used in Elizabeth Adell Cook, Ted G. Jelen, and Clyde Wilcox, *Between Two Absolutes: Public Opinion and the Politics of Abortion* (Boulder, Colo.: Westview Press, 1992). Those interested primarily in analyzing various attitudes toward abortion probably should use data from the General Social Survey.

9. Although some people view the politics of abortion as "single issue" politics, the issue has broader political significance. In their book on the subject, Cook, Jelen, and Wilcox say, "Although embryonic life is one important value in the abortion debate, it is not the only value at stake." They contend that the politics is tied to alternative sexual relationships and traditional roles of women in the home, which are "social order" issues. See *Between Two Absolutes,* pp. 8–9.

10. Ibid., p. 50.

11. The increasing wealth in industrialized societies may or may not be replacing class conflict with conflict over values. See the exchange between Ronald Inglehart and Scott C. Flanagan, "Value Change in Industrial Societies," *American Political Science Review* 81 (December 1987), pp. 1289–1319.

12. Nathan Glazer, "The Structure of Ethnicity," *Public Opinion* 7 (October/November 1984), p. 4.

13. For a review of these studies, see Robert S. Erikson, Norman R. Luttbeg, and Kent L. Tedin, *American Public Opinion,* 3d ed. (New York: Macmillan, 1988).

14. Felicity Barringer, "Census Shows Profound Change in Racial Makeup of the Nation," *New York Times,* 11 March 1991, pp. 1, 12. See also Steven A. Holmes, "Census Sees a Profound Ethnic Shift in U.S.," *New York Times,* 14 March 1996, p. A8.

15. Glazer, "Structure of Ethnicity," p. 5.

16. National Election Study for 1994, an election survey conducted by the Center for Political Studies at the University of Michigan.

17. See David C. Leege and Lyman A. Kellstedt, eds., *Rediscovering the Religious Factor in American Politics* (Armonk, N.Y.: Sharpe, 1993), for a comprehensive examination of religion in political life that goes far beyond the analysis here.

18. John Robinson, "The Ups and Downs and Ins and Outs of Ideology," *Public Opinion* 7 (February/March 1984), p. 12.

19. For a more positive interpretation of ideological attitudes within the public, see William G. Jacoby, "The Structure of Ideological Thinking in the American Electorate," paper presented at the Annual Meeting of the American Political Science Association, Washington, D.C., September 1993. Jacoby applies a new method to survey data for the 1984 and 1988 elections and concludes "that there is a systematic, cumulative structure underlying liberal-conservative thinking in the American public" (p. 1).

20. Angus Campbell, Philip E. Converse, Warren E. Miller, and Donald E. Stokes, *The American Voter* (New York: Wiley, 1960), Chap. 10.

21. See Norman H. Nie, Sidney Verba, and John R. Petrocik, *The Changing American Voter,* 2d ed. (Cambridge, Mass.: Harvard University Press, 1979), Chap. 7.

22. Some scholars believe that the methods previously used for classifying respondents as ideologues were too generous. See Robert C. Luskin, "Measuring Political Sophistication," *American Journal of Political Science* 31 (November 1987), pp. 878, 887–888. For a comprehensive critique, see Eric R. A. N. Smith, *The Unchanging American Voter* (Berkeley: University of California Press, 1989), especially Chap. 1.

23. A relationship between liberalism and political tolerance was found by John L. Sullivan et al., "The Sources of Political Tolerance: A Multivariate Analysis," *American Political Science Review* 75 (March 1981), p. 102. See also Robinson, "Ups and Downs," pp. 13–15.

24. Herbert Asher, *Presidential Elections and American Politics* (Homewood, Ill.: Dorsey, 1980), pp. 14–20. Asher also constructs a two-dimensional framework, distinguishing between "traditional New Deal" issues and "new lifestyle" issues.

25. John E. Jackson, "The Systematic Beliefs of the Mass Public: Estimating Policy Preferences with Survey Data," *Journal of Politics* 45 (November 1983), pp. 840–865.

26. Milton Rokeach also proposed a two-dimensional model of political ideology grounded in the terminal values of freedom and equality. See *The Nature of Human Values* (New York: Free Press, 1973), especially Chap. 6. Rokeach found that positive and negative references to the two values permeate the writings of socialists, communists, fascists, and conservatives and clearly differentiate the four bodies of writing from one another (pp. 173–174). However, Rokeach built his two-dimensional model around only the values of freedom and equality; he did not deal with the question of freedom versus order.

27. In our framework, opposition to abortion is classified as a communitarian position. However, the Communitarian movement led by Amitai Etzioni adopted no position on abortion. (Personal communication from Vanessa Hoffman by e-mail, in reply to my query of 5 February 1996.)

28. But a significant literature is developing on the limitations of self-interest in explaining political life. See Jane J. Mansbridge, ed., *Beyond Self-interest* (Chicago: University of Chicago Press, 1990).

29. Aaron Wildavsky, "Choosing Preferences by Constructing Institutions: A Cultural Theory of Preference Formation," *American Political Science Review* 81 (March 1987), pp. 3–21.

30. David O. Sears and Carolyn L. Funk, "Self-interest in Americans' Political Opinions," in Mansbridge, *Beyond Self-interest,* pp. 147–170.

31. Two researchers who compared the public's knowledge on various topics in 1989 with its knowledge of the same topics in the 1940s and 1950s found similar levels of knowledge across the years. They point out, however, "that knowledge has been stable during a period of rapid changes in education, communication, and the public role of women seems paradoxical." They suspect, but cannot demonstrate, that the expected increase in knowledge did not materialize because of a decline in the public's interest in politics over time. See Michael X. Delli Carpini and Scott Keeter, "Stability and Change in the U.S. Public's Knowledge of Politics," *Public Opinion Quarterly* 55 (Winter 1991), p. 607.

32. Michael X. Delli Carpini and Scott Keeter, *What Americans Know About Politics and Why It Matters* (New Haven, Conn.: Yale University Press, 1996).

33. Ibid., p. 269.

34. There is evidence that the educational system and parental practices hamper the ability of women to develop their political knowledge. See Linda L. M. Bennett and Stephen Earl Bennett, "Enduring Gender Differences in Political Interests," *American Politics Quarterly* 17 (January 1989), pp. 105–122.

35. W. Russell Neuman, *The Paradox of Mass Politics: Knowledge and Opinion in the American Electorate* (Cambridge, Mass.: Harvard University Press, 1986), p. 81.

36. Pamela Johnston Conover and Stanley Feldman, "How People Organize the Political World: A Schematic Model," *American Journal of Political Science* 28 (February 1984), p. 96. For an excellent review of schema structures in contemporary psychology—especially

as they relate to political science—see Reid Hastie, "A Primer of Information-Processing Theory for the Political Scientist," in *Political Cognition,* ed. Richard R. Lau and David O. Sears (Hillsdale, N.J.: Erlbaum, 1986), pp. 11–39.

37. John Hurwitz and Mark Peffley, "How Are Foreign Policy Attitudes Structured? A Hierarchical Model," *American Political Science Review* 81 (December 1987), pp. 1099–1220.

38. See Milton Lodge and Ruth Hamill, "A Partisan Schema for Political Information Processing," *American Political Science Review* 80 (June 1986), pp. 505–519.

39. Arthur Sanders, *Making Sense Out of Politics* (Ames: Iowa State University Press, 1990).

40. Lee Sigelman, "Disarming the Opposition: The President, the Public, and the INF Treaty," *Public Opinion Quarterly* 54 (Spring 1990), p. 46.

41. Benjamin I. Page, Robert Y. Shapiro, and Glenn R. Dempsey, "What Moves Public Opinion?," *American Political Science Review* 81 (March 1987), pp. 23–43.

42. Michael Margolis and Gary A. Mauser, *Manipulating Public Opinion: Essays on Public Opinion as a Dependent Variable* (Pacific Grove, Calif.: Brooks/Cole, 1989).

43. Daily fax assaults against the Clinton campaign in the 1992 election season are discussed in Jacob Weisberg, "True Fax: Mary Matalin, Vindicated," *New Republic,* 5 June 1993, pp. 11–12.

44. Robin Wright, "Hyper Democracy: Washington Isn't Dangerously Disconnected from the People; the Trouble May Be It's Too Plugged In," *Time,* 23 January 1995, pp. 14–31.

45. Rich Lowry, "Fax Populi: Armed with Computers and Fax Machines, Grass-Roots Organizations Are Shaking Up the Liberal Establishment," *National Review,* 7 November 1994, pp. 50–54. *Fax Congress Now* is a computer program designed to facilitate faxing government officials; see *Macworld,* May 1995, p. 48. The percentage of homes with fax machines comes from

Steve Lohr, "The Great Unplugged Masses Confront the Future," *New York Times,* 21 January 1996, sec. 4, p. 1.

46. Bill Mann, *Politics on the Net* (Indianapolis, Ind.: Que Corporation, 1995).

47. Pew Research Center for the People and the Press, "TV News Viewership Declines," press release, 13 May 1996. National survey of 1,751 adults during 19–25 April 1996.

48. Doris A. Graber, *Mass Media and American Politics* (Washington, D.C.: Congressional Quarterly Press, 1984), pp. 78–79. See also W. Lance Bennett, *News: The Politics of Illusion,* 3d ed. (White Plains, N.Y.: Longman, 1996), Chap. 2.

49. Steven Lipin and Elizabeth Jensen, "Westinghouse, Infinity Deal Sets Stage for Other Radio Groups Seeking Mergers," *Wall Street Journal,* 21 June 1996, p. A3.

50. S. Robert Lichter and Richard E. Noyes, *Good Intentions Make Bad News* (Lanham, Md.: Rowman & Littlefield, 1995), p. 26 n. 9.

51. Michael Nelson (ed.), *Guide to the Presidency* (Washington, D.C.: Congressional Quarterly Press, 1989), p. 729.

52. Graber, *Mass Media,* p. 241.

53. "America's Watching: Public Attitudes Toward Television," pamphlet published in New York by the Network Television Association and the National Association of Broadcasters, 1995, pp. 17–18.

54. Pew Research Center for the People and the Press, "TV News Viewership Declines," press release, 13 May 1996, p. 1.

55. Times-Mirror Center for the People and the Press, "The American Media," 15 July 1990.

56. This fits with findings by Stephen Earl Bennett in "Trends in Americans' Political Information, 1967–1987," *American Politics Quarterly* 17 (October 1989), pp. 422–435. Bennett found that race was significantly related to level of political information in a 1967 survey but not in a 1987 survey.

57. Times-Mirror Center for the People and the Press, press release, "The Generations Divide," 8 July 1992, p. 80.

58. One seasoned journalist argues instead that the technology of minicams and satellites has set back the quality of news coverage. Now a television crew can fly to the scene of a crisis and immediately televise information without knowing much about the local politics or culture, which was not true of the old foreign correspondents. See David R. Gergen, "Diplomacy in a Television Age: The Dangers of Teledemocracy," in *The Media and Foreign Policy,* ed. Simon Serfaty (New York: St. Martin's Press, 1990), p. 51.

59. Bennett, "Trends in Americans' Political Information." Bennett's findings are supported by a national poll in 1990 that found only 40 percent of the sample had read a newspaper "yesterday," compared with 71 percent in 1965. Times-Mirror Center for the People and the Press, "The American Media," p. 100. Two researchers who compared the public's level of knowledge in 1989 with answers to the same questions in the 1940s and 1950s found similar levels of knowledge across the years but added, "that knowledge has been stable during a period of rapid changes in education, communication, and the public role of women seems paradoxical." They suspect, but cannot demonstrate, that the lack of expected increase is because of a decline in political interest over time. See Michael X. Delli Carpini and Scott Keeter, "Stability and Change in the U.S. Public's Knowledge of Politics," *Public Opinion Quarterly* 55 (Winter 1991), pp. 583-612.

60. The Times-Mirror Center for the People and the Press, Report dated 13 January 1993.

61. W. Russell Neuman, Marion R. Just, and Ann N. Crigler, *Common Knowledge: News and the Construction of Political Meaning* (Chicago: University of Chicago Press, 1992), p. 10.

62. Neuman, Just, and Crigler, *News and the Construction of Political Meaning,* p. 113.

63. Laurence Parisot, "Attitudes About the Media: A Five-Country Comparison," *Public Opinion* 10 (January/February 1988), p. 60.

64. The statistical difficulties in determining media effects owing to measurement error are discussed in Larry M. Bartels, "Messages Received: The Political Impact of Media Exposure," paper prepared for delivery at the annual meeting of the American Political Science Association, Washington, D.C., September 1993. According to Bartels, "More direct and convincing demonstrations of significant opinion changes due to media exposure will require data collections spanning considerably longer periods of time" (p. 27).

65. A poll of 357 viewers reported in *USA Today,* 10 November 1993.

66. Benjamin I. Page, Robert Y. Shapiro, and Glenn R. Dempsey, "What Moves Public Opinion?" *American Political Science Review* 81 (March 1987), p. 31.

67. Shanto Iyengar and Donald R. Kinder, *News That Matters: Television and American Opinion* (Chicago: University of Chicago Press, 1987), p. 33.

68. Ibid., p. 60.

69. W. Russell Neuman, "The Threshold of Public Attention," *Public Opinion Quarterly* 54 (Summer 1990), pp. 159–176.

70. Robert Entman, *Democracy Without Citizens: Media and the Decay of American Politics* (New York: Oxford University Press, 1989), p. 86.

71. A panel study of ten- to seventeen-year-olds during the 1988 presidential campaign found that the campaign helped these young people crystallize their party identifications and their attitudes toward the candidates but had little effect on their political ideology and views on central campaign issues. See David O. Sears, Nicholas A. Valentino, and Rick Kosterman, "Domain Specificity in the Effects of Political Events on Preadult Socialization," paper prepared for delivery at the annual meeting of the American Political Science Association, Washington, D.C., September 1993.

72. John J. O'Connor, "Soothing Bromides? Not on TV," *New York Times,* 28 October 1990, Arts & Leisure section, pp. 1, 35.

73. James Fallows, *Breaking the News: How the Media Undermine American Democracy* (New York: Pantheon Books, 1996).

74. For analysis of elections from 1964 to 1976, see S. Robert Lichter and Stanley Rothman, "Media and Business Elites," *Public Opinion* 5 (October/November 1981), pp. 42–46. For a study of the 1980 election, see L. Brent Bozell II and Brent H. Baker (eds.), *And That's the Way It Isn't* (Alexandria, Va.: Media Research Center, 1990), p. 32.

75. "Journalism Heavy with Democrats," *Chicago Tribune,* 18 November 1992, section 1, p. 14.

76. Elizabeth Kolbert, "For Bush, More TV News Is Also Good News," *New York Times,* 22 September 1992, p. 1.

77. Elizabeth Kolbert, "Maybe the Media DID Treat Bush a Bit Harshly," *New York Times,* 22 November 1992, p. 3E.

78. *The People, The Press, and Their Leaders* (Washington, D.C.: Times-Mirror Center for the People and the Press, 1995).

79. Michael Robinson and Margaret Sheehan, *Over the Wire and on TV: CBS and UPI in Campaign '80* (New York: Russell Sage Foundation, 1983).

80. Michael J. Robinson, "The Media in Campaign '84: Part II; Wingless, Toothless, and Hopeless," *Public Opinion* 8 (February/March 1985), p. 48.

81. Maura Clancey and Michael J. Robinson, "General Election Coverage: Part I," *Public Opinion* 7 (December/January 1985), p. 54.

82. Schneider and Lewis, "Views on the News," p. 11. For similar findings from a 1994 study, see Times-Mirror Center for the People and the Press, "Mixed Message About Press Freedom on Both Sides of the Atlantic," press release of 16 March 1994, p. 65. See also Patterson, "News Decisions," p. 21.

83. "Seven Arrested for Lying About Objects in Pepsi's," *Chicago Tribune,* 18 June 1993, p. 3; and Charles M.

Madigan, "Canned Hoax: The Media and the Pepsi Scare," *Chicago Tribune*, 20 June 1993, sec. 4, p. 1.

Chapter 5 / Participation and Voting pp. 112–137

1. V. Dion Haynes, "'Normal' Folks Held in Arizona Militia Plot," *Chicago Tribune*, 4 July 1996, p. 1.

2. Patricia King, "'Vipers' in the 'Burbs," *Newsweek*, 15 July 1996, p. 23.

3. Haynes, p. 1.

4. This information is taken from the Link section of "The Militia Watchdog" at <www.greyware.com/authors/pitman/militia.htm>, updated June 16, 1996.

5. Cited in "Minuteman Press Online," obtained at <www.afn.org/~mpress/page1.html> on July 6, 1996. The "Restoring America" militia site can be found at <www.techmgmt.com/restore/restore.html>.

6. Lester W. Milbrath and M. L. Goel, *Political Participation* (Chicago: Rand McNally, 1977), p. 2.

7. See Sidney Verba, Kay Lehman Scholzman, and Henry E. Brady, *Voice and Equality: Civic Voluntarism in American Politics* (Cambridge, Mass.: Harvard University Press, 1995), pp. 40–42. In a highly publicized article, Robert D. Putnam argued that participation in politics in the United States has suffered because our nation is losing the "social capital" that is based on active participation in community life. For example, Americans are "bowling alone"–that is, they are still bowling, but not in organized leagues. See his "Bowling Alone: America's Declining Social Capital," *Journal of Democracy* 6 (January 1995), pp. 65–78. Putnam's analysis inspired related critical observations on contemporary society, but it also sparked criticism of his data and his argument. For an empirical rebuttal, see Everett C. Ladd, "The Data Just Don't Show Erosion of America's 'Social Capital,'" *Public Perspective* 7 (June–July 1996), pp. 1, 5–22.

8. Michael Lipsky, "Protest as a Political Resource," *American Political Science Review* 62 (December 1968), p. 1145.

9. William E. Schmidt, "Selma Marchers Mark 1965 Clash," *New York Times,* 4 March 1985.

10. See Sidney Verba and Norman H. Nie, *Participation in America: Political Democracy and Social Equality* (New York: Harper & Row, 1972), p. 3.

11. Russell J. Dalton, *Citizen Politics*, 2d ed. (Chatham, N.J.: Chatham House, 1996).

12. Stephen C. Craig and Michael A. Magiotto, "Political Discontent and Political Action," *Journal of Politics* 43 (May 1981), pp. 514–522. But see Mitchell A. Seligson, "Trust Efficacy and Modes of Political Participation: A Study of Costa Rican Peasants," *British Journal of Political Science* 10 (January 1980), pp. 75–98, for a review of studies that came to different conclusions.

13. Philip H. Pollock III, "Organizations as Agents of Mobilization: How Does Group Activity Affect Political Participation?" *American Journal of Political Science* 26 (August 1982), pp. 485–503. Also see Jan E. Leighley, "Social Interaction and Contextual Influence on Political Participation," *American Politics Quarterly* 18 (October 1990), pp. 459–475.

14. Arthur H. Miller et al., "Group Consciousness and Political Participation," *American Journal of Political Science* 25 (August 1981), p. 495. See also Susan J. Carroll, "Gender Politics and the Socializing Impact of the Women's Movement," in *Political Learning in Adulthood: A Sourcebook of Theory and Research*, ed. Roberta S. Sigel (Chicago: University of Chicago Press, 1989), p. 307.

15. Dalton, *Citizen Politics*, p. 65.

16. M. Kent Jennings, Jan W. van Deth, et al., *Continuities in Political Action: A Longitudinal Study of Political Orientations in Three Western Democracies* (New York: Walter de Gruyter, 1990).

17. See James L. Gibson, "The Policy Consequences of Political Intolerance: Political Repression During the

Vietnam War Era," *Journal of Politics* 51 (February 1989), pp. 13–35. Gibson found that individual state legislatures reacted quite differently in response to antiwar demonstrations on college campuses, but the laws passed to discourage dissent were not related directly to public opinion within the state.

18. See Verba and Nie, *Participation in America,* p. 69. See also John Clayton Thomas, "Citizen-Initiated Contacts with Government Agencies: A Test of Three Theories," *American Journal of Political Science* 26 (August 1982), pp. 504–522; and Elaine B. Sharp, "Citizen-Initiated Contacting of Government Officials and Socioeconomic Status: Determining the Relationship and Accounting for It," *American Political Science Review* 76 (March 1982), pp. 109–115.

19. Elaine B. Sharp, "Citizen Demand Making in the Urban Context," *American Journal of Political Science* 28 (November 1984), pp. 654–670, especially pp. 654 and 665.

20. Verba and Nie, *Participation in America,* p. 67; and Sharp, "Citizen Demand Making," p. 660.

21. See Joel B. Grossman et al., "Dimensions of Institutional Participation: Who Uses the Courts and How?," *Journal of Politics* 44 (February 1982), pp. 86–114; and Frances Kahn Zemans, "Legal Mobilization: The Neglected Role of the Law in the Political System," *American Political Science Review* 77 (September 1983), pp. 690–703.

22. *Brown v. Board of Education,* 347 U.S. 483 (1954).

23. Max Kaase and Alan Marsh, "Political Action: A Theoretical Perspective," in *Political Action: Mass Participation in Five Western Democracies,* ed. Samuel H. Barnes and Max Kaase (Beverly Hills, Calif.: Sage, 1979), p. 168.

24. *Smith v. Allwright,* 321 U.S. 649 (1944).

25. *Harper v. Virginia State Board of Elections,* 383 U.S. 663 (1966).

26. Everett Carll Ladd, *The American Polity* (New York: Norton, 1985), p. 392.

27. Ivor Crewe, "Electoral Participation,"

in *Democracy at the Polls: A Comparative Study of Competitive National Elections,* ed. David Butler, Howard R. Penniman, and Austin Ranney (Washington, D.C.: American Enterprise Institute, 1981), pp. 219–223.

28. David B. Magleby, *Direct Legislation: Voting on Ballot Propositions in the United States* (Baltimore: Johns Hopkins University Press, 1984), p. 70.

29. Thomas E. Cronin, *Direct Democracy: The Politics of Initiative, Referendum, and Recall* (Cambridge, Mass.: Harvard University Press, 1989), p 197. David B. Magleby, "Direct Legislation in the American States," in *Referendums around the World,* ed. David Butler and Austin Ranney (Washington, D.C.: American Enterprise Press, 1994), p. 232.

30. Magleby, *Direct Legislation,* p. 59. See also Ernest Tollerson, "In 90's Ritual, Hired Hands Carry Democracy's Petitions," *New York Times,* 9 July 1996, p. 1.

31. Cronin, *Direct Democracy,* p. x.

32. Cronin, *Direct Democracy,* p. 251.

33. *The Book of the States 1996–97,* vol. 28 (Lexington, Ky.: Council of State Governments, 1996), p. 150.

34. *Chicago Tribune,* 10 March 1985.

35. Crewe, "Electoral Participation," p. 232. Several scholars have successfully explained variations in voting turnout across nations with only a few institutional and contextual variables. (See G. Bingham Powell, Jr., "American Voter Turnout in Comparative Perspective," *American Political Science Review* 80 (March 1986), pp. 17–43; and Robert W. Jackman, "Political Institutions and Voter Turnout in the Industrial Democracies," *American Political Science Review* 81 (June 1987), pp. 405–423.) However, this work has been criticized on methodological grounds and also for failing to successfully explain two deviant cases, the United States and Switzerland, both of which have low voter turnout. (See Wolfgang Hirczy, "Comparative Turnout: Beyond Cross-National Regression Models," paper prepared for presentation at the an-

nual meeting of the American Political Science Association, Chicago, September 1992.)

36. Verba and Nie, *Participation in America,* p. 13.

37. Max Kaase and Alan Marsh, "Distribution of Political Action," in *Political Action,* p. 186; Dalton, *Citizen Politics,* p. 80.

38. Milbrath and Goel, *Political Participation,* pp. 95–96; Dalton, *Citizen Politics,* p. 80.

39. Verba and Nie, *Participation in America,* p. 148. For a concise summary of the effect of age on voting turnout, see Michael M. Gant and Norman R. Luttbeg, *American Electoral Behavior* (Itasca, Ill.: Peacock, 1991), pp. 103–104.

40. Richard Murray and Arnold Vedlitz, "Race, Socioeconomic Status, and Voting Participation in Large Southern Cities," *Journal of Politics* 39 (November 1977), pp. 1064–1072; and Verba and Nie, *Participation in America,* p. 157. See also Bobo and Gilliam, "Race, Sociopolitical Participation, and Black Empowerment." Their study of 1987 national survey data with a black oversample found that African Americans participated more than whites of comparable socioeconomic status in cities in which the mayor's office was held by an African American.

41. William H. Flanigan and Nancy H. Zingale, *Political Behavior of the American Electorate,* 8th ed. (Washington, D.C.: Congressional Quarterly Press, 1994), pp. 41–43.

42. Ronald B. Rapoport, "The Sex Gap in Political Persuading: Where the 'Structuring Principle' Works," *American Journal of Political Science* 25 (February 1981), pp. 32–48.

43. Bruce C. Straits, "The Social Context of Voter Turnout," *Public Opinion Quarterly* 54 (Spring 1990), pp. 64–73.

44. See Sidney Verba, Kay Lehman Scholzman, and Henry E. Brady, *Voice and Equality: Civic Voluntarism in American Politics* (Cambridge, Mass.: Harvard University Press, 1995), p. 433.

45. Stephen D. Shaffer, "A Multivariate Explanation of Decreasing Turnout in Presidential Elections, 1960–1976," *American Journal of Political Science* 25 (February 1981), pp. 68–95; and Paul R. Abramson and John H. Aldrich, "The Decline of Electoral Participation in America," *American Political Science Review* 76 (September 1981), pp. 603–620. However, one scholar argues that this research suffers because it looks only at voters and nonvoters in a single election. When the focus shifts to people who vote sometimes but not at other times, the models do not fit so well. See M. Margaret Conway and John E. Hughes, "Political Mobilization and Patterns of Voter Turnout," paper prepared for delivery at the annual meeting of the American Political Science Association, Washington, D.C., September 1993.

46. Apparently, Richard A. Brody was the first scholar to pose this problem as a puzzle. See his "The Puzzle of Political Participation in America," in *The New American Political System,* ed. Anthony King (Washington, D.C.: American Enterprise Institute, 1978), pp. 287–324. Since then, a sizable literature has attempted to explain the decline in voter turnout in the United States. Some authors have claimed to account for the decline with just a few variables, but their work has been criticized for being too simplistic. See Carol A. Cassel and Robert C. Luskin, "Simple Explanations of Turnout Decline," *American Political Science Review* 82 (December 1988), pp. 1321–1330. They contend that most of the post-1960 decline is still unexplained. If it is any comfort, voter turnout in Western European elections has seen a somewhat milder decline, and scholars have not been very successful at explaining it, either. See Richard S. Flickinger and Donley T. Studlar, "The Disappearing Voters? Exploring Declining Turnout in Western European Elections," *West European Politics* 15 (April 1992), pp. 1–16.

47. Abramson and Aldrich, "Decline of Electoral Participation," p. 519; and Shaffer, "Multivariate Explanation," pp. 78, 90.

48. The negative effect of registration laws on voter turnout is argued in Frances

Fox Piven and Richard Cloward, "Government Statistics and Conflicting Explanations of Nonvoting," *PS: Political Science and Politics* 22 (September 1989), pp. 580–588. Their analysis was hotly contested in Stephen Earl Bennett, "The Uses and Abuses of Registration and Turnout Data: An Analysis of Piven and Cloward's Studies of Nonvoting in America," *PS: Political Science and Politics* 23 (June 1990), pp. 166–171. Bennett showed that turnout declined 10 to 13 percent after 1960, despite efforts to remove or lower legal hurdles to registration. For their reply, see Frances Fox Piven and Richard Cloward, "A Reply to Bennett," *PS: Political Science and Politics* 23 (June 1990), pp. 172–173. You can see that reasonable people can disagree on this matter.

49. David Glass, Peverill Squire, and Raymond Wolfinger, "Voter Turnout: An International Comparison," *Public Opinion* 6 (December/January 1984), p. 52. Wolfinger says that because of the strong effect of registration on turnout, most rational choice analyses of voting would be better suited to analyzing turnout of only registered voters. See Raymond E. Wolfinger, "The Rational Citizen Faces Election Day," *Public Affairs Report* 6 (November 1992), p. 12.

50. Data from a League of Women Voters Study published on the NBC News Web site at <www.decision96>.msn.com/vote/motor.htm> and dated 16 May 96.

51. "Motor Voters Didn't Vote, Study Finds," *Los Angeles Times,* 21 June 1997, p. A18.

52. Recent research finds that "party contact is clearly a statistically and substantively important factor in predicting and explaining political behavior." See Peter W. Wielhouwer and Brad Lockerbie, "Party Contacting and Political Participation, 1952–1990," paper prepared for delivery at the annual meeting of the American Political Science Association, Chicago, 1992, p. 14. Of course, parties strategically target the groups that they want to see vote in elections. See Peter W.

Wielhouwer, "Strategic Canvassing by Political Parties, 1952–1990," *American Review of Politics* 16 (Fall 1995), pp. 213–238.

53. See Charles Krauthammer, "In Praise of Low Voter Turnout," *Time,* 21 May 1990, p. 88. Krauthammer says, "Low voter turnout means that people see politics as quite marginal to their lives, as neither salvation nor ruin. . . . Low voter turnout is a leading indicator of contentment." A major study in 1996 that compared 1,000 likely *non*-voters with 2,300 likely voters found that 24 percent of the non-voters said they "hardly ever" followed public affairs, versus 5 percent of likely voters. See Dwight Morris, "No-Show '96: Americans Who Don't Vote," Summary Report to the Medill News Service and WTTW Television, Northwestern University School of Journalism, 1996.

54. Crewe, "Electoral Participation," p. 262.

55. Samuel H. Barnes and Max Kaase, *Political Action,* p. 532.

56. *1971 Congressional Quarterly Almanac* (Washington, D.C.: Congressional Quarterly Press, 1972), p. 475.

57. Benjamin Ginsberg, *The Consequences of Consent: Elections, Citizen Control, and Popular Acquiescence* (Reading, Mass.: Addison-Wesley, 1982), pp. 13–14.

58. Ginsberg, *Consequences of Consent,* pp. 6–7.

59. Some people have argued that the decline in voter turnout during the 1980s served to increase the class bias in the electorate, because people of lower socioeconomic status stayed home. But recent research has concluded that "class bias has not increased since 1964" (p. 734, Jan E. Leighley and Jonathan Nagler, "Socioeconomic Class Bias in Turnout, 1964–1988: The Voters Remain the Same," *American Political Science Review* 86 [September 1992], pp. 725–736). Nevertheless, Rosenstone and Hansen say, "the economic inequalities in political participation that prevail in the United States today are as large as the racial disparities in political participation that prevailed in the 1950s.

America's leaders today face few incentives to attend to the needs of the disadvantaged," in *Mobilization, Participation, and Democracy in America,* p. 248

Chapter 6 / Political Parties, Campaigns, and Elections pp. 138–173

1. "Voter Anxiety Dividing GOP; Energized Democrats Backing Clinton," news release, 14 November 1995 (Washington, D.C.: Times-Mirror Center for the People and the Press), p. 101; and "Democratic Congressional Prospects Improve," news release, 5 April 1996 (Washington, D.C.: Pew Research Center for the People and the Press), p. 32.

2. Center for Political Studies of the Institute for Social Research, *American National Election Study 1992* (Ann Arbor: University of Michigan, 1993), p. 997.

3. David W. Moore, "Perot Supporters: For the Man, Not a Third Party," *Gallup Organization Newsletter Archive* 60, 17 August 1995; the Gallup Organization's Web page at <www.gallup.com/newsletter/aug95/>.

4. See Jerome M. Clubb, William H. Flanigan, and Nancy H. Zingale, *Partisan Realignment: Voters, Parties, and Government in American History,* vol. 108 (Beverly Hills, Calif.: Sage, 1980), p. 163.

5. See Gerald M. Pomper, "Classification of Presidential Elections," *Journal of Politics* 29 (August 1967), pp. 535–566.

6. The discussion that follows draws heavily on Austin Ranney and Willmoore Kendall, *Democracy and the American Party System* (New York: Harcourt, Brace, 1956), Chaps. 18 and 19.

7. See Steven J. Rosenstone, Roy L. Behr, and Edward H. Lazarus, *Third Parties in America: Citizen Response to Major Party Failure* (Princeton, N.J.: Princeton University Press, 1984), pp. 5–6.

8. Of these topics, reducing the deficit seems to be the most popular with American voters (although it attracts the attention of only about 50 percent of the electorate). See David W. Moore and Lydia Saad, "Americans Still Favor Independent and Third-party Candidates," *Gallup Organization Newsletter Archive* 60, 7 July 1995; see also the Gallup Organization's Web page at <www.gallup.com/newsletter/july 95/>.

9. Perot activists were mainly well-off, highly educated white males, mostly self-styled independents. See Randall W. Partin, Lori M. Weber, Ronald B. Rapoport, and Walter J. Stone, "Sources of Activism in the 1992 Perot Campaign," in *The State of the Parties,* ed. Daniel M. Shea and John C. Green (Lanham, Md.: Rowman and Littlefield, 1994), pp. 147–162.

10. Rosenstone, Behr, and Lazarus, *Third Parties in America,* p. 8.

11. See James Gimpel, *National Elections and the Autonomy of American State Party Systems* (Pittsburgh, Pa.: University of Pittsburgh Press, 1996).

12. Measuring the concept of party identification has had its problems. For recent insights into the issues, see R. Michael Alvarez, "The Puzzle of Party Identification," *American Politics Quarterly* 18 (October 1990), pp. 476–491; and Donald Philip Green and Bradley Palmquist, "Of Artifacts and Partisan Instability," *American Journal of Political Science* 34 (August 1990), pp. 872–902.

13. Rhodes Cook, "GOP Shows Dramatic Growth, Especially in the South," *Congressional Quarterly Weekly Report,* 13 January 1996, pp. 97–100.

14. There is some dispute over how stable party identification really is, when the same respondents are asked about their party identification over a period of several months during an election campaign. The research literature is reviewed in Brad Lockerbie, "Change in Party Identification: The Role of Prospective Economic Evaluations," *American Politics Quarterly* 17 (July 1989), pp. 291–311. Lockerbie argues that respondents change their party identification according to whether they think a party will help them per-

sonally in the future. But also see Green and Palmquist, "Of Artifacts and Partisan Instability."

15. Bill Keller, "As Arms Buildup Eases, U.S. Tries to Take Stock," *New York Times,* 14 May 1985; Ed Gillespie and Bob Schellhas, *Contract with America* (New York: Times Books, 1994), p. 107.

16. The Republican data came from "Delegates, Party Voters Sometimes at Odds," *Washington Post National Weekly Edition,* 12–18 August 1996, p. A8; the Democratic data were provided by Mario Brossard of the *Washington Post* via e-mail on 21 August 1996. The *Post* surveyed 505 Republican and 508 Democratic delegates. Data for registered voters came from a national survey of approximately 1,500 respondents.

17. See, for example, Gerald M. Pomper, *Elections in America* (New York: Dodd, Mead, 1968); Benjamin Ginsberg, "Election and Public Policy," *American Political Science Review* 70 (March 1976), pp. 41–50; and Jeff Fishel, *Presidents and Promises* (Washington, D.C.: Congressional Quarterly Press, 1985).

18. Robert Harmel and Kenneth Janda, *Parties and Their Environments: Limits to Reform?* (New York: Longman, 1982), pp. 27–29. See also John Huber and Ronald Inglehart, "Expert Interpretations of Party Space and Party Locations in 42 Societies," *Party Politics* 1 (January 1995), pp. 73–111; and Alan Ware, *Political Parties and Party Systems* (New York: Oxford University Press, 1996), Chap. 1.

19. Personal communication with DNC and RNC staff, 24 January 1994, and information updated from the national committees' home pages on the Web (see World Wide Web Resources for this chapter).

20. See Ralph M. Goldman, *The National Party Chairmen and Committees: Factionalism at the Top* (Armonk, N.Y.: Sharpe, 1990). The subtitle is revealing.

21. William Crotty and John S. Jackson III, *Presidential Primaries and Nominations* (Washington, D.C.: Congressional Quarterly Press, 1985), p. 33.

22. Phillip A. Klinkner, "Party Culture and Party Behavior," in Shea and Green, *The State of the Parties,* pp. 275–287; and Philip A. Klinkner, *The Losing Parties: Out-Party National Committees, 1956–1993* (New Haven: Yale University Press, 1994).

23. The Federal Election Commission, "FEC Releases Eighteen-Month Report on Political Party Finances," press release of 7 August 1996, p. 1.

24. John Frendreis, Alan R. Gitelson, Gregory Flemming, and Anne Layzell, "Local Political Parties and Legislative Races in 1992," in Shea and Green, *The State of the Parties,* p. 139.

25. Robert Biersack, "Hard Facts and Soft Money: State Party Finance in the 1992 Federal Elections," in Shea and Green, *The State of the Parties,* p. 114.

26. Martin P. Wattenberg, *The Decline of American Political Parties, 1952–1994* (Cambridge, Mass.: Harvard University Press, 1996).

27. In 1996, the Democratic National Committee mounted an unprecedented drive to organize up to sixty thousand precinct captains in twenty states, while the new Republican candidate for U.S. Senator from Illinois, Al Salvi, fired his own campaign manager and replaced him with someone from the National Republican Senatorial Campaign Committee. See Sue Ellen Christian, "Democrats Will Focus on Precincts," *Chicago Tribune,* 29 June 1996, p. 5; and Michael Dizon, "Salvi Fires Top Senate Race Aides," *Chicago Tribune,* 24 May 1996, Section 2, p. 3.

28. Barbara Sinclair, "The Congressional Party: Evolving Organizational, Agenda-Setting, and Policy Roles," in *Parties Respond,* p. 227.

29. The model is articulated most clearly in a report by the American Political Science Association, "Toward a More Responsible Two-Party System," *American Political Science Review* 44 (September 1950), Part II. See also Gerald M. Pomper, "Toward a More Responsible Party System? What, Again?," *Journal of Politics* 33 (November 1971), pp. 916–940. See also the seven essays in the symposium,

"Divided Government and the Politics of Constitutional Reform," *PS: Political Science & Politics,* 24 (December 1991), pp. 634–657.

30. This is essentially the framework for studying campaigns set forth in Barbara G. Salmore and Stephen A. Salmore, *Candidates, Parties, and Campaigns: Electoral Politics in America,* 2d ed. (Washington, D.C.: Congressional Quarterly Press, 1989).

31. Martin P. Wattenberg, *The Rise of Candidate-Centered Politics: Presidential Elections of the 1980s* (Cambridge, Mass.: Harvard University Press, 1991).

32. Michael Gallagher, "Conclusion," in *Candidate Selection in Comparative Perspective: The Secret Garden of Politics,* ed. Michael Gallagher and Michael Marsh (London: Sage, 1988), p. 238.

33. *The Book of the States,* 1996–97, vol. 31 (Lexington, Ky.: Council of State Governments, 1996), pp. 157–158.

34. Rhodes Cook, "Earlier Voting in 1996 Forecasts Fast and Furious Campaigns," *Congressional Quarterly Weekly Report,* 19 August 1995, p. 2485.

35. Ibid., pp. 2485–2487. For a description of how caucuses operate and how differently they work in the two parties, see William G. Mayer, "Caucuses: How They Work, What Difference They Make," in Mayer, *In Pursuit of the White House,* pp. 105–157.

36. Gary R. Orren and Nelson W. Polsby (eds.), *Media and Momentum: The New Hampshire Primary and Nomination Politics* (Chatham, N.J.: Chatham House, 1987), p. 23.

37. See James R. Beniger, "Winning the Presidential Nomination: National Polls and State Primary Elections, 1936–1972," *Public Opinion Quarterly* 40 (Spring 1976), pp. 22–38.

38. Michael Nelson (ed.), *Congressional Quarterly Guide to the Presidency* (Washington, D.C.: Congressional Quarterly Press, 1989), p. 1427. You can find the other exceptions there, too.

39. Harold W. Stanley and Richard G. Niemi, *Vital Statistics on American Politics,* 2d ed. (Washington, D.C.: Congressional Quarterly Press, 1990),

p. 132; and the 1992 National Election Study, Center for Political Studies, University of Michigan.

40. Rhodes Cook, "House Republicans Scored a Quiet Victory in '92," *Congressional Quarterly Weekly Report,* 17 April 1993, p. 966.

41. Quoted in E. J. Dionne, Jr., "On the Trail of Corporation Donations," *New York Times,* 6 October 1980.

42. Salmore and Salmore, *Candidates, Parties, and Campaigns,* p. 11. See also David Himes, "Strategy and Tactics for Campaign Fund-Raising," in *Campaigns and Elections: American Style,* ed. James A. Thurber and Candice J. Nelson (Boulder, Colo.: Westview Press, 1995), pp. 62–77.

43. "FEC Announces 1996 Presidential Spending Limits," Federal Election Commission press release of 15 March 1996.

44. Paul S. Herrnson, "Party Strategies and Campaign Activities in the 1992 Congressional Elections," in *The State of the Parties: The Changing Role of Contemporary American Parties,* ed. Daniel M. Shea and John C. Green (Lanham, Md.: Rowman & Littlefield, 1994), pp. 83–106; and Robert Biersack, "Hard Facts and Soft Money: State Party Finance in the 1992 Federal Elections," in Shea and Green, pp. 107–132.

45. Adam Clymer, "System to Limit Election Spending Found in Shambles," *New York Times,* 16 June 1996, p. 1.

46. Salmore and Salmore, *Candidates, Parties, and Campaigns,* p. 11.

47. David Moon, "What You Use Depends on What You Have: Information Effects on the Determinants of Electoral Choice," *American Politics Quarterly* 18 (January 1990), pp. 3–24.

48. See the "Marketplace" section in monthly issues of the magazine, *Campaigns & Elections,* which contains more than a hundred names, addresses, and telephone numbers of people who supply "political products and services"—from "campaign schools" to "voter files and mailing lists."

49. Stephen Ansolabehere, Roy L. Behr, and Shanto Iyengar, "Mass Media and Elections: An Overview," *American Politics Quarterly* 19 (January 1991), pp. 109–139.

50. See Darrell M. West, *Air Wars: Television Advertising in Election Campaigns, 1952–1992* (Washington, D.C.: Congressional Quarterly Press, 1993), p. 7.

51. Phil Kuntz, "Dole Is Lifted by the Selection of Kemp, Convention That Avoided Divisiveness," *Wall Street Journal,* 19 August 1996, p. A14.

52. Pamela Johnston Conover and Stanley Feldman, "Candidate Perception in an Ambiguous World: Campaigns, Cues, and Inference Processes," *American Journal of Political Science* 33 (November 1989), pp. 912–940.

53. Michael M. Gant and Norman R. Luttbeg, *American Electoral Behavior* (Itasca, Ill.: Peacock, 1991), pp. 63–64. The literature on the joint effects of party, issues, and candidates is quite involved. See also David W. Romero, "The Changing American Voter Revisited: Candidate Evaluations in Presidential Elections, 1952–1984," *American Politics Quarterly* 17 (October 1989), pp. 409–421. Romero contends that research that finds a "new" American voter who votes according to issues is incorrectly looking at standardized rather than unstandardized regression coefficients.

54. Conover and Feldman, "Candidate Perception," p. 938.

55. Party identification has been assumed to be relatively resistant to short-term campaign effects, but see Dee Allsop and Herbert F. Weisberg, "Measuring Change in Party Identification in an Election Campaign," *American Journal of Political Science* 32 (November 1988), pp. 996–1017. They conclude that partisanship is more volatile than we have thought.

56. For an analysis of the Republicans' problem, see Russell L. Riley, "Party Government and the Contract With America," *PS: Political Science and Politics,* 28 (December 1995), pp. 703–707.

Chapter 7 / Interest Groups
pp. 174–194

1. Michael Wines, "Congress's Twists and Turns Reshape Bill on Energy," *New York Times,* 6 June 1993, p. A1.

2. John Harwood and David Wessel, "White House Gives Ground on Energy Tax," *Wall Street Journal,* 27 May 1993, p. A3; Steven Greenhouse, "Energy Plan to Be Scaled Back, Moynihan Reports," *New York Times,* 30 May 1993, p. 1; Wines, "Congress's Twists and Turns"; Timothy Noah, "BTU Tax Is Dying Death of a Thousand Cuts as Lobbyists Seem Able to Write Their Own Exemptions," *Wall Street Journal,* 8 June 1993, p. A18.

3. Alexis de Tocqueville, *Democracy in America, 1835–1839,* reprint, ed. Richard D. Heffner (New York: Mentor Books, 1956), p. 79.

4. *The Federalist Papers* (New York: Mentor Books, 1961), p. 79.

5. Ibid., p. 78.

6. See Robert A. Dahl, *A Preface to Democratic Theory* (Chicago: University of Chicago Press, 1956), pp. 4–33.

7. Alan Rosenthal, *The Third House* (Washington, D.C.: Congressional Quarterly, 1993), p. 7.

8. This discussion follows from Jeffrey M. Berry, *The Interest Group Society* (New York: Longman, 1997), pp. 6–8.

9. William H. Honan, "With Money Threatened, Colleges Are Moving on All Lobbying Fronts," *New York Times,* 28 June 1995, p. B7.

10. John Mark Hansen, *Gaining Access* (Chicago: University of Chicago Press, 1991), pp. 11–17.

11. Anne N. Costain, *Inviting Women's Rebellion* (Baltimore: Johns Hopkins University Press, 1992).

12. David B. Truman, *The Governmental Process* (New York: Alfred A. Knopf, 1951).

13. Herbert Gans, *The Urban Villagers* (New York: Free Press, 1962).

14. Robert H. Salisbury, "An Exchange Theory of Interest Groups," *Midwest

Journal of Political Science 13 (February 1969), pp. 1–32.

15. See Mancur Olson, Jr., *The Logic of Collective Action* (New York: Schocken, 1968).

16. See Olson, *Logic.*

17. See, for example, Edward O. Laumann and David Knoke, *The Organizational State* (Madison: University of Wisconsin Press, 1987), p. 3. Cited in Robert H. Salisbury, "The Paradox of Interest Groups in Washington—More Groups, Less Clout," in *The New American Political System,* 2d ed., ed. Anthony King (Washington, D.C.: American Enterprise Institute, 1990), p. 226.

18. Dan Clawson, Alan Neustadtl, and Denise Scott, *Money Talks* (New York: Basic Books, 1992), p. 1.

19. "PAC Activity in 1994 Remains at 1992 Levels," Federal Election Commission, 31 March 1995, p. 5.

20. John R. Wright, "Contributions, Lobbying, and Committee Voting in the U.S. House of Representatives," *American Political Science Review* 84 (June 1990), pp. 417–438; and Richard L. Hall and Frank W. Wayman, "Buying Time: Money Interests and the Mobilization of Bias in Congressional Committees," *American Political Science Review,* 84 (September 1990), pp. 797–820.

21. Kay Lehman Schlozman and John T. Tierney, *Organized Interests and American Democracy* (New York: Harper & Row, 1986), p. 150.

22. Berry, *The Interest Group Society,* p. 166.

23. Yumiko Ono, "Tobacco Firms Rush to Counterattack Despite Signs of Dissension in Ranks," *Wall Street Journal,* 14 August 1995, p. A3.

24. Dirk Johnson, "Weed Killers in Tap Water in Corn Belt," *New York Times,* 18 August 1995, p. A10.

25. Berry, *The Interest Group Society,* pp. 135–137.

26. Marc K. Landy and Mary Hague, "Private Interests and Superfund," *Public Interest* 108 (Summer 1992), pp. 97–115.

27. Sidney Verba, Kay Lehman Schlozman, Henry Brady, and Norman H. Nie, "Citizen Activity: Who Participates? What Do They Say?," *American Political Science Review* 87 (June 1993), p. 311.

28. Jeffrey M. Berry, *Lobbying for the People* (Princeton, N.J.: Princeton University Press, 1977), pp. 6–10.

29. Schlozman and Tierney, *Organized Interests,* pp. 58–87.

30. Jonathan Rauch, *Demosclerosis* (New York: Times Books, 1994), p. 91.

31. Adam Clymer, "Congress Passes Bill to Disclose Lobbyists' Roles," *New York Times,* 30 November 1995, p. A1.

32. Eric Schmitt, "Order for Lobbyists: Hold the Gravy," *New York Times,* 11 February 1996, p. 30.

33. See Jonathan Rauch, *Demosclerosis.*

Chapter 8 / Congress   pp. 195–222

1. David S. Cloud, "GOP's Balancing Act Gets Tricky as Budget Amendment Sinks," *Congressional Quarterly Weekly Report,* 4 March 1995, p. 671.

2. Adam Clymer, "Americans Reject Big Medicare Cuts, a New Poll Finds," *New York Times,* 26 October 1995, p. A1.

3. Alissa Rubin and George Hager, "Chances of a Budget Deal Now Anyone's Guess," *Congressional Quarterly Weekly Report,* 13 January 1996, p. 89.

4. D'Jamila Salem Fitzgerald, "Budget Scoreboard," *Los Angeles Times,* 3 May 1997, p. A1.

5. Clinton Rossiter, *1787: The Grand Convention* (New York: Mentor, 1968), p. 158.

6. James M. Lindsay and Randall B. Ripley, "How Congress Influences Foreign and Defense Policy," in *Congress Resurgent,* ed. Randall B. Ripley and James M. Lindsay (Ann Arbor: University of Michigan Press, 1993), pp. 25–28.

7. Norman J. Ornstein, Thomas E. Mann, and Michael J. Malbin, *Vital Statistics on Congress,* 1995–1996 (Washington,

D.C.: Congressional Quarterly Press, 1996), pp. 56–58.

8. Albert R. Hunt, "In Congress, Some Things Never Change," *Wall Street Journal,* 28 March 1996, p. A15.

9. "The Critique of Congress," *American Enterprise* 3 (May–June 1992), p. 101.

10. Karlyn Bowman and Everett Carll Ladd, "Public Opinion Toward Congress: A Historical Look," in *Congress, the Press, and the Public,* ed. Thomas E. Mann and Norman J. Ornstein (Washington, D.C.: American Enterprise Institute and the Brookings Institution, 1994), p. 55.

11. "Ethics," *American Enterprise* 3 (November–December 1992), p. 84.

12. Timothy E. Cook, *Making Laws and Making News* (Washington, D.C.: Brookings Institution, 1989), p. 83.

13. Jonathan S. Krasno, *Challengers, Competition, and Reelection* (New Haven, Conn.: Yale University Press, 1994).

14. Gary C. Jacobson, "The 1994 Elections in Perspective," paper delivered at the annual conference of the Midwest Political Science Association, Chicago, April 1995.

15. Ornstein, Mann, and Malbin, *Vital Statistics,* p. 60.

16. Ornstein, Mann, and Malbin, *Vital Statistics,* pp. 22–23, 28–29.

17. Hanna Fenichel Ptikin, *The Concept of Representation* (Berkeley: University of California Press, 1967), pp. 60–91.

18. Carol M. Swain, *Black Faces, Black Interests* (Cambridge, Mass.: Harvard University Press, 1993), p. 197.

19. *Miller v. Johnson,* 115 S. Ct. 2475 (1995).

20. *Abrams v. Johnson,* __ U.S. __ (1997).

21. David G. Savage, "High Court Again Bars Race-Based Redistricting," *New York Times,* 20 June 1997, p. A12.

22. Walter J. Oleszek, *Congressional Procedures and the Policy Process* (Washington, D.C.: Congressional Quarterly Press, 1996), p. 91.

23. Roger W. Cobb and Charles D. Elder, *Participation in American Politics,* 2d ed.

(Baltimore: Johns Hopkins University Press, 1983), pp. 64–65.

24. Elizabeth Shogren, "Line Item Veto Declared Unconstitutional, U.S. Judge Rules," *Los Angeles Times,* 11 April 1997, p. A1.

25. *Raines v. Byrd,* __ U.S. __ (1997).

26. Andrew Taylor, "Congress Hands President a Budgetary Scalpel," *Congressional Quarterly Weekly Report,* 30 March 1996, pp. 864–867.

27. It was Woodrow Wilson who described the legislative process as the "dance of legislation." Eric Redman used the phrase for the title of his case study, *The Dance of Legislation* (New York: Touchstone, 1973).

28. Woodrow Wilson, *Congressional Government* (Boston: Houghton Mifflin, 1885), p. 79.

29. Lawrence D. Longley and Walter J. Oleszek, *Bicameral Politics* (New Haven, Conn.: Yale University Press, 1989), p. 4.

30. Karen Foerstal, "Gingrich Flexes His Power in Picking Panel Chiefs," *Congressional Quarterly Weekly Report,* 7 January 1995, p. 3326.

31. Joel D. Aberbach, *Keeping a Watchful Eye* (Washington, D.C.: Brookings Institution, 1990), p. 44.

32. Ornstein, Mann, and Malbin, *Vital Statistics,* pp. 131–137.

33. Gary W. Cox and Mathew D. McCubbins, *Legislative Leviathan* (Berkeley: University of California Press, 1993); and Keith Krehbiel, *Information and Legislative Organization* (Ann Arbor: University of Michigan Press, 1992).

34. Andy Plattner, "Dole on the Job," *Congressional Quarterly Weekly Report,* 29 June 1985, p. 1270.

35. Janet Hook, "Leaders Jockey Within Gingrich Power Vacuum," *Los Angeles Times,* 17 January 1997, p. A1.

36. Charles O. Jones, *The United States Congress* (Homewood, Ill.: Dorsey Press, 1982), p. 322.

37. See Jerry Gray, "Freshmen Challenge G.O.P. Elders," *New York Times,* 21 October 1995, p. 1; and Jackie Calmes,

"Militancy of GOP Freshmen May Leave Gingrich Little Room to Compromise," *Wall Street Journal,* 22 December 1995, p. A3.

38. Cox and McCubbins, *Legislative Leviathan;* D. Roderick Kiewiet and Mathew D. McCubbins, *The Logic of Delegation* (Chicago: University of Chicago Press, 1991); and Krehbiel, *Information and Legislative Organization.*

39. Dan Carney, "As Hostilities Rage on the Hill, Partisan-Vote Rate Soars," *Congressional Quarterly Weekly Report,* 27 January 1996, pp. 199–201; and Martin P. Wattenberg, *The Decline of American Political Parties, 1994* (Cambridge, Mass.: Harvard University Press, 1996), Chap. 11.

40. See Mark A. Peterson, *Legislating Together* (Cambridge, Mass.: Harvard University Press, 1990).

41. James Sterling Young, *The Washington Community* (New York: Harcourt, Brace, 1964).

42 Richard F. Fenno, Jr., *Home Style* (Boston: Little, Brown, 1978), p. 32.

43. Louis I. Bredvold and Ralph G. Ross (eds.), *The Philosophy of Edmund Burke* (Ann Arbor: University of Michigan Press, 1960), p. 148.

44. Warren E. Miller and Donald E. Stokes, "Constituency Influence in Congress," *American Political Science Review* 57 (March 1963), pp. 45–57. On minority legislators, see James B. Johnson and Philip E. Secret, "Focus and Style: Representational Roles of Congressional Black and Hispanic Caucus Members," *Journal of Black Studies* 26 (January 1996), pp. 245–273.

45. Robert Weissberg, "Collective vs. Dyadic Representation in Congress," *American Political Science Review* 72 (June 1978), pp. 535–547.

Chapter 9 / The Presidency
pp. 223–245

1. Jon Healey, "Spending Increases Come First in Rush to Pass Package," *Congressional Quarterly Weekly Report,* 20 February 1993, pp. 365–369; Jon Healey,

"Republicans Slam the Brakes on Economic Stimulus Package," *Congressional Quarterly Weekly Report,* 3 April 1993, pp. 817–819; Gwen Ifill, "White House Trying to Trim Blocked Jobs Bill, Aides Say," *New York Times,* 8 April 1993, p. D20; Ann Devroy and David S. Broder, "Missteps Mired Clinton Package," *Washington Post,* 11 April 1993, p. A1; Jeffrey H. Birnbaum and David Rogers, "GOP Filibuster Defeats Clinton Stimulus Package," *Wall Street Journal,* 22 April 1993, p. A2; and Bob Woodward, *The Agenda* (New York: Simon & Schuster, 1994).

2. See Louis Fisher, *Presidential War Power* (Lawrence: University Press of Kansas, 1995).

3. Wilfred E. Binkley, *President and Congress,* 3rd ed. (New York: Vintage, 1962), p. 155.

4. Richard E. Neustadt, *Presidential Power* (New York: John Wiley, 1980), p. 10.

5. Ibid., p. 9.

6. George C. Edwards III, *At the Margins* (New Haven, Conn.: Yale University Press, 1989). See also Jon R. Bond and Richard Fleisher, *The President in the Legislative Arena* (Chicago: University of Chicago Press, 1990).

7. See Edwards, *At the Margins,* pp. 101-125.

8. Theodore J. Lowi, *The Personal President* (Ithaca, N.Y.: Cornell University Press, 1985).

9. Richard A. Brody, *Assessing the President* (Stanford, Calif.: Stanford University Press, 1991), pp. 27–44.

10. Darrell M. West, *Congress and Economic Policymaking* (Pittsburgh: University of Pittsburgh Press, 1987), p. 33.

11. Paul Brace and Barbara Hinckley, *Follow the Leader* (New York: Basic Books, 1992).

12. Charles W. Ostrom and Dennis M. Simon, "Promise and Performance: A Dynamic Model of Presidential Popularity," *American Political Science Review* 79 (June 1985), pp. 334–358.

13. "Prepared Text of Carter's Farewell Address," *New York Times,* 15 January 1981, p. B10.

14. "Two Cheers for United Govern-

ment," *American Enterprise* 4 (January–February 1993), pp. 107–108.

15. Morris Fiorina, *Divided Government,* 2d ed. (Needham Heights, Mass.: Allyn & Bacon, 1996), p. 153.

16. See generally, Charles O. Jones, *The Presidency in a Separated System* (Washington, D.C.: Brookings Institution, 1994).

17. David R. Mayhew, *Divided We Govern* (New Haven: Yale University Press, 1991); and David R. Mayhew, "The Return to Unified Government Under Clinton: How Much of a Difference in Lawmaking," in *The New American Politics,* ed. Bryan D. Jones (Boulder, Colo.: Westview Press, 1995), pp. 111–121.

18. See Sean Kelley, "Divided We Govern: A Reassessment," *Polity* 25 (Spring 1993), pp. 475–484; and George Edwards, Andrew Barrett, and Jeffrey Peake, "The Legislative Impact of Divided Government: What *Failed* to Pass in Congress," n.d., Center for Presidential Studies, Texas A&M University.

19. For an overview of the gridlock argument, see James L. Sundquist, ed., *Back to Gridlock?* (Washington, D.C.: Brookings Institution, 1995).

20. U.S. Bureau of the Census, U.S. Department of Commerce, *Statistical Abstract of the United States, 1995* (Washington, D.C.: U.S. Government Printing Office, 1995), p. 350; and U.S. Office of Management and Budget, *Budget of the United States Government, Fiscal Year 1995* (Washington, D.C.: 1994), p. 237.

21. Jeffrey H. Birnbaum, *Madhouse: The Private Turmoil of Working for the President* (New York: Times Books, 1996).

22. Edward Weisband and Thomas M. Franck, *Resignation in Protest* (New York: Penguin, 1975), p. 139, quoted in Thomas E. Cronin, *The State of the Presidency,* 2d ed. (Boston: Little, Brown, 1980), p. 253.

23. See Richard W. Waterman, "Combining Political Resources: The Internalization of the President's Appointment Power," in *The Presidency Reconsidered,* ed. Richard W. Waterman (Itasca, Ill.: Peacock, 1993), pp. 172–210.

24. Terry M. Moe, "The Politicized Presidency," in *The New Direction in American Politics,* ed. John E. Chubb and Paul E. Peterson (Washington, D.C.: Brookings Institution, 1985), pp. 235–271.

25. *Public Papers of the President, Lyndon B. Johnson, 1965,* vol. 1 (Washington, D.C.: Government Printing Office, 1966), p. 72.

26. Kevin Phillips, *The Politics of Rich and Poor* (New York: Random House, 1990), p. 88.

27. John W. Kingdon, *Agendas, Alternatives, and Public Policies* (Boston: Little, Brown, 1984), p. 25.

28. Richard E. Neustadt, "Presidency and Legislation: The Growth of Central Clearance," *American Political Science Review* 48 (September 1954), pp. 641–671.

29. Seth King, "Reagan, in Bid for Budget Votes, Reported to Yield on Sugar Prices," *New York Times,* 27 June 1981, p. A1.

30. Jeffrey M. Berry and Kent E. Portney, "Centralizing Regulatory Control and Interest Group Access: The Quayle Council on Competitiveness," in *Interest Group Politics,* 4th ed., ed. Allan J. Cigler and Burdett A. Loomis (Washington, D.C.: Congressional Quarterly Press, 1994), pp. 319–347.

31. The extent to which popularity affects presidential influence in Congress is difficult to determine with any precision. For an overview of this issue, see Jon R. Bond, Richard Fleisher, and Glen S. Katz, "An Overview of the Empirical Findings on Presidential-Congressional Relations," in *Rivals for Power,* ed. James A. Thurber (Washington, D.C.: Congressional Quarterly Press, 1996), pp. 103–139.

32. Sidney M. Milkis, *The President and the Parties* (New York: Oxford University Press, 1993), pp. 189–191.

33. John Aloysius Farrell, "A Loyal Standard Bearer," *Boston Globe,* 7 June 1996, p. A1.

34. Fred Barnes, "Hour of Power," *New Republic,* 3 September 1990, p. 12.

35. Alexander George, "The Case for Multiple Advocacy in Foreign Policy," *American Political Science Review* (September 1972), pp. 751–782.

36. John P. Burke and Fred I. Greenstein, *How Presidents Test Reality* (New York: Russell Sage Foundation, 1989).

37. Richard E. Neustadt and Ernest R. May, *Thinking in Time* (New York: Free Press, 1986), p. 143.

38. David G. Savage, "High Court Rules Sex Suit Against Clinton Can Go On," *Los Angeles Times,* 28 May 1997, p. A1.

Chapter 10 / The Bureaucracy
pp. 246–265

1. Adam Bryant, "F.A.A. Struggles as Airlines Turn to Subcontracts," *New York Times,* 2 June 1996, p. 1.

2. James Q. Wilson, *Bureaucracy* (New York: Basic Books, 1989), p. 25.

3. Bruce D. Porter, "Parkinson's Law Revisited: War and the Growth of American Government," *Public Interest* 60 (Summer 1980), p. 50.

4. See generally Ballard C. Campbell, *The Growth of American Government* (Bloomington: Indiana University Press, 1995).

5. See Anne Schneider and Helen Ingram, "Social Construction of Target Populations: Implications for Politics and Policy," *American Political Science Review* 87 (June 1993), pp. 334–347.

6. Theda Skocpol, *Protecting Soldiers and Mothers: The Political Origins of Social Policy in the United States* (Cambridge, Mass.: Harvard University Press, 1992).

7. Linda L. M. Bennett and Stephen Earl Bennett, "Looking at Leviathan: Dimensions of Opinion About Big Government," in *Broken Contract,* ed. Stephen C. Craig (Boulder, Colo.: Westview Press, 1996), pp. 23–45.

8. John T. Tierney, "Government Corporations and Managing the Public's Business," *Political Science Quarterly* 99 (Spring 1984), pp. 73–92.

9. U.S. Bureau of the Census, *Statistical Abstract of the United States, 1995* (Washington, D.C.: U.S. Governmental Printing Office, 1995), pp. 351, 400.

10. U.S. Bureau of the Census, *Statistical Abstract of the United States, 1992* (Washington, D.C.: U.S. Government Printing Office, 1992), pp. 332–333.

11. Patricia Wallace Ingraham, *The Foundation of Merit* (Baltimore: Johns Hopkins University Press, 1995), p. 9.

12. Doris A. Graber, *Mass Media and American Politics,* 3d ed. (Washington, D.C.: Congressional Quarterly Press, 1989), p. 51.

13. Jeffrey M. Berry, *Feeding Hungry People* (New Brunswick, N.J.: Rutgers University Press, 1984).

14. Charles E. Lindblom, "The Science of Muddling Through," *Public Administration Review* 19 (Spring 1959), pp. 79–88.

15. See Michael T. Hayes, *Incrementalism and Public Policy* (White Plains, N.Y.: Longman, 1992).

16. Andrew Weiss and Edward Woodhouse, "Reframing Incrementalism: A Constructive Response to the Critics," *Policy Sciences* 25 (August 1992), pp. 255–273.

17. John Frohnmeyer, *Leaving Town Alive* (Boston: Houghton Mifflin, 1993), pp. 213, 262.

18. Thomas W. Church and Robert T. Nakamura, *Cleaning Up the Mess* (Washington, D.C.: Brookings Institution, 1993).

19. See generally Terry M. Moe, "The Politics of Bureaucratic Structure," in *Can the Government Govern?,* ed. John E. Chubb and Paul E. Peterson (Washington, D.C.: Brookings Institution, 1989), pp. 267–329.

20. See generally John J. DiIulio, Jr., Gerald Garvey, and Donald F. Kettl, *Improving Government Performance: An Owner's Manual* (Washington, D.C.: Brookings Institution, 1993).

21. David Vogel, "AIDS and the Politics of Drug Lag," *Public Interest* 96 (Summer 1989), pp. 73–85.

22. A good short introduction to TQM in government is James E. Swiss,

"Adapting Total Quality Management to Government," *Public Administration Review* 52 (July–August 1992), pp. 356–362.

23. See Donald F. Kettl and John J. DiIulio, Jr. (ed)., *Inside the Reinvention Machine* (Washington, D.C.: Brookings Institution, 1995); and Ronald Moe, "The 'Reinventing Government' Exercise: Misinterpreting the Problem, Misjudging the Consequences," *Public Administration Review* 54 (March–April 1994), pp. 111–122.

Chapter 11 / The Courts
pp. 266–290

1. Keith White, "Danforth Says Court Nominee Is Making His Own Case," Gannett News Service, 19 July 1991 (LEXIS).

2. David Brock, *The Real Anita Hill* (New York: Free Press, 1992), p. 61; Jane Mayer and Jill Abramson, *Strange Justice: The Selling of Clarence Thomas* (Boston: Houghton Mifflin, 1994).

3. Jeffrey Rosen, "Annals of Law: Moving On," *The New Yorker*, 29 April and 6 May 1996, p. 73.

4. Ibid., pp. 66–67.

5. *Missouri v. Jenkins,* 515 U.S. (1995); *Adarand v. Peña,* 515 U.S. (1995).

6. Felix Frankfurter and James M. Landis, *The Business of the Supreme Court* (New York: Macmillan, 1928), pp. 5–14; and Julius Goebel, Jr., *Antecedents and Beginnings to 1801,* vol. 1 of *The History of the Supreme Court of the United States* (New York: Macmillan, 1971).

7. Maeva Marcus (ed.), *The Justices on Circuit, 1795–1800,* vol. 3 of *The Documentary History of the Supreme Court of the United States, 1789–1800* (New York: Columbia University Press, 1990).

8. Robert G. McCloskey, *The United States Supreme Court* (Chicago: University of Chicago Press, 1960), p. 31.

9. *Marbury v. Madison,* 1 Cranch 137 at 177, 178 (1803).

10. Interestingly, the term *judicial review* dates only to 1910; it was apparently unknown to Marshall and his contemporaries. Robert Lowry Clinton, *Marbury v. Madison and Judicial Review* (Lawrence: University Press of Kansas, 1989), p. 7.

11. Henry J. Abraham, *The Judicial Process,* 6th ed. (New York: Oxford University Press, 1993), pp. 274–279; Lee Epstein et al., *The Supreme Court Compendium* (Washington, D.C.: Congressional Quarterly Press, 1994), Table 2-12.

12. *Ware v. Hylton,* 3 Dallas 199 (1796).

13. *Martin v. Hunter's Lessee,* 1 Wheat. 304 (1816).

14. *Constitution of the United States of America: Annotated and Interpreted* (Washington, D.C.: U.S. Government Printing Office, 1987) and supplements.

15. Garry Wills, *Explaining America: The Federalist* (Garden City, N.Y.: Doubleday, 1981), pp. 127–136.

16. *State Justice Institute News,* 4 (Spring 1993), p. 1.

17. Charles Alan Wright, *Handbook on the Law of Federal Courts,* 3d ed. (St. Paul, Minn.: West, 1976), p. 7.

18. Federal Court Management Statistics, October 1995, Administrative Office of the United States Courts, Statistics Division, Analysis and Reports Branch.

19. Ibid.

20. Linda Greenhouse, "Precedent for Lower Courts: Tyrant or Teacher?" *New York Times,* 29 January 1988, p. B7.

21. *Texas v. Johnson,* 491 U.S. 397 (1989); *United States v. Eichman,* 496 U.S. 310 (1990).

22. *Regents of the University of California v. Bakke,* 438 U.S. 265 (1978).

23. *Adarand Constructors v. Peña,* 515 U.S. (1995); *Miller v. Johnson,* U.S. (1995).

24. "Reading Petitions Is for Clerks Only at High Court Now," *Wall Street Journal,* 11 October 1990, p. B7.

25. H. W. Perry, Jr., *Deciding to Decide: Agenda Setting in the United States Supreme Court* (Cambridge, Mass.: Harvard University Press, 1991); Gregory A. Caldiera and John R. Wright, "The Discuss List: Agenda Building in the Supreme Court," 24 *Law & Society Review* 807 (1990).

26. Doris M. Provine, *Case Selection in the United States Supreme Court* (Chicago: University of Chicago Press, 1980), pp. 74–102.

27. Perry, *Deciding to Decide,* p. 286.

28. "Rising Fixed Opinions," *New York Times,* 22 February 1988, p. 14. See also Linda Greenhouse, "At the Bar," *New York Times,* 28 July 1989, p. 21.

29. Jeffrey A. Segal and Harold J. Spaeth, *The Supreme Court and the Attitudinal Model* (Cambridge: Cambridge University Press, 1993).

30. Thomas G. Walker, Lee Epstein, and William J. Dixon, "On the Mysterious Demise of Consensual Norms in the United States Supreme Court," *Journal of Politics* 50 (1988), pp. 361–389.

31. See, for example, Walter F. Murphy, *Elements of Judicial Strategy* (Chicago: University of Chicago Press, 1964); and Bob Woodward and Scott Armstrong, *The Brethren* (New York: Simon & Schuster, 1979).

32. Linda Greenhouse, "At the Bar," *New York Times,* 28 July 1989, p. 21.

33. Stephen L. Wasby, *The Supreme Court in the Federal Judicial System,* 3d ed. (Chicago: Nelson-Hall, 1988), pp. 107–110.

34. Sheldon Goldman, "Judicial Selection Under Clinton: A Midterm Examination," 78 *Judicature* 276 (1995). Professor Goldman kindly provided additional data from the 104th Congress.

35. *Congressional Quarterly's Guide to the U.S. Supreme Court,* 2d ed. (Washington, D.C.: Congressional Quarterly Press, 1990), pp. 878–890.

36. Maureen Dowd, "The Supreme Court: Conservative Black Judge, Clarence Thomas, Named to Marshall's Court Seat," *New York Times,* 2 July 1991, pp. A1, A16.

37. *Brown v. Board of Education II,* 349 U.S. 294 (1955).

38. Alexander M. Bickel, *The Least Dangerous Branch* (Indianapolis: Bobbs-Merrill, 1962); and Robert A. Dahl, "Decision-Making in a Democracy: The Supreme Court as a National Policy-Maker," 6 *Journal of Public Law* 279 (1962).

39. William Mishler and Reginal S. Sheehan, "The Supreme Court as a Countermajoritarian Institution? The Impact of Public Opinion on Supreme Court Decisions," *American Political Science Review* 87 (1993), pp. 87–101.

40. Thomas R. Marshall, *Public Opinion and the Supreme Court* (Boston: Unwin Hyman, 1989).

41. Marshall, *Public Opinion and the Supreme Court,* pp. 192–193; Gerald N. Rosenberg, *The Hollow Hope: Can Courts Bring About Social Change?* (Chicago: University of Chicago Press, 1991).

42. William J. Brennan, Jr., "State Supreme Court Judge Versus United States Supreme Court Justice: A Change in Function and Perspective," 19 *University of Florida Law Review* 225 (1966).

Chapter 12 / Civil Liberties and Civil Rights   pp. 291–335

1. *United States v. Baker and Gonda,* 890 F. Supp. 1375 (1995).

2. Charles Platt, *Anarchy Online* (New York: HarperPrism, 1997.)

3. *Adarand Constructors, Inc. v. Peña,* 518 U.S. (1995); Seth Mydans, "Challenging the Concept of 'Disadvantaged,'" *New York Times,* 18 June 1995, Section 1, p. 8.

4. *United States v. Baker and Gonda,* 890 F. Supp. 1375 (1995).

5. Learned Hand, *The Bill of Rights* (Boston: Atheneum, 1958), p. 1.

6. Leonard W. Levy, *The Establishment Clause: Religion and the First Amendment* (New York: Macmillan, 1986); Leo Pfeffer, *Church, State, and Freedom* (Boston: Beacon, 1953); and Leonard W. Levy, "The Original Meaning of the Establishment Clause of the First Amendment," in *Religion and the State,* ed. James E. Wood, Jr. (Waco, Tex.: Baylor University Press, 1985), pp. 43–83.

7. *Reynolds v. United States,* 98 U.S. 145 (1879).

8. *Everson v. Board of Education,* 330 U.S. 1 (1947).

9. *Board of Education v. Allen,* 392 U.S. 236 (1968).

10. *Lemon v. Kurtzman,* 403 U.S. 602 (1971).

11. *Agostini v. Felton,* — U.S. — (1997).

12. *Engle v. Vitale,* 370 U.S. 421 (1962).

13. *Wallace v. Jaffree,* 472 U.S. 38 (1985).

14. *Lee v. Weisman,* 505 U.S. (1992).

15. Michael W. McConnell, "The Origins and Historical Understanding of the Free Exercise of Religion," 103 *Harvard Law Review* 1409 (1990).

16. *Minersville School District v. Gobitis,* 310 U.S. 586 (1940).

17. *West Virginia State Board of Education v. Barnette,* 319 U.S. 624 at 642 (1943).

18. *Sherbert v. Verner,* 374 U.S. 398 (1963).

19. *Employment Division v. Smith,* 494 U.S. 872 (1990).

20. *Boerne v. Flores,* — U.S. — (1997).

21. Laurence Tribe, *Treatise on American Constitutional Law,* 2d ed. (St. Paul, Minn.: West, 1988), p. 566.

22. Zechariah Chafee, *Free Speech in the United States* (Cambridge, Mass.: Harvard University Press, 1941).

23. Leonard W. Levy, *The Emergence of a Free Press* (New York: Oxford University Press, 1985).

24. *Schenck v. United States,* 249 U.S. 47 (1919).

25. *Gitlow v. New York,* 268 U.S. 652 (1925).

26. *Dennis v. United States,* 341 U.S. 494 (1951).

27. *Brandenburg v. Ohio,* 395 U.S. 444 (1969).

28. *Tinker v. Des Moines Independent County School District,* 393 U.S. 503 at 508 (1969) .

29. *United States v. Eichman,* 496 U.S. 310 (1990).

30. Linda Greenhouse, "Supreme Court Voids Flag Law," *New York Times,* 12 June 1990, p. A1.

31. *Miller v. California,* 413 U.S. 15 (1973).

32. Donald Alexander Downs, *The New Politics of Pornography* (Chicago: University of Chicago Press, 1989), pp. 95–143.

33. *American Booksellers Ass'n v. Hudnut,* 598 F. Supp. 1316 (1984).

34. *New York Times v. Sullivan,* 376 U.S. 254 (1964).

35. *Near v. Minnesota,* 283 U.S. 697 (1931).

36. For a detailed account of *Near, see* Fred W. Friendly, *Minnesota Rag* (New York: Random House, 1981).

37. *New York Times v. United States,* 403 U.S. 713 (1971).

38. *Branzburg v. Hayes,* 408 U.S. 665 (1972).

39. *Hazelwood School District v. Kuhlmeier,* 484 U.S. 260 (1988).

40. *United States v. Cruikshank,* 92 U.S. 542 (1876); *Constitution of the United States of America: Annotated and Interpreted* (Washington, D.C.: U.S. Government Printing Office, 1973), p. 1031.

41. *DeJonge v. Oregon,* 299 U.S. 353 (1937).

42. *United States v. Miller,* 307 U.S. 174 (1939).

43. *Barron v. Baltimore,* 32 U.S. (7 Pet.) 243 (1833).

44. *Chicago B. & Q. R. v. Chicago,* 166 U.S. 226 (1897).

45. *Gitlow v. New York,* 268 U.S. at 666 (1925).

46. *Palko v. Connecticut,* 302 U.S. 319 (1937).

47. *Duncan v. Louisiana,* 391 U.S. 145 (1968).

48. *McNabb v. United States,* 318 U.S. 332 (1943).

49. *Baldwin v. New York,* 399 U.S. 66 (1970).

50. Anthony Lewis, *Gideon's Trumpet* (New York: Random House, 1964).

51. *Gideon v. Wainwright,* 372 U.S. 335 (1963).

52. *Miranda v. Arizona,* 384 U.S. 436 (1966).

53. *Wolf v. Colorado,* 338 U.S. 25 (1949).

54. *Mapp v. Ohio,* 367 U.S. 643 (1961).

55. *United States v. Leon,* 468 U.S. 897 (1984).

56. *James v. Illinois,* 493 U.S. 307 (1990).

57. Paul Brest, *Processes of Constitutional Decision-making* (Boston: Little, Brown, 1975), p. 708.

58. *Griswold v. Connecticut*, 381 U.S. 479 (1965).

59. *Roe v. Wade*, 410 U.S. 113 (1973).

60. See John Hart Ely, "The Wages of Crying Wolf: A Comment on *Roe v. Wade*," 82 *Yale Law Journal* 920 (1973).

61. *Webster v. Reproductive Health Services*, 492 U.S. 490 (1989).

62. *Planned Parenthood v. Casey*, 505 U.S. (1992).

63. *Bowers v. Hardwick*, 478 U.S. 186 (1986).

64. *The Gallup Poll Monthly*, August 1991, p. 56; Paul M. Sniderman and Thomas Piazza, *The Scar of Race* (Cambridge, Mass.: Belknap Press of Harvard University Press, 1993), pp. 133–134; Citrin, pp. 40–41.

65. *The Slaughterhouse Cases*, 83 U.S. 36 (1873).

66. *Civil Rights Cases*, 109 U.S. 3 (1883).

67. Mary Beth Norton et al., *A People and a Nation: A History of the United States*, 3d ed. (Boston: Houghton Mifflin, 1990), p. 490.

68. *Plessy v. Ferguson*, 163 U.S. 537 (1896).

69. *Plessy*, 163 U.S. at 562 (Harlan, J., dissenting).

70. *Cummings v. County Board of Education*, 175 U.S. 528 (1899).

71. *Brown v. Board of Education*, 347 U.S. 483 (1954).

72. *Brown v. Board of Education*, 347 U.S. 483, 495 (1954).

73. *Brown v. Board of Education*, 347 U.S. 483, 494 (1954).

74. *Brown v. Board of Education II*, 349 U.S. 294 (1955).

75. Jack W. Peltason, *Fifty-eight Lonely Men*, rev. ed. (Urbana: University of Illinois Press, 1971).

76. *Alexander v. Holmes County Board of Education*, 396 U.S. 19 (1969).

77. *Milliken v. Bradley*, 418 U.S. 717 (1974).

78. Norton et al., *People and a Nation*, p. 943.

79. But see Abigail M. Thernstrom, *Whose Vote Counts? Affirmative Action and Minority Voting Rights* (Cambridge, Mass.: Harvard University Press, 1987).

80. *Richmond v. J. A. Croson Co.*, 488 U.S. 469 (1989).

81. *Martin v. Wilks*, 490 U.S. 755 (1989); *Wards Cove Packing Co. v. Atonio*, 490 U.S. 642 (1989); *Patterson v. McLean Credit Union*, 491 U.S. 164 (1989); *Price Waterhouse v. Hopkins*, 490 U.S. 228 (1989); *Lorance v. AT&T Technologies*, 490 U.S. 900 (1989); and *EEOC v. Arabian American Oil Co.*, 499 U.S. 244 (1991).

82. *Saint Francis College v. Al-Khazraji*, 481 U.S. 604 (1987).

83. Dee Brown, *Bury My Heart at Wounded Knee: An Indian History of the American West* (New York: Holt, Rinehart & Winston, 1971).

84. *Muller v. Oregon*, 208 U.S. 412 (1908).

85. *International Union, United Automobile, Aerospace & Agricultural Implement Workers of America v. Johnson Controls*, 499 U.S. 187 (1991).

86. *Reed v. Reed*, 404 U.S. 71 (1971).

87. *Frontiero v. Richardson*, 411 U.S. 677 (1973).

88. *Craig v. Boren*, 429 U.S. 190 (1976).

89. *J.E.B. v. Alabama ex rel. T.B.*, 508 U.S. (1994).

90. *United States v. Virginia*, slip op. 94-1941 & 94-2107 (decided June 26, 1996).

91. Melvin I. Urofsky, *A March of Liberty* (New York: Knopf, 1988), p. 902.

92. *Harris v. Forklift Systems*, 510 U.S. (1993).

93. *Facts on File* 206B2 (4 June 1965).

94. As quoted in Melvin I. Urofsky, *A Conflict of Rights: The Supreme Court and Affirmative Action* (New York: Scribner's, 1991), p. 29.

95. *Regents of the University of California v. Bakke*, 438 U.S. 265 (1978).

96. *United Steelworkers of America, AFL-CIO v. Weber*, 443 U.S. 193 (1979).

97. *Firefighters v. Stotts*, 467 U.S. 561 (1984).

98. *Adarand Constructors, Inc. v. Peña*, 518 U.S. (1995).

99. William H. Honan, "Moves to End Affirmative Action Gain Support Nationwide," *New York Times*, 31 March 1996, p. 30; James Brooke, "Colorado Bases College Aid on Need Rather

Than Race," *New York Times,* 16
January 1996, p. A8.

100. Stephen Earl Bennett et al.,
*Americans' Opinions About Affirmative
Action* (Cincinnati: University of
Cincinnati, Institute for Policy
Research, 1995), p. 4.

Chapter 13 / Public Policy
pp. 336–357

1. Fox Butterfield, "Prison-Building Binge
in California Casts Shadow on Higher
Education," *New York Times,* 12 April
1996, p. A14.

2. The policymaking process can be
depicted in many ways. Another approach, a bit more elaborate than this,
is described in James E. Anderson,
Public Policymaking, 2d ed. (Boston:
Houghton Mifflin, 1994), p. 37.

3. See Christopher J. Bosso, "The
Contextual Bases of Problem
Definition," in *The Politics of Problem
Definition,* ed. David A. Rochefort and
Roger W. Cobb (Lawrence: University
Press of Kansas, 1994), pp. 182–203.

4. Jeffrey M. Berry, *The Interest Group
Society,* 3d ed. (New York: Longman,
1997), p. 187.

5. For a brief overview of the evolution of
AT&T and government regulation, see
Robert W. Crandell, *After the Breakup*
(Washington, D.C.: Brookings
Institution, 1991), pp. 16–42.

6. See Martha Derthick and Paul J.
Quirk, *The Politics of Deregulation*
(Washington, D.C.: Brookings
Institution, 1985); and Robert Britt
Horowitz, *The Irony of Regulatory Reform*
(New York: Oxford University Press,
1989).

7. Edmund L. Andrews, "Congress Votes
To Reshape Communications Industry,
Ending a 4-Year Struggle," *New York
Times,* 2 February 1996, p. A1.

8. Jeffrey M. Berry, "The Dynamic
Qualities of Issue Networks," paper
delivered at the annual meeting of the
American Political Science Association,
New York, September 1994.

9. Jeffrey M. Berry, "Subgovernments,

Issue Networks, and Political Conflict,"
in *Remaking American Politics,* ed.
Richard A. Harris and Sidney M. Milkis
(Boulder, Colo.: Westview Press, 1989),
pp. 239–260.

10. Thomas J. Anton, *American Federalism
and Public Policy* (Philadelphia: Temple
University Press, 1989).

11. N. Gregory Mankiw, "Symposium on
Keynesian Economics Today," *Journal
of Economic Perspectives* 7 (Winter 1993),
pp. 3–4. In his preface to four articles
in the symposium, Mankiw says, "The
literature that bears the label
'Keynesian' is broad, and it does not
offer a single vision of how the economy behaves."

12. Richard A. Musgrave and Peggy B.
Musgrave, *Public Finance in Theory and
Practice,* 2d ed. (New York: McGraw-
Hill, 1976), p. 42.

13. Mark T. Kehoe, "Clinton Veto Tally:
Up to 11," *Congressional Quarterly
Weekly Report,* 6 January 1996, p. 10.

14. George Hager, "Congress, Clinton
Yield Enough to Close the Book on
Fiscal '96," *Congressional Quarterly
Weekly Report,* 27 April 1996, p. 1155.

15. Elizabeth Kolbert, "Public Opinion
Polls Swerve with the Turns of a
Phrase," *New York Times,* 5 June 1995,
p. 1; and Adam Clymer, "Of Touching
Third Rails and Tackling Medicare,"
New York Times, 27 October 1995, p.
A11.

16. Times-Mirror Center for the People
and the Press, "Voter Anxiety Dividing
GOP: Energized Democrats Backing
Clinton," press release of 14 November
1995, p. 88.

17. Fay Lomax Cook et al., *Convergent
Perspectives on Social Welfare Policy: The
Views from the General Public, Members of
Congress, and AFDC Recipients*
(Evanston, Ill.: Center for Urban
Affairs and Policy Research,
Northwestern University, 1988), Table
4-1.

18. U.S. Bureau of the Census, U.S.
Department of Commerce, *Statistical
Abstract of the United States, 1995*
(Washington, D.C.: U.S. Government
Printing Office, 1995), p. 289.

19. Ibid., p. 480.

20. Robert Pear, "The Welfare Bill: The Overview," *New York Times,* 1 August 1996, p. Al; Jason DeParle, "Get a Job: The New Contract with America's Poor," *New York Times,* 28 July 1996, p. E1.

Index

Credits *(continued from the copyright page)*

Photos
Chapter 1: p. 1, Michael Dwyer/Stock Boston; p. 8, Dave Martin/AP/Wide World
Photos; p. 19, Bob Daemmrich/The Image Works; *Chapter 2:* p. 28,
Camerique/The Picture Cube; p. 31, Courtesy of the John Carter Brown Library
at Brown University; p. 44, Tracy W. McGregor Library, Manuscript Division,
Special Collections Department, University of Virginia; p. 49, Culver Pictures;
Chapter 3: p. 56, Bob Daemmrich/Stock Boston; p. 63, Liss/Gamma Liaison;
p. 69, International Museum of Photography; p. 73, Michael Schumann/Saba
Press; p. 77, Wide World Photos; *Chapter 4:* p. 80, Pamela Price/The Picture
Cube; p. 85, Bettmann; p. 105, James D. Wilson/Gamma Liaison; *Chapter 5:*
p. 112, Bruce Kliewe/The Picture Cube; p. 114, Sharon Henry/SABA; p. 115,
Eugene Richards/Magnum; p. 122, top, Library of Congress, bottom, Brown
Brothers; p. 133, Wide World Photos; *Chapter 6:* p. 138, Gatewood/The Image
Works; p. 139, Jennifer Waddell; p. 147, Wide World Photos; p. 164, Bob
Daemmrich/Uniphoto; *Chapter 7:* p. 174, Mark Burnet/Photos Researchers;
p. 186, Mark Asnin/SABA; p. 191, John Ficara/Woodfin Camp and Associates;
Chapter 8: p. 195, Mark Reinstein; p. 198, Mark Asnin/SABA; p. 217,
Crandall/Image Works; *Chapter 9:* p. 223, John Nordell/The Picture Cube;
p. 224, J. Ficara/Sygma; p. 244, left, Culver Pictures, right, John Fitzgerald
Kennedy Library; *Chapter 10:* p. 246, John Nordell/The Picture Cube; p. 247,
Rick Bowner/Wide World Photos; p. 257, Bettmann; p. 261, Dennis
Brack/Black Star; p. 262, Paul Conklin; *Chapter 11:* p. 266, Camerique/The
Picture Cube; p. 267, left, Markel/Gamma Liaison, right, F. Lee
Corkran/Sygma; p. 279, Ken Heinen/Wide World Photos; p. 281, Ken Heinen;
Chapter 12: p. 291, C. Blankenhorn/The Picture Cube; p. 318, Leonard
Freed/Magnum; p. 321, Michael Springer/Gamma Liaison; p. 322, Terry
Ashe/Gamma Liaison; p. 327, Houston Post; *Chapter 13:* p. 336, Myrleen
Ferguson/Photo Edit; p. 337, top left, top right, bottom, Reynolds Enterprise;
p. 342, UPI/Bettmann.

Text and Art
Figure 4.1: Gallup Report, November 1992. Used by permission of the Gallup
Poll.

Figure 4.6: Data from *1992 National Election Study,* copyright © Center for
Political Studies, University of Michigan. Reprinted with permission.

Figure 5.2: Reprinted by permission of the publisher from *American National
Election Studies Data Sourcebook, 1952–1978* by Warren E. Miller, Arthur H. Miller,
and Edward J. Schneider, Cambridge, Mass. Harvard University Press. Copyright
© 1989 by the President and Fellows of Harvard College.

Figure 7.1: Based on Jeffrey M. Berry, Kent E. Portney, and Ken Thomson, *The
Rebirth of Urban Democracy* (Washington, D.C.: Brookings Institution, 1993). Used
with permission.

Figure 9.1: Samuel Kernell, *Going Public,* 3rd ed. (Washington, D.C.:
Congressional Quarterly Press, 1997), fig. 4.2. Copyright © 1997 by
Congressional Quarterly Press. Used with permission.